W9-CGY-441

The International Library of Criminology, Criminal Justice and Penology
Series Editors: Gerald Mars and David Nelken

Titles in the Series:

The Origins and Growth of Criminology
Piers Beirne

The Psychology and Psychiatry of Crime
David Canter

Crime and the Media
Richard V. Ericson

Psychological Explanations of Crime
David P. Farrington

Terrorism
Conor Gearty

Criminal Careers, Vols I & II
David F. Greenberg

Social Control: Aspects of Non-State Justice
Stuart Henry

Professional Criminals
Dick Hobbs

Computer Crime
Richard Hollinger

Street Crime
Mike Maguire

Occupational Crime
Gerald Mars

Gender, Crime and Feminism
Ngaire Naffine

White-Collar Crime
David Nelken

Organized Crime
Nikos Passas

Criminal Statistics: Their Use and Abuse
Kenneth Pease

Police, Vols I & II
Robert Reiner

Victimology
Paul Rock

Prosecution
Andrew Sanders

Drugs, Vols I & II
Nigel South

Sex Crimes
Donald West

Social Control

Aspects of Non-state Justice

Edited by

Stuart Henry
Professor of Criminology
Eastern Michigan University

Dartmouth
Aldershot • Brookfield USA • Singapore • Sydney

C690084

141263

© Stuart Henry 1994. For copyright of individual articles please refer to the Acknowledgements.

All rights reserved. No part of this publication may be reproduced, stored in a retrieval system, or trans
mitted in any form or by any means, electronic, mechanical, photocopying, recording, or otherwise withou
the prior permission of Dartmouth Publishing Company Limited.

Published by
Dartmouth Publishing Company Limited
Gower House
Croft Road
Aldershot
Hants GU11 3HR
England

Dartmouth Publishing Company
Old Post Road
Brookfield
Vermont 05036
USA

British Library Cataloguing in Publication Data
Social Control: Aspects of Non-state
Justice. – (International Library of
Criminology & Criminal Justice)
  I. Henry, Stuart II. Series
  303.3

Library of Congress Cataloging-in-Publication Data
Social control : aspects of non-state justice / edited by Stuart
  Henry.
      p.   cm. – (The International library of criminology and
  criminal justice)
    Includes bibliographical references and index.
    ISBN 1–85521–354–0 : $129.95 (est.)
    1. Social control. 2. Criminal justice, Administration of.
  I. Henry, Stuart. II. Series.
  HM291.S5865   1994
  364–dc20   94–595
                                                                     CI

ISBN 1 85521 354 0

Printed in Great Britain by Galliard (Printers) Ltd, Great Yarmouth

Contents

0690084   T41263

Acknowledgements

The editors and publishers wish to thank the following for permission to use copyright material.

Academic Press Limited for the essay: Stuart Henry (1982), 'Factory Law: The Changing Disciplinary Technology of Industrial Social Control', *International Journal of the Sociology of Law*, **10**, pp. 365–83.

The American Society of Criminology: Arie Freiberg (1987), 'Reconceptualizing Sanctions', *Criminology*, **25**, pp. 223–55.

Blackwell Publishers for the essays: David Nelken (1989), 'Discipline and Punish: Some Notes on the Margin', *The Howard Journal of Criminal Justice*, **28**, pp. 245–54; Peter Conrad (1979), 'Types of Medical Social Control', *Sociology of Health and Illness*, **1**, pp. 1–11; Irving Kenneth Zola (1972), 'Medicine as an Institution of Social Control', *Sociological Review*, **20**, pp. 487–504.

The Cardozo Law Review for the essay: Gunther Teubner (1992), 'The Two Faces of Janus: Rethinking Legal Pluralism', *Cardozo Law Review*, **13**, pp. 1443–62. Reprinted by permission of The Cardozo Law Review.

Criminal Justice and Behavior for the essay: David B. Kalinich and Stan Stojkovic (1985), 'Contraband: The Basis for Legitimate Power in a Prison Social System', *Criminal Justice and Behavior*, **12**, pp. 435–51.

Doubleday, a division of Bantam Doubleday Dell Publishing Group for the essay: Spencer MacCallum (1967), 'Dispute Settlement in an American Supermarket: A Preliminary View', in P. Bohannan (ed.), *Law and Warfare*, pp. 291–99. Copyright © 1967 by Paul Bohannan. Used by permission of Doubleday, a division of Bantam Doubleday Dell Publishing Group, Inc.

Eric Fisher (1975), 'Community Courts: An Alternative to Conventional Criminal Adjudication', *The American University Law Review*, **24**, pp. 1253–74.

Kluwer Academic Publishers for the essay: Stanley Cohen (1979), 'The Punitive City: Notes on the Dispersal of Social Control', *Contemporary Crises*, **3**, pp. 339–63. Reprinted by permission of Kluwer Academic Publishers.

Law and Society Association for the essays: Gary Itzkowitz (1988), 'Social Theory and Law: The Significance of Stuart Henry', *Law and Society Review*, **22**, pp. 949–61; Christine B. Harrington (1988), 'Moving from Integrative to Constitutive Theories of Law: Comment on

Itzkowitz', *Law and Society Review*, **22**, pp. 963–67; Sally Engel Merry (1988), 'Lega Pluralism', *Law and Society Review*, **22**, pp. 869–96; Stuart Henry (1985), 'Community Justice Capitalist Society and Human Agency: The Dialectics of Collective Law in the Cooperative' *Law and Society Review*, **19**, pp. 303–27. Reprinted by permission of the Law and Society Association.

Osgoode Hall Law Journal and Peter Fitzpatrick for the essay: Peter Fitzpatrick (1984), 'Law and Societies', *Osgoode Hall Law Journal*, **22**, pp. 115-38.

Oxford University for the essay: M. Mellish and N. Collis-Squires (1976), 'Legal and Socia Norms in Discipline and Dismissal', *Industrial Law Journal*, **5**, pp. 164–77.

University of California Press Journals for the essays: Clifford D. Shearing and Philip C. Stennin; (1983), 'Private Security: Implications for Social Control', *Social Problems*, **30**, pp. 493–506 Susan Guarino Ghezzi (1983), 'A Private Network of Social Control: Insurance Investigatio Units', *Social Problems*, **30**, pp. 521–31. Copyright © 1983 by the Society for the study o Social Problems. Reprinted from Social Problems by permission.

The University of Minnesota Press for the essay: Nancy Fraser (1989), 'Foucault on Moder Power: Empirical Insights and Normative Confusions', in *Unruly Practices*, pp. 17–34 Copyright © 1989 by the Regents of The University of Minnesota.

Every effort has been made to trace all the copyright holders but if any have been inadver tently overlooked the publishers will be pleased to make the necessary arrangement at the firs opportunity.

Series Preface

The International Library of Criminology, Criminal Justice and Penology, represents an important publishing initiative designed to bring together the most significant journal essays in contemporary criminology, criminal justice and penology. The series makes available to researchers, teachers and students an extensive range of essays which are indispensable for obtaining an overview of the latest theories and findings in this fast changing subject.

This series consists of volumes dealing with criminological schools and theories as well as with approaches to particular areas of crime, criminal justice and penology. Each volume is edited by a recognised authority who has selected twenty or so of the best journal articles in the field of their special competence and provided an informative introduction giving a summary of the field and the relevance of the articles chosen. The original pagination is retained for ease of reference.

The difficulties of keeping on top of the steadily growing literature in criminology are complicated by the many disciplines from which its theories and findings are drawn (sociology, law, sociology of law, psychology, psychiatry, philosophy and economics are the most obvious). The development of new specialisms with their own journals (policing, victimology, mediation) as well as the debates between rival schools of thought (feminist criminology, left realism, critical criminology, abolitionism etc.) contribute overviews offering syntheses of the state of the art. These problems are addressed by the INTERNATIONAL LIBRARY in making available for research and teaching the key essays from specialist journals.

GERALD MARS
Visiting Professor of Risk Management, Cranfield University

DAVID NELKEN
Visiting Professor of Law (Criminology), University College London

Introduction

The purpose of this volume is to bring together significant theoretical and descriptive essays that examine systems of administering justice and dispensing sanctions which exist outside the state. I call these systems 'private justice' (Henry, 1983; 1987). They comprise the numerous forms of social control of crime and deviance that are part of group life, but that are not formally tied to state law. They include, for example, the practices of disciplinary bodies, boards and councils of industrial organizations, the tribunals of professional trade associations and unions, and the disciplinary committees of universities and colleges. Private justice also includes the peer sanctioning of relatively amorphous voluntary associations, such as self-help and mutual aid groups, and the informal norms and sanctions operating inside more formal control institutions, such as the informal 'code' governing police deviance or internal prisoner-to-prisoner control.

Why is consideration of such non-state justice important? First, regardless of whether state law exists and operates as a monolithic control form, its various agencies and operations are at least publicly accountable. Private forms of justice are not. While numerous refinements and endless energy are invested in public systems of criminal justice to protect the individual's right to due process and to guard against excessive or abusive use of state power, rarely are limitations on arbitrary decision making and potential abuse exercised in the day-to-day working of non-state social control.

Second, more people are governed by and controlled through these numerous interwoven non-state systems of justice on a daily basis than by the relatively distant involvement they have with state law. To twist Ehrlich's (1913) famous observation, it is non-state justice that is the 'living law' of society, the normative life of its people; however, *rarely* is it the source of legal norms and *almost never* is it subject to procedural safeguards to protect against abuses.

Let us consider one example as illustrative of the growing significance of non-state justice: private police. In the United States, according to a recent National Institute of Justice Report, 'Private security is now clearly the Nations's primary protective resource, outspending public law enforcement by 73 percent and employing $2^1/_2$ times the workforce' (Cunningham *et al.*, 1991, p. l). While public law enforcement has an annual expenditure of $30 billion and a workforce of 600,000, private security agencies spend $52 billion and employ 1.5 million. The projected average annual rate of growth in private security is 8 per cent through the year 2000 (ibid.). This partly reflects the privatization of policing functions. Indeed, since the 1950s the trend has been for private police to outnumber public police. Moreover since 1977, expenditure on private police has also exceeded expenditure on public police. But private policing is the law enforcement arm of private industry and has the sole objective of protecting the owner's private property and interests. Only occasionally are private police forces licensed. They are typically unregulated except by their membership associations (South, 1988).

Consider a second example, that of workplace discipline in the US. Although a sizeable body of law now governs the use of disciplinary and discharge measures against employees in unionized companies in the form of arbitral case law based on the 'just cause' clause in collective bargaining agreements, this does not affect the operation of internal discipline in non-unionized private industry. Arbitration of disciplinary and discharge disputes is thus restricted to those firms which have arbitration provisions in their bargaining agreements. However, only 11 per cent of US employees are union members, and the trend of declining union membership has continued every year since its peak of 36 per cent in 1945. The critical question thus becomes, what disciplinary controls befall all those employees working in non-unionized companies? Here, in spite of arguments that all employees should be protected by statutory 'just cause' termination law (Summers, 1976) and in spite of recent changes in organizational governance towards due process and alternative forms of dispute resolution (Westin and Feliu, 1988; Dobbin *et al.*, 1988) as well as some changes in law (Stickler, 1983), non-unionized employees are still generally considered to be 'employees at-will' and are largely unprotected from arbitrary employer discipline and discharge. Under this doctrine, the employer may terminate the employment relationship whether with reason, cause or no cause at all (Timmerman, 1988, pp. 1241–2). At present, and in spite of the avalanche of legislation mitigating the harsh and absolute application of the at-will doctrine for unionized employees, 'many employees still do not fit within a statutorily protected class' since, not being members of a union nor civil servants, they are 'not protected from the possibility of severe application of the at-will doctrine' (ibid., pp. 244–5). Timmerman notes that, of the approximately 70 million unprotected employees, 'disappointingly, the class that are most adversely affected by the rule are comprised disproportionately of lower-skilled employees who have the greatest need for protection'. At its most basic, then, and in spite of degrees of erosion (Naylor, 1983; Heinsz, 1983; Stickler, 1983), employers retain the absolute right to discipline and discharge employees; 'so long as discipline is not administered for an unlawful reason, the employer is free to exercise this right at will' (Redeker, 1983, p. 5). Unlike criminal law, the employer retains the right to define the offences liable to discipline or discharge. In the US two million non-probationary workers are discharged annually, and it has been estimated that 150,000 to 200,000 are discharged without good cause (Uniform Law Commissioners, 1991). Typically, at-will employees who are discharged do not have recourse to any forum for review of the decision.

Following Gurvitch (1947), it is helpful to conceive of the range of different organized, non-state forms of social control as existing on a horizontal plane. These perform the control functions of a social organization, group or sub-group. Then, for analytical purposes, consider the degree of formality of the control mechanism on a vertical plane, as ranging from informal to formal. With this schema a social formation, such as a firm, can be seen to have its own non-state form of social control which would be its system of administering internal discipline. However, its internal discipline may range from informal control methods, operating either as expectations of employees, to very formal methods, as in the written rules and procedures specified in a union contract and carried out by specialized disciplinary boards specifically organized for that purpose. Moreover, within any one setting, the number of types of non-state social control systems (horizontal plane) can vary depending upon the number of types of subgroups or subsystems, each also varying in its degree of formality (vertical plane). So, in the example of our one firm, unions may also have their own disciplinary system, being more or less formalized, as may groups of employees, work teams and other social cliques. Each subsystem of private justice exercises control over individuals and collectively vies with other private and state control forms.

Clearly any consideration of non-state forms of social control must also be an examination of the theory of 'legal pluralism' and must address the varying interrelationships between the different types of social control and between their varying levels of formality. Further, insofar as the forms of non-state control exist in an ambivalent relationship to state law – sometimes supporting it, at other times contradicting and even undermining it – consideration must also be given to how these forms relate to and even constitute the totality of control in a society.

Recognition of the significance of non-state forms of social control has led socio-legal theorists to revise their thinking about the relationship between law and society. Traditionally, as Griffiths (1979) has pointed out, the prevailing view has considered law as an object separate from, produced by and subject to the actions of external social forces, whether these be society, classes, groups or agencies. However, this perspective glosses over the possibility entertained by legal pluralism, founded in Gierke (1900), Ross (1901), Ehrlich (1913) and Gurvitch (1947), that norms and rules can be generated relatively autonomously, outside of the governmental process.

The legal pluralist idea is best expressed in Pospisil's (1971, p. 98) view that '... any human society does not possess a single legal system but as many systems as there are functioning groups'. Legal pluralists do not necessarily see groups as instrumental in shaping state law, but as developing their own 'normative orders' (Weber, 1954) or 'living law' (Ehrlich, 1913). The central idea is that societies do not possess a single legal system, but a multiplicity of contradictory law-like normative orders.

The suggestion that state law and its institutions for administering justice are but one form of social control has been a core feature of legal pluralism from the foundations of theorizing about law. However, the legal pluralist tradition has focused on the character, source and hierarchical place of non-state normative orders in relation to state law. Until the mid-1970s, much of their argument explored the relationship between indigenous tribal customs and European colonial law (Pospisil, 1971; Diamond, 1973; Hooker, 1975). This tradition saw indigenous orders as autonomous and independent, yet subordinate to colonial law. Recently, the emphasis has shifted to non-colonial societies, but retains its concern with the hierarchical power relations between dominant and subordinate law forms. Thus many critical theorists (Abel, 1981, 1982; Brady, 1981; Harrington, 1985; Cohen, 1985; Hofrichter, 1987) take informal justice institutions as the subordinate normative order and see these as serving the ideological function of blurring the power of the state so that the latter appears to be a benign part of the social fabric. They have shown that this ideological subordination is accomplished by the cooptation and exploitation of the human desire for informal and localized community justice, and that the episodic tendency towards 'informal' decentralized state control serves a dual legitimating and net-widening function for the state. These criticisms seem more applicable to the growth of state-sponsored dispute settlement institutions than to explaining the state's interrelationship with other established, formalized non-state normative orders which have largely been ignored. Only very recently, however, has attention turned to the contribution that the social relations of these non-state systems of law make in constituting state law.

Critical contributions to the legal pluralist debate argue that recognition of the interpenetrating role of non-state forms of social control requires a new conception of law in society. Hunt (1987, p. 16), for example, calls this the 'relational theory of law'; Harrington (1988) labels it the 'constitutive theory' and Santos (1987) and Teubner (1992) describe it as 'postmodernist' and 'deconstructionist' respectively.

Constitutive theory is based on the idea that law is, in part, social relations and that social relations are, in part, law (Fitzpatrick, 1983a; 1983b; 1984). It is the movement and tension whereby these are socially constituted – 'the way "society" is produced *within* "law"' (Nelken, 1986, p. 325) – rather than how they interact, that is crucial to understanding the law-society interface. Thus, instead of assuming that state law is the hub of social control whose spokes radiate as unidirectional pathways of influence to other social and normative orders, constitutive theory also directs our attention to the reverse process: forms and mechanisms whereby legal relations are penetrated by extra-legal social relations. A constitutive approach examines both the presence and the source of other social forms, 'which are not simply variant forms of legal reasoning but derive their significance and their legitimating capacity from the forms of social relations from which they originate' (Hunt, 1987, p. 18).

It is not, then, just that law is created by classes or interest groups, whether instrumentally or symbolically, to maintain or increase their power. Rather, some of the relations of these groups, particularly their rules and procedures, are, and indeed become, the relations of law. This dialectical analysis suggests that 'any site of social relations is likely to be traversed by a variety of state and non-state legal networks' and that 'what constitutes "the law" in any specific site therefore will depend upon which legal agencies (or more precisely which parts of which networks) intersect in that context, how these orders are mobilized, and how they interact' (O'Malley, 1991, p. 172).

Thus, instead of treating law as an autonomous field of enquiry linked only by external relations to the rest of society, or investigating the way 'law' and 'society' as concrete entities 'influence' or 'affect' each other, constitutive legal pluralism takes law as its subject of inquiry but pursues it by exploring the interrelations 'between legal relations and other forms of social relations' (Hunt, 1987, p. 16; Nelken, 1986, p. 324). As Hunt (1990, p. 539) observes: 'The quest is for ways of articulating the sense in which law (or better, legal relations) are generated within non-legal social relations; legal relations and social relations interpenetrate.'

One of the first to recognize the mutuality between state law and non-state forms was Moore (1973). She argues that law is not a fixed autonomous entity but a 'semi-autonomous field' which, while having rule-making and enforcement capacity, is also 'vulnerable to rules and decisions and other forces emanating from the larger world by which it is surrounded'. She claims that law is 'set in a larger social matrix which can and does affect and invade it' (Moore, 1973, p. 720).

Considering this interrelationship, some draw on Foucault's (1977) demonstration that the modern era has seen state control dispersed into the social fabric to become part of a hidden totality of surveillance (Cohen, 1979; 1985). Important too is Foucault's (1979) 'rule of double conditioning' in which power is exercised, not only from the top, but through distinct, localized machinery, which itself is effective only as part of a general overarching strategy of power. At the same time as the general strategy is distinct it is also, in turn, dependent for its effectiveness on local strategies. Similarly, Galanter (1981) argues that as formal justice moves outward, it influences indigenous orders of justice that exist in a variety of groups and organizational settings, and that this 'legal shadow' provides 'many rooms' of justice to handle the overflow from the formal state system. Central to this view is the insight that these 'rooms' also cast their own shadow on state law. The critical issue is how far these 'rooms', in their interrelationship with state law, simultaneously give identity to that law.

Developing these ideas into the concept of 'integral plurality', Peter Fitzpatrick, considerably influenced by Foucault, says that the reason state law is, in part, shaped by the plurality of other social forms, while these forms are simultaneously being shaped by it, is because '... elements of law *are* elements of other forms and *vice versa*' (Fitzpatrick, 1984, p.122; reprinted as Chapter 5). While law incorporates other forms, transforming them into its own image and likeness, the process is not unilateral but mutual, such that 'law in turn supports the other forms but becomes in the process, part of the other forms' (ibid.). As such, 'state law is integrally constituted in relation to a plurality of other social forms' and 'depends on social forms that tend to undermine it' (ibid., p. 118).

Fitzpatrick's theory of integral plurality is a considerable advance, both over earlier legal pluralism and over critical legal theory, for it demonstrates that there is not so much a unilinear relationship with other social forms, but rather that 'law is the unsettled product of relations with a plurality of other social forms. As such, law's identity is constantly and inherently subject to challenge and change' (Fitzpatrick, 1984, p.138). His fundamental insight is to recognize that state law obtains some of its identity from its interrelationship with non-state forms and vice versa; that without this connection each would be constitutively different.

In another paper, Fitzpatrick (1988) argues that the interrelations between state law and non-state normative orders form new entities as a common discourse and common set of practices, worked out between participating arenas of power. This is particularly evident in the context where law is being synthesized from other existing sets of rules and norms. Fitzpatrick says that in the process of the synopsis of existing rules and practices, the participating networks retain their own relative autonomy; however, 'integrating homologies' (corresponding structures) are formed which merge selected elements of the component networks into an emergent whole that becomes the new law. O'Malley (1991, pp. 172–3), developing this idea further, describes these attempts at legal synthesis as 'synoptic projects' which

> are characterized by the emergence of a common and integrating discourse and set of practices worked out between interacting agencies. Such negotiation involves suppression of incompatible elements of the different participating agencies' knowledges and practices, translation of other elements into more compatible forms, and the integration of all into a workable whole, albeit often inconsistent, labile and conflicting. In this process emergent, synthetic or synoptic social practices and knowledges may appear.

O'Malley claims that such 'synoptic projects' are most likely to occur where changing conditions, such as the emergence of obstacles to the continued effectiveness of existing arrangements, make their continued operation problematic. For Teubner (1992, pp. 1453–4), the process is one of 'interdiscursivity' where intraorganizational legal discourse 'productively misunderstands' and misreads (through its rereading, reinterpreting, reconstructing and reobservation) 'organizational self-production as norm production and thus invents a new and rich "source" of law'. A similar misreading occurs, says Teubner in Chapter 9, when the organization reincorporates legal rules developed and refined in disciplinary proceedings and makes use of them to restructure its organizational decision making.

In summary, developments in constitutive legal pluralism have taken a postmodernist stance (Santos, 1987; Hunt, 1990; Teubner, 1992), arguing that law is mutually constituted through social relations and discursive misreading. The discursive processes of non-state social control, with which state law is interrelated and interwoven, provide a significant context of synoptic projects wherein old power is moulded into new forms. Although constructively critical of this new legal pluralism from the perspective of legal autopoiesis, Teubner (1992, p. 1443) accurately observes that relations between the legal and the social are characterized by 'discursive interwoveness', are 'highly ambiguous, almost paradoxical: separate but intertwined, closed but open'. He argues that this new legal pluralism is 'no longer defined as a set of conflicting social norms in a given social field but as a multiplicity of diverse communicative processes that observe social action under the binary code of legal/illegal' (ibid., p. 1451). It follows, as O'Malley (1988), Merry (1988), Hunt (1987) and Santos (1985; 1987) have argued, that to understand the form and process of state law, it is crucial to establish the social sources of the non-state forms with which it is interrelated and thereby partially constituted.

Although much has been said about how law shapes social forms and about how interests shape law, little research has been done on the way that forms of semi-autonomous non-state control interrelate with and constitute state law while also being constituted by it. However, as Merry (1988, p. 881) argues in Chapter 8, although research in the 1980s emphasizes (1) 'the way state law penetrates and restructures other normative orders ...' and (2) the way non-state normative orders either 'resist or circumvent penetration' or 'capture and use the symbolic capital of state law', the study of the way non-state normative orders constitute state law is 'in its infancy'.

The research that does exist shows how individual agents can penetrate the practice of state law. For example Yngvesson's (1985) research on court clerks shows how they are able to constitute the legality of the lower courts through their understanding of the norms prevalent in the local community. Similarly, Hutton's (1986) study of the structuring of lay participation in public inquiry shows the limits of this penetration. In documenting the central role of 'The Reporter', whose control of procedure and data collection reinforces the ideologies of 'justice according to law' and 'individual responsibility', Hutton shows how forums of lay participation are occasions for reproducing the dominant ideological structure of liberal-democratic law, while restricting and diverting lay criticism. The notion of 'confinement by consent' is found in the work of Milovanovic and Thomas (1989; Milovanovic, 1988; Thomas, 1988), in their accounts of the inmate turned jailhouse lawyer who inadvertently maintains legitimation and conventional understandings of capitalist legality. This notion is paralleled in the work of Bannister and Milovanovic (1990) who show that the activist lawyer attempting to politicize a trial begins to make use of the constraining categories and legal discourse which are the very supports of the rule of law ideology. Importantly, these studies have a tendency to show how the human agents who penetrate state law are drawn to reproduce it more than they are to transform it. Neglected is the extent to which their agency contribution transforms that law in the process of constituting it. Also not researched is how more formal normative orders (such as professional self-regulatory bodies as well as industrial discipline and dismissal rules and procedures) and the variety of other non-state forms of social control are constitutive of state law.

In considering the theoretical significance of constitutive legal pluralism as an approach to understanding non-state social control, it might be worth stating the obvious. Law, and particularly statutory law creation, is often a deliberate effort to incorporate custom and practice, norms and rules prevailing in other settings. After all, is it not the job of legislators in a democratic society to synthesize the subsystems of normative life into a general legal framework? The point here, however, is that by recognizing the relative autonomy of these non-state forms of social control, and simultaneously recognizing their ability to interrelate with state law, the theory allows for the possibility that law creation will have an unpredictable outcome. In this process the eventual product is inevitably different from what its drafters will have intended. This is so precisely because of the relative autonomy of the relations of non-state law.

More broadly, the significance of this approach to law, says Nelken (1986, p. 323), is that it provides 'a useful corrective to other recent work in the sociology of law that has tended towards too radical a separation between law and society'. It allows us to move 'beyond the paradigm concerned with law's "effects" on society, without abandoning the enterprise of investigating how law enters into the production and reproduction of society' For Hunt (1990, p. 339), who is pessimistic about the destiny of the constitutive theoretical turn due to its postmodernist, nihilistic and relativistic epistemology, its value lies in the emphasis on 'the coexistence and mutual determination of practices and discourses, structure and agency'.

In taking non-state social control seriously, the contributions selected for this volume reveal a new way of thinking about the relationship between law and society which has important theoretical, practical and political implications. In so far as it exposes the extent to which private non-state social control contributes a hidden hand to state law, it will help inform policy considerations when analysing the impact of any changes in the patterns and technologies of social control.

Any attempt to suggest that there is some natural logic to the order of the contributions in this volume has been abandoned to the realistic recognition that they were written at different times, to address different themes and arguments, and are developed at varying levels of theoretical sophistication and empirical thoroughness. In my introductory comments I have attempted to address their key themes, if not every paper in detail. For convenience, the chapters have been organized into three broad categories which, while overlapping, also exhibit discrete differences. Parts I and II inform aspects of the theoretical debate whereas Part II contains more empirical contributions. Part I develops the Foucaldian contribution to this debate, by identifying the diversity of sources of power and the dispersal of social control into the subtle and not so subtle disciplinary technologies that pervade modern society. Part II redirects our thinking about the law and society relationship towards acknowledging the mutually constitutive theoretical approach outlined in my introductory comments above. It contains theoretical analyses that both review and bring together the historical development of legal pluralism with the new critical constitutive approach to law and society. Finally, Part III presents some of the empirical case studies of non-state forms of social control that have been the source for this revision of thinking. It includes examples of the more romantic vision of the role of non-state control as being harnessed to benefit society through community courts. However, it concentrates on examples which alert us to the dangers of informal control systems such as those found in prisons, private commercial and policing and corporate security, industrial discipline and workplace sanctions, corporate insurance and professional social control. In these examples we glimpse the impossibility that non-state justice can ever be freed from the wider socio-political matrix in which it is enmeshed.

Overall it is hoped that this selection of essays will provide just the right mix of theory and description to enlighten the serious student to the importance of non-state systems of social control.

References

Abel, R. (1981), 'Conservative Conflict and the Reproduction of Capitalism: The Role of Informal Justice', *International Journal of the Sociology of Law*, **9**, pp. 245–67.
Abel, R. (ed.) (1982), *The Politics of Informal Justice*, 2 vols, New York: Academic Press.

Bannister, S. and Dragan Milovanovic (1990), 'The Necessity Defense, Substantive Justice and Oppositiona Linguistic Praxis', *International Journal of the Sociology of Law*, **18**, pp. 179–98.

Brady, J.P. (1981), 'Sorting Out the Exile's Confusion: Or a Dialogue on Popular Justice', *Contemporar Crisis*, **5**, pp. 31–8.

*Cohen, S. (1979), 'The Punitive City: Notes on the Dispersal of Social Control', *Contemporary Crisis 2*, pp. 339–65.

Cohen, S. (1985), *Visions of Social Control*, Oxford: Polity Press.

Cunningham, W.C. *et al.* (1991), *Private Security: Patterns and Trends*, NIJ Research Brief.

Diamond, S. (1973), 'The Rule of Law Versus the Order of Custom' in D. Black and M. Mileski (eds) *The Social Organization of Law*, New York: Seminar Press.

Dobbin, F.R. *et al.* (1988), 'The Expansion of Due Process in Organizations' in L. Zucker (ed.) *Institutional Patterns and Organizations: Culture and Environment*, Cambridge, Mass: Ballinger.

Ehrlich, E. (1913), *Fundamental Principles of the Sociology of Law*, Cambridge, Mass: Harvard Universit Press.

Fitzpatrick, P. (1983a), 'Law, Plurality and Underdevelopment' in D. Sugarman (ed.), *Legality. Ideolog and the State*, London: Academic Press.

Fitzpatrick, P. (1983b), 'Marxism and Legal Pluralism' *Australian Journal of Law and Society*, **1** pp. 45–59.

* Fitzpatrick, P. (1984), 'Law and Societies', *Osgoode Hall Law Journal*, **22**, pp. 115–38.

Fitzpatrick, P. (1988), 'The Rise and Rise of Informalism' in R. Matthews (ed.), *Informal Justice* London: Sage.

Foucault, M. (1977), *Discipline and Punish*, Harmondsworth: Penguin.

Foucault, M. (1979), *The History of Sexuality, Volume I: An Introduction*, London: Allan Lane.

Galanter, M. (1981), 'Justice in Many Rooms: Courts, Private Ordering and Indigenous Law', *Journa of Legal Pluralism*, **19**, pp. 1–47.

Gierke, O. (1958), *Political Theories of the Middle Age*, Cambridge: Cambridge University Press, firs published in 1900.

Griffiths, J. (1979), 'Is Law Important?', *New York University Law Review*, **54**, pp. 339–74.

Gurvitch, G. (1947), *The Sociology of Law*, London: Routledge and Kegan Paul.

Harrington, C. (1985), *Shadow Justice: The Ideology and Institutionalization of Alternatives to Courts* Westport: Greenwood Press.

*Harrington, C. (1988), 'Moving from Integrative to Constitutive Theories of Law: Comment on Itzkowitz', *Law and Society Review*, **22**, pp. 963–7.

Heinsz, T. (1983), 'The Assault on the Employment At Will Doctrine: Management Considerations' Montana Law Review, **48**, pp. 855–92.

Henry, S. (1983), *Private Justice: Towards Integrated Theorizing in the Sociology of Law*, London: Routledge and Kegan Paul.

Henry, S. (1987), 'The Construction and Deconstruction of Social Control: Thoughts on the Discursive Production of State Law and Private Justice' in J. Lowman, R. Menzies and T. Palys (eds), *Transcarceration: Essays in the Sociology of Social Control*, Aldershot: Gower Press.

Hofrichter, R. (1987), *Neighborhood Justice in Capitalist Society: The Expansion of the Informal State*, Westport: Greenwood Press.

Hooker, M. (1975), *Legal Pluralism: An Introduction to Colonial and Neo-Colonial Laws*, Oxford: Clarendon Press.

Hunt, A. (1987), 'The Critique of Law: What is "Critical" about Critical Legal Theory?', *Journal of Law and Society*, **14**, pp. 5–19.

Hunt, A. (1990), 'The Big Fear: Law Confronts Postmodernism', *McGill Law Journal*, **35**, pp. 507–40.

Hutton, N. (1986), *Lay Participation in a Public Local Inquiry*, Aldershot: Gower.

*Merry, S. (1988), 'Legal Pluralism', *Law and Society Review*, **22**, pp. 869–96.

Milovanovic, D. (1988), 'Jailhouse Lawyers and Jailhouse Lawyering', *International Journal of the Sociology of Law*, **16**, pp. 455–75.

Milovanovic, D. and J. Thomas (1989), 'Overcoming the Absurd: Prisoner Litigation as Primitive Rebellion', *Social Problems*, **36**, pp. 48–60.

Moore, S. (1973). 'Law and Social Change: The Semi-Autonomous Field as an Appropriate Subject of Study', *Law and Society Review*, **7**, pp. 719–46.

Taylor, G. (1983), 'Employment At Will: The Decay of an Anachronistic Shield for Employers', *Drake Law Review*, **33**, pp. 113–31.

Nelken, D. (1986), 'Beyond the Study of "Law and Society"?: Henry's Private Justice and O'Hagan's The End of Law', *American Bar Association Research Journal*, **2**, pp. 323–38.

O'Malley, P. (1991), 'Legal Networks and Domestic Security', *Law, Politics, and Society*, **11**, pp. 171–90.

Pospisil, L. (1971), *Anthropology of Law*, New York: Harper and Row.

Redeker, J. (1983), *Discipline: Policies and Procedures*, Washington: The Bureau of National Affairs.

Ross, E. (1901), *Social Control: A Study of the Foundations of Social Order*, New York: Macmillan.

Santos, B.S. (1985), 'On Modes of Production of Law and Social Power', *International Journal of the Sociology of Law*, **13**, pp. 299–336.

Santos, B.S. (1987), 'Law: A Map of Misreading. Toward a Postmodern Conception of Law', *Journal of Law and Society*, **14**, pp. 279–302.

South, N. (1988), *Policing for Profit*, London: Sage.

Stickler, K.B. (1983), 'Limitations on an Employer's Right to Discipline and Discharge Employees', *Employee Relations Law Journal*, **9**, pp. 70–80.

Summers, C.W. (1976), 'Individual Protection Against Unjust Dismissal: Time for a Statute', *Virginia Law Review*, **62**, pp. 481–532.

Teubner, G. (1992), 'The Two Faces of Janus: Rethinking Legal Pluralism', *Cardozo Law Review*, **13**, pp. 1443–62.

Thomas, J. (1988), *Prisoner Litigation: The Paradox of the Jailhouse Lawyer,* Totowa, New Jersey: Rowman and Littlefield.

Zimmerman, T. (1988), 'Legislative Attempts to Modify the Employment At-will Doctrine: Will the Public Policy Exception be the Next Step?', *The Journal of Corporation Law*, **14**, pp. 241–64.

Uniform Law Commissioners (1991), *Model Employment Termination Act*, Chicago: National Conference of Commissioners on Uniform State Laws.

Weber, M. (1954), *On Law Economy and Society* in Max Rheinstein (ed.), New York: Simon and Schuster.

Westin, A. and A. Feliu (1988), *Resolving Employment Disputes without Litigation*, Washington DC: Bureau of National Affairs.

Yngvesson, B. (1985), 'Legal Ideology and Community Justice in the Clerk's Office', *Legal Studies Forum*, **9**, pp. 71–87.

Reprinted in this volume.

Part I
Theoretical Background:
Foucault, Power and Sanctions

[1]

Chapter 1
Foucault on Modern Power:
Empirical Insights and Normative Confusions

Until his untimely death in 1984, Michel Foucault had been theorizing about and practicing a new form of politically engaged reflection on the emergence and nature of modern societies. This reflection, which Foucault called "genealogy," has produced some extremely valuable results. It has opened up new areas of inquiry and problematized new dimensions of modernity; as a result, it has made it possible to broach political problems in fruitful new ways. But Foucault's work is also beset by difficulties. It raises a number of important philosophical questions that it is not, in itself, equipped to answer. This paper aims to survey the principal strengths and shortcomings of Foucault's work and to provide a balanced assessment of it.

Most generally, it is my thesis that Foucault's most valuable accomplishment consists of a rich empirical account of the early stages in the emergence of some distinctively modern modalities of power. This account yields important insights into the nature of modern power, and these insights, in turn, bear political sig-

---

This paper was originally written in 1980–81, before Michel Foucault's death. I cast it in the present and future tenses on the assumptions that my dialogue with him would be ongoing and that his thinking on the subjects discussed would continue to develop. Now that these assumptions no longer hold, I have had to reconsider the question of tense. I have proceeded as follows: in instances where the present or future tense seemed to me jarringly inappropriate, I have substituted the past tense; in instances where the present tense seemed to suggest, entirely rightly, the continuing relevance of Foucault's work, I have left it unchanged.

nificance—they suffice to rule out some rather widespread political orientations
as inadequate to the complexities of power in modern societies.

For example, Foucault's account establishes that modern power is "productive" rather than prohibitive. This suffices to rule out those types of liberationist
politics that presuppose that power is essentially repressive. Similarly, Foucault's
account demonstrates that modern power is "capillary," that it operates at the
lowest extremities of the social body in everyday social practices. This suffices to
rule out state-centered and economistic political praxes, since these praxes presuppose that power resides solely in the state or economy. Finally, Foucault's genealogy of modern power establishes that power touches people's lives more fundamentally through their social practices than through their beliefs. This, in turn,
suffices to rule out political orientations aimed primarily at the demystification of
ideologically distorted belief systems.

This is not to suggest that the sole importance of Foucault's account of the
nature and emergence of modern forms of power is the negative one of ruling out
inadequate political orientations. More positively, it is that Foucault enables us to
understand power very broadly, and yet very finely, as anchored in the multiplicity of what he calls "micropractices," the social practices that constitute everyday life in modern societies. This positive conception of power has the general
but unmistakable implication of a call for a "politics of everyday life."

These, in general, are what I take to be Foucault's principal accomplishments
and contributions to the understanding of modern societies. They were made possible, it seems, by Foucault's use of his unique genealogical method of social and
historical description. This method involves, among other things, the suspension
of the standard modern liberal normative framework, which distinguishes between the legitimate and illegitimate exercise of power. Foucault brackets those
notions, and the questions they give rise to, and concentrates instead upon the
actual ways in which power operates.

As I have said, Foucault's suspension of the problematic of legitimacy has unquestionably been fruitful. It is what enables him to look at the phenomenon of
power in interesting new ways and, thereby, to bring to light important new dimensions of modern societies. But, at the same time, it has given, or is likely to
give, rise to some grave difficulties. For example, it has been or may be supposed
that Foucault has given us a value-neutral account of modern power. Or, alternatively, since this does not square with the obvious politically engaged character of
his writing, that he has educed some other normative framework as an alternative
to the suspended one; or, since none is readily apparent, that he has found a way
to do politically engaged critique without the use of any normative framework;
or, more generally, that he has disposed altogether of the need for any normative
framework to guide political practice.

Clearly, a number of these suppositions are mutually incompatible. Yet Foucault's work seems simultaneously to invite all of them. He tends to assume that

his account of modern power is both politically engaged and normatively neutral. At the same time, he is unclear as to whether he suspends all normative notions or only the liberal norms of legitimacy and illegitimacy. To make matters worse, Foucault sometimes appears not to have suspended the liberal norms after all but, rather, to be presupposing them.

These, then, are what I take to be the most serious difficulties in Foucault's work. They appear to stand in a rather curious relationship to the strengths I have mentioned; it seems that the very methodological strategies that make possible the empirically and politically valuable description of power are intimately tied to the normative ambiguities.

In what follows, I propose to explore these issues systematically. First, I shall outline Foucault's genealogical method, including his suspension of the liberal normative framework of legitimacy. Next, I shall give an account of Foucault's historical insights concerning the nature and origin of modern power that the genealogical method has made possible. After that, I shall briefly discuss the valuable political implications of the view of modern power that emerges. And, finally, in the fourth and last section of the paper, I shall discuss the difficulties pertaining to the normative dimensions of Foucault's work.

1. The Genealogical Method and the Bracketing of the Problematic of Legitimacy

Following Nietzsche, Foucault calls the form of his reflection on the nature and development of modern power "genealogy."[1] What he means by this can best be approximated negatively at first, in contrast to a number of other approaches to the study of cultural and historical phenomena. Genealogy represents a break, for example, with semiology and structuralism, which analyze culture in terms of systems of signs.[2] Instead, it seeks to conceive culture as practices. Furthermore, genealogy is not to be confused with hermeneutics, which Foucault understands (no doubt anachronistically) as the search for deep hidden meanings beneath language, for the signified behind the signifier. Genealogy takes it as axiomatic that everything is interpretation all the way down,[3] or, to put it less figuratively, that cultural practices are instituted historically and are therefore contingent, ungrounded except in terms of other, prior, contingent, historically instituted practices. Foucault also claims that genealogy is opposed to critique of ideology. Again, his understanding of that enterprise is somewhat crude; he means that genealogy does not concern itself with evaluating the contents of science or systems of knowledge — or, for that matter, with systems of beliefs at all. Rather, it is concerned with the processes, procedures, and apparatuses whereby truth, knowledge, belief are produced, with what Foucault calls the "politics of the discursive regime."[4] Moreover, Foucault contends that genealogy must be distinguished from history of ideas. It does not seek to chronicle the continuous development of discursive content or practices. On the contrary, it is oriented to discontinuities. Like Thomas Kuhn, Foucault assumes the existence of a plurality of incommensurable discursive regimes that succeed one another historically. He also assumes that each of these regimes is supported by its own correlated matrix of practices. Each includes its own distinctive objects of inquiry; its own criteria of well-formedness for statements admitted to candidacy for truth and falsity; its own procedures for generating, storing, and arranging data; its own institutional sanctions and matrices.[5]

It is the whole nexus of such objects, criteria, practices, procedures, institutions, apparatuses, and operations that Foucault means to designate by his term 'power/knowledge regime'. This term thus covers in a single concept everything that falls under the two distinct Kuhnian concepts of paradigm and disciplinary matrix. But, unlike Kuhn, Foucault gives this complex an explicitly political character. Both the use of the term 'power' and that of the term 'regime' convey this political coloration.

Foucault claims that the functioning of discursive regimes essentially involves forms of social constraint. Such constraints and the manner of their application vary, of course, along with the regime. Typically, however, they include such phenomena as the valorization of some statement forms and the concomitant devaluation of others; the institutional licensing of some persons as authorized to offer authoritative knowledge claims and the concomitant exclusion of others; procedures for the extraction of information from and about persons involving various forms of coercion; and the proliferation of discourses oriented to objects of inquiry that are, at the same time, targets for the application of social policy.[6] Their obvious heterogeneity notwithstanding, all of these are instances of the ways in which social constraint, or in Foucault's terms "power," circulates in and through the production of discourses in societies.

What Foucault is interested in when he claims to be studying the genealogy of power/knowledge regimes should now be clear: he concerns himself with the holistic and historically relative study of the formation and functioning of incommensurable networks of social practices involving the mutual interrelationship of constraint and discourse.

Foucauldian genealogy is obviously a unique and original approach to culture. It groups together phenomena that are usually kept separate and separates phenomena that are usually grouped together. It does this by adhering, or professing to adhere, to a number of methodological strategies that can be likened to bracketings.[7]

'Bracketing', of course, is not Foucault's term; given its association with the phenomenological tradition to which he is so hostile, he would doubtless reject it. Nevertheless, the term is suggestive of the sort of studied suspension of standard categories and problematics that he practices. It should already be apparent, for example, that Foucault's approach to the study of power/knowledge regimes suspends the categories truth/falsity or truth/ideology. It suspends, that is, the problematic of epistemic justification. Foucault simply does not take up the question of whether the various regimes he studies provide knowledge that is in any sense true or warranted or adequate or undistorted. Instead of assessing epistemic contents, he describes knowledge production procedures, practices, apparatuses and institutions.[8]

This bracketing of the problematic of epistemic justification is susceptible to a variety of construals. It can be seen as strictly heuristic and provisional and, therefore, as leaving open the questions whether such justification is possible and, if so, in what it consists. Alternatively, it can be seen less minimally as a substantive, principled commitment to some version of epistemological cultural relativism. The textual evidence is contradictory, although the preponderance surely lies with the second, substantive, construal.

Be that as it may, Foucault's views on epistemic justification are not my primary concern here. More to the point is another sort of bracketing, one that pertains to the problematic of *normative* justification. Foucault claims to suspend such justification in his study of power/knowledge regimes. He says he does not take up the question of whether or not the various constraint-laden practices, institutions, procedures, and apparatuses he studies are legitimate or not: he refrains from problematizing the normative validity of power/knowledge regimes.[9]

A number of very important questions arise concerning the nature and extent of Foucault's bracketing of the normative. What exactly is its intended scope? Does Foucault intend to suspend one particular normative framework only, namely, the framework of modern liberal political theory, whose central categories are those of right, limit, sovereignty, contract, and oppression? This framework distinguishes between, on the one hand, the legitimate exercise of sovereign power, which stays within the limits defined by rights, and, on the other, the illegitimate exercise of such power, which transgresses those limits, violates rights, and is thus oppressive.[10] When Foucault excludes the use of the concepts legitimacy and illegitimacy from genealogy, does he mean to exclude only these liberal norms? Or, alternatively, is Foucault's bracketing of the normative rather broader? Does he intend to suspend not only the liberal framework but every normative framework whatsoever? Does he mean he will bracket the problematic of normative justification *simpliciter*? In either case, how do Foucault's proclaimed intentions square with his actual practice of genealogy? Whatever he claims to be doing, does his work in fact suspend all political norms or only the liberal ones?

Furthermore, whatever the scope of bracketing, what is its character? Is Foucault's bracketing of the normative merely a methodological strategy, a temporary heuristic aimed at making it possible to see the phenomena in fresh new ways? If so, then it would leave open the possibility of some subsequent normative assessment of power/knowledge regimes. Or, alternatively, does Foucault's bracketing of the normative represent a substantive, principled commitment to ethical cultural relativism, to the impossibility of normative justification across power/knowledge regimes?

These questions have enormous importance for the interpretation and assessment of Foucault's work. But the answers, by and large, do not lie ready to hand in his writings. To begin to untangle them, it will be necessary to look more closely at the actual concrete use he makes of his genealogical method.

2. The Genealogy of Modern Power

Foucault's empirical study of modern societies focuses on the question of the nature and emergence of distinctively modern forms of power. It is his thesis that modernity consists, at least in part, in the development and operation of a radically new regime of power/knowledge. This regime comprises procedures, practices, objects of inquiry, institutional sites and, above all, forms of social and political constraint that differ markedly from those of previous regimes.

Modern power is unlike earlier powers, according to Foucault, in that it is local, continuous, productive, capillary, and exhaustive. This is so, in part, as a consequence of the circumstances in which it arose. Foucault claims that the modern power/knowledge regime was not imposed from the top down but developed only gradually in local, piecemeal fashion largely in what he calls "disciplinary institutions," beginning in the late eighteenth century. A variety of "microtechniques" were perfected by obscure doctors, wardens, and schoolmasters in obscure hospitals, prisons, and schools, far removed from the great power centers of the *ancien régime*. Only later were these techniques and practices taken up and integrated into what Foucault calls "global or macrostrategies of domination."[11]

The disciplinary institutions were among the first to face the problems of organization, management, surveillance, and control of large numbers of persons. They were the first, that is, to face the problems that would eventually become the constitutive problems of modern government. Hence, the tactics and techniques they pioneered are, in Foucault's view, definitive of modern power.

Foucault describes a variety of new disciplinary microtactics and practices. The one for which he is best known is *le regard* or "the gaze." The gaze was a technique of power/knowledge that enabled administrators to manage their institutional populations by creating and exploiting a new kind of visibility. Administrators organized these populations so they could be seen, known, surveilled, and thus controlled. The new visibility was of two kinds, according to Foucault: synoptic and individualizing.

Synoptic visibility was premised on architectural and organizational innovations that made possible an intelligible overview of the population and of the relations among its elements. It is exemplified in the design of prisons after Bentham's Panopticon (rings of backlit cells encircling a central observation tower), in the separation of hospital patients according to their diseases, and in the arrangement of students in a classroom space articulated expressly to reflect their rank and ability.

Individualizing visibility, on the other hand, aimed at exhaustive, detailed observation of individuals, their habits and histories. Foucault claims that this visibility succeeded in constituting the individual for the first time as a "case," simultaneously a new object of inquiry and a new target of power.[12]

Both kinds of gaze, synoptic and individualizing, were micropractices linking new processes of production of new knowledges to new kinds of power. They combined scientific observation of populations and individuals, and hence a new "science of man," with surveillance. This link depended upon the asymmetrical character of the gaze: it was unidirectional—the scientist or warden could see the inmate but not vice versa. This is most striking in the case of the Panopticon. Because the unidirectionality of visibility denied the inmates knowledge of when and whether they were actually being watched, it made them internalize the gaze and in effect surveil themselves.[13] Less overtly, the forms of scientific observation in other institutions objectified their targets and pried relentlessly into every aspect of their experience.

Foucault would not, however, have us conclude that the objectifying behavioral sciences have a monopoly on the use of the gaze as a microtechnique of modern power/knowledge. He demonstrates the similar functioning of what he calls the "hermeneutics of the psyche." Practices like psychoanalysis, which constitute the individual as speaking subject rather than as behavioral object, also involve an asymmetrical, unidirectional visibility, or perhaps one should say audibility. The producer of the discourse is defined as incapable of deciphering it and is dependent upon a silent hermeneutic authority.[14] Here, too, there is a distinctive use of coercion to obtain knowledge and of knowledge to coerce.

The importance for Foucault of micropractices such as the gaze far transcends their place in the history of early disciplinary institutions. As I noted earlier, they were among the first responses to the problems of population management that later came to define modern government. They were eventually integrated into global political strategies and orientations, but even in their early disciplinary form they evince a number of the hallmarks of a distinctively modern power.

Because they cause power to operate continuously, disciplinary tactics anticipate later developments in the genealogy of modern power. Panoptical surveillance is, in this respect, very different from premodern power mechanisms. The latter operated discontinuously and intermittently and required the presence of an agent to apply force. Modern power, as first developed in disciplinary micropractices, on the other hand, requires no such presence; it replaces violence and force of arms with the "gentler" constraint of uninterrupted visibility. Modern power, then, is distinctive in that it keeps a low profile. It has no need of the spectacular displays characteristic of the exercise of power in the *ancien régime*. It is lower in cost both economically, since it requires less labor power, and socially, since it is less easily targeted for resistance. Yet it is more efficacious. Given its connection with the social sciences, modern power is capable, according to Foucault, of an exhaustive analysis of its objects, indeed of the entire social body. It is neither ignorant nor blind, nor does it strike hit or miss, as did earlier regimes. As a result of its superior hold on detail, it is more penetrating than earlier forms of power. It gets hold of its objects at the deepest level—in their gestures, habits, bodies, and desires. Premodern power, on the other hand, could strike only superficially and from afar. Moreover, modern power, as first developed in disciplinary micropractices, is not essentially situated in some central persons or institutions such as king, sovereign, ruling class, state, or army. Rather, it is everywhere. As the description of panoptical self-surveillance demonstrated, it is even in the targets themselves, in their bodies, gestures, desires, and habits. In other words, as Foucault often says, modern power is capillary. It does not emanate from some central source but circulates throughout the entire social body down to even the tiniest and apparently most trivial extremities.[15]

Taken in combination, these characteristics define the operation of modern power as what Foucault calls "self-amplifying." In this respect also it is unlike the power of the *ancien régime*. The latter operated with, so to speak, a fixed amount of force at its disposal. It expended that force via what Foucault calls "deduction" (*prélèvement*); it simply counterposed itself to the opposing forces and sought to eliminate or minimize them. Modern power, on the other hand, continually augments and increases its own force in the course of its exercise. It does this not by negating opposing forces but rather by utilizing them, by linking them up as transfer points within its own circuitry.[16] Hence, the panoptical mechanism takes up the inmate within the disciplinary economy and makes her surveil herself. It aims not at suppressing her but rather at retooling her. It seeks to produce what Foucault calls "docile and useful bodies."[17] Borrowing Marx's terminology, it may be said that whereas premodern power functioned as a system geared to simple reproduction, modern power is oriented to expanded reproduction.

Foucault's description of the disciplinary origins of modern power is extremely rich and concrete. He produced less in the way of a detailed account of the processes whereby the local, piecemeal microtechniques were integrated into global macrostrategies. The fullest account of that is the one found in volume 1 of his *History of Sexuality*. There, Foucault discusses the modern macrostrategy of "bio-power." Bio-power concerns the management of the production and reproduction of life in modern societies. It is oriented to such new objects of power/knowledge as population, health, urban life, and sexuality. It objectifies these as resources to be administered, cultivated, and controlled. It uses new quantitative social science techniques to count, analyze, predict, and prescribe. It also makes use of widely circulating nonquantitative discourses about sexuality, whose origins Foucault traces to the self-interpretation and self-affirmation of the nineteenth-century middle classes.[18]

In his Tanner Lectures of 1979, Foucault linked his work on bio-power to the problematic of political rationality.[19] Indeed, his treatment of the development and use of social science as an instrument of population resource management and social control is clearly related to more familiar treatments of modernization as a process of rationalization. But there is one striking and very important difference. Whereas for other writers the concepts of rationality and rationalization have a two-sided normative character, in Foucault's usage they do not. In the thought of Jürgen Habermas, for example, rationalization involves a contrast between instrumentalization—which is a one-sided, partial, and insufficient rationalization—and a fuller practical, political rationality. It therefore carries with it a normative standard for critiquing modern societies. Foucault's discussion of political rationality in the Tanner Lectures, on the other hand, contains no such contrast and no positive normative pole. Rationality for him is either a neutral phenomenon or (more often) an instrument of domination *tout court*.[20]

3. The Political Implications of Genealogy

Foucault's picture of a distinctively modern power that functions at the capillary level via a plurality of everyday micropractices yields a number of significant political implications. Some of these are strategic and some are normative.

Consider that Foucault's analysis entails that modern power touches individuals through the various forms of constraint constitutive of their social practices rather than primarily through the distortion of their beliefs. Foucault dramatizes this point by claiming that power is in our bodies, not in our heads. Put less paradoxically, he means that practices are more fundamental than belief systems when it comes to understanding the hold that power has on us.

It follows from this view that the analysis and critique of such practices take priority over the analysis and critique of ideology. Foucault's insight thus tends to rule out at least one rather crude version of ideology critique as strategically inadequate to the social reality of modern power. It rules out, that is, the view that given the appropriate objective material conditions, the only or main thing that stands in the way of social change is people's ideologically distorted perception of their needs and interests. When stated thus baldly, it is questionable whether anyone actually holds this view. Still, Foucault's vivid reminder of the priority of practices is a useful corrective to the potential one-sidedness of even more sophisticated versions of the politics of ideology critique.[21]

A second strategic implication of Foucault's insight into the capillary character of modern power concerns the inadequacy of state-centered and economistic political orientations. Such orientations assume that power emanates from one or the other or both of these central points in society. But Foucault's description of the polymorphous, continuous circulation of power through micropractices belies this assumption. It shows, rather, that power is everywhere and in everyone; it shows that power is as present in the most apparently trivial details and relations of everyday life as it is in corporate suites, industrial assembly lines, parliamentary chambers, and military installations. Foucault's view, therefore, rules out state-centered and/or economistic political orientations. It rules out, that is, the view that the seizure and transformation of state and/or economic power would be sufficient to dismantle or transform the modern power regime.[22]

These two strategic political implications of Foucault's empirical work can be combined and stated more positively. In revealing the capillary character of modern power and thereby ruling out crude ideology critique, statism, and economism, Foucault can be understood as in effect ruling *in* what is often called a "politics of everyday life." For if power is instantiated in mundane social practices and relations, then efforts to dismantle or transform the regime must address those practices and relations.

This is probably the single most important feature of Foucault's thought. He provides the empirical and conceptual basis for treating such phenomena as sexuality, the family, schools, psychiatry, medicine, social science, and the like as *political* phenomena. This sanctions the treatment of problems in these areas as *political* problems. It thereby widens the arena within which people may collectively confront, understand, and seek to change the character of their lives. There is no question that a new move to widen the boundaries of the political arena has been underway in the West since the 1960s. Foucault has clearly been influenced by it and has, in turn, helped to buttress it empirically and conceptually.

In the foregoing considerations of political strategy, it has been taken for granted that the modern power regime is undesirable and in need of dismantling and transformation. But that assumption pertains essentially to the normative political implications of Foucault's genealogical description. It is these that require thematization now.

I have noted several times that in Foucault's account modern power is not applied to individuals by the state or sovereign in a top-down fashion. Rather, it circulates everywhere, even through the tiniest capillaries of the social body. It follows from this, claims Foucault, that the classical liberal normative contrast between legitimate and illegitimate power is not adequate to the nature of modern power. The liberal framework understands power as emanating from the sovereign and imposing itself upon the subjects. It tries to define a power-free zone of rights, the penetration of which is illegitimate. Illegitimate power is understood as oppression, itself understood as the transgression of a limit.

But if power is everywhere and does not emanate from one source or in one direction, then this liberal framework will not apply. Furthermore, given its inapplicability, Foucault claims that the proliferation of discourse governed by this liberal framework may itself function as part of the capillary deployment of modern power. This discourse may function, in other words, to mask the actual character of modern power and thus to conceal domination.[23]

It is clear that with this last charge Foucault has crossed the line between conceptual and substantive normative analysis. In using the term 'domination' at the same time that he is ruling out the liberal normative framework, it appears that he is presupposing some alternative framework. (I will discuss the question as to what that might be in the next section of this paper.) However, if correct, Foucault's empirical thesis that modern power is capillary does not by itself dictate the adoption of any particular normative framework. At most, it undercuts one traditional basis of the liberal one.

A similar situation arises with respect to the normative political implications of Foucault's insight into the productive and self-amplifying character of modern power, his insight into its orientation to what I called "expanded reproduction." This insight belies what Foucault calls "the repressive hypothesis." That hypothesis assumes that power functions essentially negatively, through such operations as interdiction, censorship, and denial. Power, in this view, just says no. It says no to what are defined as illicit desires, needs, acts, and speech. But if Foucault is right, modern power is equally involved in *producing* all these things. His empirical account rules out the repressive hypothesis and the liberationist political orientation it supports. That orientation, which is now rather widespread in the West, aims at liberating what power represses. It makes "illicit" speech, desires, and acts into expressions of political revolt. Not only does Foucault reject it as inadequate to the true nature of modern power, but once again he suggests that it is a feature of the deployment of modern power to proliferate liberationist discourse, once again to mask the actual functioning of domination.[24]

In ruling out the repressive hypothesis, Foucault is ruling out the radical normative framework, which substitutes the contrast "repression versus liberation" for the liberal contrast "legitimacy versus illegitimacy." He has linked both of these frameworks to the functioning of what he identifies as domination. It appears, therefore, that Foucault must be presupposing some alternative normative framework of his own. What might this be?

4. Unanswered Questions concerning the Normative Dimensions of Foucault's Genealogy

It is my thesis that despite his important contributions to the study of modern societies, Foucault's work ends up, in effect, inviting questions that it is structurally unequipped to answer. A brief recap of my line of argument to this point will clarify what I mean by this allegation.

I have claimed that Foucault adopts at least the minimal heuristic principle that power regimes be broached and described as neutral phenomena, that they not, for example, be interrogated immediately from the liberal standpoint as to their legitimacy or illegitimacy. I have also claimed that the use of this methodological strategy permits him to give a perspicuous account of the emergence of the modern power regime, an account that in turn brought to light some neglected features of the operation of power in modern life. Furthermore, I have argued that Foucault's account of modern power constitutes good grounds for rejecting some fairly widespread strategic and normative political orientations and for adopting instead the standpoint of a ''politics of everyday life.''

At the same time, I have left open the question of the nature and extent of Foucault's bracketing of the problematic of normative justification of power/knowledge regimes. I have noted some indications that his description of modern power is in fact not normatively neutral, but I have not systematically pursued these. I now wish to reopen these questions by looking more closely at the politically engaged character of Foucault's work.

Let me begin by noting that Foucault's writings abound with such phrases as 'the age of bio-power', 'the disciplinary society', 'the carceral archipelago' — phrases rife, that is, with ominous overtones. I must also note that Foucault does not shrink from frequent use of such terms as 'domination', 'subjugation', and 'subjection' in describing the modern power/knowledge regime. Accordingly, the main outlines of his description can be tellingly restated as follows: In the early modern period, closed disciplinary institutions like prisons perfected a variety of mechanisms for the fabrication and subjugation of individuals as epistemic objects and as targets of power. These techniques aimed at the retooling of deviants as docile and useful bodies to be reinserted in the social machine. Later, these techniques were exported beyond the confines of their institutional birthplaces and were made the basis for global strategies of domination aimed at the total administration of life. Various discourses that have seemed to oppose this regime have, in fact, supported it, in part by masking its true character.

Put this way, it is clear that Foucault's account of power in modern societies is anything but neutral and unengaged. How, then, did he get from the suspension of the question of the legitimacy of modern power to this engaged critique of bio-power? This is the problem I want to address.

A number of possible explanations come to mind. First, one might read Foucault's critique as politically engaged yet somehow still normatively neutral. One might, that is, interpret his bracketing of the normative as covering *all* political norms, not just the liberal ones. In a variety of interviews, Foucault himself adopts this interpretation. He claims he has approached power strategically and militarily, not normatively. He says he has substituted the perspective of war, with its contrast between struggle and submission, for that of right, with its contrast between legitimacy and illegitimacy.[25] In this interpretation, Foucault's use of the terms 'domination', 'subjugation', and 'subjection' would be normatively neutral: these terms would simply be descriptive of the strategic alignments and modes of operation of the various opposing forces in the modern world.

Such an interpretation is open to a number of questions, however. It is usually the case that strategic military analyses identify the various opposing sides in the struggle. They are capable of specifying who is dominating or subjugating whom and who is resisting or submitting to whom. This Foucault does not do. Indeed, he rejects it as a possibility. He claims that it is misleading to think of power as a property that could be possessed by some persons or classes and not by others; power is better conceived as a complex, shifting field of relations in which everyone is an element.[26]

This claim does not square, strictly speaking, with the fact that Foucault seems at times to link bio-power with class domination and to implicitly accept (at least elements of) the attendant Marxian economic interpretation. Nor does it square with his tendency to identify such capillary agents as social scientists, technologists of behavior, and hermeneutists of the psyche with the "forces of domination."

But whether or not he does or can identify the forces of domination and those they dominate, the claim that his normative-sounding terminology is not normative but, rather, military runs into a second difficulty: the military usage of 'domination', 'struggle', and 'submission' cannot, in and of itself, explain or justify anyone's preference for, or commitment to, one side as opposed to the other. Foucault calls in no uncertain terms for resistance to domination. But why? Why is struggle preferable to submission? Why ought domination to be resisted? Only with the introduction of normative notions of some kind could Foucault begin to answer such questions. Only with the introduction of normative notions could he begin to tell us what is wrong with the modern power/knowledge regime and why we ought to oppose it.

It seems, then, that the assumption that Foucault's critique is engaged but non-normative creates serious difficulties for him. It would perhaps be better to assume that he has not bracketed every normative framework but only the liberal one, the one based on legitimacy. In that case, it becomes essential to discover what alternative normative framework he is presupposing. Could the language of domination, subjugation, struggle, and resistance be interpreted as the skeleton of some alternative framework?

Although this is certainly a theoretical possibility, I am unable to develop it concretely. I find no clues in Foucault's writings as to what his alternative norms might be. I see no hints as to how concretely to interpret 'domination', 'subjugation', 'subjection', and so forth in some completely new "postliberal" fashion. This is not to deny that these terms acquire rich new empirical content from Foucault's descriptions of disciplinary power; 'domination', for example, comes to include *dressage*, which involves the use of nonviolent yet physical force for the production of "normal," conforming, skilled individuals. But such important new meaning accretions and extensions are not in and of themselves tantamount to the elaboration of an entirely new normative framework. They do not, in other words, suffice to tell us precisely what is wrong with discipline in terms wholly independent of the liberal norms. On the contrary, their normative force seems to depend upon tacit appeal to the notions of rights, limits, and the like.

I suggested earlier that Foucault sometimes seems to presuppose that macro-strategies of global domination such as bio-power are connected with class dom-ination and that the Marxian account of the latter is basically right. Could it be, then, that he is presupposing the Marxian normative framework? It is character-istic of that framework, at least on one widely accepted reading, that it does not fully suspend all liberal norms. Rather, it presupposes at least some of them in its critique of capitalist social and productive relations. For example, Marx demon-strates that although the contractual exchange of labor power for wages purports to be symmetrical and free, in fact it is asymmetrical and coercive. He is not, therefore, fully suspending the bourgeois norms of reciprocity and freedom. Per-haps Foucault could be read in similar fashion. Perhaps he is not fully suspending but is rather presupposing the very liberal norms he criticizes. His description of such disciplinary microtechniques as the gaze, for example, would then have the force of a demonstration that modern social science, however much it purports to be neutral and power-free, in fact also involves asymmetry and coercion.

This reading of Foucault's work is one I am sure he would have rejected. Yet it gains some plausibility if one considers the disciplinary, or carceral, society described in *Discipline and Punish*. If one asks what exactly is wrong with that society, Kantian notions leap immediately to mind. When confronted with the treatment of persons solely as means that are causally manipulated by various institutions, one cannot help but appeal to such concepts as the violation of dig-nity and autonomy. But again, these Kantian notions are clearly related to the liberal norms of legitimacy and illegitimacy defined in terms of limits and rights.

Given that no other normative framework is apparent in Foucault's writings, it is not unreasonable to assume that the liberal framework has not been fully sus-pended. But if this is so, Foucault is caught in an outright contradiction, for he, even more than Marx, tends to treat that framework as simply an instrument of domination.

The point is not simply that Foucault contradicts himself. Rather, it is that he does so in part because he misunderstands, at least when it comes to his *own* situation, the way that norms function in social description. He assumes that he can purge all traces of liberalism from his account of modern power simply by forswearing explicit reference to the tip-of-the-iceberg notions of legitimacy and illegitimacy. He assumes, in other words, that these norms can be neatly isolated and excised from the larger cultural and linguistic matrix in which they are situ-ated. He fails to appreciate the degree to which the normative is embedded in and infused throughout the whole of language at *every* level and the degree to which, despite himself, his own critique has to make use of modes of description, interpretation, and judgment formed within the modern Western normative tradition.[27]

It seems, then, that none of the readings offered here leaves Foucault entirely free of difficulties. Whether we take him as suspending every normative framework, or only the liberal one, or even as keeping that one, he is plagued with unanswered and perhaps unanswerable questions. Because he fails to conceive and pursue any single consistent normative strategy, he ends up with a curious amalgam of amoral militaristic description, Marxian jargon, and Kantian morality. Its many valuable empirical aspects notwithstanding, I can only conclude that Foucault's work is normatively confused.

I believe that the roots of the confusion can be traced to some conceptual ambiguities in Foucault's notion of power. That concept is itself an admixture of neutrality and engagement. Take, for example, his claim that power is productive, not repressive. Throughout this paper I have supposed that this was an empirical claim about the self-amplifying nature of a distinctively modern power. But, in what is clearly an equivocation, Foucault simultaneously treats productivity as a conceptual feature of *all* power as such. He claims that not just the modern regime but every power regime creates, molds, and sustains a distinctive set of cultural practices, including those oriented to the production of truth. Every regime creates, molds, and sustains a distinctive form of life as a positive phenomenon. No regime simply negates. Foucault also makes the converse claim that no positive form of life can subsist without power. Power-free cultures, social practices, and knowledges are in principle impossible. It follows, in his view, that one cannot object to a form of life simply on the ground that it is power-laden. Power is productive, ineliminable, and therefore normatively neutral.[28]

How is this view to be assessed? It seems to me to boil down to a conjunction of three rather innocuous statements: (1) social practices are necessarily norm-governed, (2) practice-governing norms are simultaneously constraining and enabling, and (3) such norms enable only insofar as they constrain. Together, these three statements imply that one cannot have social practices without constraints and that, hence, the mere fact that it constrains cannot be held against any particular practice. This view is a familiar one in twentieth-century philosophy. It is implied, for example, in Habermas's account of the way in which the successful performance of any speech act presupposes norms of truth, comprehensibility, truthfulness, and appropriateness. Such norms make communication possible, but only by devaluing and ruling out some possible and actual utterances: they *enable* us to speak precisely insofar as they *constrain* us.

If this is what Foucault's thesis of the general productivity and ineliminability of power means, then power is a normatively neutral phenomenon indeed. But does this interpretation accord with Foucault's usage? In some respects, yes. He does include under the power/knowledge umbrella such phenomena as criteria of well-formedness for knowledge claims, criteria that simultaneously valorize some statement forms and devalue others; and he also includes social or institutional licensing of knowledge claimants, licensing that simultaneously entitles some speakers to make certain kinds of specialized knowledge claims and excludes others from so doing. If these are the sorts of things meant by power, then the thesis that power is productive, ineliminable, and therefore normatively neutral is unobjectionable.

But Foucault's power/knowledge regimes also include phenomena of other sorts. They include forms of overt and covert coercion in the extraction of knowledge from and about persons and also in the targeting of objects, including persons, for the application of policy in more subtle ways. These phenomena are far less innocuous and far more menacing. That *they* are in principle ineliminable is not immediately apparent. So if *they* are what is meant by power, then the claim that power is productive, ineliminable, and therefore normatively neutral is highly questionable.

I noted earlier that Foucault's notion of a power/knowledge regime covered a highly heterogeneous collection of phenomena. Now it appears that the difficulties concerning the normative dimension of his work stem at least in part from that heterogeneity. The problem is that Foucault calls too many different sorts of things power and simply leaves it at that. Granted, all cultural practices involve constraints—but these constraints are of a variety of different kinds and thus demand a variety of different normative responses. Granted, there can be no social practices without power—but it doesn't follow that all forms of power are normatively equivalent nor that any social practices are as good as any other. Indeed, it is essential to Foucault's own project that he be able to distinguish better from worse sets of practices and forms of constraint. But this requires greater normative resources than he possesses.

The point can also be put this way: Foucault writes as though he were oblivious to the existence of the whole body of Weberian social theory with its careful distinctions between such notions as authority, force, violence, domination, and legitimation. Phenomena that are capable of being distinguished through such concepts are simply lumped together under his catchall concept of power.[29] As a consequence, the potential for a broad range of normative nuances is surrendered, and the result is a certain normative one-dimensionality.

I mentioned earlier that though Foucault's genealogy of modern power was related to the study of modernization as rationalization, there was one very important difference. This difference was Foucault's lack of any bipolar normative contrast comparable to, say, Jürgen Habermas's contrast between a partial and one-sided instrumental rationality, on the one hand, and a fuller practical, political rationality, on the other hand. The consequences of this lack are now more fully apparent. Because Foucault has no basis for distinguishing, for example, forms of power that involve domination from those that do not, he appears to endorse a one-sided, wholesale rejection of modernity as such. Furthermore, he appears to do so without any conception of what is to replace it.

In fact, Foucault vacillates between two equally inadequate stances. On the one hand, he adopts a concept of power that permits him no condemnation of any objectionable features of modern societies. But at the same time, and on the other hand, his rhetoric betrays the conviction that modern societies are utterly without redeeming features. Clearly, what Foucault needs, and needs desperately, are normative criteria for distinguishing acceptable from unacceptable forms of power. As it stands now, the unquestionably original and valuable dimensions of his work stand in danger of being misunderstood for lack of an adequate normative perspective.

Notes

1. Foucault adopted the term 'genealogy' only relatively recently, in connection with his later writings; see, especially, "Nietzsche, Genealogy, History," in *Language, Counter-Memory, Practice: Selected Essays and Interviews,* ed. Donald F. Bouchard, trans. Bouchard and Sherry Simon (Ithaca, N.Y., 1977). Earlier he called his approach 'archaeology'; see, especially, *The Archaeology of Knowledge,* trans. A. M. Sheridan Smith (New York, 1972). For an explanation of the shift, see "Truth and Power," in *Power/Knowledge: Selected Interviews and Other Writings, 1972–1977,* ed. Colin Gordon, trans. Gordon et al. (New York, 1980).

2. Foucault, "Truth and Power." 114.

3. Foucault, "Nietzsche, Freud, Marx," in *Nietzsche* (Paris, 1967), 183–200.

4. Foucault, "Truth and Power." 118.

5. Ibid., 112–13, 131, 133.

6. Foucault, "The Discourse on Language," trans. Rupert Swyer, in *The Archaeology of Knowledge,* 216–38; "Nietzsche, Genealogy, History," 51 ff; and *Discipline and Punish: The Birth of the Prison,* trans. Alan Sheridan (New York, 1979), 17–19, 101–2, 170–73, 192.

7. That Foucault's project could be understood in terms of the concept of bracketing was first suggested to me by Hubert L. Dreyfus and Paul Rabinow. They discuss what I call below the bracketing of the problematic of epistemic justification (although they do not address what I call the bracketing of the problematic of normative justification), in *Michel Foucault: Beyond Structuralism and Hermeneutics* (Chicago, 1982).

8. Foucault, "Truth and Power," 113, and *Discipline and Punish,* 184–85.

9. Foucault, "The History of Sexuality," in *Power/Knowledge,* 184, and "Two Lectures," in *Power/Knowledge, 93, 95.*

10. Foucault, "Two Lectures," 91–92.

11. Foucault, "The Eye of Power," in *Power/Knowledge,* 158–59, and "Prison Talk," in *Power/Knowledge,* 38.

12. Foucault, "The Eye of Power," 146–65, and *Discipline and Punish,* 191–94, 201–9, 252.

13. Foucault, *Discipline and Punish,* 202–3.

14. Foucault, *The History of Sexuality, Volume I: An Introduction,* trans. Robert Hurley (New York, 1978). 61–62.

15. Foucault, "Power and Strategies," in *Power/Knowledge,* 142; "Truth and Power," 119, 125; "The Eye of Power," 151–52; "Two Lectures," 104–5; and *Discipline and Punish,* 201–9.

16. Foucault, "The Eye of Power," 160; *The History of Sexuality,* 139; and *Discipline and Punish,* 170.

17. Foucault, *Discipline and Punish,* 136–38.

34   FOUCAULT ON POWER

18. Foucault, *The History of Sexuality,* 24–26, 122–27, 139–45.

19. Foucault, "Each and Every One: A Criticism of Political Rationality," Tanner Lectures, Stanford University, October 1979 (transcribed from tapes by Shari Popen).

20. Ibid.

21. Foucault, "Truth and Power," 118, 132–33.

22. Foucault, "Truth and Power," 122; "Body/Power," in *Power/Knowledge,* 60; and "Two Lectures," 89.

23. Foucault, "Two Lectures," 95–96.

24. Foucault, "Power and Strategies," 139–41; *The History of Sexuality,* 5–13; "Truth and Power," 119; and "Body/Power," 59.

25. Foucault, "Two Lectures," 90–92.

26. Foucault, "Two Lectures," and "Power and Strategies," 142.

27. This formulation combines points suggested to me by Richard Rorty and Albrecht Wellmer.

28. Foucault, *Discipline and Punish,* 27; "Power and Strategies," 141–42; "Two Lectures," 93; and "Truth and Power," 131–33.

29. I am indebted to Andrew Arato for this point.

[2]

Contemporary Crises 3 (1979) 339–363
© Elsevier Scientific Publishing Company, Amsterdam – Printed in the Netherlands

THE PUNITIVE CITY: NOTES ON THE DISPERSAL OF SOCIAL CONTROL

STANLEY COHEN

> This, then, is how one must imagine the punitive city. At the crossroads, in the gardens, at the side of roads being repaired or bridges built, in workshops open to all, in the depths of mines that may be visited, will be hundreds of tiny theatres of punishment.
>
> Michel Foucault, *Discipline and Punish*

The study of social control must be one of the more dramatic examples in sociology of the gap between our private sense of what is going on around us and our professional writings about the social world. Our private terrain is inhabited by premonitions of *1984, Clockwork Orange* and *Brave New World*, by fears of the increasing intrusion of the state into private lives and by a general unease that more and more of our actions and thoughts are under surveillance and subject to record. Our professional formulations about social control though, reveal little of such nightmares and science-fiction projections. They tend to repeat bland structural-functional explanations about the necessity of social control or else simplistic comparisons of pre-industrial and industrial societies. There are, to be sure, powerful macro theories, especially Marxist, about the apparatus and ideology of state control and a great deal of Marcusean-like rhetoric left over from the sixties about "repression". And then there are those exquisite interactional studies about the social control dimensions in talk, gaze and gesture.

But for an overall sense of what the formal social control apparatus of society is actually getting up to, we have surprisingly little information. Those sub-fields of sociology most explicitly concerned with all this – criminology and the sociology of deviance – are not as much help as they should be, especially when trying to understand the major shifts in the ideology and apparatus of control over the last few decades. Thus writings about community control – the subject of this paper and, if my argument is

University of Essex, Essex, England

340

correct, the key area in which to find transformations in social control – are usually of a very low level. They are either blandly descriptive or else "evaluative" only in the sense of using the pseudo scientific language of process, feedback, goals, inputs, systems etc., to decide whether this or that program "works" or is cost productive. Little of this helps towards understanding basic structural and ideological trends.

Some connecting bridges have, of course, been made somewhere here between private nightmare and sociological work. This is most evident in the current wave of disenchantment about benevolent state intervention in the name of welfare or rehabilitation [1]. The historical work by David Rothman on the origins of the asylum and (from a quite different tradition) Michel Foucault's series of great works on the history of deviance control have marked a major intellectual breakthrough. The extension of this work into the contemporary scene in Scull's analysis of the decarceration movement and in the less theoretically penetrating but polemically equally compelling formulations about the "Therapeutic State" (Kittrie), "Psychiatric Despotism" (Szasz) and the "Psychological Society" (Gross) are also important. But this work is surprisingly sparse and tends anyway to concentrate on psychiatry, only one limited system of social control.

On the whole, the promise of the new sociology of deviance to deal with the "control" side of the "deviance and control" equation, has not been fulfilled. Certainly there are enough good studies of specific control agencies such as courts, prisons, police departments, abortion clinics, mental hospitals, and so on. But the problem with this ethnographic work is not so much (as the familiar criticism runs) that a pre-occupation with labelling, stigma and interaction may leave the analysis at the microscopic level. The problem is more that such studies are often curiously fragmented, abstracted from the density of urban life in which social control is embedded. It is not so much that these agencies often have no history: they also have little sense of place. They need locating in the physical space of the city, but more important in the overall social space: the master patterns of social control, the network of other institutions such as school and family, and broader trends in welfare and social services, bureaucracies and professions. This paper is a preface to a grander project of this sort.

What I want to do – largely for a sociological audience outside crime and justice professionals – is sort out some of the implications of the apparent changes in the formal social control apparatus over the last decade or so. I will concentrate on crime and juvenile delinquency though there are important tendencies – some parallel and some quite different – in such areas as drug abuse and mental illness which require altogether separate comment. I will be drawing material mainly from the United States and Britain – countries which have developed a centralized crime control apparatus

341

embedded in a more (Britain) or less (United States) highly developed commitment to welfare and more (United States) or less (Britain) sophisticated
ideologies and techniques of treatment and rehabilitation.

This paper, then, is an exercise in classification and projection, rather than
explanation.

From Prison to Community

Our current system of deviancy control originated in those great transformations which took place from the end of the 18th to the beginning of
the 19th centuries: firstly the development of a centralized state apparatus
for the control of crime and the care of dependency; secondly the increasing
differentiation of the deviant and dependent into separate types each with
its own attendant corpus of "scientific" knowledge and accredited experts:
and finally the increased segregation of deviants and dependents into
"asylums": mental hospitals, prisons, reformatories and other such closed,
purpose-built institutions for treatment and punishment. The theorists of
these transformations each place a somewhat different emphasis on just what
happened and just why it happened, but all are agreed on its essentials [2].

The most extraordinary of these three features to explain — the other two
being, in a sense, self evident in the development of the modern state — is
the growth of the asylum and its subsequent survival despite one and a half
centuries of failure. Any account of the current and future place of incarceration, must come to terms with that original historical transformation [3].

We are now living through what *appears* to be a reversal of this first Great
Transformation. The ideological consensus about the desirability and
necessity of the segregative asylum — questioned before but never really
undermined [4] — has been broken. The attack on prisons (and more
dramatically and with more obvious results on mental hospitals) became
widespread from the mid nineteen-sixties, was found throughout the
political spectrum and was partially reflected in such indices as declining
rates of imprisonment. At the end of the eighteenth century, asylums and
prisons were places of the *last* resort; by the mid-19th century they became
places of the *first* resort, the preferred solution to problems of deviancy and
dependency. By the end of the 1960s they looked like once again becoming
places of the *last* resort. The extraordinary notion of abolition, rather than
mere reform became common talk. With varying degrees of enthusiasm and
actual measurable consequences, officials in Britain, the United States and
some Western European countries, became committed to the policy labelled
"decarceration": the state-sponsored closing down of asylums, prisons and

141263

342

reformatories. This apparent reversal of the Great Incarcerations of the nineteenth century was hailed as the beginning of a golden age – a form of utopianism whose ironies cannot escape anyone with an eye on history: "There is a curious historical irony here, for the *adoption* of the asylum, whose *abolition* is now supposed to be attended with such universally beneficent consequences, aroused an almost precisely parallel set of millenial expectations among its advocates" [5].

The irony goes even further. For just at the historical moment when every commonplace critique of "technological" or "post-industrial" or "mass" society mourned the irreplaceable loss of the traditional *Gemeinschaft* community, so a new mode of deviancy control was advocated whose success rested on this very same notion of community. Indeed the decarceration movement derives its rhetoric from a much wider constituency than is implied by limited questions of how far should imprisonment be used. It touches on issues about centralization, professionalization, the rehabilitative ideal, and the limits of state intervention. The current (variously labelled) "pessimism", "scepticism", or "nihilism" about prisons, draws on all these wider themes [6].

In the literature on community treatment itself [7], two sets of assumptions are repeated with the regularity of a religious catechism. The first set is seen either as a matter of common sense, "what everybody knows" or the irrefutable result of empirical research: 1) prisons and juvenile institutions are (in the weak version) simply ineffective: they neither successfully deter nor rehabilitate. In the strong version, they actually make things worse by strengthening criminal commitment; 2) community alternatives are much less costly and 3) they are more humane than any institution can be – prisons are cruel, brutalizing and beyond reform. Their time has come. Therefore: community alternatives "must obviously be better", "should at least be given a chance" or "can't be worse".

The second set of assumptions appeal to a number of sociological and political beliefs not as self evident as the previous set, but taken by the believer to be just as well established: 1) theories of stigma and labelling have demonstrated that the further the deviant is processed into the system, the harder it is to return him to normal life – "therefore" measures designed to minimize penetration into the formal system and keep the deviant in the community as long as possible are desirable; 2) the causal processes leading to most forms of deviance originate in society (family, community, school, economic system) – "therefore" prevention and cure must lie in the community and not in artificially created agencies constructed on a model of individual intervention; 3) liberal measures, such as reformatories, the juvenile court and the whole rehabilitative model are politically suspect, whatever the

0690084

benevolent motives which lie behind them. The state should be committed to be doing less harm rather than more good — "therefore" policies such as decriminalization, diversion and decarceration should be supported.

It is the last of these beliefs which must be used to scrutinize them all — for why should community corrections itself, not be subjected to the very same suspicion about benevolent reform? A large dose of such scepticism, together with a much firmer location of the new movement in overall structural and political changes, is needed for a full scale critique of community corrections. Such a critique — not the object of this paper — would have to note at least the following doubts [8] : 1) it is by no means clear, in regard to crime and delinquency at least, that decarceration has been taking place as rapidly as the ideology would have us believe: 2) it has not been established that any community alternative is more effective in reducing crime (through preventing recidivism) than traditional imprisonment; 3) nor are these new methods always dramatically cheaper and 4) the humanitarian rationale for the move from imprisonment may be unfounded for two (opposite) reasons: a) decarceration may indeed lead to something like non-intervention or benign neglect: services are withdrawn and deviants are left neglected or exploited by private operators: b) alternatively, new forms of intervention result, which are often difficult to distinguish from the old institutions and reproduce in the community the very same coercive features of the system they were designed to replace.

However cogent this emergent critique might be, though, it comes from the margins of contemporary "corrections". Perhaps more than in any other area of social policy, crime and delinquency control has always allowed such doubts to be neutralized in the tidal wave of enthusiasm for any new "reform". There is little doubt that the rhetoric and ideology of community control is quite secure. And — whatever may be happening to overall rates of incarceration — most industrialized countries will continue to see a proliferation of various schemes in line with this ideology.

I shall take the term "community control" to cover almost any form of formal social control outside the walls of traditional adult and juvenile institutions. There are two separate, but overlapping strategies: firstly, those various forms of intensive intervention located "in the community": sentencing options which serve as intermediate alternatives to being sent to an institution or later options to release from institutions and secondly, those programs set up at some preventive, policing or pre-trial stage to divert offenders from initial or further processing by the conventional systems of justice. Behind these specific policies lies an overall commitment to almost anything which sounds like increasing community responsibility for the control of crime and delinquency.

344

Blurring the Boundaries

The segregated and insulated institution made the actual business of deviancy control invisible, but it did make its boundaries obvious enough. Whether prisons were built in the middle of cities, out in the remote countryside or on deserted islands, they had clear spatial boundaries to mark off the normal from the deviant. These spatial boundaries were reinforced by ceremonies of social exclusion. Those outside could wonder what went on behind the walls, those inside could think about the "outside world". Inside/outside, guilty/innocent, freedom/captivity, imprisoned/released — these were all meaningful distinctions.

In today's world of community corrections, these boundaries are no longer as clear. There is, we are told, a "correctional continuum" or a "correctional spectrum": criminals and delinquents might be found any-where in these spaces. So fine — and at the same time so indistinct — are the gradations along the continuum, that it is by no means easy to answer such questions as where the prison ends and the community begins or just why any deviant is to be found at any particular point. Even the most dedicated spokesmen for the community treatment have some difficulty in specifying just what "the community" is; one N.I.M.H. Report confessed that the term community treatment: ". . . has lost all descriptive usefulness except as a code word with connotations of 'advanced correctional thinking' and implied value judgements against the 'locking up' and isolation of offenders" [9].

Even the most cursory examination of the new programs, reveals that many varieties of the more or less intensive and structured "alternatives" are virtually indistinguishable from the real thing. A great deal of energy and ingenuity is being devoted to this problem of definition: just how isolated and confining does an institution have to be before it is a prison rather than, say a residential community facility? Luckily for us all, criminologists have got this matter well in hand and are spending a great deal of time and money on such questions. They are busy devising quantitative measures of indices such as degree of control, linkages, relationships, support — and we can soon look forward to standardized scales for assigning programs along an institu-tionalization-normalization continuum [10].

But, alas, there are not just untidy loose ends which scientific research will one day tie up. The ideology of the new movement quite deliberately and explicitly demands that boundaries should not be made too clear. The metaphor of "crumbling walls" implies an undifferentiated open space. The main British prison reform group, the Howard League, once called for steps to ". . . restore the prison to the community and the community to the prison" and less rhetorically, here is an early enthusiast for a model

345

"Community Correction Centre":

> The line between being 'locked up' and 'free' is purposely indistinct because it must be drawn differently for each individual. Once the client is out of Phase I, where all clients enter and where they are all under essentially custodial control, he may be 'free' for some activities but still 'locked up' for others [11].

There is no irony intended in using inverted commas for such words as "free" and "locked up" or in using such euphemisms as "essentially custodial control". This sort of blurring – deliberate or unintentional – may be found throughout the complicated networks of "diversion" and "alternatives" which are now being set up. The half-way house might serve as a good example. These agencies called variously, "residential treatment centers", "rehabilitation residences", "reintegration centers" or (with the less flowery language preferred in Britain) simply "hostels", invariably become special institutional domains themselves. They might be located in a whole range of odd settings – private houses, converted motels, the grounds of hospitals, the dormitories of university campuses or even within the walls of prisons themselves. Their programs [12] reproduce rules – for example about security, curfew, permitted visitors, drugs – which are close to those of the institution itself. Indeed it becomes difficult to distinguish a very "open" prison – with liberal provisions for work release, home release, outside educational programs – from a very "closed" half-way house. The house may be half-way *in* – for those too serious to be left at home, but not serious enough for the institution and hence a form of "diversion" – or half-way *out* – for those who can be released from the institution but are not yet "ready" for the open community, hence a form of "after care". To confuse the matter even further, the same center is sometimes used for both these purposes, with different rules for the half way in inmates and the half way out inmates.

Even this blurring and confusion is not enough: one advocate [13] draws attention to the advantages of *quarter-way* houses and *three-quarter* way houses. These "concepts" we are told are already being used in the mental health field, but are not labelled as such in corrections. The quarter-way house deals with people who need supervision on a near permanent basis, while the three-quarter way house is designed to care for persons in an "acute temporary crisis needing short term residential care and little super-vision". Then – taking the opposite tack from devising finer and finer classification schemes – other innovators argue for a multi-purpose center: some half-way houses already serve as a parolee residence, a drop-in center, a drug treatment program and a non-residential walk in center for after-care.

The fact that many of these multi-purpose centers are directed not just at convicted offenders, but are preventive, diagnostic or screening enterprises

346

aimed at potential, pre-delinquents, or high risk populations, should alert us
to the more important forms of blurring behind this administrative surreal-
ism. The ideology of community treatment allows for a facile evasion of the
delinquent/non-delinquent distinction. The British system of "intermediate
treatment" for example provides not just an intermediate possibility between sending the child away from home and leaving him in his normal
home environment, but also a new way ". . . to make use of facilities
available to children who have not been before the courts, and so to secure
the treatment of 'children in trouble' in the company of other children
through the sharing of activities and experiences within the community" [14]. There is a deliberate attempt to evade the question of
whether a rule has been actually broken. While the traditional screening
mechanism of the criminal justice system have always been influenced to a
greater or lesser degree by non-offense related criteria (race, class, demean-
our) the offense was at least considered. Except in the case of wrongful
conviction, some law must have been broken. This is no longer clear: a
delinquent may find himself in custody ("short term intensive treatment")
simply because of program failure: he has violated the norms of some other
agency in the continuum — for example, by not turning up to his therapy
group, "acting out", or being uncooperative.

We are seeing, then, not just the proliferation of agencies and services,
finely calibrated in terms of degree of coerciveness or intrusion or un-
pleasantness. The uncertainties are more profound than this: voluntary or
coercive, formal or informal, locked up or free, guilty or innocent. Those
apparently absurd administrative and research questions — when is a prison a
prison or a community a community? is the alternative an alternative? who
is half-way in and who is three-quarter way out? — beckon to a future when
it will be impossible to determine who exactly is emeshed in the social
control system — and hence subject to its jurisdiction and surveillance — at
any one time.

Thinning the Mesh and Widening the Net

On the surface, a major ideological thrust in the move against institutions
derives from a desire to limit state intervention. Whether arising from the
supposed failures of the treatment model, or the legal argument about the
over-reach of the law and the necessity to limit the criminal sanction, or the
implicit non-interventionism of labelling theory, or a general disenchantment
with paternalism, or simply the pragmatic case for easing the burdens on the
system — the eventual message looked the same: the state should do less
rather than more. It is ironical then — though surely the irony is too obvious

even to be called this — that the major results of the new movements towards "community" and "diversion" have been to increase rather than decrease the *amount* of intervention directed at many groups of deviants in the system and, probably, to increase rather than decrease the total *number* who get into the system in the first place. In other words: "alternatives" become not alternatives at all but new programs which supplement the existing system or else expand it by attracting new populations.

I will refer to these two overlapping possibilities as "thinning the mesh" and "widening the net" respectively. No one who has studied the results of such historical innovations as probation and parole should be surprised by either of these effects. As Rothman, for example, comments about the early twentieth century impact of the psychiatric ideology on the criminal justice system: ". . . rationales and practices that initially promised to be less onerous nevertheless served to encourage the extension of state authority. The impact of the ideology was to expand intervention, not to restrict it" [15].

The detailed processes through which the new community agencies are generating such expansion are not my concern here [16]. I will merely use the two strategies of "alternatives" and "diversion" to suggest how illusory is the notion that the new movement will lead to a lesser degree of formal social control.

Let us first examine community alternatives to incarceration. The key index of "success" is not simply the proliferation of such programs, but the question of whether they are replacing or merely providing supplementary appendages to the conventional system of incarceration. The statistical evidence is by no means easy to decipher but it is clear, both from Britain and America, that rates of incarceration — particularly in regard to juveniles — are not at all declining as rapidly as one might expect and in some spheres are even increasing. Critically — as one evaluation suggests [17] the "alternatives" are not, on the whole, being used for juveniles at the "deep end" of the system, i.e. those who really would have been sent to institutions before. When the strategy is used for "shallow end" offenders — minor or first offenders whose chances of incarceration would have been slight — then the incarceration rates will not be affected.

The exact proportions of these types are difficult to estimate: one English study of community service orders shows that only half the offenders sent would otherwise have received custodial sentences [18]. Leaving aside the question of the exact effects on the rest of the system, there is little doubt that a substantial number — perhaps the majority — of those subjected to the new programs, will be subjected to a degree of intervention higher than they would have received under previous non-custodial options like fines, conditional discharge or ordinary probation.

348

What all this means is that as long as the shallow end principle is used and as long as institutions are not literally closed down (as in the much publicized Massachusetts example) there is no guarantee either than incarceration will decrease dramatically or that the system will be less interventionist overall. The conclusion of the recent National Assessment of Juvenile Corrections holds true generally: although there are exceptions, "in general as the number of community based facilities increases, the total number of youths incarcerated increases" [19].

The paradox throughout all this that the more benign, attractive and successful the program is defined — especially if it uses the shallow end principle, as most do — the more it will be used and the wider it will cast its net:

> Developing and administering community programs can be a source of gratification to sincere correctional administrators and lay volunteers who believe they are 'doing good' by keeping people out of dungeons and helping them obtain social services. Judges, reluctant to send difficult children to a reformatory and equally reluctant to release them without an assurance that something will be done to prevent them from returning may be especially enthusiastic about the development of alternative dispositions [20].

Turning now to the more explicit forms of diversion, it is once again clear that the term, like the term "alternatives" is not quite what it implies. Diversion has been hailed as the most radical application of the non-intervention principle short of complete decriminalization. The grand rationale is to restrict the full force of the criminal justice process to more serious offences and to either eliminate or substantially minimize penetration for all others [21]. The strategy has received the greatest attention in the juvenile field: a remarkable development, because the central agency here, the juvenile court, was *itself* the product of a reform movement aimed at "diversion".

Clearly, all justice systems — particularly juvenile — have always contained a substantial amount of diversion. Police discretion has been widely used to screen juveniles: either right out of the system by dropping charges, informally reprimanding or cautioning, or else informal referral to social services agencies. What has now happened, to a large degree, is that these discretionary and screening powers have been formalized and extended — and in the process, quite transformed. The net widens to include those who, if the program had not been available would either not have been processed at all or would have been placed on options such as traditional probation. Again, the more benevolent the new agencies appear, the more will be diverted there by encouragement or coercion. And — through the blurring provided by the welfare net — this will happen to many not officially adjudicated as delinquent as well. There will be great pressure to work with parts of the population not previously "reached".

All this can be most clearly observed in the area of police diversion of juveniles. Where the police used to have two options – screen right out (the route for by far the *majority* of encounters) or process formally – they now have the third option of diversion into a program. Diversion can then be used as an alternative to screening and not an alternative to processing [22]. The proportion selected will vary. British research on police juvenile liaison schemes and similar measures [23] shows a clear widening of the net and one survey of eleven Californian diversion projects suggests that only 51 percent of clients were actually diverted from the system, with the rest receiving more processing than they would have received otherwise [24]. Another evaluation of 35 police departments running diversion programs concludes:

> ... the meaning of 'diversion' has been shifted from 'diversion from' to 'referral to'. Ironically, one of the ramifications of this is that in contrast to some earlier cited rationales for diversion as reducing costs, caseload and the purview of the criminal justice system, diversion may in fact be extending the costs, caseload and system purview even further than had previously been the case [25].

The key to understanding this state of affairs lies in the distinction between *traditional* or *true* diversion – removing the juvenile from the system altogether by screening out (no further treatment, no service, no follow up) – and the *new* diversion which entails screening plus program: formal penetration is minimized by referral to programs in the system or related to it [26]. Only traditional diversion is true diversion in the sense of diverting *from*. The new diversion diverts – for better or worse – *into* the system. Cressey and McDermott's laconic conclusion from their evaluation of one such set of programs might apply more generally.

> If 'true' diversion occurs, the juvenile is safely out of the official realm of the juvenile justice system and he is immune from incurring the delinquent label or any of its variations – pre-delinquent, delinquent tendencies, bad guy, hard core, unreachable. Further, when he walks out of the door from the person diverting him, he is technically free to tell the diverter to go to hell. We found very little 'true' diversion in the communities studied [27].

To conclude this section: whatever the eventual pattern of the emergent social control system, it should be clear that such policies as "alternatives" in no way represent a victory for the anti-treatment lobby or an "application" of labelling theory. Traditional deviant populations are being processed in a different way or else new populations are being caught up in the machine. For some observers [28] all this is an index of how good theory produces bad practise: each level diverts to the next and at each level vested interests (like job security) ensures that few are diverted right out. And so the justice machine enlarges itself. This looks "successful" in terms of the machine's

350

own operational definition of success, but is a failure when compared to the theory from which the policy (supposedly) was derived.

Be this as it may, the new movement — in the case of crime and delinquency at least — has led to a more voracious processing of deviant populations, albeit in new settings and by professionals with different names. The machine might in some respects be getting softer, but it is not getting smaller (and probably not more efficient — but that's another story).

Masking and Disguising

The softness of the machine might also be more apparent than real. It became common place in historical analyses to suggest that the more benign parts of the system such as the juvenile court [29] masked their most coercive intentions and consequences. This conclusion might apply with equal force to the current strategies of diversion and alternatives. Even more than their historical antecedents, they employ a social work rather than legalistic rationale; they are committed to the principle of blurring the boundaries of social control and they use the all-purpose slogan of 'community' which cannot but sound benign.

There can be little doubt that the intentions behind the new movement and — more to the point — its end results, are often humane, compassionate and helpful. Most clients, deviants or offenders would probably prefer this new variety to the stark option of the prison. But this argument is only valid if the alternatives are real ones. The net-thinning and mesh-widening effects, though indicate that the notion of alternatives can be misleading and mystifying. Note, for example, the curious claim that agencies like half-way houses are justified because they are just as successful in preventing crime as direct release into the community. As Greenberg notes, however, when such alternatives are presented as a condition of release from prison, ". . . the contrast between the brutality of the prison and the alleged humanitarianism of community corrections is besides the point, because the community institution is not used to replace the prison; instead the offender is exposed to both the prison and the community 'alternatives' " [30].

Even when the alternatives *are* real ones, it is not self evident that they are always more humane and less stigmatizing just because, in some sense they are "in the community". Community agencies, for example, might use a considerable amount of more or less traditional custody and often without legal justification. As the assessment of one experiment revealed:

When subjects failed to comply with the norms of the intensive treatment regime, or even when a program agent believes subjects might fail to comply, then, as they say in the intensive treatment circles, detention may be indicated. Both these features, and the extensive use of home placements as well, suggest that the term 'community' like the term 'intensive treatment' may come to have a very special meaning in programs designed to deliver 'intensive treatment in the community' [31].

Such disguised detention, though, is probably not a major overall source of masking. More important is the bureaucratic generation of new treatment criteria which might allow for more unchecked coercion than at first appears. In a system with low visibility and low accountability, there is less room for such niceties as due process and legal rights. Very often, for example, "new diversion" (minimization of penetration) occurs by deliberately avoiding due process: the client proceeds through the system on the assumption or admission of guilt. Indeed the deliberate conceptual blurring between "diversion" and "prevention" explicitly calls for an increase in this sort of non-legal discretion.

All this, of course, still leaves open the question of whether the end result — however mystifying some of the routes that led to it — is actually experienced as more humane and helpful by the offender. There is little evidence either way on this, beyond the rather bland common sense assumption that most offenders would prefer not to be "locked up". What is likely, is that deep end projects — those that are genuine alternatives to incarceration — have to make a trade-off between treatment goals (which favour the integrated community setting) and security goals which favour isolation. The trade-off under these conditions will tend to favour security — resulting in programs which simulate or mimic the very features of the institution they set out to replace. Let us consider two somewhat different examples.

The first is Fort Des Moines, a "Community Correctional Facility" which is part of a wider Community Corrections Program [32]. This is a 50 bed non-secure unit, housed in an ex-army base. The clients work in ordinary jobs outside and there is minimal physical security in the shape of bars or fences.

Here, though, are some of the security trade offs: 1) the low "client-counsellor" ratio — one staff person for every two clients — allows for intensive "informal observation" of the clients for security purposes. There is, for example, a "staff desk person" who signs clients in and out, recording their attitudes and activities. There is also a "floating staff person" who circulates throughout the institution, observing client behaviour, taking a count of all clients each hour (called the 'eye check') and recording the count in the log: 2) the client has to "contract" to behave well and participate actively in his rehabilitation: the sanction of being returned to prison is always present. From the beginning of his stay (when he has to sign a waiver of privacy granting the program access to information in confidential agency files) he is closely scrutinized. Besides the obvious offences like using drugs, fighting or trying to escape the failure to maintain "a

352

significant level of performance" is one of the most serious offenses a client can commit and results in immediate return to jail [33]; 3) the court retains jurisdiction over the client, receiving detailed rosters and program reports and having to authorize internal requests for work, schooling or furloughs. In addition, the local police and sheriffs departments receive weekly listings of the residents, indicating where each has to be at specified hours of each day. This information is available to patrol officers who may see inmates in the community.

These features — especially the complicated compulsory treatment process itself — suggests an intensity of intervention at least as great as that in most maximum security prisons. The commitment to a behaviourist conditioning program — a feature of many American versions of community treatment — is particularly insidious and is illustrated well in my second example, the Urbana-Champaign Adolescent Diversion Project [34]. This — unlike the first example — is genuinely enough in the community: juveniles considered as "beyond lecture and release and clearly headed for court" are referred by the police to a program of behavioural contracting organized by a university psychology department. The volunteer staff monitor and mediate contractual agreements between the youth and his parents and teachers: privileges in return for complying with curfew, house chores and personal appearance. Here are extracts from a typical day in the life of Joe, a sixteen year old who had come to the attention of the juvenile division for possession of marijuana and violation of the municipal curfew laws:

Joe agrees to:	*Joe's parents agree to:*
1. Call home by 4:00 p.m. each afternoon and tell his parents his whereabouts and return home by 5:00 p.m.	1. Allow Joe to go out from 7:30 to 9:30 Monday through Thursday evening and ask about his companions without negative comment.
2. Return home by 12:00 midnight on weekend nights.	2. Allow Joe to go out the subsequent weekend night.
3. Make his bed daily and clean his room daily (spread neat; clothes hung up).	3. Check his room each day and pay him 75 cents when cleaned.
4. Set table for dinner daily.	4. Deposit 75 cents per day in a savings account for Joe.

Bonus
If Joe performs at 80 percent or above of 1 through 4 above, his parents will deposit an additional 3 dollars in his account for each consecutive seven day period.

Sanction
If Joe falls below 60 percent in 1 and 2 above in any consecutive seven day period, he will cut two inches off his hair.

Comments about the alleged "humanitarianism" of this program are redund-
ant.

Merging Public and Private

The notion that the state should be solely responsible for crime control
only developed in England and America in the later part of the nineteenth
century. The key changes then — the removal of prisons from private to
public control and the creation of a uniformed public police force — are
taken as the beginning of the continued and voracious absorption of deviancy control into the centralized apparatus of the state. Certainly the
political and economic demands of industrial society have led to increasing
state control in the form of laws, regulations, administrative and enforcement agencies.

At a somewhat different level, though, there are other developments — in
line with the move from concentration to dispersal traced in this paper —
which are going in a somewhat different direction. Indeed some observers —
particularly in the case of the police, have gone as far as noting a tendency to
the "privatization of social control" [35]. While this might be an exagger-
ation, it is apparent that along with the other types of blurring, there has
been some merging of the obviously public and formal apparatus of control
with the private and less formal. The ideology of community implies this: on
the one hand, the repressive, interventionist reach of the state should be
blunted, on the other, the "community" should become more involved in
the day to day business of prevention and control.

It would be tempting — but too simple — to see this interpenetration of
the public and private as going back full circle to its earlier historical forms.
The connections between crime control and contractual or other forms of
profit making which emerged at the end of the seventeenth century, are not
quite the same as today's versions of private control — nor can they ever be
in the rationalized centralized state.

The increasing involvement, though — particularly in the United States —
of private enterprise in the public service sector, is noteworthy enough.
Indeed in Scull's analysis decarceration itself is attributed to a fiscal crisis:
the state divests itself of expensive crime control functions allowing private
enterprise to process deviant populations for profit. This is readily observable in the case of private clinics, hospitals or welfare hotels for the old and
mentally ill, where private agencies either serve their "own" clientele or
function under licence or contract from the state.

In the areas of crime and delinquency it is not quite as clear how ". . . the
spheres of public and private actually have become progressively less dis-

354

tinct" [36]. The term privatization does not fully cover the complicated ways in which the new community alternatives relate to the system from which they are supposedly diverting. In some cases, there *is* clear privatization in the form of half-way houses, hostels, group homes or fostering schemes being run for private profit. But the fate of most private agencies in this area — especially if they prove successful — is to become co-opted and absorbed into the formal state apparatus. This has happened even to radical self-help organizations which originated in an antagonistic relationship to the system. In the case of diversion, the ideal non-legal agency (free from system control, client oriented, with voluntary participation, independent of sponsor's pressure) often becomes like the various "para-legal" agencies closely connected to the system and dependent on it for space, referrals, accountability and sponsorship [37]. Various compromises on procedure are made as temporary tactics to deflect suspicion and criticism, but are then institutionalized. The private agency expands, for example, by asking for public funding and in turn might change its screening criteria to fit the official system's demands. It becomes increasingly difficult to assign the status of private or public to these agencies.

At the same time as private agencies find it difficult not to be co-opted, the public sector responds to pressures (some fiscal and some sincerely deriving from the community ideology) by using more private resources, especially in the form of volunteers. Ex-offenders treat offenders, indigenous community residents are recruited to probation or voluntary "big brother" type schemes, family members and teachers are used in behavioural contracting programs or university students take on counselling functions as part of their course work.

All this is a fairly long way removed from the pre-nineteenth century forms of privatization. The closest parallels to this might be in the area of policing. In both Britain and the United States private policing has become a massive industry. In the United States, private police outnumber their counterparts in the public sector — a growth attributed to the increasing involvement of the ordinary police in human services "dirty work", leaving large corporations dependent on private protective and investigative services in areas such as pilferage, security checks, industrial espionage and credit card scrutiny.

Alongside all this, there have been changes in police methods which have some other curious historical parallels — to the time when the dividing lines between the civilian population and a uniformed, centralized police force were not at all clear. There has been considerable expansion in the use of informers, secret agents, undercover work, agents provocateurs — all those disguised operations in which the police are made to look more like citizens and citizens more like the police. There is a great deal of evidence about the infiltration of social movements by informers and agents provocateurs [38] while undercover work and entrapment in the field of victimless crime or vice (drugs, gambling, prostitution) has become — if this is not a contradiction — open knowledge. Here, police work is less re-active than pro-active: aimed at anticipating and preventing crimes not yet committed through such methods as police posing as criminals (prostitutes, fences, pornographic book dealers) or as victims (for example, as elderly citizens to attract mugging).

Leaving aside the surrealistic possibilities this opens up (agents who are themselves under surveillance selling drugs to and arresting other agents), and the implications for civil liberties and conceptions of trust and privacy [39] it directs attention to further twists and ambiguities in the already complex relationship between deviance and social control. While some parts of police work are becoming more underground and secretive, others are trying to reach out more openly into the wider community. Schemes for "community based preventive policing" are now well established in Britain and America. Community relations officers, juvenile liaison bureaus. school-linked officers are all involved in establishing closer links with the community, humanizing the face of police work and encouraging early reporting and surveillance. Official law enforcement agencies also actively support various projects aimed at encouraging early reporting of crime through such methods as building up neighbourhood "whistle alert networks" or citizen band radio reporting. A more obvious form of privatization is the development of unofficial residents patrols to maintain surveillance over neighbourhoods as well as mediating between the police and residents [40].

It might be premature to cite these developments as heralding a quite new mode of law enforcement. The appeal of the ideology of citizen involvement in crime prevention, though, is strong and shares the very same roots as the broader movement to the community. Here is an official version:

> ... Crime prevention as each citizen's duty is not a new idea. In the early days of law enforcement well over a thousand years ago (sic) the peacekeeping system encouraged the conceopt of mutual responsibility. Each individual was responsible not only for his actions but for those of his neighbours. A citizen observing a crime had the duty to rouse his neighbours and pursue the criminal. Peace was kept for the most part, not by officials but by the whole community [41].

Needless to say, today's forms of peacekeeping by the community are not quite the same as those golden days of "mutual responsibility". Closed circuit television, two way radios, vigilante patrols and police decoys hardly emulate life in a pre-industrial village. This is not for want of trying. In some large stores, private security police are posing as employees. They conpicuously steal and are then conspicuously "discovered" by the management and ceremonially disciplined, thus deterring the real employees. They

356

then presumably move on to stage somewhere else another such Durkheimian ceremony of social control.

Absorption, Penetration, Re-integration

The asylum represented not just isolation and confinement — like quarantining the infected — but a ritual of physical exclusion. Without the possibility of actual banishment to another society, the asylum had to serve the classic social function of scapegoating. The scapegoat of ancient legend was an animal driven to the wilderness, bearing away the sins of the community.

In the new ideology of corrections, there is no real or symbolic wilderness — just the omnipresent community into which the deviant has to be unobtrusively "integrated" or "reintegrated". The blurring of social control implies both the deeper penetration of social control into the social body and the easing of any measures of exclusion, or status degradation. For the apologists of the new corrections, the word "re-integration" has a magic ring. Thus Empey [42] argues that we are in the middle of a third revolution in corrections: the first from Revenge to Restraint (in the first part of the nineteenth century), the second from Restraint to Reformation (from the late nineteenth to the early twentieth century) — and now from Reformation to Re-integration. Leaving aside the historical inaccuracy of this sequence, it does not actually tell us what this new utopia will look like.

In the most immediate sense, what is being proposed is a greater direct involvement of the family, the school and various community agencies in the day to day business of prevention, treatment, and resocialization. This implies something more profound than simply using more volunteers or increasing reporting rates. It implies some sort of reversal of the presumption in positivist criminology that the delinquent is a different and alien being. Deviance rather is with us, woven into the fabric of social life and it must be "brought back home". Parents, peers, schools, the neighbourhood, even the police should dedicate themselves to keeping the deviant out of the formal system. He must be absorbed back into the community and not processed by official agencies [43].

The central role allocated to the family — part of the broader movement of the rediscovery of the family in sociology and social policy — is a good example of the integration ideology. Well established methods such as foster care, substitute homes and family placements are being extended and one enthusiast looks forward to "... the day when middle class American families actually wanted in large numbers to bring juvenile and pre-delinquent youths into their homes as a service commitment" [44]. The family having a delinquent living with them is seen as a "remarkable correctional resource" for the future. In Britain and Scandinavia a number of alternative systems of family placement besides salaried foster parents have been tried — for example "together at home", the system of intensive help in Sweden in which social workers spend hours sharing the family's life and tasks. Alongside these diversionary alternatives, parents and schools are also encouraged to react sooner to early signs of trouble.

Going beyond the family setting, the stress on community absorption has found one of its most attractive possibilities in the system of community service orders developed in England. Under this system, offenders are sentenced to useful supervised work in the community: helping in geriatric wards, driving disabled people around, painting and decorating the houses of various handicapped groups, building children's playground etc. This is a particularly attractive scheme because it appeals not just to the soft ideology of community absorption, but the more punitive objectives of restitution and compensation.

Needless to say, there are profound limits to the whole ideology of integration — as indeed there are to all such similar patterns I have described. The "community" — as indicated by the standard local reaction to say, half-way houses or day centers being located in their own neighbourhood — is not entirely enthusiastic about such "integration". In the immediate future the segregation of the deviant will remain as the central part of the control apparatus. The established professionals, agencies and service bureaucracies are not going to give up so easily their hard won empires of "expertise" and identity in the name of some vague notion of integration. Nevertheless at the rhetorical and ideological levels, the move to a new model of deviancy control has been signalled. On this level at least, it may not be too dramatic to envisage the distinction between cannibalism and anthropemy becoming less relevant:

> If we studied societies from the outside, it would be tempting to distinguish two contrasting types: those which practise cannibalism – that is which regard the absorption of certain individuals possessing dangerous powers as the only means of neutralising those powers and even of turning them to advantage – and those which, like our own society, adopt what might be called the practice of anthropemy (from the Greek *èmai'*, to vomit); faced with the same problem the latter type of society has chosen the opposite solution, which consists of ejecting dangerous individuals from the social body and keeping them temporarily or permanently in isolation, away from all contact with their fellows, in establishments especially intended for this purpose [45].

Conclusion — Towards the Punitive City

These emerging patterns of social control — dispersal, penetration, bluring, absorption, widening — must be seen as no more than patterns: repre-

358

sentations or models of what is yet to be fully constructed. Historians of
social policy can use the emergent final system to validate their reading of
such early, tentative patterns; the student of contemporary policy has no
such luxury. The largest question mark must hang over the future role of the
prison itself in the total system. The rhetoric of community control is now
unassailable, but it is not yet clear how *far* the prison will be supplemented
and complemented by these new forms of control.

It is, eventually, the sheer proliferation and elaboration of these other
systems of control — rather than the attack on prison itself — which impres-
ses. What is happening is a literal reproduction on a wider societal level of
those astonishingly complicated systems of classification — the "atlases of
vice" — inside the nineteenth century prison. New categories and sub-
categories of deviance and control are being created under our eyes. All these
agencies — legal and quasi-legal, administrative and professional — are mark-
ing out their own territories of jurisdiction, competence and referral. Each
set of experts produces its own "scientific" knowledge: screening devices,
diagnostic tests, treatment modalities, evaluation scales. All this creates new
categories and the typifications which fill them: where there was once talk
about the "typical" prisoner, first offender or hardened recidivist, now there
will be typical "clients" of half-way houses, or community correctional
centers, typical divertees or predelinquents. These creatures are then fleshed
out -- in papers, research proposals, official reports — with sub-systems of
knowledge and new vocabularies: locking up becomes "intensive placement", dossiers become "anecdotal records", rewards and punishments become "behavioural contracts".

The enterprise justifies itself: there is hardly any point in asking about "success — this is not the object of the exercise. Research is done on the
classification system *itself* — working out a "continuum of community
basedness²", prediction tables, screening devices — and one does not ask for a
classification system to "work". In one massive American enterprise [46]
some 10 Federal agencies, 31 task forces and 93 experts got together simply
to study the ways of classifying various problem groups of children.

The overwhelming impression is one of bustling, almost *frenzied* activity:
all these wonderful new things are being done to this same old group of
troublemakers (with a few new ones allowed in). It might not be too far
fetched to imagine an urban ethnographer of the future, that proverbial
Martian anthropologist studying a day in the life of this strange new tribe,
filing in a report something like this [47]:

> Mr. and Mrs. Citizen, their son Joe and daughter Linda, leave their suburban home after
> breakfast, saying goodbye to Ron, a fifteen year pre-delinquent who is living with them under the
> LAK (Look After a Kid) scheme. Ron will later take a bus downtown to the Community
> Correctional Center, where he is to be given two hours of Vocational Guidance and later tested

on the Interpersonal Maturity Level Scale. Mr. C. drops Joe off at the School Problems Evaluation Center from where Joe will walk to school. In his class are five children who are bussed from a local Community Home, four from a Pre-Release Facility and three, who, like Ron live with families in the neighbourhood. Linda gets off next – at the GUIDE Center (Girls Unit for Intensive Daytime Education) where she works as a Behavioural Contract Mediator. They drive past a Threequarter-way House, a Rape Crisis Center and then a Drug Addict Cottage, where Mrs. C. waves to a group of boys working in the garden. She knows them from some volunteer work she does in RODEO (Reduction of Delinquency Through Expansion of Opportunities). She gets off at a building which houses the Special Intensive Parole Unit, where she is in charge of a five year evaluation research project on the use of the HIM (Hill Interaction Matrix) in matching group treatment to client. Mr. C. finally arrives at work, but will spend his lunch hour driving around the car again as this is his duty week on patrol with TIPS (Turn in a Pusher).

Meantime, back in the ghetto . . . .

The logic of this master pattern – dispersal, penetration, spreading out – as opposed to its particular current forms, is not at all new. Its antecedents can be traced though, not to the model which its apologists cite – the idyllic pre-industrial rural community – but to a somewhat later version of social control, a version which *in theory* was an alternative to the prison. When, from the end of the eighteenth century, punishment started entering deeper into the social body, the alternative vision to the previous great concentrated spectacles of public torture, was of the dispersal of control through "hundreds of tiny theatres of punishment" [48]. The eighteenth century reformers dreamed of dispersal and diversity but this vision of the punitive city was never to be fully realized. Instead punishment became concentrated in the coercive institution, a single uniform penalty to be varied only in length. The earlier "projects of docility" which Foucault describes – the techniques of order, discipline and regulation developed in schools, monasteries, workshops, the army – could only serve as models. Panopticism (surveillance, discipline) began to spread: as disciplinary establishments increased, ". . . their mechanisms have a certain tendency to become 'de-institutionalized', to emerge from the closed fortresses in which they once functioned and to circulate in a 'free' state; the massive compact disciplines are broken down into flexible methods of control, which may be transferred and adapted" [49].

This principle of "indefinite discipline" – judgements, examinations and observations which would never end – represented the new mode of control is much as the public execution had represented the old. Only in the prison, though, could this utopia be realized in a pure, physical form. The "new" move into the community is merely a continuation of the overall pattern established in the nineteenth century. The proliferation of new experts and professionals, the generation of specialized domains of scientific knowledge, the creation of complicated classification systems, the establishment of a

360

network of agencies surrounding the court and the prison – all these developments marked the beginning a century ago of the widening of the "carceral circle" or "carceral archipelago".

The continuous gradation of institutions then – the "correctional" continuum" – is not new. What is new is the scale of the operation and the technologies (drugs, surveillance and information gathering techniques) which facilitate the blurring and penetration which I described. Systems of medicine, social work, education, welfare take on supervisory and judicial functions, while the penal apparatus itself becomes more influenced by medicine, education, psychology [50]. This new system of subtle gradations in care, control, punishment and treatment is indeed far from the days of public execution and torture – but it is perhaps not quite as far as Foucault suggests from that early reform vision of the punitive city. The ideology of community is trying once more to increase the visibility – if not the theatricality – of social control. True, we must not know quite what is happening – treatment or punishment, public or private, locked up or free, inside or outside, voluntary or coercive – but we must know that something is happening, here, in our very own community.

An obvious question: is all this good or bad? Most of us – consciously or not – probably hold a rather bleak view of social change. Things must be getting worse. My argument has obviously tilted towards this view of the world by dwelling on the undesirable consequences – some unintended and others not too unintended – of the emerging social control system. The consequent series of all-purpose radical assumptions, though – that things must always be getting worse; that all reforms, however well intentioned ultimately lead to more repression and coercion; that industrial capitalism contains the seeds of its own destruction – need some correction. Undoubtedly some programs of community treatment or diversion are genuine alternatives to incarceration and in addition are more humane and less intrusive. Sometimes the programs might succeed in avoiding the harsh effects of early stigmatization and brutalization. In addition, all these terrible sounding "agents of social control" instead of being disguised paratroopers of the state, might be able to deploy vastly improved opportunities and resources to offer help and service to groups which desperately need them. These possibilities must not be ignored for a minute, nor should the possibility that from the delinquent or criminal's own subjective personal experience, these new programs might indeed be preferable – whatever the overall consequences as depicted by any outside sociologist.

Many of these possibilities are yet to be resolved by more or less empirical evidence. But in the long run – as they say – social control is in the interests of the collective, not the individual. It could hardly be otherwise.

Notes

1 In the United States, some recent and explicit versions of this disenchantment – framed in the language of embittered liberalism – may be found in the various essays in Gaylin, W. et al (1978). *Doing Good: The Limits of Benevolence*, New York: Pantheon Books. In Britain, despite the fact that substantial cuts in welfare services have occurred, the commitment to the welfare state is more entrenched and consequently a liberal disenchantment with "doing good" has not yet surfaced.

2 Rusche, G. and Kircheimer, O. (1938). *Punishment and Social Structure*, New York: Russell and Russell; Foucault, M. (1967). *Madness and Civilisation*, London: Tavistock and (1977). *Discipline and Punish: The Birth of the Prison*, London: Allen Lane; Rothman. D. J. (1971). *The Discovery of the Asylum*, Boston: Little Brown.

3 For various relevant attempts, see Cohen. S. (1977). "Prisons and the Future of Control Systems" in M. Fitzgerald et al (eds.) *Welfare in Action*, London: Routledge, pp. 217–228; Scull, A. (1977). *Decarceration: Community Treatment and the Deviant*, London: Prentice Hall; and Rothman, D. "Behavioural Modification in Total Institutions: A Historical Overview", *Hastings Centre Report*, 5: 17–24.

4 Scull, op. cit., documents both the presence at the end of the nineteenth century of the equivalent of today's liberal/social scientific critique of institutions and the reasons for the failure of this earlier attack. For him, the origins of current policy lie in certain changing features of welfare capitalism. Crudely expressed: it no longer "suits" the state to maintain segregative modes of control based on the asylum. In relative terms (and hence the appeal to fiscal conservatives) such modes become costly, while the alternative of welfare payments allowing subsistence in the community, is easier to justify and can be sold on humanitarian and scientific grounds. Scull's argument is a useful corrective to accounts purely at the level of ideas, but it places too much importance on the supposed fiscal crisis, it is less relevant to Britain and America and far less relevant for crime and delinquency than mental illness. In regard to crime and delinquency the picture is not the non-interventionist one Scull implies but – as this paper suggests – the development of parallel systems of control.

5 Scull. op. cit., p. 42.

6 See Gaylin et al. op. cit. and Von Hirsh, A. (1976). *Doing Justice: The Choice of Punishments*, New York: Hill and Wang.

7 The most informative sources in the United States would be journals such as *Crime and Delinquency* and *Federal Probation* from the mid-sixties onwards and the various publications from bodies such as the National Institute of Mental Health and, later, the Law Enforcement Assistance Administration. A representative collection of such material is Perlstein, G. R. and Phelps, T. R. (eds.) (1975). *Alternatives to Prison: Community Based Corrections*. Pacific Palisades, Calif: Goodyear Publishing Co., In Britain the ideology of community control has been slower and less obvious in its development. though it can be traced in various Home Office publications from the end of the nineteen sixties. See also Blom-Cooper, L. (ed.) (1974). *Progress in Penal Reform*, Oxford: Oxford University Press and Tutt, N. (ed.) (1978). *Alternative Strategies for Coping with Crime*, Oxford: Basil Blackwell.

8 Some of these may be found in Scull, op. cit. and Greenberg, D. F. (1975). "Problems in Community Corrections", *Issues in Criminology*, 10: 1–33.

9 National Institute of Mental Health (1971). *Community Based Correctional Programs: Models and Practices*, Washington, D.C.: U.S. Government Printing Office, p.1.

10 Coates, K. B., et al (1976). "Social Climate, Extent of Community Linkages and Quality of Community Linkages: The Institutionalisation Normalisation Continuum" unpublished Ms., Centre for Criminal Justice, Harvard Law School.

11 Bradley, H. B. (1969). "Community Based Treatment for Young Adult Offenders", *Crime and Delinquency*, 15 (3): 369.

12 For a survey, see Seiter. R. P. et al (1977). *Halfway House*, Washington, D.C.: National Institute of Law Enforcement and Criminal Justice, L.E.A.A.

362

13 Fox, V. (1977). *Community Based Corrections*, Englewood Cliffs: Prentice Hall, pp. 62–63.
14 Hinton. N. (1974). "Intermediate Treatment" in Blom Cooper (ed.) op. cit., p. 239.
15 Rothman (1975). op. cit., p. 19.
16 The most exhaustive research here deals with the two Californian projects – Community Treatment and Probation Subsidy – widely hailed as exemplars of the new strategy. See, especially, Lerman, P. (1975). *Community Treatment and Social Control: A Critical Analysis of Juvenile Correctional Policy*, Chicago: University of Chicago Press and Messinger, S. (1976). "Confinement in the Community: A Selective Assessment of Paul Lerman's 'Community Treatment and Social Control' ", *Journal of Research in Crime and Delinquency*, 13 (1): 82–92. Another standard Californian study of the diversion strategy is Cressey, D. and McDermott (1974). *Diversion from the Juvenile Justice System*, Washington, D.C.: National Institute of Law Enforcement and Criminal Justice. L.E.A.A. For two useful general evaluations of the field, see Rutherford, A. and Bengur, O. (1976). *Community Based Alternatives to Juvenile Incarceration*, Washington, D.C., National Institute of Law Enforcement and Criminal Justice. L.E.A.A.; Rutherford, A. and McDermott, R. (1976). *Juvenile Diversion*, Washington, D.C.: National Institute of Law Enforcement and Criminal Justice, L.E.A.A.
17 Rutherford and Bengur, op. cit.,
18 Pease. K. (1977). *Community Service Assessed in 1976*, Home Office Research Unit Study No. 39 London: H.M.S.O.
19 Quoted in Rutherford and Bengur. op. cit., p. 30.
20 Greenberg. op. cit., p. 23.
21 A clear statement of this rationale and the legal problems in implementing it, is to be found in Law Reform Commission of Canada (1975). *Working Paper No. 7: Diversion*, Ottawa: Law Reform Commission of Canada.
22 Dunford, F. W. (1977). "Police Diversion – An Illusion?". *Criminology*, 15 (3): 335–352.
23 Morris, A. (1978). "Diversion of Juvenile Offenders from the Criminal Justice System" in Tu (ed.), op. cit., pp. 50–54.
24 Bohnstedt. M. (1978). "Answers to Three Questions about Juvenile Diversion", *Journal of Research in Crime and Delinquency*, 15 (1): 10.
25 Klein, M. W. et al (1976). "The Explosion in Police Diversion Programmes: Evaluating the Structural Dimensions of a Social Fad", in M. W. Klein (ed.) *The Juvenile Justice System*, Beverley Hills: Sage, p. 10.
26 Rutherford and McDermott. op. cit.
27 Cressey and McDermott, op. cit., pp. 3–4.
28 Rutherford and McDermott, op. cit., pp. 25–26.
29 See. especially, Platt, A. M. (1969). *The Child Savers: The Invention of Delinquency*. Chicago: Chicago University Press.
30 Greenberg, op. cit., p. 8.
31 Messinger, op. cit., pp. 84–85.
32 Boorkman, D. et al (1976). *An Exemplary Project: Community Based Corrections in Des Moine:* Washington, D.C.: National Institute of Law Enforcement and Criminal Justice, L.E.A.A.
33 Ibid., pp. 35–36.
34 Ku. R. and Blew, C. (1977). *A University's Approach to Delinquency Prevention: The Adolescent Diversion Project*, Washington, D.C.: National Institute of Law Enforcement and Criminal Justice, L.E.A.A.
35 Spitzer. S. and A. T. Scull (1977a). "Social Control in Historical Perspective: From Private to Public Responses to Crime" in D.F. Greenberg (ed.) *Corrections and Punishment*, Beverley Hills: Sage, pp. 265–286 and Spitzer, S. and A. T. Scull (1977b), "Privatisation and Capitalist Development: The Case of the Private Police", *Social Problems*. 25 (1): 18–29.
36 Spitzer and Scull (1977a) op. cit., p. 265.
37 For a description of this process, see Rutherford and McDermott. op. cit.
38 Marx. G. T. (1974). "Thoughts on a Neglected Category of Social Movement Participant: The agent provocateur and informant", *American Journal of Sociology*, 80 (2): 402–442.
39 Marx, G. T. (1977). "Undercover Cops: Creative Policing or Constitutional Threat?", *Civil Liberties Review*, pp. 34–44.

40 For approved examples of these new forms of policing, see Bickman, L. et al (1977). *Citizen Crime Reporting Projects*, Washington, D.C.: National Institute of Law Enforcement and Administration of Justice and Yin, R. K. et al (1977). *Citizen Patrol Projects*, Washington, D.C.: National Institute of Law Enforcement and Criminal Justice, L.E.A.A.

41 National Advisory Commission on Criminal Justice Standards and Goals (1973). *Community Crime Prevention*, Washington, D.C.: U.S. Government Printing Office, p. 7.

42 Empey, L. T. (1967). *Alternatives to Incarceration*, Washington, D.C.: U.S. Government Printing Office.

43 For typical statements about absorption, see Carter, R. M. (1972). "The Diversion of Offenders", *Federal Probation* 36 (4): 31–36.

44 Skoler, D. (1975). "Future Trends in Juvenile and Adult Community Based Corrections" in Perlstein and Phelps (eds.), op. cit., p. 11.

45 Levi Strauss, C. (1977). *Tristes Tropiques*, Harmondsworth: Penguin, p. 508.

46 Hobbs, N. (1975). *Issues in the Classification of Children*, San Francisco: Jossey Bass Publishers.

47 Strangers to the world of community corrections should be informed that all the projects named in this imaginary report are *real* and current.

48 Foucault (1977), op. cit., p. 113.

49 Ibid., p. 211.

50 Ibid., p. 306.

[3]

The Howard Journal Vol 28 No 4. Nov 89
ISSN 0265-5527

Discipline and Punish: Some Notes on the Margin

DAVID NELKEN

Reader in Law, University College, London

Abstract: This paper re-analyses a debate between Cohen and Bottoms over the alleged growth of the 'disciplinary society'. It then takes as a test case empirical evidence concerning a new technique of social control used by social workers, namely the use of 'contracts' in welfare interventions, especially with parents suspected of maltreating their children. It argues that this form of social control illustrates the limitations of the analytical framework used by both Cohen and Bottoms and suggests that a characteristic of modern control techniques may be the way they fuse together disciplinary and juridical elements.

In this paper I shall review and attempt to take further an important and still unresolved debate between Stan Cohen and Tony Bottoms. This concerns the question of whether recent developments in criminal justice reflect the growth of a 'disciplinary society', by which is meant the complex of social, educational and medical technologies of regulation delineated by Foucault (Foucault 1977). I shall first set out some of the crucial issues in the debate and then introduce some empirical evidence of my own from a recent project investigating one of the new methods of social control discussed in it. The example will be used to show the strengths and weaknesses of the framework around which this debate is constructed. Because both authors draw heavily on the work of Foucault, this discussion could be seen as a contribution to the literature deriving from *Discipline and Punish* (Foucault 1977). But it is intended even more to serve as a study of practices at the margin between 'discipline' and 'punishment'.

The Debate over 'The Punitive City'

The claim that new methods of crime control carried out in 'the community' represented the consolidation of the 'disciplinary society' was put forward by Stan Cohen in his widely quoted paper entitled 'the punitive city' (Cohen 1979). Tony Bottoms then criticised Cohen's conclusions in the course of a magisterial and wide-ranging review of changes in penal sanctions in Britain since the second world war (Bottoms 1983). More recently, Cohen has defended and reformulated his views in his new book *Visions of Social Control* (Cohen 1985).

Cohen concentrates his analysis on initiatives in America and Britain

245

such as community crime prevention schemes, diversion programmes and professional mediation and treatment techniques. Like a number of other writers he sees these so-called 'alternatives' to criminal justice as in fact enlarging its reach (Nelken 1985). In his metaphors, these developments 'blur' the distinction between institutional and non-residential means of crime control: they widen the 'net' of criminal justice by increasing the number of people subjected to forms of crime prevention and they 'thin the mesh' by increasing the degree of interference in the lives of those involved in treatment and control programmes. All this means that it becomes increasingly difficult to tell where the official system of crime control ends and ordinary life in the 'family' and the 'community' begins. We may end up living in the 'punitive city' (Cohen 1979).

Bottoms, on the other hand, focusses on what he calls 'some neglected features of criminal justice systems', in particular the continued heavy reliance on the fine in Britain. Drawing support from criminal statistics, as well as other evidence, he suggests that it is this penalty (and others not requiring continuing supervision by a penal agent), together with community service and compensation orders, which are characteristic of modern penality. The centrality of the fine is seen to contradict Cohen's thesis because it represents an exemplary neo-classical *juridical* form of punishment. The fine works by communicating public messages concerning the blameworthiness and costs of wrong-doing rather than seeking to train, re-socialise or otherwise 'discipline' the offender (Bottoms 1983, pp. 179–80, 183). Moreover, in the modern context, the fine has taken on new life not only in the sanctioning of motoring offences, but as an adjunct to the regulatory activities of the national and local state (Bottoms 1983, pp. 187–90). The measures described by Cohen, on the other hand, form a small and relatively declining part of the contemporary penal scene. They can be sufficiently explained by the need for more options to deal with rising crime, or the willingness to report crime, and by changes in the burden of welfare responsibilities carried out by the state (Bottoms 1983, pp. 184, 193–4). The initiatives which Cohen describes do *not* represent the fulfilment of the nineteenth century disciplinary project: the *dispersal* of control should not be seen as the spread of 'the disciplines'. The modern trend is towards greater *indirect* control of groups and activities instead of concentrating on the individual. It demonstrates that '*disciplinary punishment is not necessary to achieve control*' (Bottoms 1983, p. 187, italics in original).

The Point of the Argument

What is to be made of this debate? It depends what it is really about. If it concerns the leading characteristics of modern criminal justice systems, especially in Britain, then Bottoms has the better of the argument. Some commentators have indeed drawn this conclusion, describing Bottoms's paper as an ideal illustration of the way 'the qualitative understanding of changing ideologies of social control can be addressed through statistics of punishment' (Bottomley and Pease 1986, p. 94). But this begs the question of whether Cohen and Bottoms share the same concerns. Unlike

Bottoms, Cohen was not interested in criminal justice as such, *except* as an illustration of wider changes in 'social control'. His task, as originally conceived, was to locate 'courts, prisons and police . . . in an overall social space, the master patterns of social control behaviours of other institutions such as school and family, and broader trends in welfare and social services' (Cohen 1979, p. 340). But this means that developments which are marginal to criminal justice may well be central to wider changes in social control. And it is questionable how far it is possible to rely on 'penal statistics' in an argument concerning 'changing ideologies of social control'.

I would suggest that two issues underly the debate and give it its point. The first problem is how to relate developments in criminal justice to wider changes in social control. The second issue concerns the correct interpretation of Foucault's contrast between 'juridical' and 'disciplinary' punishment.

The debate arises because neither author confines himself to criminal justice on the one hand, or social control on the other. Bottoms also discusses the modern bureaucratic systems (both public and private) which he admits exist outside the criminal justice system proper and use penal sanctions only as a last resort (Bottoms 1983, pp. 186–7). Again, he suggests that Cohen's argument about the growth of diciplinary punishment may be applicable to the United States where the criminal justice system takes on many of the roles which are performed in England and Wales by the more extensive welfare system and by 'informal structures of society' (Bottoms 1983, p. 194). But he insists that Cohen's examples, most of which are drawn from American probation and prosecution initiatives, would be found *outside* the criminal justice system in Britain. Bottoms's overall argument, therefore, is that discipline, in the strictly Foucauldian sense, may be of relatively declining significance within the penal system (as opposed to the social control system as a whole) (Bottoms 1983, p. 191). To this Cohen could reply that he is more interested in the wider scene. But Cohen lays himself open to Bottoms's critique by choosing his examples too squarely from initiatives within criminal justice and by confining his remarks to what he characterises as the domain of 'formal social control'. Bottoms, for his part, claims too much whenever he extends his argument to embrace all of social control, generalising from evidence restricted to penal developments. For example, he concludes his paper by explaining that it, 'has been concerned merely to show that there are plausible ways of theorizing about a possible relative decline in the significance of disciplinary punishment within *the total apparatus of social control*' (Bottoms 1983, p. 195, italics added).

But there is also a wider disagreement over the very meaning of disciplinary control. Bottoms distinguishes carefully between 'corporal', 'juridical' and 'carceral' mechanisms of punishment. He identifies 'discipline' with 'carceral' methods of training, which generally take place within institutions and involve 'knowledge of the offender as a whole person'. And his review of penal developments is intended to show the lack of evidence of any growth in such measures. Bottoms also criticises

247

Cohen's adoption of a Foucault quotation which describes 'the punitive
city' as a locus of 'hundreds of tiny theatres of punishment'. He claims that
this deals with the classical reformers' dream of a widely diffused scheme
of *juridical* punishment rather than with the extension of disciplines
(Bottoms 1983, p. 177; Foucault 1977, p. 113). Cohen has now conceded
this exegetical point. In his new book he adds to the Foucault quotation
the qualifying rider 'each a perfect arithmetical representation of the
bourgeois social contract' (Cohen 1985, p. 85). He even goes further and
admits that Foucault's approach does not take sufficient account of the
continued vitality of the neo-classical juridical approach to punishment
shown by the success of the fine (Cohen 1985, p. 152). But he repeats
Foucault's argument that in the nineteenth century the reformer's *juridical*
project was 'replaced, or rather overladen with the carceral or *disciplinary*
vision' (Cohen 1985, p. 85). And he continues to defend the applicability
of Foucault's programmatic statement at the end of *Discipline and Punish* in
which he describes the disciplines as poliferating beyond their original
institutional settings (Foucault 1977, p. 306).

In order to take this debate further, it is important to see what the
protagonists have in common as well as what divides them. Their most
important point of agreement is that they both rely heavily on Foucault's
dichotomy between 'juridical' and 'disciplinary' punishment. Cohen
needs to show that disciplinary punishments are replacing and obscuring
juridical penalties whilst Bottoms wants to insist that the few examples of
discipline can be *differentiated* clearly from other types of sanctions.
This means that both authors are uninterested in examining the
various ways in which disciplinary and juridical modes of control may
be mutually 'constitutive', and the way they supplement each other in
modern forms of social regulation (Fitzpatrick 1984). There are hints of
such possibilities, as when Bottoms observes that community service
contains both juridical and disciplinary elements, but these are not
followed up. Rather than pursuing this argument at an abstract level,
however, I shall now turn to a specific example to illustrate the value of
opening up such questions.

The Normalising Contract

The research I shall draw on here concerns the use of contracts and
working agreements in social work. It involved interviewing social
workers, lawyers, clients and others about the way this technique was
employed, when and why it was used, and the practical meanings of
'success'. The main sample of 85 social workers was taken from both basic
and managerial grades working in ten local authorities in London in
fieldwork and residential settings. I hope to publish the full results of this
study in due course and I shall be concerned here only with those findings
which have implications for the Cohen–Bottoms debate.

The growing interest in contracts in the United States, Britain and
other European countries is the result of internal and external influences
on social work (Nelken 1987). The development of the task-work

248

approach, the rise of consumerism, increasing legal challenges at court, all, in different ways, encourage greater clarity and documentation of social work decision making. Contracts also play an important co-ordinating role as social welfare comes to rely more heavily on community and 'lay' social work assistance, for example in showing increasing recognition of the role of foster parents. Although the use of detailed and signed formal agreements still represents the exception rather than the rule they play a strategic role, as will be seen, in some of the most serious and troublesome social work cases.

The special relevance of re-examining contracts in this context is that they are used by Cohen as an illustration of the growth of disciplinary punishment (Cohen 1979, 1985, pp. 72–4). His dismissal of the value of this technique was one of the stimuli which led me to initiate this research project. The example Cohen describes deals with a contract drawn up by a university psychology department in the United States. The agreement was intended to help achieve a mediated settlement of a dispute between an adolescent and his family. The boy was the subject of a diversion project following charges of curfew breaking and mahrijuana use. The details of this techniques therefore provide a good example of the interpenetration of education, family, and criminal justice systems – the blurring of boundaries characteristic of 'the punitive city'. The contract terms required the boy to call home to tell his parents where he was in the evenings, to return home by midnight, to make his bed, and to help in the house. His parents had to agree to allow him out on some evenings, to refrain from criticising his friends and to pay him for cleaning his room. The penalties for non-performance by the son involved progressive cuts in pocket-money and in the length of his hair, his reward was to be increased pocket money. Cohen was highly critical of the 'alleged humanitarianism' of this programme, which he saw instead as an imposed behavioural instrument of manipulation and surveillance. More recently Cohen has described the term 'contract' as an example of a 'control talk' euphemism by which a behaviourist technique is disguised as an instance of voluntary agreement (Cohen 1985, p. 22). Many of Cohen's suspicions may be well warranted. But in his desire to unmask the misuse of contract he does not give sufficient attention to the variety of uses of contract inside and outside the criminal justice system and the disparate elements which constitute this style of work.

It is these issues which I want to consider, using the framework of the Cohen–Bottoms' debate as a starting point. Firstly, do social work contracts belong inside or outside the criminal justice system? The answer appears to be both. My research uncovered some cases where contracts formed part of diversion schemes and intermediate programmes (as in Cohen's illustration). Social workers used them as a device for securing initial agreement to acceptance on a scheme and for monitoring progress thereafter. They also often serve as a basis for mediating problems in families with children in trouble. Contracts are also found within residential institutions as rules of the house and as personal treatment plans for individual inmates. They are used to organise liaison between

residential and community supervision of offenders and as a basis of
community care programmes where children from institutions are placed
temporarily with substitute families.

But contracts are used even more *outside* the field of criminal justice.
The social work literature in fact recommends them for virtually all types
of intervention (Corden and Preston-Shoot 1987). In my research I too
found a variety of diverse uses of contracts. But almost all respondents
saw contracts as particularly essential in statutory-based child-care,
especially in working with parents who were suspected of injuring or
neglecting their children. Most of the formal contracts I was shown dealt
with the minimal requirements of 'normal parenting', including the
protection of children from sources of harm, and compliance with
measures allowing the social work department to monitor children's
progress. Amongst the reasons for this was the fact that in this type of
social work it was important to be able to show, if necessary at court,
whether parents had reached the prescribed standards of parenting.

Contracts are therefore used both inside and outside criminal justice.
But their significance would not be well captured by arguing that they are
quantitatively marginal to criminal justice (Bottoms) or, alternatively, by
insisting that they extend the reach of the system (Cohen). Interestingly,
contract is a technique which social workers use for similar purposes of
increasing control both inside and outside the criminal justice system.
Thus one social worker justified his use of contracts in *child-care* by
explaining: 'A lot of social workers have a problem about power. They
keep it out of view, deny that we're social policemen'. An officer of the
N.S.P.C.C. (the quasi-official charity which deals with many of the most
serious cases of children 'at risk') used similar language: 'People tend to
come into the profession to be things other than policemen, but of course a
lot of social work involves very heavy policing'. Even the choice of when
and how to introduce contracts in particular interventions was to be
understood in these terms. As another worker argued: 'When things are
getting out of control is when people start thinking about contract. That
might be the wrong way with it . . .'.

In fact, some social workers made efforts to avoid or reduce what they
saw as the abuse of contracts as a method of social control (Nelken 1988).
But, surprisingly they thought that social control needed to be more
limited in the context of *criminal justice* rather than in the more usual child-
care situations. Thus one residential social worker commented critically
that: 'It actually quite often is a mechanism for control . . . A member of
staff can say "you've broken the contract, now I can do so and so" '.
Similarly, a worker on a diversion project was actually one of the most
determined opponents to the use of contract for purposes of control,
explaining:

We've found that social services children homes are very keen to actually use it as
an extension of their control systems. To put things in the contract like 'If he
misbehaves in the children's home he will be punished by us by not being allowed
as much free time or something'. We've just refused to do that.

Attitudes to the dangers of contracts as a method of control did not always fall into this pattern. But we could make sense of any apparent paradox by arguing that contracts are valuable for control precisely in those situations where social workers most feel the need to clarify and strengthen their powers. It could be for this reason that they are more likely to be needed for social control purposes in settings *other* than criminal justice. Cohen is certainly right to argue there is some difficulty in even drawing this distinction, given that the same technique can be used in both contexts and that both are characterised as involving 'social policing'. But this does not necessarily show, as he assumes, that criminal justice is losing its boundaries. For this depends on the point of reference. A more apt way of putting it would be to argue that the notion of social control itself belongs to the sphere of 'the social' which is superimposed over the conventional divide between criminal justice and what lies outside it. The practice and discourse of social workers and others when constructing and administering the realm of the 'social' may often not recognise the boundaries between criminal justice and the rest of social life. But for other purposes and discourses the distinction may continue to be recognisable and recognised.

Having re-examined the place of social work contracts in terms of the problem of criminal justice and its boundaries we may now turn to the alleged contrast between disciplinary and non-disciplinary sanctions. Although some case can be made for seeing social work contracts as an extension of 'the disciplines' it is important to see that they also show the continuing vitality of the juridical approach. What is of special interest is to understand how contracts combine both elements in a way which both Bottoms's and Cohen's approaches fail to illuminate.

On the one hand, there is much in Foucault's description of 'the disciplines' (whether interpreted by Cohen or by Bottoms) which seem to fit contracts very well. Whatever their other manifest or latent functions, the typical use of contracts, as in child-care cases, is as a method for managing and 'training' clients. In this they are unlike the impersonal regulatory techniques which Bottoms sees as typical of modern social control. Even the language used by partisans of the technique is sometimes closely reminiscent of Foucault. As one informant explained: 'It's one way of breaking down these events and developments into meaningfully attainable elements'. Contracts are drawn up by social workers using their specialised expertise, and they depend on a process of previous clarification and assessment of the client's 'problem'. The local authority's legal department plays little or no part in these contracts unless the cases actually come to court. Moreover the contract continues to be used throughout the intervention as a *diagnostic* tool and not just as 'an agreement'. Social workers claim to be able to 'learn' from the client's response to the contract, however it turns out. From that point of view the contract can never 'fail'. The decision whether to apply to remove the child from home or to re-negotiate the contract will depend on social workers' appraisal of the parents' achievement of the required standards of behaviour. Because contracts are used in the maintenance of liaison and co-ordination between social work agencies and others such as day nurseries, they also satisfy Bottoms's definition of disciplinary techniques as involving a combination of both 'training' and 'surveillance'.

On the other hand, there is also an undeniably legalistic side to contracts which is sometimes inconsistent with their disciplinary function. This is not only because their popularity coincides with a period in which social workers and other professions are being called to account for the exercise of their power. Contracts do not have the status of binding private agreements it is true but they can make clearer what the social work department expects and what it is prepared to offer. In child-care cases, for example, they spell out the actual meaning of statutory requirements and they are written partly with an eye to what the court may later decide. Social work contracts have one other feature which is particularly important in terms of Bottoms's understanding of the differences between 'carceral' and 'juridical' techniques. As compared to traditional casework, contracts treat a client more like an ordinary citizen who has defaulted rather than as an 'object' of re-training. This brings them closer to his juridical model which allows individuals to 're-integrate' themselves into society by their own efforts.

There are issues of symbolism and procedure as well as substance. The use of the term 'contract', for all that it is inappropriate and even manipulative, does signify the importance of the ideal which agreement represents. Some social work authors are trying hard to gain acceptance for the 'legal' model of contracts, as compared to the 'behaviourist' one, and recognise that this would entail considerable changes in existing social work practice (Corden and Preston-Shoot 1987). It would be unduly cynical to explain all calls for empowering clients, foster parents and others – some of which come from the interested parties themselves – as efforts to increase social work control. One further sign of the extent to which the legal analogy is taken seriously is the willingness of some social workers to accept that they can be placed in an adversarial position towards their clients. The N.S.P.C.C., for example, encourages clients to have their contracts checked by their own lawyers. As one inspector commented: 'almost inevitably at some point we're going to have a fight with them'. Social workers re-thinking their commitment to increasing the autonomy of their clients find the legal approach quite congenial. If autonomy is the ultimate goal, they reason, perhaps it should also be the starting point of intervention, especially as the automatic compliance aimed at by 'the disciplines' is neither feasible nor suitable in non-institutional settings. If clients must somehow be taught to choose for themselves so as to be capable to guiding their own behaviour, a juridical model for encouraging appropriate choices seems more apt than the imposition of control.

What this shows is that social work contracts can be properly understood neither as disciplinary nor as juridical techniques since they contain elements of both. Contrasts between the 'disciplinary' and the 'juridical' (Foucault 1977), 'tutelage' and 'contract' (Castel 1976; Donzelot 1980) or 'bureaucratic' and 'gesellschaft' law (Kamenka and

Tay 1975) may be misleading even as heuristic ideal-types when it is their interrelation which is important (Nelken 1982). The significance of techniques such as social work contracts may be that they show the necessity of replacing existing conceptual distinctions between civil and criminal sanctions, law and welfare etc. in order to capture the properties of marginal emergent phenomena. It may in fact be a more plausible account of Cohen's argument to interpret it in this way rather than to see it as a claim about the boundaries of criminal justice as such. This is not to deny that, in Cohen's terms, social work contracts are closer to a disciplinary than to a juridical technique. Their aim is the 'normalisation' of the role behaviour of parents, spouses, adolescents and others, whilst their method is regulation through self-regulation. From this point of view the apparent extension of the 'social contract' to include welfare clients, offenders, children and the mentally ill may represent little more than a more demanding form of paternalism. All this can be accepted as long as it is also remembered that the combination of legal and behaviourist models cuts *both* ways and is embodied in the technique itself.

The peculiar mixture of characteristics represented by social work contracts is not only a matter of theoretical interest. In order to decide whether or not such developments represent a move towards greater accountability we will need to examine whether the juridical element actually limits discretionary power or only serves to protect social work decision making from closer scrutiny. For example, contracts may enable social workers to appeal, as and where necessary, either to social work discourse and expertise or to legal processes and models of expected conduct (either serially or simultaneously). This means that in practice contracts can increase rather than reduce social workers' room for manoeuvre. As Rose has argued in connections with psychiatry (Rose and Miller 1986, pp. 168–99) a stress on clear-cut rights as the enemy of discretion can in fact help to co-ordinate the activities of different professionals quite as much as it enhances the status of clients. In the end law and social work can come together to provide 'a rationale for the "contractualization" of subjectivity' (Rose and Miller 1986, p. 128) rather than the empowerment of the previously powerless.

Conclusion

This paper began by reconsidering the debate between Cohen and Bottoms over the alleged rise of the 'punitive city'. By bringing to bear new information concerning one of the techniques in dispute I sought to show the limitations of the questions and the conceptual categories used by both parties to the debate.

My major claim has been that in seeking to understand marginal forms of crime control, such as the use of contracts by social workers, only limited insight is gained by arguing whether they count as extensions of the criminal justice system (Cohen 1979) or whether they belong outside it (Bottoms 1983). They are, after all, marginal practices. Instead their specific characteristics need to be identified for their own sake. It is clear that the rise of the disciplinary society has both challenged and transformed criminal justice. More significantly it has reduced its relative importance as a source of official social control. We may be tempted to conclude that it is criminal justice which is now only a marginal form of social control. Yet the continued strength of juridical forms and processes can be demonstrated from the mix of features which characterise some of the most modern of disciplinary techniques.[1]

Notes

[1] I am grateful for the valuable comments of Professor Peter Fitzpatrick and the journal's referees.

References

Bottomley, A. K. and Pease, K. (1986) *Crime and Punishment*, Milton Keynes: Open University Press.

Bottoms, A. E. (1983) 'Some neglected features of modern penal systems', in: D. Garland and P. Young (Eds.), *The Power to Punish*, London: Heinemann.

Castel, R. (1976) *L'ordre Psychiatrique*, Paris: Editions de Minuit.

Cohen, S. (1979) ' "The punitive city": notes on the dispersal of social control', *Contemporary Crises*, 2, 339–65.

Cohen, S. (1985) *Visions of Social Control*, Oxford: Polity Press.

Corden, J. and Preston-Shoot, M. (1987) *Contracts in Social Work*, London: Gower.

Donzelot, J. (1980) *The Policing of Families: Welfare versus the State*, London: Hutchinson.

Fitzpatrick, P. (1984) 'Law and societies', *Osgoode Hall Law Journal*, 22, 115.

Foucault, M. (1977) *Discipline and Punish: The Birth of the Prison*, London: Allen Lane.

Kamenka, E. and Tay, A. E-S. (1975) 'Beyond bourgeois individualism: the contemporary crisis in law and legal ideology', in: E. Kamenka and R. S. Neale (Eds.), *Feudalism, Capitalism and Beyond*, London: Edward Arnold.

Nelken, D. (1982) 'Is there a crisis in law and legal ideology?', *Journal of Law and Society*, 9, 177–89.

Nelken, D. (1985) 'Community involvement in crime control', *Current Legal Problems*, 38, 239–61.

Nelken, D. (1987) 'The use of "contracts" as a social work technique', *Current Legal Problems*, 40, 207–32.

Nelken, D. (1988) 'Social work contracts and social control', in: R. Mathews (Ed.), *Reconstructing Criminal Justice*, London: Sage.

Rose, N. and Miller, P. (1986) *The Power of Psychiatry*, London: Polity Press.

[4]

RECONCEPTUALIZING SANCTIONS

ARIE FREIBERG
Monash University
Melbourne, Australia

This article is an attempt to extricate sanction analysis from its criminological context and to focus on the sanction as an independent realm of knowledge. A framework for the study of sanctions based on power relations is suggested which has three major aspects: first, sanction form, of which seven types are identified (physical, economic, social, informational, political, privacy, and legal); second, sanction mode (postulated as either positive or negative); and third, arena of deployment, being either public or private. The advantages of this type of analysis over other sanction taxonomies are briefly discussed.

The study of sanctions as an independent realm of knowledge is a relatively recent development. Working within, but not necessarily bounded by, the framework of criminology, sanction theorists have tended to regard the sanction primarily as a penal entity, the consequence of crime, or, when rarely extended, as an appendix to the civil law (Rusche and Kirchheimer, 1939: 5). Sanctions have been understood from their ends alone, either the reduction of crime or its just desert. This "peripheralization" of sanctions (Spitzer, 1985: 576) has resulted in a neglect of the study of sanctions as social phenomena in their own right.

However, as Foucault states (1979: 24), we should "rid ourselves of the illusion that penality is above all (if not exclusively) a means of reducing crime." Rather, "punishment must be understood as a social phenomenon freed from both its juristic context and its social ends" (Rusche and Kirchheimer, 1939: 5). Durkheim was one of the first to explore the links between sanctions and social structure in preference to the nexus between sanctions and the type or amount of crime (Durkheim, 1933, 1969), and the recent resurgence of interest in this aspect of his work (Spitzer, 1974; Sheleff, 1975; Turkel, 1979; Garland, 1983; Lukes and Scull, 1983) is evidence of the overdue return to research in the sociology of sanctions.

The sanction is important for a number of reasons. First, it is the crucial concept said to distinguish law from nonlaw. Second, because norms and sanctions tend to be conceptually linked, both definitions of crime and deviance refer to sanctions (Gibbs, 1966: 147; Schwartz and Orleans, 1967: 274). Finally, and perhaps most importantly, it provides a key to understanding the nature and structure of societies and of the power relationships within societies. Foucault has shown the utility of connecting "a special object, like penality, with what are taken to be general and central sociological concepts like social structure or power" (Garland and Young, 1983: 8).

A major factor inhibiting a broad-based and more powerful analysis of sanctions has been the inability, of lawyers in particular, to discard the traditional legal positivist categories which have confined the study of sanctions within the bounds of a narrow correctionalism (compare Garland and Young, 1983). The intimate association of sanctions with the penal law has resulted in a gross neglect of the study of the nature and range of sanctions in the civil law. As the vast majority of disputes are resolved within the civil sphere, such neglect creates serious distortions in an understanding of the distribution and forms of power in society. Durkheim, for one, grasped the significance of the role of nonpenal law in industrialized societies and, in so doing, provided "an important corrective for sociological perspectives on law, given the orientation of criminology and the tendency in some sociological writings to concentrate on penal law as necessarily the dominant type and to underemphasize the sociological interest of non-penal law" (Cotterrell, 1977: 251). Concentration on the substance of penal sanctions has also resulted in the neglect of the study of the significance of the changing boundaries between the civil, criminal, and administrative branches of the law (compare Freiberg and O'Malley, 1984) as well as of the boundaries between the legal and nonlegal. Such "boundary" studies are rare and Turk, among others (1976: 283), has pointed to the need for "historical and anthropological studies to determine the specific conditions where . . . [a distinction] is introduced . . . in social life." Instead of assuming that distinctions are the inevitable product of some supra-human evolutionary process, they should be regarded as historically specific accomplishments (Turk, 1976: 282-283).

TOWARD A RECONCEPTUALIZATION

The equation of "punishment" with "sanction" is conceptually, heuristically, and semiotically unfortunate. For a start, the terms "punishment" or "penalty" connote pain, loss, or suffering, and so exclude positive sanctions or rewards from the field of study. Second, the focus on "punishment" tends to create confusion between the sanction itself and the purpose or justification for its imposition. Traditional studies of punishment have focused almost exclusively upon the relationship between punishment and justification (Greenawalt, 1983)[1] or have tended to take the form of listing the multitude of sanctions or, more particularly, the selection of one penalty and the examination of its history, use, effectiveness, and, sometimes, its relationship to

---

1. It is interesting to note that the entry for "sanctions" in the *Encyclopedia of Crime and Justice* contains no text but merely refers to other headings including capital and corporal punishment, prisons, and punishment.

other penalties. Ultimately, such approaches are limited because each sanction tends to be viewed in isolation, its resemblance to other sanctions ignored
or unrealized. They have added little to our understanding of "statecraft"
which Turk (1982: 160) has defined as "the art and science of social control."
This is related to the third problem, that of nomenclature. The ostensible
range of sanctions appears enormous (Cohen, 1985, 40-41). It includes
imprisonment, attendance center orders, community-based orders, weekend
imprisonment, probation orders, care orders, supervision orders, parole, work
release, periodic detention, hospital orders, suspended sentences, deferred
sentences, bonds, recognizances, discharges, dismissals, work orders, borstals,
youth training centers, youth attendance orders, and a host of others. On the
"civil" side one can find damages, divestiture orders, restitution and compensation orders, confiscation orders, injunctions, warnings, cease and desist
orders, license revocation, suspension or cancellation, and many more.

The purpose of this article is to sketch a framework for a model[2] of sanctions which, it is hoped, will clarify certain concepts which appear central to
research in social control, penology, and the sociology of law. It is an exercise in conceptual homology. This framework postulates a set of "ideal
types" of sanctions which approximate, but do not necessarily reflect reality
(Rheinstein, 1966: xxxviii). It draws heavily from the literature of politics,
especially upon political conceptions of power. Sanctions, it will be argued,
are expressions of power relations and taxonomic analyses of the forms of
power are regarded as providing a valuable basis for an analysis of sanctions.
The model has three basic dimensions: first, the sanction form itself, of which
seven types are identified; second, the sanction mode, postulated as being
either positive or negative; and third, the arena of deployment, either public
or private.

SANCTIONS AND POWER

Lawyers have long been aware that the debate about sanctions is ultimately
a debate about the use of power. Concentration on the criminal sanction has
occurred because it has appeared as the paradigmatic case of the controlled
use of power within a society. Yet, deprivations are imposed and indulgences
bestowed by officials as part of a larger system of the management of conflict,
and it is that larger context which must be addressed by sanction analysis

---

2. "A model or paradigm is a convenient shorthand, a device for presenting a suc-
cinct codification of an area of analysis. Models are tentative and limited, yet they are the
building blocks of theory and interpretation. They are less vague than a perspective, for
they provide a systematic, specific and often logically exhaustive set of categories for
research and speculation. At the same time they are less than a theory. A model provides
a 'language, a set of interrelated questions, but no account of validated propositions'"
(Dyson, 1980: 77).

(Probert, 1964: 293). Lukes and Scull, in criticizing Durkheim for his neglect of the phenomenon of power, write (1983: 24):

> Recent work has rightly seen systems of punishment as inextricably linked with the asymmetric relationships of control and dependency characteristic of the larger society, and has stressed their connections with the changing forms and extent of state power and economic organization. Law, after all, is one of the focal points of conflict and struggle in modern societies, a major means by which power is legitimized, and the form in which coercion is most routinely exercised.

The concept of power is an essentially contested one (Lukes, 1974: 9). All social relations can be viewed as power relations and the range of words used to signify power relations (including power, influence, authority, control, persuasion, might, force, coercion, manipulation, and others) testifies to the breadth of the concept (Dahl, 1970: 15; Tedeschi et al., 1970: 523).

Power, like social control, has been a concept in eclipse but, like social control, is undergoing somewhat of a revival (Cohen and Scull, 1983; Cohen, 1985; Mann, 1986). Debates about power have been bogged down in sterile debates about pluralism versus centralism, functionalism versus structuralism, zero-sum versus positive sum, and others. Without wishing to embark upon an extensive justification of the following definition, power is here defined as the ability of A to get B to do something he would not otherwise do, or not do something he otherwise would. A and B include groups as well as individuals, and "do something" includes attitudes as well as overt conduct (compare Lukes, 1974: 12).

There are a number of preliminary comments to be made about this conception of power. First, that it is a social relation, not a property of a person or a group. Second, society can be regarded as a network of power structures, many of them overlapping and competing (Stone, 1966: 711). Power is not the sole possession of the state. It does not have a central source, but is diffused throughout society—that is, it is "micro-physical" (Foucault, 1979; Hirst, 1985: 181). However, although power is not the exclusive province of a group or of the state, that is not to say that it cannot be concentrated. The state can be seen as a linking together of micropowers, of the numerous forms of power existing at all levels of social life with an overall strategy. Cotterrell writes (1984: 316) that "Power is not a derivation from the state but the state is the crystallization and organization of the dispersed forms of power which are ubiquitous in social life." Finally, power need not be repressive but can produce things, induce pleasure, and form knowledge (Foucault, 1980: 119).

Since the time of Aristotle, it has been common to relate differences in power to the differential distribution of resources, or assets among individuals, classes, or groups within society (Etzioni, 1970: 19; Dahl, 1968: 409). The hypothesis is that the greater one's resources, the greater the power

(Wrong, 1979: 125). Despite its widespread use, the concept of resource is not clearly understood. Turk defines a resource as "anything of cultural significance for human welfare" (1976: 280) and power as the control of resources (1982: 14). Clearly the range of things which have biological or cultural significance is very broad indeed. Food has a biological significance while money has a cultural significance. Anything which can be unequally distributed and which is valued or desired can become the basis of power (Wrong, 1979: 48).

The key concept in this approach is that of "value" which forms the basis of "significance" or "desire." The exercise of power presupposes the existence of values.[3] Similarly, the use of sanctions presupposes values. Power is the effective manipulation of values, either in the form of penalties or inducements, to obtain a desired result. The values of a society are not static, nor are values constant across societies. The ways that deprivations or indulgences of values are manifested are not in any way predetermined. The types of power which are employed, or the character of the sanctions used in a particular society, will be "inextricably associated with and dependent on the cultural values of the state that employs them" (Sellin, 1939: vi). Thus, "a prior condition to the emergence of the prison is the generality of the presumption that individuals both possess a right to freedom and that deprivation of it constitutes a penal sanction" (Young, 1983: 93).

What then are these resources or values? Resource taxonomies have been developed by a number of writers including Dahl (1968),[4] Schermerhorn (1961),[5] Russell (1938), and Turk (1976, 1982: 15).[6] Lasswell and Kaplan (1950) developed a scheme of base values and identified eight such values.[7] From this analysis Arens and Lasswell subsequently developed a model of sanctions which combined the notion of values with legal sanction and produced a scheme which attempted to transcend the traditional boundaries of civil, criminal, and administrative law (Arens and Lasswell, 1961, 1964; Lasswell and Arens, 1967). The foundation for this approach is best stated by Etzioni (1970: 24):

> The conversion of assets into power generates a variety of sanctions, rewards, and instruments to penalize those who resist, to reward those

---

3. Power and values are related in another way. Values are the product of many influences, including the type of information a person receives. As will be argued below, however, control of information can itself shape values.

4. Patterns of social standing, distribution of cash credit and wealth, access to legality, popularity, and control over jobs and information (1968: 409).

5. Military, economic, political, ideological, and diversionary. See also Mann, 1986.

6. Physical, economic, political, ideological, and diversionary.

7. Power, respect, well-being, rectitude, affection, wealth, skill, and enlightenment (1950: 74).

228   FREIBERG

who assist, to remove those who block, and to provide facilities for those who implement a collectively-set course of action.

Sanctions are thus conceived as the intentional manipulation of values. From the wide range of posited resources or types of power, seven basic sources of power or sanction have been identified: (1) *Physical*—this is narrowly conceived of as relating to the use of, or control over the body. The use of the body for labor, the regulation of its movement, and the use of, or threat of use of, means of hurting or incapacitating the body are all contained within this sanction. (2) *Economic*—this is a broad concept encompassing the "control of the production, allocation and/or use of the material resources," material resources comprising money and its equivalents, and property, both corporeal and incorporeal (Turk, 1976: 280). (3) *Social*—social power is premised upon a person's essentially gregarious nature. It is conceived as taking two forms—reputational, based on the value of community esteem, and interactional, based on the need for human contact. (4) *Informational*—this power is based on the "control of definitions of access to knowledge, beliefs, values" (Turk, 1976: 280) and encompasses not only the control or regulation of knowledge and information but also special forms of knowledge such as skill. (5) *Political*—this is used in a broad sense to refer not only to access to state or governmental decision-making organs, but to the decision-making process in general. (6) *Privacy*—this power is based on the need of social man to have some element of spiritual or personal autonomy. Control of the means of infringing that autonomy by surveillance or inspection is the basis of this sanction. (7) *Legal*—this is the power to invoke or regulate the mechanisms of the legal apparatus for the purpose of applying or not applying other resources through a legitimated authority.

A single penalty such as imprisonment may represent the concatenation of a number of sanctions as here conceived. Imprisonment may include the physical sanction (restriction of movement), the economic sanction (for example, loss of earnings), the privacy sanction (surveillance of activity), and the social sanction (deprivation of desired companionship). One of the reasons that imprisonment has proved to be such a popular and entrenched penalty may well be its "sanctional complexity" or density of value deprivations (compare Garland and Young, 1983: 23). A detailed discussion of these sanctions must be postponed until the matters of sanction mode and arena are reviewed.

SANCTION MODE

The effects of an action of one person upon another range from the beneficial or pleasurable to the harmful or painful. As with all polarities, reward and punishment can best be understood as points on a continuum. Positive sanctions have been termed variously gains, rewards, benefits, advantages, inducements, incentives, indulgences, or generally the "compensatory power" (Galbraith, 1983: 16), but so deeply has sanction analysis been rooted in the punishment model that little attention has been paid to sanctions in the positive mode (compare Freiberg, 1986).[8] Because of a preoccupation with punitive models of sanctions, there has been a tendency to overlook major changes in the nature of social control which have seen allocational sanctions, based on the ability to regulate access to scarce resources, supplement or replace criminal sanctions as a major force of modern government (Kreimer, 1984: 1,295).

Reward and punishment are, of course, matters of perception, and there should be no assumption that because an act is intended as punitive (or nonpunitive) it is necessarily so perceived by the recipient (Gibbs, 1975: 99). There are severe phenomenological problems in deciding where, on the positive-negative continuum, a particular sanction lies (Sebba, 1978; Christie, 1981: 9), and these phenomenological (and terminological) problems have not been assisted by the introduction into penal law of a whole array of therapeutic techniques such as community corrections, half-way houses, and the rest, which has blurred the lines between coercion and persuasion, treatment and punishment (Cohen, 1979, 1985; Aubert, 1983).

The relevance of sanction mode to this discussion of sanctions and power is that power relations ought not to be seen in terms of coercion. The actions of others can be equally if not more affected by inducement and reward as by coercion. The choice of positive or negative sanction may be relevant to questions of effectiveness or cost but not to the essential nature of power. Thus, conceptions of law which confine law only to state imposed negative sanctions are considered too narrow, and Black's view of law as governmental social control, whereby compliance can be sought either by positive or negative sanctions, has much to commend it in this respect (Black, 1976: 2).

A change in sanction mode from negative to positive ought not to be seen as necessarily a change from more to less repressive or from "worse" to "better." Nor, necessarily, should changes in types of sanctions. The presumption that punishment has steadily progressed from a state of barbarism to one of enlightenment is deeply embedded in the social psyche. The abolition of mutilation, torture, capital punishment, and the pillory, and their replacement by community corrections and psychiatric treatment, are presented as evidence for this thesis (compare Christie, 1968: 161; Miller, 1974: 93). However, it has been cogently argued that changes in sanctions do not in fact reflect the transformation of forms from the less to the more humane, but rather reflect the search for more efficient methods of social control (Sellin,

---

8. Sanction modality is, in this analysis, considered to be distinguishable from the content of the sanction.

1939: vi; Rusche, 1978: 5). In Foucault's view, reform strategies do not represent progress but are merely refinements in the technology of punishment or redistributions of the power to punish (Foucault, 1979: 23-24). Reform, or rather change, it is argued, is the effort to bring sanctions into accord with the base values which at that time predominate among those exercising power. Cruelty, therefore, is a relative phenomenon which can only be understood in terms of the social relationships prevailing in any given period (Rusche and Kirchheimer, 1939: 23).

ARENAS: PUBLIC OR PRIVATE

Criminology has tended to be preoccupied by analyses of state-imposed sanctions (compare Shearing and Stenning, 1983), although sociological analyses of social control have been less neglectful of other arenas in which power is exercised. Foucault has urged us to "escape from the limited field of juridical sovereignty and State institutions, and instead [to] base our analysis of power on the study of the techniques and tactics of domination" (1980: 102; Palmer and Pearce, 1983).

The private/public or state/civil society distinctions represent classic divisions in orthodox political theory (Cohen, 1985: 134; Cotterrell, 1984: 262). If the division ever existed, it has now been severely eroded by the increasing intrusion of state or governmental controls into the family, the school, and the church. The "practices comprising the private sphere of life . . . are inextricably linked to, and are at least practically constituted by politics and law'" (Klare, 1982: 1,417).

A taxonomic approach to sanctions and sanctioning encounters some difficulty when it comes to distinguishing state-imposed from privately imposed sanctions (Griffiths, 1984). Dichotomization is unnecessary if law or the state can be regarded as degrees of organization or specialization in the division of the labor of social control. Thus, no sharp distinctions need be made between formal/informal or legal/nonlegal sanctioning which, instead, can be regarded as points on a continuum, points which themselves ought to be regarded as appropriate subjects of study (Griffiths, 1984: 47; Stone, 1966. 753). Grabosky (1984: 181) argues that the most basic change in the form of punishment lies in the transition from informal sanctioning to the formal administration of penalties and that the form of punishment appears to be a function of both the size of a collectivity and its relationship to the host society.

According to Weber, the state is that organization which successfully upholds a claim to the monopoly of the legitimate use of physical force in the enforcement of its order. But it does not necessarily follow from this that the state is the only organization that can or does *use* force: "penality need not always be conceived of as the property of a centralized and national state"

(Garland and Young, 1983: 33). Ignatieff (1983: 77) asserts that revisionist accounts of history contain a basic misconception that the state enjoys a monopoly over punitive regulation of behavior in society, that its moral authority and practical power are the binding sources of social order, and that all social relations can be described in the language of subordination. His point has much substance, for although state power may be the most visible and concentrated manifestation of power, recognition of this fact ought not to render one oblivious to power diffused throughout society in nonstate institutions such as the family, the school, or the church (Humphries and Greenberg, 1984: 176; Jenkins and Potter, 1984: 160). These institutions are said to live in the "shadow" of the state (Cohen, 1985: 134; Abel, 1982: 275). However, what distinguishes the state from other institutions is that it "has the exclusive authority to set the limits within which force may legitimately be used" (Dahl, 1970: 12). As von Ihering stated, state force must be superior to every other power within the jurisdiction, so that every person or association within that territory which wishes to execute force or coerce its members derives its power from, or is dependent upon, the cooperation of the state (1968: 235, 240). Although all sanctions ultimately *derive* from the state, this is not to argue that all sanctions are *approved* by it. Force can be, and is, used widely in a society by private armies, street gangs, criminals, and others (Black: 1984: 13). Theft is simply an unauthorized transfer of property. What distinguishes the use of force by the state (or by those acting on its behalf or with its consent) is that it is authoritative—that is, legitimate (Dyson, 1980: 208).

The blurring of the private/public distinction is evident in the growth of the so-called noncustodial sanctions. State-imposed sanctions such as probation require private individuals such as volunteer probation officers to supervise probationers. Private half-way houses are funded by the state. Prisons are now run by private profit-making organizations on behalf of governments and private therapeutic interventions are often made the conditions of bonds or probation.

The model of sanctions and sanctioning briefly sketched thus far has three basic dimensions: the sanction form itself, of which more in the succeeding sections; the sanction mode, which is the continuum running along the positive/negative axis; and the arena, which requires analysis of the sanctioning agency. In diagrammatic form it can be presented in the following manner:

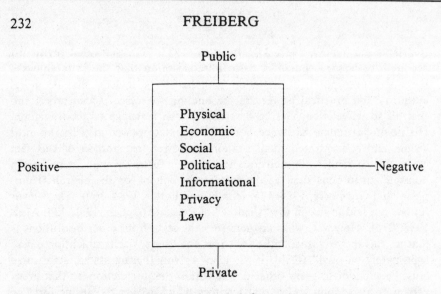

Each sanction can therefore be regarded, for analytical purposes, as a cluster or combination of these elements in more or less pure form. Thus, to take a simple example, smacking a child for disobedience may be seen as a negative/physical/private sanction. Capital punishment is a negative/physical/public sanction. Bestowing a medal of honor on a war hero may be a positive/social/public sanction, while rewarding a person for returning a lost object is a positive/economic/private sanction. The variations are great but not infinite and, in many cases, there may be difficulty in determining how many sanctions are in fact operating in a given action. Very rarely will a sanction form be pure. Thus, a whipping in front of an audience may involve not only the physical sanction but may include the social because of the humiliation involved. Despite these problems, for reasons to be outlined below it appears that this approach has a number of advantages over traditional analyses of sanctions.

The author turns then to a brief discussion of each of the sanctions and prefaces it with the caveat that considerations of space preclude the use of a great deal of exemplifying material to illustrate how a number of past and present sanctions would fit into the proposed scheme.

THE PHYSICAL SANCTION

In its broadest sense, the physical sanction refers to anything that relates to the body and control over the body, directly or indirectly. It is comprised of three closely related elements: (1) action on the body itself; (2) regulation of movement of the body; and (3) use of the body. For purely analytical purposes, "action on the body" can be further subdivided into four categories: (a) the infliction of pain simpliciter, (b) alteration to the appearance of the body (with or without the infliction of pain), (c) destruction of part or parts of the body (with or without the infliction of pain), (d) death (with or without pain).

The number of methods of inflicting pain is limited only by the imagination and is determined by the limits of technology and the social context. Flogging, lashing, birching, and so on are all primitive forms of inflicting pain. Today, forms of isolation and sensory deprivation of light, sound, and touch have emerged as potent weapons against the body as have techniques of medical control either by surgery or through chemical means (Ackroyd et al., 1977: 237). Techniques of altering or mutilating the body, either temporarily or permanently, and with or without pain, have long histories, though some of these methods pertain more to the social than the physical sanction, being designed as forms of social degradation through ridicule and contempt. Historically, many physical sanctions were determined by the talionic principle that the punishment should resemble the crime: hence rape would be dealt with by castration, theft by the loss of a hand, and scurrilous gossip by the excision of the tongue.

Movement of the body can be regulated by both physical and nonphysical means. The physical means can be as close as handcuffs or straightjackets or as broad as the open prison. It can be permanent, temporary, or intermittent (for example, weekend imprisonment). Penology's concentration on the prison as the major, if not sole, means of deprivation of liberty has distorted understanding of the physical sanction (Young, 1983: 100).

Nonphysical means of restraining movement include licensing (for example, to drive a car), removal of travel documents, injunctions, expulsion from particular places or to particular places, prohibition from specified areas, exile, and transportation.

Human labor has always been a valuable resource, and its control and regulation has been widely used as a negative sanction. Control over the person can vary along two dimensions, the length of time and the degree of control. Slavery can be understood as the complete control of a person for an indefinite period and has been used as a sanction for crime (Sellin, 1976). Forced labor has been employed when labor is short and employers are unwilling or unable to adequately remunerate the labor force. Impressment into the armed services, work in mines or in inhospitable regions, and the settlement and development of colonies are all tasks which have been carried out by convicts.

Institutions whose functions are primarily segregative such as the House of Correction, Bridewells, workhouses, and the prisons have, through the centuries, tried to make labor productive. Noninstitutional techniques currently in use such as attendance centers and community service orders focus on reform and compensation through labor.

The physical sanction, often characterized as force or violence, has often

234   FREIBERG

been declared as the main or ultimate form of power. Machiavelli and Hobbes both regarded force as central to the organization of society. The physical sanction is regarded as the sanction of last resort, to be used, for example, when all other sanctions fail. Sanctions are, in this sense, hierarchical. Sanctions are sometimes seen to be climbing a " 'ladder of escalation' from the mildest and most consensual to the most punitive form of power in order to obtain compliance" (Wrong, 1979: 71).

THE ECONOMIC SANCTION

Economic power refers to the "control of the production, allocation, and/ or use of material resources" (Turk, 1976: 280), though not included here is the human material resource which is classified under the physical sanction. Societies that have moved beyond mere subsistence economies to those where there is differential access to the means of production will make extensive use of economic sanctions (Wrong, 1979: 451). The transformation from a feudal society, based on personal service, to a modern industrial society resulted in an enormous increase in economic power. Societies in which economic exchange is the predominant interpersonal transaction will set great store on economic assets and will therefore strongly emphasize economic sanctions (Wrong, 1979: 46).

Economic assets take two major forms, money (including notes, coins, credit, checks, and so on) and property, both corporeal and incorporeal. Economic sanctions are concerned with the flow of economic resources. Whether a sanction is positive or negative depends on the direction of the flow.

Public positive economic sanctions can be conceived of as the transfer or creation of wealth. Thus taxation deductions, depreciation allowances, grants, bounties, and subsidies are all wealth transfers as is the system of welfare benefits. All can be means of social control (Schmidt, 1964; Melossi, 1980; Garland, 1981). The granting of licenses, patents, and monopolies are other means of creating wealth.

In the modern administrative state, government is a major source of wealth. In Australia, over one quarter of the population receives some form of direct grant from the state and even more are the recipients of tax expenditures. Aubert argues (1983: 53) that

> The transition from the "nightwatchman's" state to the industrial or
> post-industrial welfare or interventionist state is certainly one of the
> momentous events of recent history. . . . Most citizens . . . are enmeshed
> in a network of access to "alienable goods" (resources that can be taken
> away from them). Legal rules may stipulate the conditions under which
> this may be done, either as a sanction or for some other purpose such as
> the redistribution of income or wealth. The state is in charge of the dis-
> tribution of a large share of these resources and can, to some extent, use

its command of resources to reward desirable behavior and to penalize noncompliance.

The strength of the modern state now seems to depend less on the state's powers of coercion than upon its ability to satisfy the material demands of its citizens.

Negative economic sanctions are involuntary transfers of money or property. Involuntary transfers to the state in money terms take the form of fines and taxes; involuntary transfers to individuals are called compensation or damages. The loss of an opportunity to earn money, for example by the denial of access to employment, by demotion, suspension, or dismissal, can be economic sanctions as can the loss of one's credit rating. Involuntary transfer of property, goods, or land took or takes the form of deodand, seizure and/or forfeiture, attainder, divestment, destruction, forced transfer, sequestration, cancellation, suspension, or transferal of licenses.

THE SOCIAL SANCTION

The social sanction is the most pervasive of the sanctions, founded as it is on the existence of social organization. It is based on the premise that people are social beings who value interaction with other human beings and require their affection, love, and approbation. People who are loved or admired obtain power over those who love or admire them.[9] Two major elements of the social sanction can be identified—first, the reputational aspect which emphasizes a person's need to be esteemed and, second, the "interactive" component, which stresses the value of gregariousness.

REPUTATION

Reputation can be defined as the estimation in which one is generally held. Good fame, credit, honor, or respectability are all facets of this, and Bentham referred to this sanction as the "moral" sanction[10] (Bentham, 1970: 453). Corporations or business firms may also possess reputations which are regarded as business assets to be bought and sold. However, reputation here is regarded as a value in itself.

Citations, awards, medals, decorations, and honorific occasions are all means of enhancing reputation. The law protects reputation through the laws of defamation, suppression of information relating to trials, and the like.

---

9. Weber identified this form of power as "charisma"; see (Wrong, 1979: 60-64).
10. Who steals my purse, steals trash; 'tis something, nothing;
      But he that filches from me my good name
      Robs me of that which not enriches him,
      And makes me poor indeed.

                                        Shakespeare, _Othello_
                                        Act III, Scene iii

236   FREIBERG

The range of techniques for bringing ignominy, obloquy, dishonour, shame, or disgrace is large.

Legislatures can damage reputation by the publicity which attends their hearings; the executive can do so by the publication of the names of miscreants in annual reports and elsewhere. For example, the Australian Taxation Office was, until recently, required by law to publish an annual list of the names, addresses, and occupations of people who have contravened sections of the Income Tax Assessment Act and other cognate Acts. Judicial degradation is the most frequent public use of this sanction. Apart from the process of the trial itself which formally ritualizes the creation of shame, there are a number of penalties which are infamizing. The stocks, the pillory, the ducking stool, and many forms of mutilation were prevalent when societies were more parochial. Offenders were often also required to perform degrading or humiliating acts in public—for example, displaying an offending object, such as underweight bread. Such penalties could also be posthumous. Bodies of traitors were publicly displayed and executed felons were denied ordinary burials. Blacklisting is a form of private destruction of reputation. Stigma may be the result of these processes and labeling theory is, in essence, the study of the creation, maintenance, and amplification of poor reputation.

INTERACTION

Few people can exist without some amount of social intercourse, though individuals vary widely in the amount they require. Imprisonment and, in particular, solitary confinement, has the effect of isolating the person from contact. Sanctions along this line include restricted visiting and letter writing privileges and the denial of sexual association. Forced association with people one may not wish to associate with may also be considered as a form of punishment. Enforced isolation was a feature of early 19th century prison philosophies based on penitence and reform through inner renewal. Solitary confinement, however, turned out to be an instrument of exquisite suffering leading to an increase in the rates of death and suicide (Ignatieff, 1978: 78).

THE INFORMATIONAL SANCTION

To control or regulate the amount and flow of information or knowledge is to control what is today perhaps the most important resource of all: "knowledge is its own form of power" (Cohen, 1983: 109; Miller, 1971: 23; Fardon, 1985). It has been consistently argued over the last few decades that western societies have moved from an industrial to a postindustrial phase (Bell, 1970: 394), that physical and economic power no longer form the primary bases of social control but have been replaced by power based on knowledge, skill, and information. Olsen states (1970: 371-372) that

A fully developed "post-industrial" society would undoubtedly contain a

SANCTIONS 237

wide variety of important new power sources, including administrative and managerial abilities in operating complex organizations, scientific and technological expertise, teaching and mass communication skills and even artistic and aesthetic talents. The common element in all these kinds of resources is knowledge, since the functional requirement in such a society would be expert knowledge and accompanying skills. The scientific-educational-informational network would replace the economy as the major sphere of power in society and those individuals and organizations who performed such activities would be able—because of their functional dominance—to control numerous resources and exert intensive social power.

Such power is not distributed equally in a society. Informational power is capable of being "structured and organized, allocated and applied in much the same way as other kinds of power" (Etzioni, 1970: 25). It can, like other forms of power, be coalesced, concentrated, oligopolized, or monopolized by the state or other bodies (Wrong, 1979: 33; Russell, 1938: 147).

Foucault, in particular, has observed the change from highly visible, physical forms of power to the more subtle, nonphysical forms, suitable to mass society (Foucault, 1979). He has, in essence, conflated the concepts of power and knowledge and "emphasized the relation of knowledge and truth to the network of power" (Fardon, 1985: 15).

Three aspects of the informational sanction require particular attention: knowledge, skill, and ideology.[11]

KNOWLEDGE

The total control of information is indoctrination (Turk, 1982: 129), but, although information control is generally less intense, nowhere is it totally unregulated (Wilsnack, 1980). In the public domain the transmission of information through the broadcast media, the press, the postal services, and even (or especially) access to government information are all the subject of extensive legislation. Banning orders, official secrets Acts, censorship laws, and the laws of evidence all inhibit the flow of information. Private collection and dissemination of information through the data bases of credit agencies

---

11. I am ambivalent about including Foucault's concept of "discipline" here, or under the privacy sanction, to which it is clearly linked in Foucault's own work. Because his concept of discipline is a process rather than a resource, it is difficult to accommodate within this scheme. However, to the extent that discipline has as its purpose the coercive training of the soul (Bottoms, 1983: 178), the author would include it under the ideological part of this sanction discussed below. The concept of discipline is not, of course, new. Stone, in his discussion of power in 1945 (1966: 603), wrote of "the undoubted stabilizing effect on power relations . . . of learned routines of response to certain stimuli." Foucault did, however, emphasize the centrality of discipline to an understanding of power.

238   FREIBERG

banks, medical funds, and interlocking corporations is also extensive (Rule, 1973).

The organization of knowledge itself can be regarded as a major form of social control. In his review of Foucault's book *The History of Sexuality Volume I: An Introduction*, Lasch writes of the medicalization of deviance (1980: 27-28; see also Cohen, 1979: 359-360):

> In place of moral norms, the new style of social discipline substituted a set of medical and psychological norms from which moral questions, questions of commendation and censure, were rigorously excluded. Doctors, criminologists, alienists, and other members of the learned professions—to which in the twentieth century were added social workers, psychiatrists, educators, marriage counsellors, child development experts, pediatricians, parole officers, judges of juvenile courts, in short the modern apparatus of resocialization—governed society not by right but by technique, not by law, but by control.

SKILL

Skill is a form of specialized knowledge, and skill-related sanctions have become increasingly common. Occupations, trades, and professions are collections of people with similar skills and the state can, through law, control the entry of people to a profession or occupation, establish standards for the exercise of that skill, and prevent persons from exercising their skill by suspending or cancelling their license or registration. The use of licensing as a form of control has been a feature of 20th-century society with some hundreds of trades, professions, or activities now requiring some form of certification or state approval.

IDEOLOGY

This aspect refers to the control over beliefs and value systems, and includes religion, education, and propaganda and therapy. The ability to successfully influence the thoughts and values of others is a form of power "because it represents a means by which an actor may achieve an intended effect on another's behaviour" (Wrong, 1979: 32). Belief systems are obviously shaped by the type and amount of information available, and ideological power can be organized, either publicly or privately. The priestly classes of earlier societies may now have been replaced by the class of educationists and the organized professions (Mann, 1986: 22).

Therapy as sanction has long been a feature of the sentencing process. Counselling, therapy, or reeducation, whether within prison or as a condition of a noncustodial sentence, are accepted modes of attempting to alter personality and overt behaviors (Castel, 1983; Horwitz, 1984: 215). The emergence of a class of "mind bureaucrats" of "knowledge professionals" both in the public and private arenas has been noted by Cohen (1985: Chapter 5), although for reasons such as professional autonomy, contradictory values, and others this administrative class cannot, in the West, be regarded as mere tools of the state. This may be less true in other societies (Brown, 1983).

The co-option of religious ideology to the aid of penology in the late 18th century provides an example of ideology as sanction. John Howard, the English penal reformer, believed in the reform of criminals through work, physical abstemiousness, and "religious exercises" (Webb and Webb, 1963: 32). The penitentiary was a place of salvation where prisoners could be bound with "cords of love." The prison chaplain "would persuade offenders to accept their sufferings as an impartial and benevolent condemnation. He would force them to accept their own guilt. It was he who would enclose them in the ideological prison" (Ignatieff, 1978: 75).

Compulsory "reeducation," retraining programs, and the inculcation of discipline are all examples of ideological or informational sanctions. Ideological power can entrench other forms of power by legitimizing it, by creating the belief that the given order of resource distribution is generally accepted and right (Turk, 1982: 30). In Gramscian terms it may be called "hegemonic power" (Benney, 1983).

THE POLITICAL SANCTION

This sanction refers to access to, or control of, decision-making processes in the private or public realms (Turk, 1976: 280). Participation in decision making, be it in the local council, the affairs of a company, a sporting club, or in the process of electing a government is, in many societies, highly valued.

Sanctions of this type include loss of the right to vote or to stand for office or to retain office and may be consequent upon conviction for criminal offenses, conflict of interest provisions, impeachment, misconduct, bankruptcy, or insanity.

THE PRIVACY SANCTION

Privacy is a complex phenomenon and is a value which is perhaps the most culturally variable. Privacy can be regarded as a kind of autonomy or independence from intrusion into one's personal or spiritual concerns (Rossiter, 1958: 15-17). It is the right to keep one's thoughts and judgments to oneself, to be free to act in a particular way without being observed or listened to, to "maintain one's person, personality or individuality inviolate" (Australian Law Reform Commission, 1980: 12).

The potency of privacy as a power resource has only been recognized relatively recently, though its possibilities were envisaged by Bentham in the late 18th century. The privacy sanction represents a progression from a concern with the body or the material possessions of a person to a concern with the

240   FREIBERG

nature and quality of that person's existence in society. Its main form is surveillance.[12]

Concern over privacy is not new. Orwell, in his book *Nineteen Eighty-Four*, graphically anthropomorphized surveillance in his "Big Brother," but one of the first to articulate the immense implications of the power of invasion of privacy was Michel Foucault in his book entitled *Surveiller et Punit*, (translated into English as *Discipline and Punish*). The translator of the book considered that "surveillance" was not a suitable translation of the French term, being too restricted and technical (Foucault, 1979: Translator's Note), and that words such as inspect, observe, and supervise were too neutral or had unsuitable connotations. However, the word perfectly describes this sanction. The apotheosis of the concept of surveillance as an instrument of power is found in Bentham's *Panopticon*, written in 1791. It reflected, if it did not influence, the changing power relations of the 18th and 19th centuries. Foucault finds in it the embodiment of a new social order. The Pantopticon was more than a building, it was a

> new principle of construction applicable to any sort of establishment, in which persons of any description are kept under inspection; and in particular to penitentiary-houses, prisons, houses of industry, work-houses, poor-houses, manufactories, mad-houses, lazarettos, hospitals and schools (Bentham, cited in Melossi, 1980: 385).

Modern technology has enabled surveillance to escape from any physical confines and has created "opportunities for punitive surveillance that hitherto were not feasible" (Gibbs, 1975: 67). Telemetric devices now enable the monitoring of movements and even bodily states from a distance (Ingraham and Smith, 1972). Listening and optical devices, remote sensing devices, infra-red photography, and closed-circuit television have all been refined to a stage where observation may be continuous, intense, and unknown to the observed (Mathiesen, 1983; Miller, 1971: 26; Ackroyd et al., 1977: Chapter 14).

Institutions of surveillance such as police and inspectorate forces have burgeoned. Governmental agencies maintain detailed files on large sections of the population, and identification cards are now mandatory in many countries. Chan and Ericson have termed the police a human panopticon, keeping the population in a state of "conscious and permanent visibility" (1981: 63; Rule, 1973: Chapter 2). Or as Foucault notes (1979: 214), the police power was "the instrument of permanent, exhaustive, omnipresent surveillance; capable of making all visible, so long as it itself could remain invisible. It had to be like a faceless gaze that transformed the whole social body into a field of perception: thousands of eyes posted everywhere, mobile attentions ever on the alert, a long hierarchical network. . . ." The computer revolution has

---

12. There is a relationship between the information and privacy sanctions in that surveillance includes, but is not confined to, the gathering of information about the person.

SANCTIONS 241

made the "faceless gaze" a practical reality. Extensive mass surveillance of "activities, habits and associations" (Miller, 1971: 39), of financial transactions and interactions with government can now be carried out with minimal human resources. Orwell's model of surveillance was a centralized one, but Foucault sees surveillance as being distributed and embedded throughout the whole of society. Both have, however, identified this as a form of control.[13]

Other forms of punitive surveillance include probation, parole, supervision orders, release on recognizances, reporting requirements, compulsory counselling, and the like, all of which employ the threat of always watching together with the threat of the invocation of other sanctions (Chan and Ericson, 1981: 62-63; Greenberg, 1975: 9). Singer argues (1980: 273) that the probation or parole order is "a precisely conceived juridical technology of surveillance. The subject must visit and be visited by the probation officer who watches over both his private and public lifestyle." The Manual of Probation Practice and Procedure in the State of Victoria states openly (1981: 2-3) that the aim of probation is, inter alia, "to provide surveillance, direction, counselling and support."

The community corrections movement is the manifestation of the change from the incarcerative, or physical sanction, to the informational/privacy sanction. Unlike physical power/sanctions, which are "added on from the outside, like a rigid, heavy constraint to the functions it invests," this power/sanction is "a lighter, more rapid, more effective" form of coercion (Foucault, 1979: 206 and 209; Smart, 1983: 66).

THE SANCTION OF LAW

Law is a major societal resource. The ability to change and create laws or the ability to invoke the machinery of the law or even to prevent or curtail its operation is a major form of power (Turk, 1976: 276). Law represents a process whereby other resources such as the physical, economic, social, and the others can be applied, granted, or removed through a legitimated authority structure. Thus, law has an intrinsic duality—it is both a resource in itself, for which people contend, as well as being the conduit for other resources. Law can legitimate physical violence, it can control or regulate the flow of economic resources, it provides the model and the framework for decision making, and the concept of legalism itself provides "the cultural bedrock of political order" (Turk, 1976: 281).

Positive "law" sanctions are those that prevent or mitigate the operation of other sanctions or protect the individual from the operation of the legal system. Examples of such sanctions include the pardon, which is a form of

---

13. It should be emphasized that the intrusion into privacy is a sanction in itself and not just a means of detecting deviance leading to the imposition of other sanctions (compare Rule, 1973: 40).

242   FREIBERG

release from punishment, remissions of sentence, the suspending and dispensing powers vested in the Crown but now illegal,[14] the institutions of benefit of clergy and sanctuary, as well as the whole range of immunities. Immunity is the protection a person has from legal action and through history has included sovereign or crown immunity, parliamentary immunity, diplomatic and consular immunities, and informer's immunity.

Negative "law" sanctions are those where the protection of the law is refused or where access to law is barred or diminished. Nullity is perhaps the best (and most contentious) example of such a sanction. Nullity can be defined as the refusal by the state to assist a person guilty of an act or forbearance prohibited by law to gain any legal advantage by his conduct (Jenks, 1933: 136). Where, for example, the law prescribes a particular mode of procedure, and that procedure is not followed, that transaction fails to attract to it any legal consequences. Thus, a will which is not properly witnessed has no force in law and contracts which are void or illegal will not be enforced. Nullity is unusual in that, unlike traditional sanctions, such as the fine or imprisonment, which are directed against defendants and usually follow some official action, nullity is "imposed" upon an unsuccessful plaintiff and there need be no action by ministerial officers (Hall, 1973: 107).

Outlawry was an extreme form of the denial of the protection of law and was only abolished in England in criminal matters in 1938. An outlaw was literally a person who was put outside the protection of the law: his body was completely unprotected and he was deprived of all proprietary, possessory, contractual, and testatory rights (Pollock and Maitland, 1898: Vol. 1: 477).

Denial of access to the courts is another form of "law" sanction. Statutory provisions exist in many jurisdictions which deprive a person of the ability to go to law to recover money owing to him, for example, because he is unlicensed or unregistered. Convicts were, by "civil death" statutes, incapable of commencing action for the recovery of any property, debt, or damage, or of alienating or charging any property, or of making any contract.

Finally, legal persons such as corporations, which exist only because of the legal status accorded to them, may be sanctioned by having their legal recognition forfeited or suspended.

CONCLUSION

The model of sanctions presented in this paper is an attempt to develop a broad conceptual framework within which techniques of power, particularly in the legal context, can be understood. The divisions suggested are not rigid or precise, having been formulated as "ideal" rather than "real" types. Some

---

14. The term "suspend" is generally applied to the abrogation of a statute so that it loses its binding force; the term "dispense" is applied to a permission given to an individual to disobey a statute (Holdsworth, 1956: Vol. 6, 217).

of the sanctions are concentrated and some are diffuse. The author has not been so bold as to attempt to develop a history and theory of power relations in all human societies (compare Mann, 1986), yet believes that this kind of analysis, which attempts to give a "collective organization and unity to the infinite variety of social existence" (Mann, 1986: 28) is preferable to previous attempts to conceptualize sanctions on the basis of source, effect, purpose, temporal sequence, and others (Bentham, 1970; Kelsen, 1961; Pound, 1917; Kocourek, 1924; Gibbs, 1975). The reasons are varied.

First, this approach separates sanctions completely from their justifications of purposes. Although the two are related, breaking this nexus allows changes in sanction form, mode, and arena to be studied separately from changes in justification, which may vary independently. The terms "punishment," "compensation," and "therapy" are too imprecise to be useful analytical tools because of this confusion between sanction and purpose (compare Black, 1976). Second, as already noted, the focus on the "penal" sanction has denied the impact of "civil" sanctions and allowed systems to develop in which there are few legal safeguards available to civil defendants because of a misplaced belief in their innocuousness (compare Freiberg and O'Malley, 1984). Spitzer (1979: 172) has observed that

> the control of domestic populations may depend to a far greater extent on economic and ideological regulation than the direct use of coercive force against evil doers. Regulations which are generally considered to lie outside the punitive realm may actually be far more important in establishing a structure of domination than the most visible and documented forms of legal coercion.

Another untoward effect of this sanction myopia is that sweeping attempts to attribute changes in the nature and use of sanctions to single causes, such as the mode of production (Rusche and Kirchheimer, 1939), have been inadequate primarily because of their failure to take account of the whole range of legal sanctions, civil, criminal, and administrative. Statements concerning the role of economic wealth in a society that are based only upon the use of the fine and that do not as well include civil damages are bound to be misleading.

The third advantage of this approach is that it avoids any concepts of developmentalism or progress. Implicit in many accounts of sanctioning is that history is the story of the decline of barbarity and the victory of humanitarianism. Instead, it allows a focus, as O'Malley suggests (1983: 150) on why certain sanction forms and modes are predominant under given social conditions and why some forms are considered more severe than others, and by whom. In other words, it is a study of changes in "patterns of valuation" in cultures (Lasswell and Kaplan, 1950: 94).

Fourth, by concentrating on social values and social relations rather than

244   FREIBERG

legal or other labels, it may assist in cross-cultural research which is often
hampered by inconsistent or unintelligible nomenclature (Schumann, 1983:
274).

Fifth, this approach may assist in the task of developing sanction hierarchies. Sanction hierarchies, which have to date tended to be implicit in sentencing structures, are needed for four main reasons: to undertake research
on deterrence (which requires measures of severity against which to measure
relative effectiveness); to develop just deserts models which require graduated
sanction scales to match the newly developed graduated scales of offense hei-
nousness; to mitigate problems of sentence severity; and, finally, to facilitate
the development of rational sentencing codes or statutes (Sebba and Nathan,
1984; Freiberg and Fox, 1986).

Sixth, by focusing upon patterns of valuation in cultures, comparisons may
be drawn between sanction type and distribution and the substantive law.
The relationship between sanction forms and its changes and the content of
the substantive law have not been the subject of extensive investigation, but it
would seem that the pattern of values embodied in the substantive law should
be reflected in the pattern of sanctions employed to reinforce those laws.

Finally, and most importantly, a power analysis of sanctions can provide a
useful tool for the mapping of changes in social relations within a society and
for comparing societies (Cohen, 1985: Chapter 3). Spitzer writes (1979: 208)
that if we

> assume that changes in the kind and degree of punishment reveal some-
> thing about the basic structure of the societies in which they are found,
> then it makes sense to give careful attention to both changes in the sanc-
> tioning of disobedience within a specific society over time and the differ-
> ences in punitive controls that exist between different societies at a fixed
> point in time.

If the concept of "sanction" in its broadest form were substituted for the
term "punishment" or its equivalents, his insight would be more powerful.
Many of the studies of sanctions in recent years which have attempted to
discern changes in sanctioning patterns have, to a degree, been hampered by a
lack of a clear and consistent conceptual base. Some of the findings of these
studies include:

The shift from the physical sanction. This trend has been widely noted
(Foucault, 1979; Cohen, 1985: 13-14, 26; O'Malley, 1983) but the focus has
been upon the public/physical/negative sanction, in particular, capital punishment. The trend is dated from the late 18th to the early 19th century and
is said to coincide with the rise of the prison (Ignatieff, 1983: 79). It has been
recognized by some, however, that the institution of prison existed for hundreds of years prior to this time (Pugh, 1968) but that what in fact changed

was the *purpose* of imprisonment; that is, it was no longer merely incapacitative but transformative through techniques of reform, discipline, and education (O'Malley, 1983: 153).

Reading back through recent changes in the use of the physical sanction, for example, the reemergence of capital punishment in the United States may reveal a great deal about the ethicojuridical homogeneity of that society (Sorokin, 1937; Grabosky, 1984) or about the changing conception of the role of the state under a conservative or neoconservative hegemony (Cohen, 1985: 127).

The growth in use of the fine. It is said that the fine is the typical punishment of modern society (Rusche and Kirchheimer, 1939: 7), and that is typical of societies where money is a universal form of exchange. While this is true of many modern Western societies, it may not be true of the United States (Bottoms, 1983). As argued previously, the centrality of the negative economic sanctions must be understood in the light of the use of other monetary sanctions such as damages.

The predominance of the fine as a sanction appears at first sight as inconsistent with Foucault's contention that the concept of discipline is central to an understanding of modern techniques of power since the fine contains neither disciplinary nor surveillance components (Bottoms, 1983). However, discipline can be understood in a broader sense, in relation to the control of population as well as individuals. When the fine is allied to "law" as a sanction, then its growth may be better understood. The creation of the "obedient subject" can be effected through large-scale regulation, through the imposition of numerous minor sanctions upon the bulk of the population rather than through the imposition of massive, punitive sanctions upon a few, highly visible individuals. The technique is to maintain a sustained demand for strict compliance with detailed and punctilious rules (Ball and Friedman, 1965: 220). The law itself, therefore, forms part of the "culture of discipline" (Carson, 1980: 150) with all its minutiae of rules and subrules, regulations, orders, and licenses. Compliance, repeated to the point of unthinkingness, lays an ideological basis for the extension of similar social norms to analogous situations (Ball and Friedman, 1965: 220). Hence the move from the gallows to the fine.

The change in the nature of the privacy sanction. The transition of punishment from the physical to the mental, from the body to the mind, from terror to discipline has been explained as a new form of power (O'Malley, 1983: 154), an incorporative rather than segregative power (Cohen, 1985: 266). However, what has probably occurred is the transfer of the privacy sanction from the *private* to the *public* arena. Merry (1984) notes that small societies are characterized by conditions of little privacy where every event is common

246   FREIBERG

property, where observation and judgment are intense. In such groups the power of public opinion (the social sanction) is great. What may be occurring in this transition from the small society to the larger is the divorce of the privacy sanction from the social. Whereas previously the power to watch was allied with the power to comment, now watching itself is the sanction, something made possible by the technological advances of our times.[15]

Marx (1985) notes that the new, modern technological surveillance methods such as computer matching, eavesdropping and viewing devices, telemetric devices, and the like differ from traditional forms of surveillance in that they transcend distance, darkness, and physical barriers, transcend time, are capital- rather than labor-intensive, and have low visibility or are invisible.

A graphic example of the attempt to utilize the privacy sanction on a massive scale as a consequence of the almost complete failure of traditional law enforcement techniques is found in Australia. As a result of the perpetration of large-scale tax and welfare frauds and an unwillingness or inability by government to devote police resources or invoke the criminal law, a national identity card system (the "Australia Card") was to be introduced. The proposed legislation, which was defeated in the Australian Senate in December, 1986, required every person in Australia to be registered and would have required the production of the card for, among other things, payment of wages, welfare payments, health insurance claims, transfers of land, opening of bank accounts, and income tax returns. The "panoptic" qualities of such a scheme did not go unobserved (Ware, 1986).

The development of the public social sanction. The community corrections movement represents an attempt to revive the social sanction by recapturing the sense of belonging, intimacy, and shared social values which was said to typify preindustrial society (Cohen, 1979, 1985: 78, 118). Community treatment rests on the notion of *gemeinschaft*, though paradoxically the loss of *gemeinschaft* is oft bemoaned (Cohen, 1979: 356). It is the "community" which, though having failed in its task in the first place (as evidenced by the deviant), is expected to reintegrate that deviant through some osmotic process. Community treatment programs are comprised of three major elements as presented in this model—surveillance, ideology, and social interaction. As Cohen notes (1985: 118), the quest for the return to the "community" is unreal because of the inability, and perhaps the inappropriateness, of reproducing the power structures of small communities.

---

15. Foucault's myopic research techniques, his concentration on French history and historiography, have been rightly criticized (Turner, 1985: 211), and perhaps comparative research on such societies as Switzerland and Japan, where the combination of private social and privacy sanctions is still dominant, would place statements about the nature of power in modern societies in some perspective.

SANCTIONS   247

The move to control through positive sanctions. The work of Foucault and others has shown that modern social control depends less on punishment and coercion through negative forms and more on rewards and upon agents of normalization in the spheres of health, education, and welfare (Garland, 1981: 29). Reward is not a new invention, but what has changed is the growth in the economic power of the state, its absorption of an increasing proportion of the gross national product, and the institutionalization of the distribution of largesse in the public realm. Hay has argued that in the 18th century, the system of social control was founded on mechanisms of contingent benevolence backed by coercion (1975: 62). But, in the 20th century, patronage has become welfare and has passed from private to public hands (Garland, 1981; Freiberg, 1986).

Fluctuations in the role of the state. The increased role of the state in the business of deviancy control, the development of a centralized, rationalized, and bureaucratic apparatus for the control and punishment of crime and delinquency, and the care and cure of other types of deviance have been well documented (Cohen, 1985: 13). The informalism or delegalization movement (Abel, 1982) can be seen as an attempt to move the arena of sanctions from the public back to the private again, to divest the state of some of its control functions. Shifts along the public/private continuum can have paradoxical results, depending upon whence the impetus comes. The "sentimental anarchists" (Cohen, 1985: 127) desire a return to a premodern sanctioning system which relies primarily upon the social and the ideological sanctions. Minimal state neoconservatives demand decline in positive economic sanctions (welfare systems) and the state privacy sanction (surveillance), to replace it instead with traditional sanctions such as hanging and imprisonment, which hark back to the days of the weak, rather than the minimal central state.

A fruitful area for research in this field is the relationship between state and private sanctioning systems. Henry's work on social control systems in factories charts the complicated interplay between factory-based informal systems and the state system which is required to reinforce the informal system when it fails (Henry, 1983: 198). Thus, sanction hierarchies can be discerned in sanctions arenas as well as types.

Sanctions are pervasive. There can be no escape from the power of others, either individually or collectively. The nature of social power, the reasons for its exercise, the variations in its use historically and cross-culturally, the impact of factors such a class, technology, and economic development upon the way in which specific sanctions are generated and the protections, legal and otherwise, against the use of power are all appropriate subjects for the study of sanctions. Criminology may focus upon state or public sanctions, but, as this paper argues, such sanctions ought to be seen as only one part of

248   FREIBERG

the sanctioning spectrum, the dimensions and divisions of which are themselves problematic. What this reconceptualization may lose in fine detail
may, it is hoped, be more than compensated for by the minimization of the
distortions which present sanction analyses have created or perpetuated.

REFERENCES

Abel, Richard
    1982   The Politics of Informal Justice. New York: Academic Press.

Ackroyd, Carol et al.
    1977   The Technology of Political Control. Harmondsworth: Penguin.

Arens, Richard and Harold D. Lasswell
    1961   In Defense of Public Order. New York: Columbia University Press.
    1964   Toward a general theory of sanctions. Iowa Law Review 49: 233-276.

Aubert, Vilhelm
    1983   In Search of Law: Sociological Approaches to Law. Oxford: Robertson.

Australian Law Reform Commission
    1980   Privacy and intrusions. Discussion Paper No. 13. Canberra: Australian
              Government Printing Service.

Ball, Harry V. and Lawrence M. Friedman
    1965   The use of criminal sanctions in the enforcement of economic legislation: A
              sociological view. Stanford Law Review 17: 197-223.

Bell, Daniel
    1970   Notes on the post industrial society. In Marvin E. Olsen (ed.), Power in
              Societies. New York: Macmillan.

Benney, Mark
    1983   Gramsci on law, morality and power. International Journal of the Sociology
              of Law 11: 191-208.

Bentham, Jeremy
    1970   An Introduction to the Principles of Morals and Legislation. London:
              Athlone.

Black, Donald
    1976   The Behavior of Law. New York: Academic Press.
    1984   Crime as social control. In Donald Black (ed.), Toward a General Theory
              of Social Control, Vol. 2. New York: Academic Press.

Bottoms, Anthony E.
    1983   Neglected features of contemporary penal systems. In David Garland and
              Peter Young (eds.), The Power to Punish. New Jersey: Humanities Press.

Brown, Julie
    1983   Psychiatrists and the state in Czarist Russia. In Stanley Cohen and Andrew
              Scull (eds.), Social Control and the State. Oxford: Robertson.

Carson, Kit W. G.
    1980   The institutionalization of ambiguity: Early British factory acts. In Gilbert
              Geis and Ezra Stotland (eds.), White-Collar Crime: Theory and Research.
              Beverly Hills: Sage.

SANCTIONS 249

Castel, Robert
   1983   Moral treatment: Mental therapy and social control in the nineteenth
           century. In Stanley Cohen and Andrew Scull (eds.), Social Control and the
           State. Oxford: Robertson.

Chan, Janet B. L. and Richard V. Ericson
   1981   Decarceration and the Economy of Penal Reform. Toronto: Centre of
           Criminology, University of Toronto.

Christie, Nils
   1968   Changes in penal values. In Scandinavian Studies in Criminology, Vol. 2.
           Oslo: Universitetforlaget.
   1981   Limits to Pain. Oxford: Robertson.

Cohen, Stanley
   1979   Book review: Decarceration. British Journal of Sociology 30: 250.
   1983   Social control talk: Telling stories about correctional change. In David
           Garland and Peter Young (eds.), The Power to Punish. New Jersey:
           Humanities Press.
   1985   Visions of Social Control: Crime Punishment and Classification. Oxford:
           Polity.

Cohen, Stanley and Andrew Scull
   1983   Social Control and the State. Oxford: Robertson.

Cotterrell, Roger B.
   1977   Durkheim on legal development and social solidarity. British Journal of
           Law and Society 4: 241-252.
   1984   The Sociology of Law: An Introduction. London: Butterworths.

Dahl, Robert A.
   1968   Power. In D. L. Sills (ed.), International Encyclopedia of the Social
           Sciences. New York: Macmillan.
   1970   Modern Political Analysis (2nd ed.). New Jersey: Prentice Hall.

Durkheim, Emile
   1933   The Division of Labor in Society. New York: Macmillan.
   1969   Two laws of penal evolution. University of Cincinnati Law Review 38: 32-
           60.

Dyson, Kenneth H. F.
   1980   The State Tradition in Western Europe. Oxford: Robertson.

Etzioni, Amitai
   1970   Power as a societal force. In Marvin E. Olsen (ed.), Power in Societies.
           New York: Macmillan.

Fardon, Richard
   1985   Power and Knowledge: Anthropological and Sociological Approaches.
           Edinburgh: Scottish Academic Press.

Foucault, Michel
   1979   Discipline and Punish. Victoria: Penguin.
   1980   Power/Knowledge: Selected Interviews and Other Writings. Colin Gordon
           (ed.). London: The Harvester Press.

Freiberg, Arie
   1986   Reward, law and power: Toward a jurisprudence of the carrot. Australian
           and New Zealand Journal of Criminology 19: 91-113.

250   FREIBERG

Freiberg, Arie and Richard Fox
    1986   Sentencing structures and sanction hierarchies. Criminal Law Journal 10:
              216-235.

Freiberg, Arie and Pat O'Malley
    1984   State intervention and the civil offense. Law and Society Review 18: 373-
              394.

Galbraith, John K.
    1983   The Anatomy of Power. Boston: Houghton Mifflin.

Garland, David
    1981   The birth of the welfare sanction. British Journal of Law and Society 8: 29-
              45.
    1983   Durkheim's theory of punishment: A critique. In David Garland and Peter
              Young (eds.), The Power to Punish. New Jersey: Humanities Press.

Garland, David and Peter Young
    1983   Toward a social analysis of penality. In David Garland and Peter Young
              (eds.), The Power to Punish. New Jersey: Humanities.

Gibbs, Jack P.
    1966   Sanctions. Social Problems 14: 147-159.
    1975   Crime, Punishment and Deterrence. New York: Elsevier.

Grabosky, Peter N.
    1984   The variability of punishment. In Donald Black (ed.), Toward a General
              Theory of Social Control, Vol. 1. New York: Academic Press.

Greenawalt, Ken
    1983   Punishment. In Sanford H. Kadish (ed.), Encyclopedia of Crime and
              Justice. New York: Free Press.

Greenberg, David F.
    1975   Problems in community corrections. Issues in Criminology 10: 1-33.

Griffiths, John
    1984   The division of labor in social control. In Donald Black (ed.), Toward a
              General Theory of Social Control, Vol. 1. New York: Academic Press.

Hall, Jerome
    1973   Foundations of Jurisprudence. Indianapolis: Bobbs-Merrill.

Hay, Douglas
    1975   Property, authority and the criminal law. In Douglas Hay, Peter Linebaugh,
              John A. Rule, E.P. Thompson, and Carl Winslow (eds.), Albion's Fatal
              Tree. New York: Pantheon.

Henry, Stuart
    1983   Private Justice: Towards Integrated Theorising in the Sociology of Law.
              London: Routledge and Kegan Paul.

Hirst, Paul Q.
    1985   Constructed space and the subject. In Richard Fardon (ed.), Power and
              Knowledge: Anthropological and Sociological Approaches. Edinburgh:
              Scottish Academic Press.

Holdsworth, William
    1956   A History of English Law (7th ed.). London: Methuen.

SANCTIONS 251

Horwitz, Allan V.
1984   Therapy and social solidarity. In Donald Black (ed.), Toward a General
        Theory of Social Control, Vol. 1. New York: Academic Press.

Humphries, Drew and David F. Greenberg
1981   The dialectics of crime control. In David F. Greenberg (ed.), Crime and
        Capitalism. Palo Alto: Mayfield.
1984   Social control and social formations: A Marxian analysis. In Donald Black
        (ed.), Toward a General Theory of Social control, Vol. 2. New York:
        Academic Press.

Ignatieff, Michael
1978   A Just Measure of Pain: The Penitentiary in the Industrial Revolution
        1750-1850. London: Macmillan.
1983   State, civil society and total institutions: A critique of recent social histories
        of punishment. In Stanley Cohen and Andrew Scull (eds.), Social Control
        and the State. Oxford: Robertson.

Ingraham, Barton L. and Gerald W. Smith
1972   The use of electronics in the observation and control of human behavior and
        its possible use in rehabilitation and parole. Issues in Criminology 7: 35-53.

Ihering, R. von
1968   Law as a Means to an End. New Jersey: Rothman Reprints.

Jenkins, Philip and Gary W. Potter
1984   The dominance of authority: Austin Turk and political criminality.
        Contemporary Crises 8: 157-165.

Jenks, Edward
1933   The New Jurisprudence. London: Murray.

Kelsen, Hans
1961   General Theory of Law and State. New York: Russell and Russell.

Klare, Karl E.
1982   The public/private distinction in labor law. University of Pennsylvania Law
        Review 130: 1,358-1,422.

Kocourek, Albert
1924   Sanctions and remedies. University of Pennsylvania Law Review 72: 91-110.

Kreimer, Seth F.
1984   Allocational sanctions: The problem of negative rights in a positive state.
        University of Pennsylvania Law Review 132: 1,293-1,397.

Krislov, Samuel
1982   The politics of control and the control of politics. In Jack Gibbs (ed.),
        Social Control. Beverly Hills: Sage.

Lasch, Christopher
1980   Life in the therapeutic state. New York Review, June 12: 24-32.

Lasswell, Harold D. and Richard Arens
1967   The role of sanctions in conflict resolution. Journal of Conflict Resolution
        11: 27-39.

Lasswell, Harold D. and A. Kaplan
1950   Power and Society. New Haven: Yale University Press.

252 FREIBERG

Lukes, Steven
   1974   Power: A Radical View. London: Macmillan.

Lukes, Steven and Andrew Scull
   1983   Durkheim and the Law. Oxford: Robertson.

Mann, Michael
   1986   The Sources of Social Power, Vol. 1: A History of Power from the
           Beginning to A.D. 1760. Cambridge: Cambridge University Press.

Marx, Gary
   1985   The new surveillance: Its basic dimensions, social dynamics and some
           theoretical implications. Presented at the annual Law and Society Confer-
           ence.

Mathieson, Thomas
   1983   The future of control systems—The case of Norway. In David Garland and
           Peter Young (eds.), The Power to Punish. New Jersey: Humanities Press.

Melossi, Dario
   1980   Strategies of social control in capitalism: A comment on recent work.
           Contemporary Crises 4: 381-402.

Merry, Sally E.
   1984   Rethinking gossip and scandal. In Donald Black (ed.), Toward a General
           Theory of Social Control, Vol. 1. New York: Academic Press.

Miller, Arthur R.
   1971   The Assault on Privacy. Ann Arbor: University of Michigan Press.

Miller, Martin B.
   1974   At hard labour: Rediscovering the nineteenth century prison. Issues in
           Criminology 9: 91-114.

Olsen, Marvin E.
   1970   Power as a social process. In Marvin E. Olsen (ed.), Power in Societies.
           New York: Macmillan.

O'Malley, Pat
   1983   Law, Capitalism and Democracy. Sydney: Allen and Unwin.

Palmer, Jerry and Frank Pearce
   1983   Legal discourse and state power: Foucault and the juridical relation.
           International Journal of the Sociology of Law 11: 361-383.

Pollock, Frederick and Frederick W. Maitland
   1898   The History of English Law (2nd ed.). Cambridge: Cambridge University
           Press.

Pound, Roscoe
   1917   The limits of effective legal action. American Bar Association Journal 3: 55.

Pugh, Ralph Bernard
   1968   Imprisonment in Medieval England. Cambridge: Cambridge University
           Press.

Probert, Walter
   1964   Creative judicial sanctioning: Application in the law of torts. Iowa Law
           Review 49: 277-324.

Rheinstein, Max
1966   Max Weber on Law in Economy and Society. Cambridge: Harvard
        University Press.

Rossiter, Clinton, L.
1958   The pattern of liberty. In Milton R. Konvitz and Clinton L. Rossiter (eds.),
        Aspects of Liberty. New York: Cornell University Press.

Rule, James B.
1973   Private Lives and Public Surveillance. London: Lane.

Rusche, Georg
1978   Labor market and penal sanction: Thoughts on the sociology of criminal
        justice. Crime and Social Justice 10: 1-8.

Rusche, Georg and Otto Kirchheimer
1939   Punishment and Social Structure. New York: Columbia University Press.

Russell, Bertrand
1938   Power: A New Social Analysis. London: Allen and Unwin.

Schermerhorn, Richard A.
1961   Society and Power. New York: Random House.

Schmidt, Robert M.
1964   Federal taxation—A lesson in direct and indirect sanctions. Iowa Law
        Review. 49: 474-497.

Schumann, Karl F.
1983   Comparative research on legal sanctions: Problems and proposals. Interna-
        tional Journal of the Sociology of Law 11: 267-276.

Schwartz, Richard D. and Sonya Orleans
1967   On legal sanctions. University of Chicago Law Review 34: 274-300.

Sebba, Leslie
1978   Some explorations in the scaling of penalties. Journal of Research in Crime
        and Delinquency 15: 247-265.

Sebba, Leslie and G. Nathan
1984   Further explorations in the scaling of penalties. British Journal of
        Criminology 24: 221-249.

Sellin, Thorsten
1939   Forward to Rusche and Kirchheimer's Punishment and Social Structure.
        New York: Columbia University Press.
1976   Slavery and the Penal System. New York: Elsevier.

Shearing, Clifford and Phillip C. Stenning
1983   Private security: Implications for social control. Social Problems 30: 493.

Sheleff, Leon S.
1975   From restitutive law to repressive law: Durkheim's The Division of Labor
        in Society revisited. Archives Europeennes de Sociologie 16: 16-45.

Singer, Lawrence R.
1980   Supportive surveillance: Probation as discipline. International Journal of
        the Sociology of Law 8: 251-275.

254   FREIBERG

Smart, Barry
    1983   On discipline and social regulation: A review of Foucault's genealogical
              analysis. In David Garland and Peter Young (eds.), The Power to Punish.
              New Jersey: Humanities Press.

Sorokin, Pitirim
    1937   Socio-cultural Dynamics. New York: American Book.

Spitzer, Steven
    1974   Punishment and social organization: A study of Durkheim's theory of penal
              evolution. Law and Society Review 9: 613-637.
    1979   Notes towards a theory of punishment and social change. In Research in
              Law and Sociology, Vol. 2. Greenwich, CT: J.A.I.
    1985   Review essay. Criminology 23: 575-581.

Stone, Julius
    1966   Social Dimensions of Law and Justice. Sydney: Maitland.

Tedeschi, James, Thomas V. Bonoma, Barry R. Schlenker, and Svenn Lindskold
    1970   Power, influence and behavioral compliance. Law and Society Review 4:
              521-544.

Turk, Austin T.
    1976   Law as a weapon in social conflict. Social Problems 23: 276-291.
    1982   Political Criminality. Beverly Hills: Sage.

Turkel, Gerald
    1979   Testing Durkheim: Some theoretical considerations. Law and Society
              Review 13: 721-738.

Turner, Bryan S.
    1985   The practices of rationality: Michael Foucault, medical history and
              sociological theory. In Richard Fardon (ed.), Power and Knowledge:
              Anthropological and Sociological Approaches. Edinburgh: Scottish Aca-
              demic Press.

Victoria,
    1981   Manual of Probation Practice and Procedures. Melbourne: Department of
              Community Services.

Ware, Diane
    1986   Bentham's panopticon downunder: The Australia card program. Legal
              Service Bulletin 11: 198-201.

Webb, Sydney and Beatrice Webb
    1963   English Prisons under Local Government. London: Cass.

Wilsnack, Richard W.
    1980   Information control: A conceptual framework for sociological analysis.
              Urban Life 8: 467.

Wrong, Dennis H.
    1979   Power. New York: Harper and Row.

Young, Peter
    1983   Sociology, the state and penal relations. In David Garland and Peter Young
              (eds.), The Power to Punish. New Jersey: Humanities Press.

SANCTIONS   255

Arie Freiberg is a Senior Lecturer in Law at Monash University, Melbourne, Australia, specializing in criminal law and criminology. He is coauthor of *Sentencing: State and Federal Law in Victoria* and has published in the areas of the mentally disordered and the law, Aborigines and the criminal justice system, quasi-criminal sanctions, and victimology. His current research interest is tax compliance.

Part II
Rethinking the Law and Society Relationship: From Legal Pluralism to Postmodernism

[5]

LAW AND SOCIETIES

By Peter Fitzpatrick*

Professor Fitzpatrick offers an examination of bourgeois legality as the concrete embodiment of modern law. Citing examples from the prison system and the workplace, he finds that modern law exists in certain relations of opposition and support with other social forms. From these relations, certain modes of convergence and separation between law and other social forms are identified and explored. To test the utility of this analysis, Fitzpatrick provides an extended application to traditional scholarship about the nature of law and its relation to society. The central focus in this enquiry is the idea of integral plurality as a vehicle by which the abstracted, unitary and universalistic pretensions of the modern legal system may be exposed.

. . .and even the sensitive animals tell that we're not very surely at home here in this encodified world. Perhaps we have still one special tree on the hillside we pass every day that we notice, we still possess yesterday's street and the devoted persistence of an old habit which decided it liked us and stayed with us.[1]

I. INTRODUCTION

"Law and Societies" is a gentle play on the title of the lecture series, "Law and Society," held at Osgoode Hall Law School in 1981-82. In various ways, that series provided the origins for this paper.[2] The title encapsulates the central theme of the paper: that state law is integrally constituted in relation to a plurality of social forms.[3] This is called the theme of 'integral plurality.' In its development, the theme exposes the limits of viewing law as "typically public, unified and direct in its operation."[4] This idea of law creates a distortion; liberation from it opens up radical possibilities for the study and the politics of law.

In outline, the paper takes the familiar academic field of legal plu-

---

© Copyright, 1984, P. Fitzpatrick.

* Senior Lecturer in Law and Interdisciplinary Studies at the University of Kent at Canterbury, England. In working on this piece, I deeply appreciated the intellectual companionship of Rue Bendall and Dave Reason. Noel Machin provided his incomparable translation of Rilke. The faculty and students at Osgoode Hall Law School provided a most stimulating and a most convivial setting for introducing the ideas elaborated in this paper.

[1] Rilke, *Duino Elegies* I, translated by Noel Machin.

[2] The paper is mostly a compendium of several presentations at Osgoode during a visit in January 1982 to deliver a lecture on "Law, Plurality and Historical Materialism" as part of this series.

[3] Here "form" is not used as something devoid of 'content,' but rather as content rendered determinate.

[4] Galanter, "Legality and Its Discontents: A Preliminary Assessment of Current Theories of Legalization and Delegalization," in Blankenburg, Klausa and Rottleuthner, eds., *Alternative Rechtsformen und Alternativen zum Recht, Jahrbuch fur Rechtssoziologie und Rechtstheorie, Band VI* (1980) 20.

ralism as a point of departure. In sustaining the idea of a persistent
plurality of legal orders, legal pluralism has proved an enduring, if
marginal affront to unitary, state-centred theories of law. Yet its own
relation to the state, and to state law, has been distinctly ambivalent.
Some of its adherents attribute no special pre-eminence to the state
and even see it as subordinate to other social forms. In this view, there
is left an unstructured and promiscuous plurality. Other adherents pre-
maturely reduce or subordinate plurality to some putative totality, usually the state or state law. I want to argue that both these stands are
'right'; they are not opposed, but rather, reflect mutual elements of a
wider process. State law does take identity by deriving support from
other social forms. Thus, it would appear to be one social form among
many, even as a subordinate form. But in the constitution and maintenance of its identity, state law stands in opposition to and in asserted
domination over social forms that support it. There exists a contradictory process of mutual support and opposition. This process is tested
and given more specific elaboration in instances of the relations between state law and other social forms, including the prison and the
capitalist labour relation. Further, the academic utility of the analysis
is found in the light it throws on certain perennial concerns: the gap
between law and social reality; the link between law and consensus; and
stages of legal development.

II. LEGAL PLURALISM

Using legal pluralism as a starting point, I will draw a distinction
between two approaches to it: the diffusive and the centerist.[5] Ehrlich,
the ancestor of the diffusive, remains an apt example. For him, the very
basis of state law was a prior "social law" or "living law" which was
the "inner order of associations."[6] Although the state is one of a plurality of associations, state law is subordinate to "living law." In the event
of a conflict between the two, it would be ineffective. Attempts in this
tradition to integrate state law and other legal orders have similarly
been in denial of the originality of state law. An example is Bohannan's
famed attempt at integration in which state law results from a "double
institutionalization of norms" in which some "customs", operative
within "social institutions" are "reinstitutionalized at another level" as
state law.[7] There is nothing in such a reconciliation that would accord

---

    [5] These approaches are treated in more detail in Fitzpatrick, *Marxism and Legal Pluralism*
(1983), 1 Aust. J. L. & Soc'y 45.

    [6] Ehrlich, *Fundamental Principles of the Sociology of Law* (1936) at 39-82.

    [7] Bohannan, "The Differing Realms of Law," in Bohannan, ed., *Law and Warfare: Studies*

state law any distinctness and identity, much less accord it the original efficacy that, on occasion, it manifestly has. As well, that element of the tradition that would treat all legal orders equally fails to account for conflict between orders, a conflict that may point towards some overarching status for state law.

As for the centerist stand, a start should be made with Gierke. Like Ehrlich, Gierke saw associations as having a life of their own. The state was one such association. However, with Gierke's organic theory of society, the state is an association which embraces all other associations and has ultimate authority over them.[8] Whilst advancing theories of pluralism, legal scholars have been prone to make a pre-emptory ascription of ultimate domination to state law. This is well established in Griffith's acute and relentless analysis of legal pluralists which underlines the obduracy of "legal centralism" in this scholarship.[9] Both the diffusive and centerist strands encapsulate processes constituting state law in its relation to other social forms. Accordingly, it is necessary to move on to state law and its relation to a plurality of social forms. To this extent, the paper ceases to be exclusively about legal pluralism, but, insofar as social forms are integral to non-state law, the discussion remains one about legal pluralism, at least for those who wish to read it as such.

III. INTEGRAL PLURALITY AND STATE LAW

Social forms are constituted in contradictory relations of support and opposition with a plurality of other social forms.[10] I tentatively suggest that the more social forms stand in a relation of integral support, the sharper is the opposition between them: "the more alike, the more dissimilar."[11] To establish the first proposition, I will take one idea of law, that of bourgeois legality or the rule of law, and show that

---

in the Anthropology of Conflict (1967) 43 at 47-48.

[8] See Hallis, *Corporate Personality: A Study in Jurisprudence* (1930) at 140-65.

[9] Griffiths, *What is Legal Pluralism?*,(paper presented at the Annual Meeting of the Law and Society Association, Amherst, June 12-14, 1981). Griffiths' valuable account extends also to the diffusive strand in legal pluralism.

[10] This, and the method of analysis that follows, could be seen as a crude derivation from Hegel's ideas of contradiction and the dialectic but one which differs in several basic ways from Hegel: see Taylor, *Hegel* (1975) at 104-106, 227-31 and 238. Of course, the germ of these ideas is not exactly unusual: *cf.* McDonald. *The Legal Sociology of Georges Gurvitch* (1979), 6 Brit. J. L. & Soc'y 24 at 30-31.

[11] One of "a motley collection of maxims to disguise our epistemological nakedness" from Reason, *Generalization from the Single Case: Some Foundational Considerations*, (paper presented at the Conference on The Formal Analysis of Qualitative Data, University of Surrey, Guildford, Apr., 1983) at 32.

certain other social forms are conditions of its existence. The prison and the capitalist labour relation will be used as examples. The next step involves showing that the relations between bourgeois legality and these other social forms are contradictory. Bourgeois legality depends on social forms that tend to undermine it. The case of the dependency of other social forms on law is considered only incidentally. In the next section, the analysis becomes more concrete in its consideration of the operative modes taken by the contradictory relations of opposition and support. The present analysis is only a beginning, an open and prelimi- nary enquiry the coverage and bounds of which are not comprehensive. It celebrates the particular, and pries open holistic, unitary conceptions of law. As such, this exercise is not at one with mainstream pluralism for it does not seek to deny overarching and integrating structures of domination.[12]

To ground the analysis, I will begin by looking briefly at bourgeois legality and the prison before taking the wage labour relation as my main example. There are several, more or less subtle ways in which bourgeois legality depends on the prison but, in the broad approach being used here, it is sufficient to point to the prison, in particular, as the ultimate enforcer of law. Moreover, it is an exemplar of a perva- sive, disciplinary power that typifies modern society and that effects particularist coercions which leave bourgeois legality 'free' to assume its aspects of equality and universality.[13] The relation of bourgeois le- gality to the prison is a contradictory one. It is increasingly evident that prisons in 'liberal democracies' necessarily operate on the basis of arbi- trary, authoritarian and Draconic power and that their operation would be impossible if the rule of law extended to relations within the prison.[14] Conversely, if bourgeois legality did so extend, it would lose identity as bourgeois legality. The prison is part of the necessary "dark side" of bourgeois legality.[15] Yet it is of the essence of bourgeois legal- ity that the rule of law be universal. Consequently, bourgeois legality is asserted through the legal supervision by law of relations in the prison. This supervision is, however, always limited and marginal in its opera- tion. It serves to set boundaries beyond which law will not proceed. When the judiciary reach these bounds, its inability to proceed further is justified on such evasive, but indicative grounds as the public interest

---

[12] *Cf* Fitzpatrick, "Law, Plurality and Underdevelopment," in Sugarman, ed., *Legality, Ide- ology and the State* (1983) 159.

[13] For a fuller treatment see Fitzpatrick, *supra* note 5.

[14] See, *e.g.*, Abbott, *In the Belly of the Beast: Letters from Prison* (1972) and Zdenkowski and Brown, *The Prison Struggle: Changing Australia's Penal System* (1982).

[15] Foucault, *Discipline and Punishment: The Birth of the Prison* (1979) at 222.

and the smooth running of the prison regime.[16]

To approach, in good company, the relation between bourgeois legality and the labour relation,

> Marx reveals that the the fundamental condition of existence of the legal form is rooted in the very economic organization of society. In other words, the existence of the legal form is contingent upon the integration of the different products of labour according to the principle of economic exchange. In so doing, he exposes the deep interconnection between the legal form and the commodity form.[17]

Bourgeois legality derives its constituent elements of freedom and equality from commodity exchange. Where labour power cannot be obtained 'freely' through its exchange as a commodity, direct compulsions in the field of production become necessary. However, this is incompatible with bourgeois legality. Commodity exchange can only be the realization of what is produced and production under capitalism is based on coercion and inequality. The freedom and equality imported by commodity exchange has to be kept separate from immediate relations of production. Bourgeois legality depends on the separation. The separation is achieved in an enthrallingly neat manner. Immediate relations of production, characterized by coercion and inequality, are necessarily entered into *via* the elements of freedom and equality imparted by commodity exchange. The element of compulsion, the necessity to labour for a wage, is general; it is not confined to or even specific to any particular employment relation.

Immediate relations of production come into being through the 'voluntary' and 'personal' commitment of the worker as an individual legal subject entering into a contract of employment. Bourgeois legality creates what is opposed to it, but it blunts the contradiction by investing its creation with its own aura. Life within the workplace becomes a matter of 'private' and 'economic' relations; outside is a matter of 'public' and 'political' relations. But immediate relations of production are also political relations which are ultimately based on compulsion. They are political relations of control over the worker and over production of hierarchic subordination and inequality.[18] They have to be kept apart from the contrary rationalities of bourgeois legality. If relations of equality and freedom pervaded the workplace or if there were a reverse process, there would be a very different type of law to that characterized by bourgeois legality. This is revealed in the necessary respect

---

[16] See, *e.g.*, *Becker* v. *Home Office*, [1972] 2 Q.B. 407 and *Payne* v. *Lord Harris of Greenwich*, [1981] 2 All E.R. 842.

[17] Pashukanis, *Law and Marxism: A General Theory* (1978) at 63.

[18] See Wood, *The Separation of the Economic and the Political in Capitalism* (1981), 127 New Left Rev. 66.

which bourgeois legality shows for the integrity of the regime of the work-place in the severely limited effect of anti-discrimination law on the labour relation. Such legislation cannot displace the opposing practical rationalities of the immediate relations of production.[19]

IV. MODES OF RELATION

To make the analysis more concrete and more complex, I will present a more historically specific aspect of the wage labour relation. There has been a remarkable increase in the formalization of "workplace discipline" in British factories in the last twenty years.[20] Stuart Henry charts "a dramatic change . . . in the form of disciplinary technology during the period in question towards the formalization of rules and procedures."[21] These are rules and procedures internal to the factory. During the same period, there was a large increase in external state regulation of the labour relation. A guiding code of practice was promulgated, legislation on "employment protection" was enacted (providing, for example, a remedy against "unfair dismissal") and "industrial tribunals" were established to deal with a range of employment disputes.

The main thrust of these developments is the link between internal and external changes. Henry finds that "the evidence . . . supports the view that formalization takes place as a result of government and legislative pressure."[22] The *how* of it is fascinating. The state's code of practice provides recommended rules and procedures only. However, internal disciplinary proceedings tend to follow the code since, as one manager put it, "going about these things in a different way might lead towards an Industrial Tribunal."[23] Such an outcome does not seem a matter of direct justiciability, but a breach of the code could be damaging evidence in a justiciable claim, such as in one for unfair dismissal. Yet the state's involvement does not seem to constrain management greatly. As the same manager put it: "[t]he Code does in fact reflect the practice of industry . . . there has been a pressure on us to mold things into the shape of the Code but only minor things. The general

---

[19] *Cf.*, Mayhew, "Stability and Change in Legal Systems," in Barber and Inkeles, eds., *Stability and Social Change* (1971) 187.

[20] Henry, *Factory Law: The Changing Disciplinary Technology of Industrial Social Control* (1982), 10 Int'l. J. Soc. L. 365.

[21] *Id.* at 369.

[22] *Id.*

[23] *Id.* at 370.

philosophy is identical to the Code."[24] Indeed, Henry considers that formalization has operated to support management by giving it, in the face of counter-assertions of power by workers, a 'legitimate' means to dismiss.[25] To generate such legitimacy internally, it would be necessary for formalization to be of some, even if mixed, benefit for workers. This is the case. There are many measures supporting workers and, in a related development, there has been a growth in the participation of workers "in rule creation," "in establishing procedures" and "in administration."[26]

Henry emphasizes the limits of these changes. Thus, he found that "what is formalized is largely procedural," and "the due process-like model typically has representative participation only in its warning, procedural and appeals stages, and crucially important, not in its rule making or sanctioning stages." As well, "unions participate far more in creating procedures than in making rules, and far more in representing employees, than in deciding their fate."[27] There is a strong suggestion that these changes are, in total, a strategy for containing workers and unions. Not that this is a fixed resolution. Henry finds some "tension" between the involvement of workers and the potentiality of the situation to "undermine managements' ability to control."[28] "Automatic employee self-discipline" does, however, restrain the demands put on participation.[29] Overall, it seems there has been no significant change in the type of behaviour punished nor in the nature of the sanctions imposed.[30] There is continuity in the substantive law of the factory despite procedural changes. As for substantive law, it is indicative to find the law of the workplace dealing with such matters as "theft of company property . . . violence and assault, fraud . . . [and] damage to property."[31]

These and other instances can be used to map out modes of relation between law and other social forms. In fact, this mapping could be developed into a complex of contradictions. I will do little more than intimate that conclusion. The mapping is founded on the dichotomy of convergence and separation between law and other social forms. The dichotomy is further divided into positive and negative aspects. This

[24] *Id.*
[25] *Id.*
[26] *Id.* at 371-73.
[27] *Id.* at 370-71, 377.
[28] *Id.* at 374.
[29] *Id.* at 371-73.
[30] See, *id.* at 375-77.
[31] *Id.* at 375.

creates a quadruple division: convergence/positive; convergence/negative; separation/positive; separation/negative.

Integral relations of mutual support between law and another social form tend towards their convergence. It is not such a matter of distinct influence operating from the outside. Elements of law *are* elements of other social forms and *vice versa.* So, with Bohannan's "double institutionalization of norms," some state law results by absorbing material by custom.[32] Custom supports law, but law transforms the elements of custom that it appropriates into its own image and likeness.[33] Law in turn supports other social forms, but becomes in the process part of the other forms. Henry's account of the strategic intervention of law in support of the regime of the workplace showed law subsuming itself to the alien rationalities of this other form. Non-state legal orders will often appropriate legal contents and techniques taken from the state. For instance, Santos provides a case study of how an urban community in Brazil constructed its own legality in drawing considerably on state law.[34] Supportive interactions are, however, much more complex, layered, and even dialectical. So, to use Henry's case study, the state "code" applying to the factory was derived largely from the practice of the factory, but it modified that practice. This becomes relevant to claims before the State's industrial tribunals and their treatment of such claims shapes the practice. And so it goes on.

To take another example, law, in support of the regime of the workplace, is supporting that which supports it. As we saw in Henry's account, the workplace deals with much crime on behalf of the state. More generally, I have considered the dependence of bourgeois legality on the wage labour relation. Along with the labour relation, I would suggest that a further example is the most significant for societies of advanced capitalism.[35] It is not infrequently said that law is increasingly dependent on and being displaced by 'science', that is, by the operation of the sciences of man and society in such forms as state administration and therapy.[36] Doubtless, law is integrally dependent on science, but science depends also on law and law's coercive power for its social operation. If science had to effect its own coercion, it would

---

[32] Bohannan, *supra* note 7.

[33] See note 42, *infra.*

[34] Santos, *The Law of the Oppressed: The Construction and Reproduction of Legality in Pasargada* (1977), 12 Law & Soc. Rev. 5.

[35] Fitzpatrick, *supra* note 5.

[36] A formidable statement of the case can be found in Thomson, *Law and Social Sciences - The Demise of Legal Autonomy* (paper presented at the Conference on Critical Legal Scholarship, University of Kent at Canterbury, Mar.- Apr., 1981).

lose its essential concern for the neutrally or objectively factual. Its political constitution would be revealed, the basis of its legitimation in modern society would disappear and its own identity would change radically. With an audacity matching law's part in constituting the wage labour relation, that very coercion is also a social expression of freedom. For bourgeois legality has it that such coercive interactions in the lives of 'free' legal subjects must be justified in law. So the sphere outside of this legal coercion is one of 'freedom', but within that sphere come the myriads of 'normal', often more subtle, but still deeply coercive operations of science.

Accordingly, law and other social forms take identity from each other in positively supportive ways, but the resulting convergence has its negative aspect in its tendency towards dissolution. Hence, much of the lamentation over 'the death of the law' sees bourgeois legality being inexorably undermined by the intrusion of administration or science.[37] Such unidirectional scenarios do accurately perceive that law is open to penetration by corrosive social forms. However, they are at best preemptory. Law relates to opposing social forms in ways that constitute it positively. In this, law is separated from other social forms. It assumes some separate and autonomous identity in positive constitutive relations to other social forms. These are the relations of separation in their positive aspect. Law would not be what it is if related social forms were not what they are. This argument has just been illustrated in the instances of the prison, the wage labour relation and, summarily, that of science.

This leaves the last relational mode in our quadruple division, that of separation in its negative aspect. In this mode, identity is asserted or maintained in the rejection of other social forms. The most straightforward case is that of outright rejection. Law's coverage is confined by formal jurisdictional limits and in the range of issues recognized as legally significant. Some legal systems, such as that of Imperial China, drastically limit the range of state law and fundamentally discourage resort to law.[38] For legal systems with pretensions to popular access and broad coverage, especially those committed to a 'universal' rule of law, oblique rather than direct rejections are necessary if law is to exclude elements threatening its identity. Most obviously, this occurs in the vaunted problem of access to legal services and the exclusion of many people through the differential effect of the cost of litigation, lack

---

[37] *Cf.* the acute critique in Nelken, *Is there a Crisis in Law and Legal Ideology?* (1982), 9 J. L. & Soc. 177.

[38] Needham and Ronan, 1 *The Shorter Science and Civilization in China: An Abridgement of Joseph Needham's Original Text* (1970) at 276-84, and van der Sprenkel, *Legal Institutions in Manchu China: A Sociological Analysis* (1962).

of cultural compatibility with law's processes and the allocation of inadequate resources to handle disputes.[39]

The Hunts' graphic account of the state court system in a region
of Mexico illustrates this rejection.[40] More exactly, I will take one
strand of the case study, the relation between the state court and the
local Indian community. Their incompatibility may be dramatic, but it
is not atypical. The state court operates along highly formalized and
bureaucratic lines. It serves the dominant group in the region adequately. In the operation of the court, that group's local interests tend
to override the state's interests. Yet the socially subordinate Indian
community almost always dislikes taking cases to the court. This is
partly a manifest matter of Indian custom. For example, customary
marriages are not recognized in state law and cannot be dealt with in
state courts. Also, the court usually imposes fines that Indians cannot
afford or metes out inept punishments. Elopement, although deserving
only passing admonition in the Indian view, is punished in state courts
with prison sentences ranging from six months to six years and with
heavy fines. There are other more covert and illuminating rejections.
When the state court *does* recognize Indian claims, these will often be
distorted in ways alien to the community. An action brought against a
witch who failed to bring rain, when paid to do so, was treated as one
of fraud. In the Indian view, the resulting fine was too light. An application to the court for protection from charges of witchcraft was
treated inadequately as libel.[41]

Nor does the court modify its own demands to be more accommo-
dating. If Indians tried to overcome the usual inability to pay a fine in
cash by tendering corn, they would be mocked by officials and even
imprisoned. More subtly, the very constitutive rationalities of the court
serve to repel Indian involvement. For an Indian, coming to court as a
witness is put aside if some significant agricultural task has to be carried out. It is not too speculative to say that something as basic as
different and incompatible notions of time are involved. The same incompatibility underlies the complaint of a judge who claims not to have
time to accommodate Indian modes of disputation. In peasant societies,
time fits within social relations; in capitalist societies, social relations fit
within time. Cumulatively, these rejections encourage Indians to settle

---

[39] See generally, Galanter, *Why the "Haves" Come Out Ahead: Speculations on the Limits
of Legal Change* (1974), 9 Law & Soc. Rev. 95.

[40] Hunt and Hunt, "The Role of Courts in Rural Mexico," in Bock, ed., *Peasants in the
Modern World* (1969) 109.

[41] These two examples are from another region. Indians from the region studied would not
even bring such cases because of the courts' inability to deal aptly with them, *id.* at 131-32.

disputes within their own community. Judges believe that by rejecting Indian cases, they are eliminating Indian law. They are doing the opposite.

Outright rejection is not the only mode of effecting separation. There remains the paradoxical mode of rejection through acceptance. The Hunts' case study also illustrates this. The cases of witchcraft were accepted by the state court, but transformed in its own terms. Also, there are many studies showing that when custom is penetrated by state law, its nature changes fundamentally and it becomes part of state law.[42] The mere formal presentation of custom is incompatible with the persistence of custom.[43] This point has profound resonances in debates over the use of folk classifications in legal anthropology.[44] Nor is the inability of custom to survive in an encodified world only a matter of presentation. The issue of presentation is integral to a more comprehensive division between worlds. This is aptly encapsulated in the admonition of a magistrate of the Village Court in Papua New Guinea to a crowd outside the courthouse. The magistrate applies 'custom' through formal legal procedures characteristic of capitalist societies and this contrasts with the traditional mode of dispute settlement through popular participation. He said:

> [t]his is not the good old times when every person, whether he is a party to the dispute or not, could crowd around to hear and talk about the disputes. The village court is a completely different institution running under a new law. We must all respect the village court. It is only those people who are concerned that can come to the village court to settle their disputes. Everybody else must go home and involve themselves in coffee gardening, businesses and their families.[46]

Legal procedures characteristic of capitalist societies are incompatible with the communal expression of interest and, hence, with the

---

[42] See generally, Diamond, "The Rule of Law Versus the Order of Custom," in Black and Mileski, eds., *The Social Organization of Law* (1973) 318 and specifically Burman, *Chiefdom Politics and Alien Law: Basutoland under Cape Rule, 1871-1884* (1981); Chanock, *Neotraditionalism and Customary Law in Malawi* (1978), 16 Afr. L. Stud. 80; Le Roy, *Local Law in Black Africa: Contemporary Experiences of Folk Law Facing State Law and Capital in Senegal and Some Other Countries* (paper presented at the meeting of the Commission on Folk Law and Legal Pluralism, Villa Servelloni, Bellagio, Sept., 1981); and Snyder, "Colonialism and Legal Form: The Creation of 'Customary Law' in Senegal," in Sumner, ed., *Crime, Justice and Underdevelopment* (1982) 90.

[43] See Galanter, *The Displacement of Traditional Law in Modern India* (1968), 24 J. Soc. Issues 65, and Twining, *The Place of Customary Law in the National Legal Systems of East Africa* (1964).

[44] See Bohannan, "Ethnography and Comparison in Legal Anthropology," in Nader, ed., *Law in Culture and Society* (1969) 401.

[46] See Paliwala, "Law and Order in the Village: Papua New Guinea's Village Courts" in Sumner, *supra* note 42, 192 at 213 for the general point and also, in the same volume, Fitzpatrick, "The Political Economy of Dispute Settlement in Papua New Guinea" at 228.

adequate expression of communal interests. More broadly, these are simply instances of reification in and through law. Law transforms social issues into its own terms of communication or substantive content.[46] In this way, law protects its own identity against contrary demands made on it. Also, there are other ways in which such demands can be absorbed and their danger contained. One admits the demand initially, but then allows it only an anaemic existence at the level of enforcement, as in the failures of enforcement in racial discrimination actions.[47] Another mode of shaping what is allowed into the sanctum of law and of rejecting what is not apt involves the use of broad discretionary standards, such as reasonableness and good faith. Such obfuscating forms of dispute settlement as conciliation and the judicial review of administrative action also allow a broadly similar discretion.[48] The implied term in contract law is another example which serves to instance the most oblique type of rejection through acceptance. The mechanism of the implied term imports the immediate relations of production into the contract of employment;[49] workers thereby 'agree' to their own subjection in those relations.

In such instances, law sets and maintains an autonomy for opposing social forms, keeping them apart from itself and purporting to exercise an overall control. Yet this control is merely occasional and marginal. In such instances, the balance between autonomy and control is most often struck by law's intervention being comprehensive in terms but limited in operation. Administrative law provides numerous examples. Again the analysis of Henry's case study showed that law's intervention in factory 'discipline' was limited operatively to procedural elements, leaving substantive elements unchanged. The balance can be more intricate. In the same case study, the law's immediate intervention in factory 'discipline' took the form of a non-obligatory code which was nevertheless enforced obliquely through its relevance to cases before industrial tribunals; in this way state law came to the aid of capital without being compromised in too intimate and too revealing an involvement in the regime of the workplace and without manifestly undermining the integrity of that regime. In the limited nature of its involvement with other social forms, law accepts the integrity of that

---

[46] See, *e.g.*, Gabel, "Reification in Legal Reasoning," in Spitzer, ed., 3 *Research in Law and Sociology: A Research Annual,* (1980) 25.

[47] See, *e.g.*, Marshall *et al., Employment Discrimination: Impact of Legal and Administrative Remedies* (1978).

[48] See Arthurs, *Rethinking Administrative Law: A Slightly Dicey Business* (1979), 17 Osgoode Hall L.J. 1, and, *e.g.*, Mullard, *Black Britain* (1973) at 75-87.

[49] See Napier, *Discipline* (1980).

which it controls. Its penetration is bounded by the integrity of the opposing social form. In exceptional instances, such bounds are explicit, even audacious. Accordingly, the maintenance of secrecy in the operation of the prison or of the capitalist enterprise has been given explicit protection and law will rarely penetrate beyond those bounds of secrecy.[50] In judicial review of administrative action, the law's restraint in deference to the integrity of administration is on occasion open and unqualified.[51] More often the bounds are fudged in terms of what is "reasonable" and other such discretionary gateways. When a judge, or another of law's gatekeepers, leaves the law at the prison gate in "the public interest" or "implies" immediate relations of production in a contract of employment - an operation that would rarely fit law's own constitutive test of an "implied term"[52] - transparencies emerge through which the contingencies of law's identity can be glimpsed. If identity is to be maintained, borders become places of danger and anomaly, not to be too often explicitly confronted.[53] Indeed, the (common) law is not "a brooding omnipresence in the sky,"[54] but law's operatives have to view it so because of the dangers of confronting law's terrestrial connections. Law cannot bear very much reality.[55]

V. ACADEMIC UTILITIES

There are various academic strategies which protect law from too much reality and serve to maintain its integrity as an object of study. An extreme is 'legal positivism.' It asserts the self-contained nature of law and law's moral and political neutrality. However, I will concentrate on and explore critically a cluster of academic strategies in the field of 'law and society' to test the utility of the idea of integral plurality. These comprise the gap between law and social reality, the link between law and consensus, and the conception of modern law as a stage of legal development.

The gap between law and social reality is sometimes seen as the law's lack of responsiveness to society and sometimes in terms of its efforts to bring society into line with it. Other approaches partially en-

---

[50] See, *e.g.*, *Home Office* v. *Harman*, [1981] 2 All E. R. 349, and *Nasse* v. *Science Research Council*, [1979] 3 W.L.R. 762.

[51] See, *e.g.*, *Local Government Board* v. *Arlidge*, [1915] A.C. 120.

[52] *Cf.* Napier, *supra* note 49, at 5 and 12.

[53] Douglas, *Purity and Danger: An Analysis of Concepts of Pollution and Taboo* (1970).

[54] Holmes as quoted in Megarry, *Miscellany-at-Law: A Diversion for Lawyers and Others* (1955) at 268.

[55] *Cf.* Eliot, *Murder in the Cathedral* (1935) at 49.

compass both these, such as the gap between law in books and law in action or between what law says and what it does.[56] For all these approaches, the gap is a bridgeable one. At least, it is held to be so in an unspecified range of relations between law and society. Alternatively, none of these approaches envisages the unbridgeability of the gap in any specific instance. On the contrary, their impetus is a concern to bridge the gap through changing the content or operation of law.[57] No specific challenge to law's integrity is admitted. Law is thus preserved as a unitary object of study immune to the challenges of the plurality of its constitutive social forms. Not being restrained in any specific relation with other social forms, law has an unspecific potential efficacy. This is nothing more than the academic analogue of bourgeois legality. With bourgeois legality, law must appear comprehensively capable of rule or, at least, not be seen to be specifically incapable. There is no need to labour the differences between these approaches and that of integral plurality. For integral plurality, law is constituted in relations of opposition and support with other social forms to the effect that there are necessarily unbridgeable gaps between law and other social forms. Perceptions of a gap are accurate to the extent that they accommodate social forms opposed to law. But the gap cannot be bridged, for law depends on these opposed social forms. It depends integrally on what is contrary to it. The gap is set. There is not in the gap some vague, but remediable derogation from the efficacy of law; rather, there is something constitutive of law itself.

"Consensus" is one way of bridging the gap. "It is possible," Talleyrand said, "to do many things with a bayonet, but one cannot sit on one."[58] So with law, it cannot coerce comprehensively and must depend, so it is said, on consensus. In a valuable and wide-ranging survey, Hunt finds a unity between "contemporary Marxist and non-Marxist theories of law" in a shared and fundamental concern with "the dichotomy between coercion and consent" in the constitution of law. In this, there is a particular concern with consent.[59] The immediate problem in dealing with consent is to give it some content. In "dichotomy between coercion and consent," consent emerges from the framing of the prob-

---

[56] For illustrations of some of these approaches and an analysis broadly similar to that offered here see Fitzpatrick, "Law, Modernization and Mystification" in Spitzer, *supra* note 46, at 161.

[57] See, for an analysis of some instances, Gurvitch, *Sociology of Law* (1947) at 122-35.

[58] As quoted in Nwafor, *History and the Intelligence of the Disinherited* (1975), 7 The Rev. of Radical Political Econ. 43.

[59] Hunt, *Dichotomy and Contradiction in the Sociology of Law* (1981), 8 Brit. J. L. & Soc'y 47 at 47, 62 and 73.

lematic. Coercion is not sufficient to secure compliance with law. Therefore, there must be consent as well. Consent acquires identity and coherence in binary opposition to coercion. For the non-Marxist theories of law, this leaves consent conveniently vague. Any compliant behaviour not coerced through law becomes consent. Hence, the operative or factual validity of bourgeois legality is given in the constitution of the problematic. To adopt Foucault's argument, power is presented through law as a negative constraint, leaving a measure of freedom intact. In this way, the coercive operation of other social forms is masked and the exercise of a coercive, disciplinary power outside of law is rendered acceptable.[60]

Marxist theories of law fare little better. They seem to rely on a similar constitutive dynamic in the formation of 'consent'. The emphasis on consent, as Fryer *et al.* indicate, emerges in reaction against a so-called "rather naive and instrumental version of Marxism, which treated law exclusively as a coercive apparatus wielded at will by a malevolent ruling class."[61] The emphasis on coercion cannot account, as Gramsci has argued, for "the 'spontaneous' consent given by the great masses of the population to the general direction imposed on social life by the dominant fundamental group."[62] With the Marxist variant, consent seems to merge into the oblique or elusive coercions of some Gramscian notion of "hegemony", but 'consent' still means a significant consent and it is still set against coercion.[63] Under such a view then, law must be seen, as constituted, in significant part through general consent. This general consent maintains law as autonomous or 'relatively autonomous' both as an object of study and as a field of political action.[64] Law cannot be reduced to dominant class and economic elements. Thus, the integrity and unitary nature of 'law' is maintained.

---

[60] Foucault, *Power/Knowledge: Selected Interviews and Other Writings 1972-1977* (1980) at 104; Foucault, *The History of Sexuality, An Introduction*, No. 1 (1981) at 86, 144.

[61] Fryer *et al.*, "Law, State and Society," in Fryer *et al.*, eds., *Law, State and Society* (1981) 9 at 11.

[62] As quoted in Hunt, *supra* note 59, at 62.

[63] *Cf.* Althusser's neo-Gramscian notion of Ideological State Apparatuses which comprise such as educational and religious institutions and the family and operate basically as "ideology". These are contrasted with a "*Repressive* State Apparatus" (emphasis added). Law functions in both the "ideological" and the "repressive" spheres. See, Althusser, *Lenin and Philosophy and Other Essays* (1971) at 124-49.

[64] Hunt, *supra* note 59, at 62-65 and 67-72. General consent is not necessarily the sole support for such autonomy. Engels, among others, would add there is a need for modern law to be "an *internally coherent* expression"; letter to Conrad Schmidt, as quoted (with the emphasis) in Cain and Hunt, *Marx and Engels on Law* (1979) at 57. It is not infrequently also said that some 'relative autonomy' of the state and of law is needed because of the limited rule of the bourgeoisie; see, *e.g.*, Poulantzas, *Political Power and Social Classes* (1973) at 284-85; this is congruent with a need for some general consent. Compare, *infra* note 78.

In the perspective of integral plurality, consenting persons are nor-
malized through a diversity of coercions operating in a constellation of
social forms, usually constituted and maintained by law, and in the
general standards cited in these forms. Such social forms include the
prison, the workplace, the family, various therapeutic regimes, monito-
rial schooling and state welfare regimes. The effect is that consent is
pre-shaped to conform to extant structures of domination.[65] It is not a
matter of people being influenced by other social forms and then adopting an attitude of consent towards law, either specifically or as a diffused part of "the general direction imposed on social life by the dominant fundamental group."[66] Rather, it is a more contemporaneous and
more intimate matter. Consenting persons are constituted in and by
these social forms, which interact concurrently with-in law and so operate to constitute law. In short, the inter-relations between law, consent
and coercion are closer and more complex than the simple dichotomy
between coercion and consent can even remotely allow. These same inter-relations undermine the efficacy of solitary consent as a basis for
the autonomy and integrity of law.

The analysis of the conception of modern law as a 'stage' in legal
development can be stated with the words of Karl Marx:

> The so-called historical presentation of development is founded, as a rule, on the
> fact that the latest form regards the previous ones as steps leading up to itself,
> and, since it is rarely and only under quite specific conditions able to criticize
> itself — leaving aside, of course, the historical periods which appear to them-
> selves as times of decadence — it always conceives them one-sidedly. The Chris-
> tian religion was able to be of assistance in reaching an objective understanding
> of earlier mythologies only when its over self-criticism had been accomplished to
> a certain degree. . . . Likewise, bourgeois economics arrived at an understanding
> of feudal, ancient, oriental economics only after the self-criticism of bourgeois
> society had begun. In so far as the bourgeois economy did not mythologically
> identify itself altogether with the past, its critique of the previous economies,
> notably of feudalism, with which it was still engaged in direct struggle, resem-
> bled the critique which Christianity levelled against paganism, or also that of

---

[65] The argument is developed further in Fitzpatrick, *supra* note 5. There are other relevant
aspects which deserve some mention but are not immediately relevant to "the dichotomy between
coercion and consent." Generally, the positing of a vague, unitary 'consent' has a flattening effect
in analytical and political terms. That is, such 'consent' obscures a significant diversity of behaviour. In an illuminating analysis of the limits of the notions of consensus, legitimacy and the like,
Rootes draws attention to a large "*dissensus* . . . even in those states that are apparently politically stable": Rootes, *Intellectuals, the Intelligentsia and the Problem of Legitimacy*, (paper
presented to the Workshop on "The Politics of Intellectuals, the Intelligentsia and Educated Labour," European Consortium for Political Research, Joint Session, Freiburg-im-Breisgau, Mar.,
1983, at 1 (his emphasis)). And he proceeds to consider how compliance is secured short of active
consent. For example, "Subordination to authority at work does . . . have consequences for the
way working people think: it promotes the . . . inability to conceptualize either the structural
sources of their troubles or the alternatives to them." *Id.* at 4.

[66] See, *supra* note 62, and the accompanying text.

Protestantism against Catholicism.[67]

The modern age is not unique in its self-conception as both the culmination and rejection of all that has preceded it. Modern law is at one with the age. Its culmination is as a universalist, unitary and state-centred form. In this, law is seen as evolving from, yet set against, a plurality of particularist social forms. Its integrity as a distinct stage of legal development is achieved, in part, in the ostensible rejection of such social forms. It is possible to provide an initial indicative sketch of the emergence of modern law in its relation to this plurality. I will use the sketch to account for the stage of modern law as a unitary, state-centred conception and introduce alternative conceptions of law responsive to the idea of integral plurality.

The sketch of the emergence of modern law is presented around the three merging lines of the economic, the political and the line of mentalities. It has been said that modern law emerges in the triumph of the bourgeoisie. Law, developing closely with the constitution of individual property, becomes and takes identity as an instrument in the historically necessary universalism of the rule of the bourgeoisie.[68] It becomes so as a distinct form of law and not as operatively integrated with other social forms.[69] As such, law is not only a social presentation set against lesser, particularist orders, but is used in their elimination and in the constitution of an alternative site of power.[70] Giddens pithily adds the wider perspective and points towards deeper dimensions:

> The vast extension of time-space mediations made structurally possible by the prevalence of money capital, by the commodification of labour and by the transformability of the one into the other, undercuts the segregated and autonomous character of the local community of producers. Unlike the situation in most contexts in [pre-capitalist] class-divided societies, in capitalism class struggle is built into the very constitution of work and the labour setting.[71]

Jakubowski finds that the "dissolution of traditional entities such as the corporations and estates places individuals alongside each other as independent, private persons whose special links take mainly legal forms"[72] and the constitution of the "individual" as legal subject are, in

---

[67] Marx, *Grundrisse: Foundations of the Critique of Political Economy* (1973) at 106.

[68] See Unger, *Law in Modern Society: Toward a Criticism of Social Theory* (1976) and, *cf.*, Poulantzas, *supra* note 64, at 284-85.

[69] See Arthur, "Editor's Introduction," in Pashukanis, *supra* note 17, at 14, 16.

[70] See, *e.g.*, Horwitz, *The Transformation of American Law, 1780-1860* (1977) at 253 and Thompson, *Whigs and Hunters: The Origins of the Black Act* (1977).

[71] Giddens, *A Contemporary Critique of Historical Materialism* (1981) at 121.

[72] Jakubowski, *Ideology and Superstructure in Historical Materialism*, translated by A. Booth (1976) at 95.

132   OSGOODE HALL LAW JOURNAL   [VOL. 22, NO. 1

turn, integrally tied to "commodification."[73] Law encompasses and me-
diates between the individual and the general relations made possible
by "the prevalence of money capital, by the commodification of labour
and by the transformability of the one into the other."[74] Law is impli-
cated in that basic contradiction in the constitution of modern society
so vividly described by Marx:

> Only in the eighteenth century, in 'civil society', do the various forms of social
> connectedness confront the individual as a mere means towards his private pur-
> poses, as external necessity. But the epoch which produces this standpoint, that
> of the isolated individual, is also precisely that of the hitherto most developed
> social (from this standpoint, general) relations.[75]

Other heralds of modern society have, of course, discerned a similar
division and have seen law as of particular significance in this. For
Durkheim, progress towards "organic solidarity" entails increasing collaboration between individuals through law which, in turn requires increasing "administration" by the state as the operative representation
of general social relations.[76] This utter centrality of law is revealed in a
Marxist perspective for it is one that squarely confronts class division.
Class division cuts across the idylls of "organic solidarity" or "civil society," and the like positing of an harmonious integration, through law
or otherwise, of the individual and general social relations. No longer is
class division contained in "the segregated and autonomous character
of the local community of producers" but "is built into the very constitution of the 'work and labour setting'."[77] This setting is founded on
coercion and inequality. Further, there results from this change in the
effectivity of class division a potential for the working class to act at
the level of general social relations. The combination of this potentiality
and this subordination in relations of coercion and inequality is ominous for the dominant class. It is in the prospect of class division that
modern law, as bourgeois legality, comes into its own in effecting the
'voluntary' and 'equal' adherence of the legal subject to certain coercive
and unequal relations of production and in guaranteeing equal and universal rule outside of those relations, countering, in both instances, the
effects of class subordination. In this, law cannot be reduced to a strategic position adopted by the bourgeoisie for it is also something won
by the working class.[78] As well as operating directly or in its own right,

---

[73] Pashukanis, *supra* note 17.

[74] Giddens, *supra* note 71, at 121.

[75] Marx, *supra* note 67, at 84.

[76] See Gurvitch, *supra* note 57, at 86. Compare, *id.* at 87.

[77] Giddens, *supra* note 71, at 121.

[78] See, *e.g.*, Weitzer, *Law and Legal Ideology: Contributions to the Genesis and Reproduc-*

modern law has further significance in mutual inter-connections with the state. It is the state which is the prime mediator between the individual and general social relations and which compensates most comprehensively for the effects of class division or which otherwise acts to contain it.[79] As part of and apart from the state, law is a symbolic and an operative embodiment and guarantor of the equality and universality of state rule and a factor of cohesion in state activity.

In short, a distinct, certain and bounded identity for law is at the core of the making and the maintenance of modern society. Law is an encompassing of the individual and general social relations formalized in universal and equal rule. As such, it is integrally set against social relations of a lesser scale or of a particularistic nature. This opposition was manifested in struggles against agrarian use rights, customs and notions of property antithetical to the advance of the bourgeoisie. However, once so cast, law's identity in opposition could and did extend to comparable social forms whether continuing in spite of law and modernity or appearing as new or as qualitatively different. The family, the penitentiary and various welfare regimes could be taken as instances. For the maintenance of law's identity, these social forms had to be subordinate to law and this subordination is effected in law's constitution and control of such social forms. In the process these social forms are endowed with a supportive aura of universal right.

In terms of mentalities and the supportive complicities of scholarship, law becomes associated with what is effective, that which acts and controls, rather than that which is acted on and controlled. It dominates rather than reflects nature. It partakes of the rationally constructivist rather than the organic, of the universalist rather than the particularist, of the determinant rather than the contingent, of effective change rather than residual continuity. Once its new stage was secure, law could draw on traditions and arrogate some legitimation in continuity. The fusion of the innovative and *stasis* was achieved in notions of evolution:

> [I]n the second half of the nineteenth century . . . it is no longer the analysis of the legal form, but, the problem of justifying the binding force of legal regulation which becomes the focal point of interest for juridical theory. The result is a strange mixture of historicism and juridical positivism which is reduced to negat-

---

tion of Capitalism (1980), 25 Berkeley J. Soc. 137 at 146-47. It may be revealing to consider a dynamic "reciprocity" between classes here, instead of a static consensus: see Sugarman, "Theory and Practice in Law and History: A Prologue to the Study of the Relationship between Law and Economy from a Socio-historical Perspective," in Fryer *et al., supra* note 61, at 92-94.

[79] This again (*cf. ,supra* note 10) could be seen as Hegel scaled down: see, Wellmer, *Critical Theory of Society* (1971) at 76-77.

ing every law except the official law.[80]

It was in the latter half of the nineteenth century that law's "own self-criticism had been accomplished to a certain degree."[81] This was accompanied by an informed critique and, in part, an adoption of earlier legal forms.[82] Notions of evolution provided some resolution of contradictions between critique and adoption. In terms of the origins of the scholarship of 'law and society,' it is notions of evolution and quasi-Hegelian equivalents that set the seal on the modern idea of law. As Gurvitch shows in his seminal account of the "forerunners and founders" of the sociology of law, contemporary scholarship tied law to the state in a culmination of legal development that displaced or incorporated prior forms of law and custom. This outcome is extended, at least implicitly, to favour generally the claims of the "inclusive" society over all "included" social forms.[83] In this, the state-centered, formalistic "prejudices of the dogmatic jurists" are upheld.[84]

To pursue an instance into the twentieth century, this sketch of origins may prompt questioning of the central interest of sociological jurisprudence with the effectiveness of law. The summary response is that this concern is an expression of class interests. The bluntness of the answer can be mitigated, but is not qualified, in placing those class interests and their relation to law at the heart of the constitution of modern capitalist society. The resulting 'law', in a unitary and state-centred conception, continues to set the very bounds for legal scholarship. It elevates certain lines of enquiry and subordinates or excludes others. Sociological jurisprudence and legal realism are certainly concerned with the limiting and undermining effect that other social forms have on law.[85] But the presentation of this concern is precisely limited. Law, as 'law in books,' may be seen as subordinate to interests reflected in law or to what officials actually do about disputes. The focus of the concern remains formal legal process and formal legal doctrine - the

---

[80] Pashukanis, *supra* note 17, at 69.

[81] See note 67 *supra*, and the accompanying passage. An example of "self-criticism . . ., to a certain degree" would be von Ihering's influential account of law in terms of "interest": see generally Stone, *Social Dimensions of Law and Justice* (1966) at 164-98. The self-criticism is preceded and accompanied by law's self-realization to a certain degree, as exemplified in the work of Austin.

[82] See, *e.g., id.* at 86-118.

[83] Gurvitch, *supra* note 57, at 72-96. Important as Gurvitch's work is, it leaves large gaps which would have to be made good in a less abbreviated account than that offered here. The difficult case of Marx is not considered. Weber is too summarily dismissed: *id.* at 30. And the central significance of Maine is not adequately confronted: *cf., id.* at 74-75.

[84] The phrase comes from *id.* at 77.

[85] See, generally, Hunt, *The Sociological Movement in Law* (1978).

"prejudices of the dogmatic jurists." The range of social forms considered relevant is set from within a pre-constituted 'law'. Academic legal knowledge is generated by applying a certain idea of law to the world. This approach cannot extend to social forms which do not find expression in terms of legal process or doctrine. The integrity of 'law' is thus obliquely but potently affirmed in areas of scholarship that claim to be fundamentally sceptical of it.

In crude summary, modern law can be seen as a distinct stage of development only because of the conditions of its emergence. These entailed a specific dynamic of identity and a specific constitutive connection between 'law and society.' This specific connection and the resulting distinctness of law cannot be a general basis for a theory of stages or types of law. Yet it is implicitly so used when different stages or types of a reified 'law' are seen to result from different stages or types of 'society'. As Nelken so aptly puts a contrary suggestion, "as we move to an increasingly 'managed' society," it does not follow "that law must necessarily follow suit and be shaped accordingly."[86] Against the more familiar argument, it can be said that the apparent increase in state administration may not promote "bureaucratic-administrative law" at the expense of bourgeois legality. It may lead to an increased reliance on bourgeois legality.[87] In the perspective of integral plurality, there is a range of 'legal' types in society - "a kind of regulatory continuum"[88] - and a persisting interaction between them. Hence Galanter's challenging argument that:

> [o]nce we put aside the notion that law is typically public, unified and direct in its operations, we can formulate the question of the change of the role of law in modern society as a question of changing relations between the big (public, national, official) legal system and the lesser normative orderings in society.[89]

Galanter offers an illustration of one such "change of the role of law in modern society." He adopts familiar assertions that there is currently an increasing social ordering through "technocratic controls and communal arrangements."[90] In the perception of this increase, conventional views predict the demise of bourgeois legality. On the contrary, Galanter finds an increasing resort to bourgeois legality "to monitor and oversee" these "alternative" modes of ordering and to effect their

---

[86] *Supra* note 37, at 184.

[87] *Cf.* Kamenka and Tay, "Beyond Bourgeois Individualism: the Contemporary Crisis in Law and Legal Ideology," in Kamenka and Neale, eds., *Feudalism, Capitalism and Beyond* (1975) 126.

[88] Cotterrell, *The Sociological Concept of Law* (in press), J. L. & Soc'y.

[89] Galanter, *supra* note 4, at 20.

[90] *Id.* at 21.

136   OSGOODE HALL LAW JOURNAL   [VOL. 22, NO. 1

"articulation . . . to other social ordering."[91] However, the conventional view does not miss the point entirely. The increasing differentiation and independence of alternative modes of ordering intensify law's difficulties in controlling these other modes; control through law is increasingly ineffective and consigned to the symbolical.[92] A congruent example will help broaden the analysis. Stewart's account of "the reformation of American administrative law" deals, in part, with law's response to the increase in and the intractability of administrative discretion, in the face of which:

> [C]ourts have changed the focus in judicial review (in the process expanding and transforming traditional procedural devices) so that its dominant purpose is no longer the prevention of unauthorized intrusions on private autonomy, but the assurance of fair representation for all affected interests. . . .[93]

This example shows law responding to the claims of another social form by limiting precisely, but not denying, its own power of intervention. This suggests that there is a diversity and a complexity in the relation between law and other social forms lying between a comprehensive control by law of these forms and a retreatist symbolism in the face of their advance. This diversity and complexity have already been explored in the earlier account of modes of relation between law and other social forms. The relation between law and another social form involved a necessary separation between them. If the integrity of the other social form was to be maintained, law could not control it comprehensively. Law would be left with a certain want of power which its own pretentions to comprehensive rule would not allow it to recognize. It is from this fissure in the effective identity of law that a certain symbolism emerges.

Even if, as Galanter says, law is increasingly symbolical, it cannot, in terms of his analysis, be so merely because it takes on a direct effectiveness in the cause of ordering through administration and community. If law's effectiveness in this changed, such ordering would also change. To provide a full explanation, it is necessary to return to the constitutive, but contradictory relations of support and opposition between law and other social forms. Within these relations, the fixity of such categories as 'administration' and 'community' as outright challenges to the integrity of law cannot stand. The apparent resort to community ordering has been validly seen, not so much as a challenge to

---

[91] *Id.*

[92] *Id.* at 19.

[93] Stewart, *The Reformation of American Administrative Law* (1975), 88 Harv. L. Rev. 1669 at 1712.

state law but as a mode of its extension.[94] More common, of course, is the assumption that the inexorable advance of state administration is the expense of law.[95] There is much about law that these premature scenarios overlook, but, most immediate to the present analysis, they fail to confront the integral dependence of administration on law.[96]

VI. CONCLUSION

There is no better way to expose the limits of an enquiry than to try to bring it to a close. In my presentation, I have taken a part of the Hegelian notion of dialectical contradiction and transmogrified it in application to a particular social sphere.[97] This contrasts with positing a social form and then seeing its connection to the world as a matter of 'external' relations. Rather, "this positedness is *in itself*."[98] A social form takes identity "in itself," yet relationally by being in opposition to the social forms that support it. Accordingly, law establishes identity in conterminous relations of opposition and support with a plurality of other social forms. This integral plurality entails a convergence, yet necessitates separation between law and these other social forms. This method of enquiry does not match the ostensible confidence of that agenda. A specific, operative idea of modern law, that of bourgeois legality, was taken as a starting point. It was found to exist in certain relations of opposition and support with other social forms. From these relations, certain modes of convergence and separation between law and other social forms were identified and explored. The utility of the analysis was tested through an extended application to persistent academic issues about the nature of law and its relation to society.

This was to be an open and an opening enquiry. The exploration of the connections between law and specific social forms cannot claim to

---

[94] See Abel, ed., *The Politics of Informal Justice, The American Experience*, No. 1 (1982).

[95] This characterizes even such penetrating accounts as Donzelot, *The Policing of Families: Welfare versus the State* (1980) at 116 and Foucault, *Power/Knowledge, supra* note 60, at 107-108.

[96] A similar dependence is elaborated on in Fitzpatrick, *supra* note 5. Habermas provides an analysis relevant here, one sensitive to the identity and limits of social forms, including administration; he finds a particular need in present-day society to maintain separate from administration "expressive symbols" involved in, amongst other things, "the symbolic use of hearings" and "juridical incantations": Habermas, *Legitimation Crisis* (1976) at 69-70, *et passim*. This particular need is based on the perceived politicization of the relations of production within societies of advanced captialism, a perception that I have implicitly viewed as overdrawn in the earlier analysis of the capitalist labour relation.

[97] The difficulties skirted around in this abrupt process are considerable. For an exploration of this, and for literature by and about Hegel that is unusually lucid see Norman and Sayers, *Hegel, Marx and Dialectic: A Debate* (1980).

[98] Hegel, *Hegel's Science of Logic* (1969) at 488 - emphasis in the original.

be more than illustrative. No comprehensive claims could be made about law's constitutive relations with other social forms. Similarly, no settled alternative view of law could be offered, nor the identification of some stage or tendency in the development of law. Instead, the concern was to employ and to establish in use the idea of integral plurality in the 'deconstruction' of such conceptions and of related academic complicities. As Marx said, the dialectic "lets nothing impose upon it."[99] Nonetheless, I have asserted, the central significance of modern law's relation to particular social forms, especially the capitalist labour relation.[100] Linked with the idea of integral plurality, this assertion serves to identify limits on the necessarily universalistic pretentions of bourgeois legality and serves to explain the hold and the obduracy of abstracted, unitary conceptions of law. Not that the analysis has been set against abstraction. It has been set against an abstraction that forgets too much of its beginnings, and loses too much on the voyage out. I have been concerned to show that the selection necessitated by abstraction, the inclusion of some things and the exclusion of others, is itself an arrogation of power. In contrast to the comforts of premature abstraction, I have tried to stress that law is the unsettled product of relations with a plurality of social forms. As such, law's identity is constantly and inherently subject to challenge and change. Our enquiries into law have to be more diverse and more wide-ranging. Although they may seem perpetually open-ended, such inquiries should, dialectically speaking, reveal unifying and cohering elements as well.

---

[99] Marx, *Capital*, No.1 (Afterword to the Second German Edition, 1954) at 29.

[100] Modern law's relation with science was also said to be central but it was touched on only briefly. For a fuller development, see Fitzpatrick, *supra* note 5.

[6]

SOCIAL THEORY AND LAW: THE SIGNIFICANCE OF STUART HENRY

GARY ITZKOWITZ

I. INTRODUCTION: INTEGRATIVE THEORY AND THE SOCIOLOGY OF LAW

The interrelationship between the formal structures of law and the informal social control structures originating at the private and community level/(private justice) poses difficult questions for lawyers and sociologists alike. For the legal profession the question concerns the impact of law on social institutions, the community, and on the individual. For the sociologist the inverse question must also be included; that is, what is the impact of various sociopolitical levels of society on the formation of law?

Historically, there have been two divergent approaches to analyzing the interrelationship between formal law and private community justice. Most macrotheorists suggest formal law plays a coercive role in maintaining the status quo within society. Moreover, macro-theorists define private justice either as a reflection of formal law (Marx, 1947) or as a social control mechanism that fulfills a particular need or desire of society (Parsons, 1962). Micro-theories of law, by comparison, emphasize social interaction as people develop social control mechanisms, and isolate these informal structures from any relationship with the formal structures of society (Mead, 1934; Piaget, 1951).

Dissatisfied with the presuppositions and dichotomy of both the macro and micro schools of thought, Stuart Henry, the British sociologist of law, explores how the two might be integrated into a more complete sociology of law. In an important but largely overlooked book, *Private Justice: Towards Integrated Theorising in the Sociology of Law* (1983) Henry develops the thesis that formal law and private justice are integrally related; some of the relations of one are the relations of the other. Thus, while formal law relies on private justice to execute some social control functions, private law relies on formal structures to establish a parameter for its discipline.

I am particularly indebted to Professor Ronald Collins of the Syracuse University College of Law for his encouragement and reading of an early draft of this essay, and to Professor David Scover of the University of Puget Sound Law School for his comments on this essay. I also especially thank D'Anne DuBois for her comments, editorial assistance, and continual enthusiasm for my work.

Henry develops this thesis in two main sections of his book. The first is an analysis of past and present theories of the sociology of law (Ibid.: 1–69). Here he sets the stage for his integrated theoretical perspective. To uncover the concrete principles that underlie the theory, section two (Ibid.: 70–219) outlines his research of varied workplace settings as examples of where formal law and private justice intermix.

Henry has two goals in this work. The first is to show that private justice is a legitimate, often ignored, area of inquiry. The second is to develop a theoretical framework that may act as a springboard for an integrative sociology of law. While the author attains the first goal with much persuasiveness, he is much less successful in reaching the second goal. The essential problem in Henry's theory is that it encourages a static description of law, rather than an explanation of law's development. The positive and negative aspects of this work are illustrated in the author's critique of theorists of the sociology of law and in his analysis of workplace discipline.

II. HENRY'S CRITIQUE OF THE SOCIOLOGICAL THEORIES OF LAW

Professor Henry begins his theoretical review by crediting classical macro-sociologists of law (e.g., Durkheim, 1964; Weber, 1947; Maine, 1912) with attempting to place law in its sociopolitical context and with exploring when and why people will legitimate and obey laws. Henry also gives credit to the classical theorists for "debunking" natural law theorists and their notion that "law is a spontaneous and uncontrived product of the continuous flow of life" (1983: 1). Such theorists believe law has evolved naturally, distinct from other private and community rules and customs (e.g., Austin, 1832; Hobbes, 1964). Natural theories of law have been considered positivist because they assume law is a separate, self-contained element of society.

In more modern times, functional theorists have advanced beyond earlier positivist arguments by placing law in a social context whereby law supplies society with a buffer to resolve conflicts (e.g., Parsons, 1954; Merton, 1969). Functional theory makes its own positivist assumptions, however, by viewing the development of the structures of society as an independent, evolutionary process, while private justice is seen merely as fulfilling a structural need. Functional theory, therefore, fails critically to assess the interrelationship between formal and informal structures. The inherent problem within this modern positivist school of law is that it is not able to analyze the formulation of law, or its use by various social actors (Henry, 1983: 4).

Henry also criticizes the most recent defenders of the positivist school, structural theorists (e.g., Unger, 1976; Kamenka and

Tay, 1980). This school of thought advances beyond some of the
obvious pitfalls of functional theory by understanding the independent nature of other elements of law besides the formal.
Nevertheless, structuralists either connect private justice to formal
law according to a preconceived theory or consider individual
forms of private justice as completely isolated elements (ideal-
types) separate from formal law.

Henry's critique of theory is not limited to macro-theory, however. On the micro level, he argues that major schools can be
identified (1983: 33). The first is comprised of legal realists such as
Llewellyn, who encourages study of the actual behavior of the
courts (1930: 431) and the sociological jurisprudence of Pound, who
called for the study of law as it actually is (1943: 60–94). Henry argues that common to these trends is an understanding of the role
of the informal functions of law that impose order on the formal.
This belief has given rise to a wealth of empirical research on
many aspects of law. Henry holds that the problem with the real-
ist practice of empirical research is that it never questions its ideological assumptions, even when arguing for its reform.[1]

Henry holds a similar criticism for community justice reformers. These reformers believe formal law has become bureaucratic
and argue for a popular, decentralized form of justice. In contrast,
he argues that the question is not how to decentralize law, but
rather what is the state of law and the interrelation of formal law
and private justice that allows for the centralization to exist.

For Henry, then, an integrated approach to a sociology of law
must begin at the point where law is constituted; where people interact and create and recreate its formation. To do so not only requires an analysis of the agencies and procedures of formal law,
but also an analysis of social interaction where formal and private
justice blend together and interrelate with sociopolitical structures.

Thus, in place of currently accepted micro and macro theories
Henry argues for a "genuine pluralism" (1983: 30) in theory that
would allow for the autonomy of independent forms of law, each
generated by a different source, and each operating at various
levels of society. Such a theoretical perspective requires a methodology that is "a more micro-analytical, interpretive perspective
which takes seriously the meaning and conceptions of law for the
participants. . . ." (Ibid.) Only then can the social construction of
law be uncovered.

It is important to note that Henry is not the first sociologist of
law to raise such issues. Ehrlich was a Professor of Law at Czernowitz University in Czernowitz, which was then the capital of the

---

[1] For an example of the reforms that Henry critiques see Bush, "Dispute
Resolution Alternatives and the Goals of Civil Justice: Jurisdictional Principles for Process Choice," 84 *Wisconsin law Review* 893 (1984).

952   HENRY'S SOCIOLOGY OF LAW

Austro-Hungarian province of Bucovina. His studies pointed to
many of the same ideas discussed by Henry. In his important
work, *Fundamental Principles of the Sociology of Law*, first published in 1913, Ehrlich explained his approach to the interrelation
of formal and private justice.

For Professor Ehrlich, the source of legal development lies
within society as a whole (Ibid.: 391–411). While the state has a
monopoly on the formal creation of legal statutes, the state alone
cannot regulate all of human conduct (Ibid.: 161–163). Laws created by the state have the power to enforce compliance, but most
people adhere to laws willingly with little thought of the formal
justice system. Moreover, people also conform to many social control mechanisms of private justice that have no formal sanctions at
all (Ibid.: 162).

Professor Ehrlich further suggests that the existence of associations of like-minded individuals is critical to private justice
and these associations are almost exclusively organized in the form
of economic associations that must conform to existing methods of
the production, exchange and consumption of goods (Ibid.: 43). "A
man therefore conducts himself according to law, chiefly because
this is made imperative by his social relations (Ibid.: 64).

It follows, then, that Professor Ehrlich believes that changes
in formal law must be historically relevant and connected to the
source of the private means of social control (moral, religious, ethical, and cultural mores), but just as importantly, formal law itself
changes as a result of social and economic changes effected by
members of associations within the society at large (Ibid: 394–411).

For his part, Henry is critical of Ehrlich on two main points:
first, Ehrlich is seeking a universal source of law instead of distinguishing between different sources for different associations; and
second, Henry maintains that Ehrlich does not fully appreciate the
impact that state law has on private justice. In short, while Ehrlich's work may be considered a plural approach to law it is not
plural enough (1983: 50).

To correct this mistake, Henry suggests that a plural legal
methodology must operate at various horizontal and vertical levels
of society. The horizontal level encompasses law originating in different groups or institutions, while the vertical level includes law
that operates within various layers of society that range "from a
superficial formality down to a spontaneous, unorganized informality" (Ibid: 47). Thus, an adequate theory of law must account
for both the totality of social structures in all layers of society and
the particularity of human conduct found in man's social interactions.[2]

To bring his argument from the theoretical to the concrete,

[2] For a discussion of Weber's similar but contradictory conclusions see
Trubek, Book Review, 37 *Stanford Law Review* 919 (1985).

Henry chose to study private justice forms of discipline as they occurred in different workplace settings ranging from a factory to a
worker-cooperative (Ibid.: 70–219). What he found was that, no
matter how work was organized, similar aspects of private justice
could be uncovered. Factories based on the private control of
property and containing standard methods of hierarchical management not only used coercion by management to gain social control,
but also peer pressure by the workers. At the same time, worker-
cooperatives, which were not based on private control, and instead
extolled collective decisionmaking, nevertheless, also exhibited
forms of hierarchical management.

These findings lead to Henry's fundamental conclusion: private justice is not only an autonomous element of law, but an active, creative element containing its own dynamic. Private justice,
therefore, does not "merely serve to legitimate the existing social
order, but it also claims some of its territory. . . . (Ibid.: 221).

Next Henry argues that such conclusions have serious ramifications for the sociology of law. First, the notion that a change in
formal law equals concrete changes in social control mechanisms
at the community level is erroneous because formal law is only
one element of the continuum of law. Indeed, when changes in
formal law do not account for existing forms of private justice, the
formal change either is likely to be absorbed into the established
social relations or discarded. Here, Henry follows Montesquieu
(1900: 58–80) who has argued that excessive punishment hinders
the execution of laws and that manners and customs cannot be
changed by law, and Ihering (1914: 178–179) who has suggested
that government is bound by laws that cannot and should not be
all encompassing since laws exist for the sake of society, not society for the sake of law. Moreover, Henry further argues that the
inverse relationship in the development of law is also true: any
change in private justice that does not account for the existing
structure of formal law will be adapted to the formal system of social control.

Thus, change in law must simultaneously recognize the autonomous yet interrelated elements and layers of law. Moreover, if
legal change is to occur, participants must "not create idealistic alternatives but reflect upon how human experience is related to the
totality of which it is a part. . . . Such change requires revelation
not revolution" (Henry, 1983: 93).

III. IMPLICATIONS FOR THE SOCIOLOGY OF LAW

To his credit Professor Henry points out the necessity for the
sociology of law to recognize that private justice exists as an element of law in its own right and has a definite impact on the structure of law. This theoretical recognition is of vital importance and
overcomes limitations of past and present theories that either ele-

954   HENRY'S SOCIOLOGY OF LAW

vate or ignore private justice. Henry argues forcefully and shows concrete evidence that private justice does indeed exist. Henry's argument for the integration of theory is much less successful. There are problems in both his theoretical construct and suggested methodology. Henry's theory may be condensed to five main points:

    1.   Various formal, structural elements of law and informal, micro-elements of social control (private justice) combine to create horizontal and vertical layers of law.

    2.   Taken together, these layers make up the continuum of law.

    3.   Structural and micro-layers of law are autonomous in that they are distinct and observable, but are also integrated in that each reacts to and helps shape the other.

    4.   Change within the continuum of law is caused by the interrelationship of structural and micro-layers.

    5.   Change is possible, therefore, only when participants realize the totality and interrelation of the elements of law.

There are several areas of critique where Henry's thesis appears to falter. The first is his theory of separate yet integrated elements and layers of law. His aspiration not to separate the elements contained within the continuum of law, nor determine private justice from formal structures has led Henry to develop a theory that is all encompassing, but difficult to apply concretely. If all elements are separate, yet all have some of the relations of the other, it becomes difficult to know where the analysis should begin: an infinite number of elements and layers seemingly relate to an infinite number of other elements and layers. Regrettably, Henry does not outline a clear construct to escape this dilemma. Moreover, the few times he does attempt to develop theoretical principles Henry runs into analytical walls.

To begin with, other than private justice we are told very little about potential elements and layers in the law continuum. Indeed, we are told that to categorize elements formally would destroy the integrative approach since all elements share relations with all other elements.[3] Thus, when Henry analyzes private justice and, in particular, discipline in the workplace, he does not view it as an isolated element, but rather as an interrelated part of the law continuum. Private justice, itself, is made up of semiautonomous elements, which Henry places into three layers to study workplace discipline: the state, economy and society; industry, organization, and management; and unions, co-workers and individual workers (1983: 97). These are interdependent parts of the whole continuum, each sharing social relations and distinguishable by the

---

    [3] For a similar use of private and formal law see Glennon, "The Use of Custom in Resolving Separation of Power Disputes," 64 *Boston University Law Review* 109 (1984).

source of their autonomy. Thus, some elements are structural and rest outside the organization where the discipline takes place, some are at the organizational level, and some elements are within it. Each has the ability to penetrate and shape the other (1983: 30). One can be left only with the conclusion that these elements are equal and moreover are never ending.

This is just what Henry seems to argue by announcing the need for a genuine pluralism in approach that utilizes a micro-analytic interpretative perspective that concentrates on the participants in the social construction of law (1983: 27). To engage in such a theoretical undertaking would be to dive into an ever-flowing stream of elements and layers, each sharing relations and helping to shape the other. While Henry does tell us that such an approach allows for one element or layer to dominate another, there is no theoretical impetus to uncover this and make the task easier. Rather, Henry's theory continuously calls on the analyst to find new interrelated elements and layers along the continuum of law.

If, in a relatively small unit of analysis such as work discipline, the analyst must take into account the breadth of elements and layers, each impacting the other, how are more general conclusions regarding the sociology of law to be made?

Henry does seem to come to the aid of the analyst by suggesting that similar interactions take place between elements no matter what the organization of work. A rigid control over discipline by management, a participatory form of joint management, and workers' control of decision-making all share the same interaction of elements within the law continuum. Thus, while the number of interrelated elements within the continuum of law may be infinite, Henry does outline some universal attributes as clues for research. But this raises another perplexing problem. How does law change? If the semiautonomous elements are universally evident, what difference does the form of work make, or the organization in which the work takes place, or the sociopolitical context in which the organization exists? Indeed, societal change seems to have relatively little impact on the elements of law. These theoretical constructs seem to dismiss the very potential of an integrative theory. While Henry's integrative theory allows for the dominance of one element over another because of historical conditions, it is the mere presence of the elements and their universal qualities that seem to interest him the most. In fact, the emphasis should be on the inverse relationship: that is, integrative theory should search for the dynamics that make law different, not universal.

In this regard, the author's work is a regression, and not an improvement, on the work of Ehrlich who not only integrated formal law with the development of private justice, but interrelated the development of law to the general development of society. Justice Benjamin Cardozo also has seen the importance of the dy-

956   HENRY'S SOCIOLOGY OF LAW

namic relationship of law to society. He has argued that the judicial process has a combination of forces including logic, history,
custom and utility; which force will dominate depends on the social interest served or impaired (Cardozo, 1921). In contrast,
Henry seems most interested in developing a theoretical construct
allowing for the mere existence of elements and layers rather than
the dynamics of their integration.

By misplacing the theoretical emphasis, Henry has formed unnecessary and troublesome assumptions. First, he suggests that
the entire interrelated continuum of law is designed to act as a
mechanism for social control. Indeed, this is the theoretical and
ideological underpinning of his entire work, but if one element of
law can dominate another, the legal dynamic might include a reaction by the social actors that may alter or dramatically change the
formal law.[4]

One may look at many social movements as examples where
the social actors played a definite role in shaping formal law far
beyond any definition of social control. In regard to the United
States, the populist movement of the 1890s, the union movement
of the 1930s, and the civil rights movement of the 1960s come to
mind. But if we seek to understand these legal changes originating
at the nonstructural level, the mechanisms by which the dynamic
interrelationship of elements occurs must be uncovered. A static
view of time and space in history is not enough.[5] The potential of
integrative theory can be unlocked when integrative theorists resist assumptions about social control and ask the following and
many similar questions. When does private justice come into conflict with formal law? How does one element of the continuum
gain dominance over another element? Are there any signals
within the development of the continuum that may alert a sociologist of law to a future legal crisis?

Thus, the thesis that law can be conceived of only as an agent
of social control is theoretical abortion to integrative theory.
When feudal law gave way to capitalist law during the Middle
Ages in Europe, laws protecting the right to private property
(which were developed as a result of dynamic changes in formal
and private justice) were designed not only to maintain social control, but to institute a social change (e.g., Anderson, 1974: 397–431).

If one element has the capacity to gain dominance over another, a theorist must also allow for the potential that either a
macro- or micro-bias may be correct.[6] That is, given certain condi-

---

[4] As an example of how private justice can impact formal law see Stein-
berg, "Church Control of a Municipality: Establishing a First Amendment Institutional Suit," 38 Stanford Law Review 1327 (1986).

[5] A similar point was made in Kelman, "American Labor Law and Legal
Formalism: How Legal Logic Shaped and Vitiated the Rights of American
Workers," 58 St. John's Law Review 1 (1983).

[6] For an example of how formal law can impact private justice see Simon,

tions and circumstances, a theorist may be correct in emphasizing
micro-social interaction, or macro-structures. Henry is correct that
neither may be seen in a determinist fashion: neither micro- or
macro-elements or layers can fully determine the shape and relations of law in the other, but while each interacts and together
form the law continuum, this supposition must not lead the analyst to preconceive an equality between elements. What exists in
concrete reality should be the guiding force in uncovering the form
of the interrelationship.[7]

If the possibility of dominance were left open, an integrative
theory that allows for, indeed looks for, such dynamics may lead to
a fruitful analysis. For example, in hunting and gathering societies
there was little or no hierarchy of government. In many of these
societies elders of both sexes acted as advisors but had no formal
institutional power to enforce their decisions. The daily demands
of existence required a consensus decision-making process. The result was little or no antisocial behavior (e.g., Goodman and Marx,
1978: 240–242). In such a society it is not difficult to see the dominance of private justice over structural forms of social control.
That is not to say, however, that structural conditions did not help
shape the form of private justice. Hunters and gatherers were nomadic and moved from area to area as the conditions of food and
weather prescribed. This structural reality had an effect on the
form of private justice, albeit a subordinate one.

In tribal societies the situation was much different. Here it
may be possible to argue that there was a more equal interrelationship between private and structural justice. Rather than being
nomadic, tribes became more stationary, cultivating the land and
domesticating animals for food. Most important for this discussion
was the rise of quasi-legal forms in the administration of justice.
Law and order was maintained through blends of authoritative
and public justice. As in decision-making, most tribes settled disputes through a combination of kinship ties, public opinion, and
authority figures related to the chieftan (Schapera, 1967: 135–202).
Thus, in a tribal society the dynamic relationship between private
and structural justice was more flexible and active as compared to
feudalism, for example, when royalty emerged with absolute
power and the interrelationship became heavily weighted toward
formal law (Anderson, 1974).

In this same vein, some general conclusions may be proposed
for modern industrial societies. In modern societies the structural
elements in the continuum of law have gained dominance over
micro-elements. This conclusion is based on the fact that the na-

"Rights and Redistribution in the Welfare System," 38 *Stanford Law Review*
1431 (1986).

    [7] For a particularly acute example of the potential inequality of elements
in their interrelation see Gordon, "Indian Religious Freedom and Governmental Development of Public Lands," 94 *Yale Law Journal* 1447 (1985).

958   HENRY'S SOCIOLOGY OF LAW

ture and impact of the community on the individual is far less direct than in hunting and gathering societies. Modern societies exhibit a more complex division of labor and relative reduction in the structural importance of community, as well as family. This does not mean that community and family values and socialization have evaporated, but only that relative to previous societies social discipline and socialization have taken on a more formal function through various institutions including education, work, and the criminal justice system. These institutions must be considered more structurally related to macro-social and macro-political developments than in previous social formations, resulting in a dominance of the structural elements of law.[8]

Again, this idea is not to suggest that structural elements determine the nature of private justice. It simply allows for the possibility that if certain historical conditions exist in specific periods of time, the dominance of one element of law over another may develop. Moreover, the degree of domination and the length of time of its existence is variable and can be changed by the social actors, particularly during general periods of social change.

This conclusion raises a further issue. If it is true that an integrative approach to the sociology of law must not simply describe the various elements of the continuum of law, is it not also true that general sociological theory must search for dynamic interrelations throughout the whole of society? Moreover, if general sociology must focus on dynamic interrelationships, law can be understood only in its interrelation to the rest of society and must not be viewed in isolation from the other elements.[9] The potential of an integrative approach is now greater: if an understanding of the dynamic of law and society is gained, and if the interrelationship of the structure and nonstructural elements within, outside, and through law is made clear, then a complete integrative understanding of the sociology of law becomes possible.

One last implication of Henry's integrative theory merits discussion. He argues that only when social actors realize the interrelated nature of law elements can constructive changes be applied. His argument is based on the belief that actions within the continuum often are focused on a particular aspect of law rather than on its totality. It is this "diversification with its powers of mystification which stifles the possibility of liberation" (1983: 181).

Putting aside Henry's overemphasis of law's social control

---

[8] Institutional influence on private justice often is caused by direct governmental involvement. Private justice is monitored and steps toward mitigating its impact often are suggested by federal government institutions. For example, see Kerwin, "Assessing the Effects of Consensual Processes in Regulatory Programs: Methodological and Policy Issues," 32 *American University Law Review* 401 (1983).

[9] For an example of how societal development can affect law see Bell, "The 1983 James McCormick Mitchell Lecture—A Hurdle Too High: Class Based Roadblocks to Racial Remediation," 33 *Buffalo Law Review* 1 (1984).

function and the extreme difficulty in understanding all of the elements and layers contained within his integrative theory, Henry's belief in the power of revelation is at best still only an idealistic hope. People are concerned with particular elements of the law continuum because of the activity of their everyday lives. To ask someone to step outside that existence and become fully integrated is surely wishful thinking. While it is true that people are not mere dupes of circumstance and have the ability to act on those circumstances, actions are not divorced from the social context. Within the continuum of law, the structural and nonstructural elements have long interrelated dynamic histories. An analysis of the dynamic may well lead to an understanding of conditions, which may in turn lead to change, but the theory itself has relatively little direct impact. Rather it is people dynamically acting on and reacting to concrete elements of the law continuum that cause change. They do so, however, because of the conditions found within the dynamic, not the theory. Law, itself, contains internal and external interrelations and changes continuously, and therefore, whether or not a proposed legal change is possible depends not only on the level of consciousness of the social actors, but on the conditions and development of the legal dynamic, as well as the conditions and dynamic of the society as a whole. The purpose of an integrative theory of law, therefore, should be to uncover the interrelated conditions of formal law and private justice, for not only does this outline the concrete conditions of the continuum, but having accomplished this, may point to a potential consciousness that is not only raised, but constructively directed.

IV. TOWARD AN INTEGRATIVE THEORY FOR THE SOCIOLOGY OF LAW

There are several points in Henry's proposal for an integrative theory of law that are useful starting points. His insistence on looking at law as continuous, interrelated parts indeed has merit. Moreover, his desire to view social actors in their everyday life is equally correct. Law is not an abstract category that can be understood apart from human beings. Rather, law is a human creation that acts and reacts to all elements contained within it. However, an integrative theory should not be concerned only with a description of various elements of the law. Rather, the main focus of integrative theory should be on uncovering the dynamic activity within and between elements.

In attempting to employ such a theory it must be understood that people cannot simply change law as they see fit. This is not to view micro-elements of law as rigid or predetermined by the macro-elements; both structural and private justice elements are simply parts of the specific history and conditions of the law continuum. Change occurs when the dynamic between private justice

and formal law gives rise to concrete conditions that allow for
legal change, but these conditions are always connected with the
general development of society.

Thus, the goal of integrative theory should be to create a clear
picture of the dynamic. And Henry has outlined the first crucial
step for this by calling attention to the interrelated nature of the
continuum of law. What is needed next is a clearer understanding
of the processes of both micro- and macro-forces that combine to
make up the law continuum, and how those forces relate to the
macro-structures of society.

To begin the task of exploring the dynamic of integrated theory requires a rejection of two main approaches influencing the
study of the sociology of law. In the United States the approach
has traditionally emphasized the mechanism for, and the function
of, consent to law. Implicit in this approach is that law is utilized
at all levels of society as a means for consolidating the consensus
of values and for social control. As Henry has argued, social control will not be effective if it is inconsistent with the psyche, or
culture as expressed at the private and community level. Nor, it is
important to add, will social control be effective if it is at odds with
the current political and economic structures. When congruent
with social development, formal law sanctions and private legitimizing functions of law have powerful impacts. They are not,
however, inevitable and universal ramifications of law.

Simultaneously, an integrative theory of law must leave open
the possibility that law is not simply reflective of the macro-social
structures. Often implicit in this second major approach is the notion that there is a direct relation of law to economic structures,
power, and ideology, and that these structures determine the
shape and impact of law. It should follow that as laws are adhered
to at the private and community level, it is because of some form
of false consciousness.

While the reduction of law from macro-structures can provide
critical, even necessary, insights connecting law with other social
structures within society, that connection is not necessarily unidirectional. In periods when society is reproducing effectively, law
and other macro-structures may indeed be in relative unison and
greatly influence private means of law, particularly when historical conditions allow macro-structures to gain dominance. However, during these periods the consent to law is not merely a false
consciousness, but is internalized and promoted at the micro-level.
This does not preclude change originating at the micro-level, however. If it did, not only would all changes in law simply mirror
macro-structures, but the many examples of legal change sought
by groups and classes within society would appear negated.

An integrative theory of law requires a different approach.
Whether or not law is a mechanism for social control through private consent, or whether changes in macro-social structures di-

rectly influence formal and private law, or whether private forms emerge to challenge existing principles of formal law and indirectly macro-social structures, are questions to be studied and not assumed by theoretical principle.

An integrative theory may provide not only an explanation of the development of law, but of a great deal of other social phenomena as well.

GARY ITZKOWITZ is Assistant Professor of Sociology at the University of Wisconsin, Stevens Point, teaching theory and macro-sociology. He is co-author of *How the Poor Would Remedy Poverty*, (Washington, D.C.: Coalition on Human Needs, 1988).

REFERENCES

ABEL, Richard (1982) *The Politics of Informal Justice.* New York: Academic Press.

ANDERSON, Perry (1974) *Lineages of the Absolutist State.* London: New Left Books.

AUSTIN, John (1832) *Lectures on Jurisprudence.* London: John Murray.

CARDOZO, Benjamin (1921) *The Nature of the Judicial Process.* New Haven: Yale University Press.

COLLINS, Randall (1981) "On the Microfoundations of Macrosociology," 86 *American Journal of Sociology* 984.

EHRLICH, Eugen (1913) *Fundamental Principles of the Sociology of Law.* Cambridge, MA: Harvard University Press.

GOODMAN, Norman, and Gary T. MARX (1978) *Society Today.* New York: Random House.

GIDDENS, Anthony (1979) *Central Problems in Social Theory.* London: Macmillan.

GURVITCH, Georges (1947) *Sociology of Law.* London: Routledge & Kegan Paul.

HENRY, Stuart (1983) *Private Justice: Towards Integrated Theorising in the Sociology of Law.* London: Routledge & Kegan Paul.

IHERING, Rudolph von (1914) *Law as a Means to an End.* Boston: Boston Book.

KAMENKA, Eugene, and Alice TAY (1980) *Law and Social Control.* London: Edward Arnold.

KNORR-CETINA, K., and Arron CICOUREL (1981) *Advances in Social Theory and Methodology: Toward an Integration of Micro-, and Macro-Sociologies.* London: Routledge and Kegan Paul.

LLEWELLYN, Karl (1930) "A Realistic Jurisprudence—the Next Step," 30 *Columbia Law Review* 431.

MARX, Karl (1965) *The German Ideology.* London: Lawrence & Wishart.

MONTESQUIEU, Baron de (1900) *The Spirit of Laws.* New York: D. Appleton.

PARSONS, Talcott (1937) *The Structure of Social Action.* New York: McGraw-Hill.

POUND, Roscoe (1903) *Outlines of Lectures on Jurisprudence.* Cambridge, Mass.: Harvard University Press.

SANTOS, Benedito (1980) "Law and Community: The Changing Nature of State Power in Late Capitalism," 8 *International Journal of the Sociology of Law* 379.

SCHAPERA, I. (1967) *Government and Politics in Tribal Societies.* New York: Schocken Books.

UNGER, Roberto (1976) *Law in Modern Society.* New York: Free Press.

[7]

MOVING FROM INTEGRATIVE TO CONSTITUTIVE THEORIES OF LAW: COMMENT ON ITZKOWITZ

CHRISTINE B. HARRINGTON

Private Justice examines disciplinary practices in different workplace settings (i.e., hierarchical, participatory, and cooperative) in light of theoretical debates about the relationship between social structure and human agency, on the one hand, and the relationship between formal and informal law, on the other hand. This book challenges us to rethink how these relationships are conceptualized in a wide range of sociolegal theories and it examines the organization of "private justice" or nonstate law, in workplace discipline. Itzkowitz states that Henry succeeds in showing the "existence" of private justice, but he argues beyond that Henry's integrated theory of law is limited in a number of ways. Among its limitations, according to Itzkowitz, is that the aspiration of integrated theory *not* to separate parts (i.e., structure and action, formal and informal law) makes it "difficult to know where the analysis should begin" (p. 954). Rather than oppose the aspiration for integrated theory, Itzkowitz argues that "an integrative theory of law requires a different approach" (p. 960). Itzkowitz's disagreements with Henry exemplify some of the contemporary debates in law and social theory. In particular, as I read Itzkowitz's comment on *Private Justice*, he takes issue with two aspects of Henry's approach. First, he questions the utility of legal pluralism as a methodology and/or basis for integrated theory. Second, he questions the value of approaches that deconstruct relations of social control as opposed to those that predict which forms of law will prevail under certain social conditions.

Although Itzkowitz embraces legal pluralism, for him it is only a way of describing the existence of different legal systems. He argues that Henry has "misplac[ed] the theoretical emphasis" by focusing on "the mere existence of elements and layers rather than the dynamics of their integration" (p. 956). But Henry wants more from legal pluralism than simply descriptions of multiple legal forms. In his study, Henry uses legal pluralism as both a framework for describing semiautonomous legal forms (formal and informal), and a methodology for studying disciplinary practices at work. Both applications are at odds with Itzkowitz's implicit understanding of legal pluralism. Legal pluralism for Itzkowitz organizes "various formal, structural elements of law

964   COMMENT ON ITZKOWITZ

and informal, micro-elements of social control (private justice)"
along what he calls "the continuum of law" (p. 954). In contrast,
Henry seeks to avoid the kind of legal pluralism that assumes an *a
priori* ordering or hierarchy among legal forms.

Instead Henry designs an analytical map made up of different
layers of sociolegal relations. With this map as his guide, Henry
examines the relationship *between* semiautonomous and interdependent legal forms (formal and informal) in the *context* of everyday experiences that are also comprehended as part of a larger social structure or "totality." Henry finds fault with traditional
theories of legal pluralism and the ethnography of dispute processing literature, because both fail to "achieve a dialectical analysis"
of relationships of social control that, for Henry, explain the constitution of workplace discipline (1983: 57). For Henry, legal pluralism is a dialectical theory of sociolegal integration.

If, however, Henry said more about what a successful dialectical analysis was and paid less attention to restacking the lumber of
previous generations of sociolegal theorists with whom he takes issue, we might have a clearer sense of his contribution to integrated
theory. It is conceivable that a reader, even one who is more theoretically sympathetic thàn Itzkowitz, might not fully appreciate
Henry's project because there is a lingering ambivalence in his
work about the connection between where we have been and
where we are heading in the "sociological movement of law."[1] For
instance, Henry objects to approaches that link social structure
and law in a correspondence fashion (e.g., formal law corresponds
to hierarchial organization and informal law corresponds to cooperative organizations).[2] He also does not want to argue for what
he calls "macro" theories, which emphasize structural determi-
nants of workplace discipline (i.e., economy and state) over the
meaningful actions by managers, union leaders, or workers. Nor
does he claim to privilege "micro" theories that focus on motives
and interests of managers and workers. Nonetheless, Henry re-
trains the macro/micro distinction in his own study, albeit with the
purpose of integra.ing them. He takes us back to what he has argued are limiting paradigms and says it is "necessary to explore
the processes of interpenetration of the micro-structures with the
macro and vice versa" (ibid.: 62). Toward the end, Henry appears
to let go of these paradigms when he says it is "not necessary that
the two explanations given above [micro and macro] are mutually
exclusive," but then he returns to them when he concludes that
"an adequate theory of law must address both the macro and the
micro without losing the autonomy of either" (ibid.: 216). Henry

---

[1] This phrase is borrowed from the title of Hunt's (1978) book on the intellectual roots of sociolegal theory.

[2] Similarly, Nelken (1986) argues that Henry is ambivalent in his treatment of the "correspondence thesis."

seeks to transform the dominant explanations into distinct but compatible analytical frameworks.

Is integration a theoretical problem that demands attention, or is it a barrier to the larger theoretical project Henry wants to advance? I am inclined to argue that it is a barrier, but join with Henry's aspiration to build a social theory that does not reduce law to an outcome of behavior or social structure. His larger claim is that (ibid.: 61):

> By recognising the dialectical relationship between structure and social action and how these are interdependent and mutually implying, we begin to see the possibility of transcending the view that law is either the product of structure, or the outcome of interaction. We begin to glimpse how informalism is not so much an alternative form of law but a necessary part of the ideological process whereby the crystallised, formalised, objective-like qualities of law are created and sustained in an on-going manner. It is necessary to reveal the ways in which in acting at the informal spontaneous level of interaction, total social structures are conceptualised and implied as though they were objective realities having real consequences.

Instead of calling this move an effort to establish integrated theory, it might be more accurate to call it a constitutive theory of law. As Henry himself states (ibid.: 68):

> An adequate theory of law, then, must be sufficiently sensitive to capture both the totality of social structure and the particular of human action, the macro and the micro, without absorbing the one into the other. Neither is a product of the other, but each implies the other. Both have autonomy but neither is completely free from the influence of the other. From the integrated theoretical perspective then, law can only be adequately analysed through the processes whereby it is constituted.

His study of discipline at work focuses on "the ways people in their doings with each other construct and reconstruct the manifest appearances of law" (ibid.). Thus, similar to some contemporary studies of legal ideology,[3] Henry's study of factory law takes us beyond the task of bridging structure and action and moves us toward a constitutive theory of workplace discipline.

Itzkowitz holds on to the macro/micro distinction, but for reasons other than those mentioned by Henry. Specifically, Itzkowitz wants an integrated theory that is able to *predict* which factors are likely to determine the form of law. Henry is instead engaged in the deconstruction of factory law; "showing what is taken to be the reality of private justice . . . is merely one surface appearance of a wider range of social control" (ibid.: 98). Henry argues that the nature of factory law itself "is actually part of the process whereby

---

[3] For example, see the "Special Issue on Law and Ideology," 22 *Law & Society Review* (1988).

966   COMMENT ON ITZKOWITZ

it [factory law] is constituted as a reality, separate from the actions
of those who create it" (ibid.: 71). Thus, while Itzkowitz seeks an
integrative theory that can predict which factors determine law,
Henry's approach takes us in the opposite direction—toward an
analysis of the ways in which factory law is constituted as a reality
about the workplace.

In addition, Itzkowitz questions whether a theory can address
the "possibility of dominance" (p. 956) if it does not specify which
elements of law will prevail under particular social conditions.
Under what conditions might semiautonomous legal forms come
into conflict with one another and as a result become relatively
less "semiautonomous?" This raises an important yet difficult issue for Henry's approach because in his study private justice is
thoroughly imbricated in workplace discipline. Yet the question of
dominance is central to Henry's study. British workers in companies with joint management-worker disciplinary processes, for example, speak of "aspects of the social control package," and from
their narratives Henry concludes that "although some general protection exists through union involvement in many cases it would
seem that management were able to impose their own views on
what should happen" (1983: 165). What follows from these insights is not a set of general principles or a hypothesis on the relationship between social structure and social action, but an approach to sociolegal research that "emphasise the *partiality* of any
particular form and the interdependence of it with the totality"
(ibid.: 216, emphasis added).

The problem of linking human agency and social structure in
studies of law is a common problem whether one's goal is to predict or deconstruct sociolegal relations. It is also not a new problem. There are, however, new sets of issues that have come into
the discussion concerning agency and structure. Integrative approaches that unite macro- and micro-perspectives in a single theoretical framework (see Giddens, 1979) may provide new insights
concerning law in society such as the partiality thesis. Beyond
merely reformulating the relationship between micro- and macro-
explanations, they may also raise additional theoretical problems.
For as Henry notes, "above all else [an integrative approach]
recognises that action and structure presuppose one another and as
such cannot be addressed separately" (ibid.: 64).

CHRISTINE B. HARRINGTON is an Assistant Professor at New
York University in the Department of Politics. She has written a
book entitled, *Shadow Justice* (1985) and published several articles
on the alternative dispute resolution movement in the United
States. The politics of a new informalism movement in administrative law and its relationship to regulatory litigation activity is
examined in a recent article, "Reforming Regulation: Creating

Gaps and Making Markets," *Law & Policy* (1988). She is engaged in a study of the formation of federal administrative law practice which focuses on the regulatory bar in the U.S. Circuit Courts of Appeals and the role of the legal profession in shaping this practice.

REFERENCES

GIDDENS, Anthony (1979) *Central Problems in Social Theory: Action, Structure and Contradiction in Social Analysis.* New York: Macmillan.

HENRY, Stuart (1983) *Private Justice: Towards Integrated Theorising in the Sociology of Law.* London: Routledge and Kegan Paul.

HUNT, Alan (1978) *The Sociological Movement in Law.* London: Macmillan.

LAW & SOCIETY REVIEW (1988) "Special Issue on Law and Ideology," 22 *Law & Society Review.*

NELKEN, David (1986) "Beyond the Study of 'Law and Society'?," 1986 *American Bar Foundation Research Journal* 323.

[8]

LEGAL PLURALISM

SALLY ENGLE MERRY

I. INTRODUCTION

The intellectual odyssey of the concept of legal pluralism moves from the discovery of indigenous forms of law among remote African villagers and New Guinea tribesmen to debates concerning the pluralistic qualities of law under advanced capitalism. In the last decade, the concept of legal pluralism has been applied to the study of social and legal ordering in urban industrial societies, primarily the United States, Britain, and France. Indeed, given a sufficiently broad definition of the term legal system, virtually every society is legally plural, whether or not it has a colonial past. Legal pluralism is a central theme in the reconceptualization of the law/society relation.

Early twentieth century studies examined indigenous law ways among tribal and village peoples in colonized societies in Africa, Asia, and the Pacific. Social scientists (primarily anthropologists) were interested in how these peoples maintained social order without European law (e.g., Malinowski, 1926). As they documented the rich variety of social control, social pressure, custom, customary law, and judicial procedure within small-scale societies, these anthropologists gradually realized that colonized peoples had both indigenous law and European law. Colonial law was reshaping the social life of these villages and tribes in subtle ways, even when it seemed remote. Indeed, as Chanock observed for colonial Africa, "The law was the cutting edge of colonialism, . . ." (1985: 4). Tribes and villages had some law developed over the generations on to which formal rational law was imposed by the European colonial powers. The imposed law, forged for industrial capitalism rather than an agrarian or pastoral way of life, embodied very different principles and procedures. Scholars termed these situations legal pluralism. They recognized that the introduction of European colonial law created a plurality of legal orders but overlooked, to a large extent, the complexity of previous legal orders.

For the proponents of empire in the nineteenth century, this imposition of European law was a great gift, substituting civilized

This article was completed in February, 1988 and covers literature from 1978 to early 1988. I am grateful to Peter Fitzpatrick, John Griffiths, Christine Harrington, Robert Hayden, Stuart Henry, and June Starr for helpful suggestions and comments on earlier drafts.

870   LEGAL PLURALISM

law for the anarchy and fear that they believed gripped the lives of
the colonized peoples, freeing them from the scourges of war,
witchcraft, and tyranny (Ranger, 1983). In Africa, the British and
the French superimposed their law onto indigenous law, incorporating customary law as long as it was not "repugnant to natural
justice, equity, and good conscience," or "inconsistent with any
written law," (Okoth-Ogendo, 1979: 160; Adewoye, 1986: 60; Bentsi-
Enchill, 1969). The repugnancy principle was used to outlaw unacceptable African customs. That the European legal system also
helped to mold a cooperative labor force to serve the new extrac-
tive industries or to produce cash crops for export was probably
not lost on the colonial administrators (cf., Chanock, 1985;
Comaroff, 1985; Comaroff and Comaroff, 1986; Moore, 1986a).

Yet, legal pluralism goes far deeper than the joining of European and traditional forms of law. We are only now beginning to
explore the extent to which previously colonized societies are legally and culturally plural. The Europeans were not the first
outside influence bringing a new legal system to many Third
World peoples. Indigenous law had been shaped by conquests and
migrations for centuries. For example, Geertz describes the legal
complexity of Java as the product of the encounters of an original
group of settlers from South China and north Vietnam with India
states, Chinese trading communities, Islamic missionaries, Dutch
and British colonizers, Japanese occupation forces, and presently,
the Indonesian state (1983: 226). As we engage in careful historical
study, we throw off the notion that the pasts of traditional societies were unchanging (Ranger, 1983; Chanock, 1985).

What is legal pluralism? It is generally defined as a situation
in which two or more legal systems coexist in the same social field
(Pospisil, 1971; Griffiths 1986a; Moore, 1986a).[1] Pospisil, in his pio-
neering work on legal levels, claims that "every functioning subgroup in a society has its own legal system which is necessarily different in some respects from those of the other subgroups" (1971:
107). By subgroups he means units such as family, lineage, community, and political confederation that are integral parts of a ho-
mogenous society, hierarchically ranked, and essentially similar in
rules and procedure. Recent work defines "legal system" broadly
to include the system of courts and judges supported by the state
as well as nonlegal forms of normative ordering. Some of these
are part of institutions such as factories, corporations, and universities and include written codes, tribunals, and security forces,
sometimes replicating the structure and symbolic form of state law
(Macaulay, 1986; Henry, 1983). Other normative orders are informal systems in which the processes of establishing rules, securing

---

[1] In an important essay on the definition of legal pluralism, Griffiths defines it as "that state of affairs, for any social field, in which behavior pursuant
to more than one legal order occurs (1986a: 2)."

compliance to these rules, and punishing rulebreakers seem natural and taken for granted, as occurs within families, work groups, and collectives (Abel, 1982; Henry, 1985). Thus, virtually every society is legally plural. This approach runs the risk of defining legal system so broadly that all social control forms are included (see further Comaroff and Roberts, 1981).

Griffiths distinguishes between the "social science" view of legal pluralism as an empirical state of affairs in society (the coexistence within a social group of legal orders that do not belong to a single "system") and what he calls a "juristic" view of legal pluralism as a particular problem of dual legal systems created when European countries established colonies that superimposed their legal systems on preexisting systems (1986a: 5, 8). A legal system is pluralistic in the juristic sense when the sovereign commands different bodies of law for different groups of the population varying by ethnicity, religion, nationality, or geography, and when the parallel legal regimes are all dependent on the state legal system. This situation creates a range of complex legal problems, such as the need to decide when a subgroup's law applies to a particular transaction or conflict, to what group particular individuals belong, how a person can change which law is applicable to him or her (educated Africans in the colonial era, for example, chafed at being judged under African law rather than European law), choice of law rules for issues between people of different groups, and determinations of which subjects, particularly family law, and in which geographical areas subgroup law should be accepted (Griffiths, 1986a: 7). It is often difficult to determine what the subgroup's rules are, particularly when they are not part of a written tradition. As we will see below, even those legal systems with written codes, such as Islamic law, are often embedded in very different ways of thinking about the fact/law dichotomy, the nature of evidence, and the meaning of judging (Rosen, 1980–81; Geertz, 1983; Messick, 1986).

Hooker provides a masterful and comprehensive overview of legal pluralism in this sense, surveying plural legal systems in Asia, Africa, and the Middle East (1975). He defines legal pluralism as circumstances "in the contemporary world which have resulted from the transfer of whole legal systems across cultural boundaries" (Ibid.: 1). Legal problems of the juristic kind confront leaders of many post-colonial societies, who widely regard their complex legal systems as frustrating, messy, and obstructive to progress (Bentsi-Enchill, 1969; Griffiths, 1986a). Contemporary elites in Africa see modernization and nation-building as requiring a unified legal system, often drawing on models of European law (Okoth-Ogendo, 1979: 165).[2] As post colonial societies endeavor to adopt uniform state law, however, they meet with pockets of in-

---

[2] To this extent, they appear to have accepted the dominant legal ideology of Western society (see Merry, 1986).

872   LEGAL PLURALISM

tense resistance from those groups whose law has been preserved in some fashion (see further, Geertz, 1983: 228).

This review discusses primarily the social science version of legal pluralism. According to the design of the Fifth Issue, the review focuses on literature from the past decade, although I have included earlier work when it is important for my argument. I focused on materials published in English, although there is a substantial non-English literature. Central resources in the study of legal pluralism are the new *Journal of Legal Pluralism and Unofficial Law*, created in 1981,[3] and several important international conferences along with the books they have generated.

II. CLASSIC LEGAL PLURALISM AND THE NEW LEGAL PLURALISM

Research on colonial and post-colonial societies produced a version of legal pluralism I call "classic legal pluralism." This is the analysis of the intersections of indigenous and European law. Beginning in the late 1970s, there has been an interest among sociolegal scholars in applying the concept of legal pluralism to noncolonized societies, particularly to the advanced industrial countries of Europe and the United States. This move produces a version of legal pluralism I call the "new legal pluralism." A number of studies explore contemporary legal pluralism in the United States (e.g., Moore, 1973; Forer, 1979; Merry, 1979; Engel, 1980, 1984, 1987; Nader, 1980; Greenhouse, 1982, Buckle and Thomas-Buckle, 1982; Macaulay, 1986), Britain (e.g., Henry, 1983; 1985), and the Netherlands (e.g., van den Bergh *et al.*, 1980; Strijbosch, 1985; van den Bergh *et al.*, 1980). There are also several historical studies of legal pluralism in these countries (e.g., Auerbach, 1983; Arthurs, 1985; Bossy, 1983). Case studies on legal pluralism presented at a conference on the imposition of law included the American Indians, Hungarian farm cooperatives, British trade unions, British game laws, and the American death penalty along with the more traditional topics of legal pluralism in New Guinea, Kenya, and Niger (Burman and Harrell-Bond, 1979). Legal pluralism has expanded from a concept that refers to the relations between colonized and colonizer to relations between dominant groups and subordinate groups, such as religious, ethnic, or cultural minorities, immigrant groups, and unofficial forms of ordering located in social networks or institutions (Woodman,

---

[3] This journal, under the editorship of John Griffiths in the Netherlands, incorporates international scholarship on legal pluralism to a far greater extent than the *Law & Society Review*. The *Journal of Legal Pluralism* includes important theoretical articles, book reviews, and case studies on diverse subjects such as the role of public letter writers in the development of the legal profession in Ibadan, Nigeria between 1904 and 1960 (Adewoye, 1986), the coexistence of indigenous, Islamic, British colonial, and post-colonial Nigerian law in Northern Nigeria (Salamone, 1983), and the acquisition of indigenous Hawaiian lands through legal means (Lam, 1985).

1987–88: 3–4; Macaulay, 1986). Moore provides a useful summary of concepts of legal and social pluralism in her overview of ways of comparing legal systems of the world (1986b: 15–24).

According to the new legal pluralism, plural normative orders are found in virtually all societies. This is an extraordinarily powerful move, in that it places at the center of investigation the relationship between the official legal system and other forms of ordering that connect with but are in some ways separate from and dependent on it. The new legal pluralism moves away from questions about the effect of law on society or even the effect of society on law toward conceptualizing a more complex and interactive relationship between official and unofficial forms of ordering. Instead of mutual influences between two separate entities, this perspective sees plural forms of ordering as participating in the same social field. In his remarks at the Bellagio Conference on People's Law and State Law (see Allott and Woodman, 1985), Francis Snyder argues that any dualistic distinction, such as that between folk and state law, is misleading because plural normative orders are part of the same system in any particular social context and are usually intertwined in the same social micro-processes (Griffiths, 1985: 17–18). The particulars of the relationship in any social location are historically derived and unsettled.

The new legal pluralism draws on the rich ethnographic and theoretical work from classic legal pluralism. Among the significant contributions of classic legal pluralism there are, I think, three of particular importance. First is the analysis of the interaction between normative orders that are fundamentally different in their underlying conceptual structure. Second is an attention to the elaboration of customary law as historically derived. Third is the delineation of the dialectic between normative orders. In classic legal pluralism, this dialectic takes place in situations in which different orders are readily identified and the dynamics of resistance and restructuring by groups experiencing the imposition of a very different normative order are relatively easy to see. When Pospisil reports the Kapauku Papuans' response to the introduction of Dutch law, for example, it is relatively easy to identify the actors, since Kapauku law and Dutch law are quite distinct. In this situation there are clearly limits to the penetration of Dutch law, areas in which the Kapauku have taken Dutch law and made it their own, and areas in which Dutch law has become part of the political struggle between different factions, some more attuned to the colonial order than others (1981).

In societies without colonial pasts, however, the nonstate forms of normative ordering are more difficult to see. They blend more readily into the landscape and, aside from some notable exceptions (such as Ehrlich's concept of "living law," (1913), Gurvitch's "social law," (1947) and Macaulay's work on private ordering (1963)) were generally ignored until the mid 1970s. To rec-

874   LEGAL PLURALISM

ognize legal pluralism at home required rejecting what Griffiths
calls the "ideology of legal centralism," the notion that the state
and the system of lawyers, courts, and prisons is the only form of
ordering (1986a). Indeed, scholars trained in legal positivism are
taught that law and ordering take place in courthouses and law offices, not in corporate gossip, university regulations and tribunals,
or neighborhood bars (on this point, see Arthurs, 1985). It is probably no accident that many of the prominent scholars in the new
legal pluralism, such as Richard Abel, David Engel, Marc Galanter, Peter Fitzpatrick, Sally Falk Moore, Boaventura de Sousa
Santos, and Francis Snyder began their sociolegal research in post-
colonial societies in which legal pluralism was an obvious and unambiguous fact of life.

     In sum, research on legal pluralism began in the study of colo-
nial societies in which an imperialist nation, equipped with a centralized and codified legal system, imposed this system on societies
with far different legal systems, often unwritten and lacking formal structures for judging and punishing. This kind of legal pluralism is embedded in relations of unequal power. The concept
has been expanded in recent years to describe legal relations in advanced industrial countries, but here, discussions of legal pluralism
are quite different. They center on a rejection of the law-centered-
ness of traditional studies of legal phenomena, arguing that not all
law takes place in the courts (e.g., Nader and Todd, 1978; Arthurs,
1985). The concern is to document other forms of social regulation
that draw on the symbols of the law, to a greater or lesser extent,
but that operate in its shadows, its parking lots, and even down the
street in mediation offices. Thus, in contexts in which the dominance of a central legal system is unambiguous, this thread of argument worries about missing what else is going on; the extent to
which other forms of regulation outside law constitute law.

     These two contexts make odd companions. Their central ad-
versaries, the positions against which they are arguing, are quite
different. They come out of different scholarly traditions. The nature of the relationship between the systems seems quite different.
In the former, there is an unambiguous imposition or dominance
of one system over the other; in the latter, the nature of the
linkage is more fluid and opaque. Yet, on closer inspection, even
dominant colonial legal orders failed to penetrate fully, encountered pockets of resistance, and were absorbed and co-opted, as
Kidder has shown clearly in the Indian case (1974; 1979). Further,
in industrial societies, despite the apparent autonomy of nonjudicial spheres, the legal system stands in a relation of superior power
to other systems of regulation as the ultimate source of coercive
power (Abel, 1982; Merry, 1986; Yngvesson, 1985). Thus, there are
ways in which joining these two contexts of legal pluralism enhances our understanding of the interaction of plural orders rather
than obstructing it.

III. FOLK LAW, INDIGENOUS LAW, STATE LAW, LAWYER'S LAW: DEFINING THE TERMS

There are a wide variety of terms used to discuss the parts which make up legally plural societies: the systems or normative orders that make up a legally plural situation. Each is discredited in various ways because the term carries with it unwanted perjorative implications. The terminological debate concerning state law is the easier one: commonly used terms are law, state law, lawyers' law, official law, and bourgeois legality. Names for nonstate law form a far greater tangle. The early work in classic legal pluralism referred to a distinction between law and custom. Diamond, in an influential article, described the relations dichotomously (1973: 322–323):

Custom—spontaneous, traditional, personal, commonly known, corporate, relatively unchanging—is the modality of primitive society; law is the instrument of civilization, of political society sanctioned by organized force, presumably above society at large, and buttressing a new set of social interests. Law and custom both involve the regulation of behavior but their characters are entirely distinct; no evolutionary balance has been struck between developing law and custom, whether traditional or emergent.

Rejecting the notion that custom is a form of primitive law that will gradually develop into state law, Diamond argues instead that the advance of law contradicts and extinguishes custom.

But what is custom? In colonial settings, pre-colonial law recognized or accepted by the colonial rulers after conquest or takeover was labeled customary law (e.g., Hooker, 1975). This law was often predominantly oral rather than written and derived from sources of authority outside the colonial state (Snyder, 1981b: 49). Yet, a rich body of recent ethno/historical research in Africa, Indonesia, and Papua New Guinea argues that the notion of an unchanging custom or even customary law was a myth of the colonial era, while customary law itself was a product of the colonial encounter (Colson, 1976; Benda-Beckmann, 1979; Fitzpatrick, 1980; Snyder, 1981a, 1981b; Ranger, 1983; Chanock, 1985; Gordon and Meggitt, 1985; Moore, 1986a; Starr and Collier, 1987, 1989).

Snyder, for example, argues that customary law was not simply an adapted or transformed version of indigenous law, but a new form created within the context of the colonial state (1981b). Through a detailed history of the changing social position of the rain priest among a group of rice farmers in Senegal, Snyder shows how customary law was created. Senegalese more familiar with European languages and customs served as intermediaries, interpreters of indigenous law to Europeans. The Europeans, in turn, accepted those versions of customary law which meshed best with their own ideology of land ownership as well as other legal relations. Snyder concludes (Ibid.: 74, 76):

876   LEGAL PLURALISM

Customary law in the Casamance [Senegal], as elsewhere,
was a concept and a legal form that originated in specific
historical circumstances, namely the period in the transformation of pre-capitalist social relations that saw the consolidation of the colonial state. . . . Produced in particular historical circumstances, the notion of 'customary law' was an
ideology of colonial domination. The concept of 'customary
law' itself manifested an attempt to reinterpret African
legal forms in terms of European legal categories, which
formed part of the ideology of those classes most closely
associated with the colonial state. The designation of African law as 'customary' because it was oral, though apparently technical, embodied and masked an essentially political conclusion that it was subordinate to the colonial law
of European origin.

Snyder urges a full reanalysis of the role law plays in post-colonial societies from the perspective of dependency theory rather
than from that of modernization theory (1980). Rather than viewing plural legal orders as barriers to modernization, he suggests
that their creation was a product of the expansion of the European
capitalist order throughout the world over the last 400 years, an
expansion which has gradually incorporated the most remote societies into a single economic system despite its fractionated political
structures. These traditional forms of law were constructs of the
European expansion and capitalist transformation, as were also the
tribes, villages, chiefs and many other features of apparently traditional social systems (Wolf, 1982). Ranger argues, for example,
that the vision of a traditional, unchanging African past ruled by
long-established custom was a creation of colonial administrators
of the early twentieth century in an effort to restore some order
after the chaotic years of the nineteenth century (1983: 250–251).

If the nonstate forms of social ordering in legally plural situations are not customs or customary law, then what can we call
them? A symposium in 1978, The Social Consequences of Imposed
Law, debated using imposed law but abandoned the term as inadequate since all law is experienced as imposed in some ways, yet all
law is also to some degree accepted rather than simply imposed
(Burman and Harrell-Bond, 1979: 2). Kidder, pointing to the enthusiasm with which Indians adopted British law, suggested instead the concept of external law, which takes into account the
"sources of power at different levels of externality" (1979: 296).
He suggests thinking of multiple layers of legal organization at
various levels of externality with struggles between these levels,
rather than just law and custom (Ibid.: 299).

In a later paper, Galanter suggests the terms indigenous ordering and indigenous law to refer to forms of ordering outside the
official system (1981: 17). But recent work indicates that even
those societies analyzed as if they were untouched by European
culture, and in that sense "indigenous," were vulnerable to outside

influences at the time of early ethnographic research (Fitzpatrick, 1985). Indeed, Pospisil, an anthropologist who worked during the early contact period between a group of New Guinea peoples and the Dutch government and authored a classic text on indigenous law, points out that he himself was an important pawn in local politics, co-opted by one faction (1979). On a second trip to the Kapauku, he was surprised to find that the Dutch colonial administrators were using his book on Kapauku law as the basis for their determinations of customary law (Ibid.: 132). As anthropologists examine more carefully the situations in which early ethnographic accounts were produced they discover ways in which these accounts were structured by the colonial encounter (Marcus and Fisher, 1986).

At a 1981 conference on people's law and state law, participants discussed using the term folk law, but there was concern over whether the term romanticized folk law or minimized it (Roberts, 1986). The participants concluded that there is no such type of law as folk law distinct from state law, but instead a continuum of differentiation and organization of the generation and application of norms, a conception suggested by Galanter (Allott and Woodman, 1985).

Within the new legal pluralism, Macaulay proposes the concept of "private government," which he defines as that governing done by groups not part of federal and state constitutions but which may mimic symbols and structures of the public legal system (1986). He advocates a "private government perspective," which recognizes private associations that affect governing and also treats distinctions between public and private as problematic (1983: 2). He envisions a private government landscape as follows: ". . . While it may be necessary to draw a sharp line between public and private government even to think about law, actually there is no such line but situations of interpenetration, overlapping jurisdictions, and opportunities for harmony and conflict (Ibid.: 1)." Henry suggests the term "private justice" to refer to nonstate systems that "include practices of such institutions as the disciplinary bodies, boards, and councils of industrial and commercial organizations, professional and trade associations and unions, down to the peer sanctioning of relatively amorphous voluntary associations such as local self-help and mutual aid groups (1985: 89)."

Private justice does not exist in isolation but interrelates with the more formalized state order in a semiautonomous way (Henry, 1985: 89). As with Macaulay's private governments, private justice institutions can be formally constituted with written rules and procedures or informally constituted, generated spontaneously by members who share only tacit assumptions and who do not necessarily recognize that they are part of a system of normative ordering. Private government or private justice often replicates aspects of the legal order, such as security forces and tribunals, and

878   LEGAL PLURALISM

mimics its symbols with similar police uniforms, lights, codes, and systems of judgment. However, there are also occasions when it takes an oppositional form, as it does with the law of cooperatives in a capitalist society (Henry, 1985; 1987).

The most enduring, generalizable, and widely-used conception of plural legal orders is Moore's notion of the semiautonomous social field, a concept developed to describe multiple systems of ordering in complex societies (1973). The semiautonomous social field is one that (Ibid.: 720):

> can generate rules and customs and symbols internally, but that . . . is also vulnerable to rules and decisions and other forces emanating from the larger world by which it is surrounded. The semi-autonomous social field has rule-making capacities, and the means to induce or coerce compliance; but it is simultaneously set in a larger social matrix which can, and does, affect and invade it, sometimes at the invitation of persons inside it, sometimes at its own instance.

The advantages of this concept are that the semiautonomous social field is not attached to a single social group, that makes no claims about the nature of the orders themselves or their origin (whether traditional or imposed), and that it draws no definitive conclusions about the nature and direction of influence between the normative orders. The outside legal system penetrates the field but does not dominate it; there is room for resistance and autonomy.

Galanter, building on this model, argues that indigenous ordering persists not in bounded groups so much as in more open social networks that are regulated largely by reciprocity and shared but tacit understandings (1981: 22). Societies contain many partially self-regulating sectors organized along geographical, ethnic, or familial lines, often in fragmentary and overlapping social networks (Ibid.: 19–20). Galanter states (Ibid.: 22):

> If we have lost the experience of an all-encompassing inclusive community, it is not to a world of arms-length dealings with strangers, but in large measure to a world of loosely joined and partly overlapping partial or fragmentary communities. In this sense, our exposure to indigenous law has increased at the same time that official regulation has multiplied.

Macaulay's conception of private government is very similar: he envisions ordering through open social networks as well as within more organized and established institutional frameworks (1986).

Why is it so difficult to find a word for nonstate law? It is clearly difficult to define and circumscribe these forms of ordering. Where do we stop speaking of law and find ourselves simply describing social life? Is it useful to call all these forms of ordering law? In writing about legal pluralism, I find that once legal centralism has been vanquished, calling all forms of ordering that are not state law by the term law confounds the analysis. The literature in this field has not yet clearly demarcated a boundary between normative orders that can and cannot be called law. I think one of the difficulties lies in the tremendous variation in normative orders and the diversity of particular situations. The move to include noncolonized societies under the framework of legal pluralism adds to the complexity. However, there is general agreement that pluralism does not describe a type of society but is a condition found to a greater or lesser extent in most societies, with continuous variation between those that are more and those less plural (Galanter, 1981; Griffiths, 1986a).

Defining the orders which make up legal pluralism raises other issues as well. Does it make a difference that these plural legal orders vary greatly in power, in coercive potential, in symbolic strength, in attachment to class groupings? Are state and nonstate forms of ordering similar, or are there ways in which the state-law system is fundamentally different from all other forms of ordering? I think it is essential to see state law as fundamentally different in that it exercises the coercive power of the state and monopolizes the symbolic power associated with state authority. But, in many ways, it ideologically shapes other normative orders as well as provides an inescapable framework for their practice.

IV. RELATIONS BETWEEN NORMATIVE ORDERS: EXPLORING THE INTERACTIONS

Legal pluralism not only posits the existence of multiple legal spheres, but develops hypotheses concerning the relationships between them. The existence of legal pluralism itself is of less interest than the dynamics of change and transformation. Historically, there has been a shift in the way the interaction between legal orders, particularly between state law and nonstate law, has been described. Early research in classic legal pluralism saw normative orders as parallel but autonomous. During the 1960s and early 1970s, several studies demonstrated the power of state law to reshape the social order, suggesting the dominance of this form of law over other normative orders (e.g., Massell, 1968; Diamond, 1973; Burman and Harrell-Bond, 1979). Law appeared to be a potent tool for modernization in Third World countries (see Gardner, 1980; Lynch, 1983) and for creating social justice in the First World during this period.

But, it has not always worked that way, as law and development scholars discovered and as American social reformers found (Trubek and Galanter, 1974). In the 1970s, a more cautious and limited view of law's potential to reshape other social orders emerged. Some studies showed limits to the capacity of law to transform social life. The comparative examination of imposed law showed that sometimes it had powerful consequences for

880   LEGAL PLURALISM

change but that at other times the consequences were unexpected or negligible (Burman and Harrell-Bond, 1979). In contrast to Massell's analysis of the revolutionary impact of new laws on the status of women in the Islamic societies of Soviet Central Asia (1968), for example, Starr and Pool showed that the drastic law reforms introduced into Turkish society in 1926 that swept away Islamic Ottoman law in favor of the Swiss civil code produced relatively little change in the normative ordering of local villages (1974: 534). The vast majority of the Turkish population continued to follow customs incompatible with the new codes (Ibid.). Instead of revolutionary transformation, Starr and Pool document gradual, incremental change as, for example, women began to use the courts more frequently for family problems.

The creation of customary law, to give another example, was an ongoing, collaborative process in which power was clearly unequal, but subordinate groups were hardly passive or powerless. For example, Adewoye describes the development of public letter writers in Ibadan, Nigeria, between 1904 and 1960 (1986). These Africans drafted and produced legal documents in the absence of trained lawyers, shaping the forms of sale and land ownership contracts. Moore's model of the semiautonomous social field was in part an effort to explain why new laws or other attempts to direct change did not always produce the anticipated results or brought unplanned or unexpected consequences (1973: 723):

> This is partly because new laws are thrust upon going social arrangements in which there are complexes of binding obligations already in existence. Legislation is often passed with the intention of altering the going social arrangements in specified ways. The social arrangements are often effectively stronger than the new laws.

Moore's careful historical study of customary law among the Chagga of Tanzania documents this process more fully (1986a). Here she defines customary law as a cultural construct with political implications, a set of ideas embedded in relationships that are historically shifting (Ibid.: xv). Franz von Benda-Beckmann points out that the particular areas of resistance or acquiescence to imposed colonial law are complex and historically situated, depending to some extent on the processes of imposition themselves, which are highly variable (1981).

Research in the 1980s has increasingly emphasized the dialectic, mutually constitutive relation between state law and other normative orders. I think this reflects a new awareness of the interconnectedness of social orders, of our vulnerability to structures of domination far outside our immediate worlds, and of the ways implicit and unrecognized systems of control are embedded in our day-to-day social lives. Moreover, analysis of this dialectic is enriched by recent interpretations of law as a symbolic and ideological system (c.f., *Law & Society Review Special Issue on Law and*

Ideology, 1988). Research in the 1980s emphasizes the way state law penetrates and restructures other normative orders through symbols and through direct coercion and, at the same time, the way nonstate normative orders resist and circumvent penetration or even capture and use the symbolic capital of state law. In a final turn, some research explores the way nonstate normative orders constitute state law. Beyond well-known research on phenomena such as plea bargaining and courtroom workgroups, however, this study is in its infancy.

I will begin by describing research that focuses on the ways state law shapes other normative orders. Auerbach's study of the history of nonjudicial forms of dispute resolution in the United States demonstrates how state law gradually infiltrates and restructures alternatives so that they come to resemble state law (1983; see also Arthurs, 1985). This and other studies of the progressive reconstitution of alternatives as legalistic forums illuminate the expansion of state law into other normative orders over time (Nader, 1984; Harrington, 1985; Arthurs, 1985). But, subordinate groups may also choose to draw on the symbols and meanings of the state legal system. Santos's well-known study of law in the *favelas* of Brazil describes how residents of an illegal squatter settlement create their own legality using the forms and symbols of state law, the "law of the asphalt," as they call it (1977). Here, legal orders are attached to classes. Legal pluralism describes the relations between a dominant class and an oppressed urban class, relations that reflect the class hierarchy of Brazilian society, its structure of domination and unequal exchange. Squatters pursue a strategy of implicit confrontation at the same time as they adapt in order to survive (1977).

In another context, Westermark documents the practices of new village courts in Papua New Guinea, created in 1973 as informal, conciliatory alternatives to the state courts (1986). But the courts he studied replicated the state courts in architecture and furniture, using tables, chairs, the national flag, notes, and stone-lined walkways to an enclosed building (1986). Equipped with handbooks and badges, the magistrates pressed for uniforms and handcuffs. These village courts dispense what they call government law.

In an American study, John Brigham argues that legal discourse constitutes the discourse and practices of some American social movements (1987). Using examples from the gay rights movement, the anti-pornography movement, and the alternative dispute resolution movement, Brigham shows how references to rights or to the failures of law enter into and thus constitute movement discourse and even the strategies and tactics of the movements. Other studies have begun to explore the widespread legal consciousness of American society (Scheingold, 1974; Merry, 1986;

882   LEGAL PLURALISM

Macaulay, 1987) but there has been relatively little investigation of
how this consciousness shapes other normative orders.

Symbolic appropriation works the other way around as well:
state law may borrow the symbols of other normative orders.
Government reformers sometimes promote new state judicial institutions with traditional symbolic trappings, claiming to reinstitute
traditional law. The Philippine *katarungang pambarangay*,
(neighborhood justice) or Indian *nyaya panchayats* (justice village
councils) (Silliman, 1985; Meschievitz and Galanter, 1982; Hayden,
1984) illustrate this practice. The Philippine system is called
neighborhood justice but is administered by state officials called
neighborhood captains (Silliman, 1985). Many have argued that
American neighborhood justice is another example of state law
masquerading under the symbolic trappings of nonstate normative
orders (Santos, 1982; Abel, 1982; Harrington, 1985; Harrington and
Merry, 1988). New state judicial institutions clothed in revolutionary symbols have been created in the service of social transformation, as in Allende's Chile (Spence, 1978) and Castro's Cuba (Salas,
1983).

Studies of the micro-level processes of legal action, disputing,
and case processing describe the dynamics of the symbolic radiation and imposition of state law, its appropriation within other
normative orders, and forms of resistance to its penetration. The
rich ethnographic studies of local dispute processes reported in Nader and Todd (1978) provide numerous examples of individuals
pursuing dispute strategies in legally plural arenas (see, e.g., Ruffini, 1978). Even when state law is not used, it constitutes bargaining and regulatory endowments, to use Galanter's terms (1981). In
these situations, the contours of local disputing are inextricably
connected with local political struggles between those whose authority claims rest on kinship or religion and those whose claims
rest on knowledge of the state, education, or connections with the
government. Moore's description of a dispute among the Chagga
illustrates this dynamic, pointing to the linkage between local
political competition for power and knowledge of and access to village and state legal systems (1977). Based on her analysis of disputing in a legally plural arena in Indonesia, Keebet von Benda-
Beckmann proposes a model of forum shopping and social change
that provides a way of understanding how local processes of disputing reshape legally plural situations (1981). Disputants shop for
forums for their problems and forums compete for disputes, which
they use for their own local political ends (Ibid.: 117). There are
constraints on disputants, however. For example, state courts re-
fuse to hear claims by women for rice plots since only the official
representative of the lineage is entitled to sue, thus preventing women from appealing to the state courts to escape the control of the
lineage head over their land (Ibid.: 143).

Abel (1979a) and Merry (1982) also develop models of disputing and legal change which argue that the cumulative effect of litigant choice of forum affects dispute institutions at the same time as dispute institutions are themselves changing along with developments in the political economy. Starr's analysis of disputing strategies during a period of capitalist transformation in Turkey carefully analyzes this process as well (1974; see also Abel, 1979b). Peter just explores the manipulation of evidence as a strategy for providing justice while conforming to law (1986).

Another new area of research examines how state law both constitutes and is constituted by the normative orders of which it is composed. Fitzpatrick's concept of "integral plurality" focuses on the interaction between normative orders, positing that state law is integrally constituted in relation to a plurality of social forms (1984). His work draws on Foucault's analysis of the emergence of modern law (Fitzpatrick 1983a: 176). Fitzpatrick argues that we need to look at law not simply as domination but also as constitutive of social life. Both state law and semiautonomous social fields are constituted in significant part by their interrelations with one another: the family and its legal order are shaped by the state, but the state in turn is shaped by the family and its legal order because each is a part of the other (Ibid.: 159). Here, Fitzpatrick makes the turn from seeing the semiautonomous social field as constituted by state law to seeing state law shaped by its constituent normative orders and vice versa.

In Fitzpatrick's theory, state law takes identity from and derives support from other social forms, but these forms both support and oppose state law. Bourgeois legality, for example, depends on social forms such as the prison and capitalist labor relations that both support and undermine it. The prison is a condition of the existence of bourgeois legality, since prison serves both as the ultimate enforcer of law and as an example of a pervasive disciplinary power that typifies modern society, yet it cannot itself incorporate bourgeois legality in its functioning. It coerces outside this structure while leaving bourgeois free to be equal and universal (1984: 116).

Integral relations of mutual support between law and other social forms tend toward convergence as elements of law are elements of the other social forms and vice versa. For example, science is incorporated into elements of law, and law supports and reinforces science: the two take identity from each other in positively supportive ways (Fitzpatrick, 1984). Similarly, custom, when penetrated by state law, changes its nature fundamentally and becomes part of state law. In his words, "Custom supports law but law transforms the elements of custom that it appropriates into its own image and likeness. Law, in turn, supports other social forms but becomes, in the process, part of the other forms" (1984: 9). Not a unitary phenomenon, law is constituted by a plurality of social forms. Since law is constituted in relations of oppo-

884   LEGAL PLURALISM

sition and support to other social forms, however, there is a gap between law and other social forms that cannot be bridged; law
depends on these opposed social forms. Integral pluralism is part
of a dialectic of power and counter power. Fitzpatrick concludes,
that "law is the unsettled resultant of relations with a plurality of
social forms and in this law's identity is constantly and inherently
subject to challenge and change" (Ibid.: 138).

Henry's work on law in collectives and cooperatives in Britain
further develops this model of integral plurality (1983; 1985; 1987;
see also Nelken, 1986). Henry argues that the relations between
state law and other normative orders now appear very complicated, requiring attention to history, human agency, local contexts,
and culture (1985: 315). Conflicting normative orders, such as
those of the cooperative and the capitalist state, may challenge and
oppose each other, both by outright rejection (when the state prohibits conflicting normative orders, for example), or by accepting
and recognizing the autonomy of a separate normative order
within that sphere. Thus, the law refuses to intervene in the cooperative because some matters are seen as the private concern of
the co-op (Ibid.: 314). The members of the cooperative, on the
other hand, can reject and to some extent undermine capitalist legality. Henry proposes a dialectical model, in which "[a]lternative
institutions and their associated normative orders do not work
transformations on capitalist structures and rule systems but instead interact with them in a dialectical way such that both the alternative system and the capitalist order are vulnerable to incremental reformulations" (Ibid.: 324). Drawing on Giddens' analysis
of structure and action according to which action shapes structure
and structures constrain and enable actions, an integrated theory
that provides some space for individual actions to "make a difference," even for the powerless, Henry adds the dimension of individual action to Fitzpatrick's model of integral plurality. Individuals within communitarian organizations, he argues, are likely to
interject communitarian elements into capitalist society as long as
they are not totally marginal or separated from that society. Thus,
the impact of communitarian organizations within capitalist society may be greater than that of marginal collectives (Ibid.).

Of particular interest, yet also particularly unstudied, is the
way constituent normative orders shape state law. Yet, this describes how groups in power attempt to control state law and
shape it to their ends at the same time as they are limited by the
plural normative orders of which they are a part. Careful empirical work such as Henry's study of workplace discipline (1983) or
Silbey's and Bittner's study of consumer protection reveal the importance of constituent normative orders within regulatory activities (1980–81, 1982). Yngvesson's ethnographic studies on local-
level legal processes in American courts demonstrate how court
clerks constitute the legality of the lower courts through their un-

derstanding of community norms of justice (1985, 1988). Sarat and Felstiner, listening to the way lawyers talk to clients, hear the construction of a vision of legality for the client which seems to reflect the local normative order of lawyers (1986).

David Sugarman develops the mutually constitutive understanding of state law and nonstate normative orders in his edited volume, *Legality, Ideology, and the State* (1983). State law is itself plural: it contains procedures for establishing facts, general substantive rules that guide citizen action, enforcement of judgments, provisions for physical punishment, modes of appeal, insurance against loss, ideological and symbolic dimensions, and the ability to provide a degree of private ordering through facilitative laws (1983: 230–231). Law and legal institutions mean different things to different people. There are tensions between local and central regulation, indigenous and state conceptions of legality, discretionary practices and enforcement, and arbitration and other extralegal mechanisms for dispute resolution. In eighteenth and nineteenth century Britain, there were struggles between local courts, special courts, and the formal state system of courts. Arthurs demonstrates these struggles in British administrative law (1985) and Provine describes analogous debates over local lay judges in the United States (1986).

Sugarman explores the plurality of law through his discussion of facilitative law, law that functions not by imposing obligations but by providing individuals with facilities for realizing their wishes through conferring legal powers on them, such as the powers to construct marriages, wills, contracts, companies, trusts, and so forth (1983). This law permits private law-making and affords the opportunity to bypass the legal obligations of the state. Facilitative laws simultaneously define and constrain permissible conduct and enable individuals to expand or contract their autonomy, thus promoting, qualifying, or subverting state policy (Sugarman, 1983: 217).

In his review of this book, Freeman sees the move in British critical legal scholarship toward seeing law as pluralistic—as having many sides and many determinations—as analogous to the American critical legal studies' move to deconstruction (1986: 840). Freeman claims that, in an effort to avoid simple reductionist views of law as the product of the ruling class, British critical legal studies scholars argue that law is pluralistic just as Americans argue that it is indeterminant and incoherent. Yet, Freeman concludes, pluralism, just as deconstruction, ultimately ends in immobilization, since if everything is complex and variable, just as if everything is a matter of interpretation, how can one say anything?

The turn toward a dialectic analysis of the relations between plural legal orders, particularly between state law and other normative orders, comes primarily from work within the new legal

pluralism: that is, from those who have used the model of legal
pluralism to understand legality in the First World. Yet, this dialectic analysis is equally fruitful for a reanalysis of classic legal
pluralism materials, as the example of the reanalysis of customary
law demonstrates. In none of these analyses, however, is there an
implication that the power relations between plural legal orders
are equal: the theme instead is the penetration and dominance of
state law and its subversion at the margins.

V. PLURAL LEGALITIES AND LOCAL KNOWLEDGE

Another aspect of legal pluralism is the study of law as a system of meanings, a cultural code for interpreting the world.
Geertz, a preeminent spokesman for this perspective, has developed an interpretive view of legal pluralism, one richly evocative
of cultural diversity (1983). Law is understood as a system of symbols, of meanings. Unlike the research tradition discussed above,
there is little attention here to relations of power or to the political economy of legal pluralism, but there is a substantial interest
in history and context.

In *Local Knowledge*, Geertz urges a focus on structures of
meaning, especially on the symbols and systems of symbols
through whose agency such structures are formed, communicated,
and imposed, in the comparative analysis of law as in the comparative analysis of myth, ritual, ideology, art, or classification systems
(1983: 182). In his words, . . . " 'law' here, there, or anywhere, is
part of a distinctive manner of imagining the real (Ibid.: 184)." He
conceives of law as a species of social imagination. Starting with
basic words or concepts, he compares the "legal sensibilities" of
three cultures, using these words to orient the reader to different
senses of law. This is a hermeneutic project; the words are keys to
understanding the social institutions and cultural formulations
that surround them and give them meaning (1983: 187). For example, in the Islamic world he discusses the concept *haqq* which
means reality, truth, or validity, and in various permutations and
combinations, God, fact, actuality, right, duty, claim, obligation,
fair, valid, just, or proper (1983: 188). In Islamic legal sensibility,
to determine the empirical situation is to determine the jural principle. Facts, in other words, are normative; there is no fact/law dichotomy. Facts are estimates of character assumed by background
and demeanor as much as they are weightings of notarized documents presented (Rosen, 1980–81: 231; see also Messick, 1986).[4] Because the law itself is certain and comprehensive, although what is
just and unjust is not, it is in the recounting of incident and situa-

---

4 The *qadi* or judge takes into account the relationship between the parties, their social background, each person's location in the system of ordering,
their kin connections, residence, and occupation as evidence as to the likely
way that the person acted in any situation (Rosen, 1980–81: 229). The standard of conduct to which a person is held depends on who he or she is.

tion that value balancing comes in. To achieve the proper recounting of a situation, the court needs morally upright people who can testify about cases. In classical times these people were chosen by the *qadi* and appeared before the court over and over (Geertz, 1983: 191–192). Geertz argues that even in secular courts, one can see the lingering influence of the notion of the virtuous witness speaking moral truth in the persistence of certified truth bringers and other examples of normative witnessing in these courts (Ibid.: 193).[5] A hermeneutic approach applied to legally plural situations describes sets of meanings joined together in a "polyglot discourse" (Ibid.: 226). These views do not cohere into a systematic position, but bounce off one another. This means viewing the situation as one of several, incommensurate local expressions of legal sensibilities. The diversity and mingling of legal sensibilities is not likely to end, in Geertz's opinion, but may increase; it is something that Indonesians and other Third World peoples live with as they try to construct principled lives, as do many First World peoples as well.

In a recent paper that develops these themes, Santos asserts that legal pluralism is the key concept in a postmodern view of law (1987: 297). Using the metaphor of the map to discuss law, he suggests that law is a system of signs that represents/distorts reality through the mechanisms of scale, projection, and symbolization. As do maps, different legal orders have different scales, different forms of projection and centering, different systems of symbolization. Thus, another way of discussing legal pluralism is to talk about the different symbolic systems inscribed in each normative order.

Santos delineates two ideal-typical sign systems by means of which law symbolizes reality. The first he labels the Homeric style, in which (to shorten his description) everyday reality is described in abstract and formal terms through conventional cognitive and referential signs. A second, the biblical style, presupposes an image-based legality in which (again condensed) interactions are inscribed in multilayered contexts and described in figurative and informal terms through iconic, emotive, and expressive signs (1987: 295). These styles are perpetually in tension, with variations in dominance during particular historical periods. He suggests that the modern state legal order is predominantly Homeric. In Cape Verde, the tension between these two types of legal symbolization appears in the system of popular justice, which fuses both customary law and state law (Ibid.: 296). The tension crops up in the way judges settle disputes: some judges adopt one, some the other, some shift from one to another depending on the case and their familiarity with it. He concludes that the legal pluralism he is

---

[5] Hayden provides an analysis of forms of speaking and consideration of facts in Indian caste panchayts, government courts, and United States courts (1984; 1987).

describing is not the legal pluralism of traditional legal anthropology (what I have called classic legal pluralism) but (Ibid.: 297–298)

> rather the conception of different legal spaces superimposed, interpenetrated, and mixed in our minds as much as in our actions. . . . Our legal life is constituted by an intersection of different legal orders, that is, by *interlegality*. Interlegality is the phenomenological counterpart of legal pluralism and that is why it is the second key concept of a postmodern conception of law.

Bentley develops the culturally constructive role of law in his analysis of disputing among the Maranao in the Philippines (1984). He argues that disputing is an expression of competing visions of social reality, an arena for constructing and expressing alternative visions of the world. In the society he studied, which combines custom (*adat*), Islamic law, and Philippine civil and criminal law, the manipulation of the different legal systems is part of the effort to construct an interpretation of truth in the world in a way that others will accept. He argues that the complexity and fluidity of the arenas of contest appears to enhance the range of manipulation and contest. In the same vein, O'Connor makes the intriguing argument that law is an indigenous social theory, using Thai ethnography (1980).

Foucault's conceptions of the forms of power and discipline of modern society provide yet another take on legal pluralism (1979), a perspective that is being developed by Fitzpatrick (1983b). If the nature of law that has emerged in the wake of capitalism is fundamentally different from that of pre-capitalist societies in what Foucault refers to as its "disciplinary technologies"—productive forms of power such as the timetable, the cell, and the panopticon—the encounter between these forms of power and discipline and those of noncapitalist societies takes on new meaning. Power, in Foucault's theory, is not simply based on prohibition but also on the positive formation of norms and shaping of individuals to fit these norms (Fitzpatrick, 1983b: 50). Law gives shape to institutions that supervise rather than contain; it creates new technologies of discipline that stretch from the prison to the factory to the military to the school (Fitzpatrick, 1983b; Foucault, 1979).

In an intriguing illustration of the meaning of these shifts in forms of power and discipline, Pospisil describes the dismay of the Kapauku Papuans at the use of jail as a punishment, one that to them seems extraordinarily severe since it separates the individual from the essential cooperation of soul and body, the linkage between one's actions and one's own free decisions (1979: 141). In their words, in jail, "The man's vital substance deteriorates and the man dies" (Ibid.: 142). Indeed, the Dutch colonial administrators found that Kapauku tended to pine and die if imprisoned long, despite the administrators' conviction that prison had a positive, civilizing effect.

VI. CONCLUSIONS AND DIRECTIONS FOR FUTURE RESEARCH

What are the implications of focusing on legal pluralism for future sociolegal research? My review of this literature suggests at least five ways in which viewing sociolegal phenomena as plural expands the research framework. First, a concern with legal pluralism moves away from the ideology of legal centralism—the predisposition to think of all legal ordering as rooted in state law—and suggests attention to other forms of ordering and their interaction with state law. It highlights competing, contesting, and sometimes contradictory orders outside state law and their mutually constitutive relations to state law.

Second, this perspective requires a shift away from an essentialist definition of law to an historical understanding since any situation of legal pluralism develops over time through the dialectic between legal systems, each of which both constitutes and reconstitutes the other in some way. Defining the essence of law or custom is less valuable than situating these concepts in particular sets of relations between particular legal orders in particular historical contexts. Plural normative orders, once created, can persist with tenacity justifying themselves by appeals to tradition, or they can be radically reformed in the contest between opposing orders, a process exemplified by the creation of customary law in colonial societies.[6] Or they may change incrementally through small additions, subtractions, and reinterpretations. The papers from a recent conference, Ethnohistorical Models for the Evolution of Law within Specific Societies, provide rich descriptions of these historical processes of change and transformation in legally plural societies (Starr and Collier, 1988).[7]

Third, viewing situations as legally plural leads to an examination of the cultural or ideological nature of law and systems of normative ordering. Rather than focusing on the particular rules applied in situations of dispute, this perspective examines the ways social groups conceive of ordering, of social relationships, and of ways of determining truth and justice. Law is not simply a set of rules exercising coercive power, but a system of thought by which certain forms of relations come to seem natural and taken for granted, modes of thought that are inscribed in institutions that exercise some coercion in support of their categories and theories of explanation.

Fourth, examining the plurality of legal situations facilitates

---

[6] Starr and Collier describe this process in terms of "historical struggles between native elites and their colonial and postcolonial rulers" (1987: 368).

[7] As the twenty participants in this 1985 conference concluded, societies may be characterized as having multiple legal systems that are not autonomous but negotiated in relation to an encompassing political structure and particular assymetrical relations of power (Starr and Collier, 1987: 371; see further, Starr and Collier, 1989).

890   LEGAL PLURALISM

the move away from an exclusive focus on situations of dispute to
an analysis of ordering in nondispute situations (see further, Collier, 1973; Engel, 1980). Holleman suggests the study of "trouble-
less cases" rather than situations of trouble, arguing that disputes
are exceptional events and therefore misleading guides to the nature of ordering (1986).[8] The study of facilitative law and historical studies of legal change similarly move away from an exclusive
focus on dispute.[9]

Fifth, the dialectical analysis of relations among normative orders provides a framework for understanding the dynamics of the
imposition of law and of resistance to law, for examining the interactive relationship between dominant and subordinate groups or
classes. It offers a way of thinking about the possibilities of domination through law and of the limits to this domination, pointing
to areas in which individuals can and do resist. This is a difficult
area for research. On the one hand, attention to law in its ideological role points to its power to construct modes of thinking and implicit understandings as a central aspect of its power. On the other
hand, attention to plural orders examines limits to the ideological
power of state law: areas where it does not penetrate and alternative forms of ordering persist, groups that incorporate the symbols
of state law but oppose it, perhaps becoming expert in its intrica-
cies and forms of power as in colonial India, and situations in
which other forms of ordering are so embedded in the administration of law that they subvert its actual implementation. Here, of
course, we are on the familiar terrain of plea bargaining, courtroom workgroups and agency capture, but instead of explaining
why the law on the books and the law in action differ according to
gap theory, we could understand this well-documented characteristic of legal life as one of plural legal orders within the courthouse,
the police station, or the regulatory agency, some of which are organized around standards of community justice, others around
rule-of-law standards, and others around the cultural predispositions of particular groups in power. Indeed, state law is itself plural. Despite efforts to root out pluralism such as attacks on "rough
justice," on lay justices of the peace (Provine, 1986), and on police
discretion, new plural orderings continually spring up. These plural orderings constitute state law.

---

[8] The Dutch tradition of the anthropology of law, which is premised on
assumptions of legal pluralism, indicates the potential of an approach to sociolegal phenomena that looks at systems of ordering within arenas of social life
such as the family, land tenure, inheritance, commercial transactions, and so
forth, examining day-to-day peace rather than rare moments of trouble (Griffiths, 1986b). Griffiths suggests that perhaps the Anglo-American common law
tradition leads British and American anthropologists to focus on moments of
dispute rather than on systems of ordering embedded in the wider domain of
uncontested social life (1986b; see also Ietswaart, 1986).

[9] As Starr and Collier point out, the dispute paradigm has become too
normative and positivistic for many researchers, leading to a turn to historical
research as a way of considering legal change (1987: 367).

However, for some problems the concept has limitations. One is in the analysis of change within a single social field and a second is in the attention to the specific characteristics of particular social locations. A legal pluralist analysis tends to emphasize changes that occur through interactions between social fields but not those taking place within a social field. It is likely to miss the way a particular social field is gradually reshaped by a variety of ideological and political forces both within and outside it. For example, in their study of the impact of European missionaries on South Africa during the colonial period, Comaroff and Comaroff argue that the missionaries introduced new concepts of time, space, work, personhood, and so forth, at a variety of particular locations throughout the country over a period of years, gradually shifting the consciousness of the Africans they encountered and converted and paving the way for the colonial conquest of these people despite the missionaries' efforts to oppose it (1986).[10] Although this historical shift in consciousness could be described in terms of legal pluralism—the interaction between the African and the missionary legal orders—the concept tends not to highlight the intricate relations between ways of thinking and knowing within a social field, the ways they change over time, and the ways symbols seep into and out of legal systems in large cities, small towns, and provincial places.

Moreover, the concept of legal pluralism can press too quickly toward analyses of systems to the neglect of the variation in particular local places. It is difficult to understand the particularity of small situations and the interaction of large systems at the same time. Thinking of legal pluralism seems likely to get us out of the courtroom and the lawyers's office, but once outside, legal pluralist analyses could lead away from detailed examinations of particular local places. To examine the ever-changing conceptions of the normal and the cultural and the constant struggle of interpretation of the symbols and forms of legality in small places and large legal systems at the same time is, at the least, challenging.

In sum, the new legal pluralism has opened up questions of dialectic and resistance that build on the sophisticated theoretical traditions and rich ethnography of classic legal pluralism. There is much in these traditions that could serve as the basis for exciting new directions in law and society research. However, the concept requires refinement as we work to develop it, including attention to the specificity of each situation, to the variations in minute so-

---

[10] By introducing new symbols such as the moral worth of work, wealth, belief in free choice, liberal democracy, impersonal forms of regulation such as the clock, and conceptions of political authority as distinct from religious authority and power, the missionaries gradually transformed the taken-for-granted world of the Tswana people and, despite their explicit opposition to taking political power or fostering imperialist expansion, facilitated the political absorption of the Tswana into the colonial state (Comaroff and Comaroff, 1986; see also Comaroff, 1985).

892   LEGAL PLURALISM

cial processes, and to the complex texture of ideological meanings formed within particular historical situations. This is no small project.

SALLY ENGLE MERRY is Associate Professor of Anthropology at Wellesley College, Wellesley, Mass. She is the author of a monograph on urban crime, *Urban Danger: Life in a Neighborhood of Strangers*, and numerous articles on legal ideology and legal consciousness, mediation in American society and in cross-cultural perspective, and urban social order. She is currently completing a manuscript describing the people who bring interpersonal problems to court and the nature of their legal consciousness.

REFERENCES

ABEL, Richard L. (1982) *The Politics of Informal Justice*, 2 Vols. New York: Academic Press.
———(1979a) "Western Courts in Non-Western Settings: Patterns of Court Use in Colonial and Neo-Colonial Africa," in Sandra B. Burman and Barbara E. Harrell-Bond (eds.), *The Imposition of Law*. New York: Academic Press, pp. 167–200.
———(1979b) "The Rise of Capitalism and the Transformation of Disputing: from Confrontation over Honor to Competition for Property," 27 *UCLA Law Review* 223.
ADEWOYE, Omoniyi (1986) "Legal Practice in Ibadan, 1904–1960," 24 *Journal of Legal Pluralism* 57.
ALLOTT, A.N., and G.R. WOODMAN, (eds.). (1985) *People's Law and State Law: The Bellagio Papers*. Dordrecht: Foris.
ARTHURS, H.W. (1985) *Without the Law: Administrative Justice and Legal Pluralism in Mid 19th-Century England*. Toronto; University of Toronto Press.
AUERBACH, Jerold S. (1983) *Justice Without Law?* New York: Oxford University Press.
BENDA-BECKMANN, Franz von (1981) "Some Comments on the Problems of Comparing the Relationship between Traditional and State Systems of Administration of Justice in Africa and Indonesia," 19 *Journal of Legal Pluralism* 165.
———(1979) *Property in Social Continuity: Continuity and Change in the Maintenance of Property Relationships through Time in Minangkabau, West Sumatra*. The Hague: Nijhoff.
BENDA-BECKMANN, Keebet von (1981) "Forum Shopping and Shopping Forums—Dispute Settlement in a Minangkabau Village in West Sumatra," 19 *Journal of Legal Pluralism* 117.
BENDA-BECKMANN, Keebet von, and Fons STRIJBOSCH (eds.) (1986) *Anthropology of Law in the Netherlands: Essays in Legal Pluralism*. Dordrecht and Cinnaminson: Foris.
BENTLEY, G. Carter (1984) "Hermeneutics and World Construction in Maranao Disputing," 11 *American Ethnologist* 642.
BENTSI-ENCHILL, Kwamena (1969) "The Colonial Heritage of Legal Pluralism," 1 *Zambia Law Journal* 1.
BOSSY, John (ed.) (1983) *Disputes and Settlements: Law and Human Relations in the West*. Cambridge: Cambridge University Press.
BRIGHAM, John (1987) "Right, Rage, and Remedy: Forms of Law in Political Discourse," in *Studies in American Political Development*. New Haven: Yale University Press.
BUCKLE, Leonard, and Suzann R. THOMAS-BUCKLE (1982) "Doing unto Others: Dispute and Dispute-Processing in an Urban American Neighbor-

hood," in Roman Tomasic and Malcolm Feeley (eds.), *Neighborhood Justice.* New York: Longman.

BURMAN, Sandra, and Barbara E. HARRELL-BOND (eds.) (1979) *The Imposition of Law.* New York: Academic Press.

CHANOCK, Martin (1985) *Law, Custom, and Social Order: The Colonial Experience in Malawi and Zambia.* Cambridge: Cambridge University Press.

COLLIER, Jane (1973) *Law and Social Change in Zinacantan.* Stanford, CA: Stanford University Press.

COLSON, Elizabeth (1976) "From Chief's Court to Local Court: The Evolution of Local Courts in Southern Zambia," in M.J. Aronoff (ed.), *Freedom and Constraint.* Amsterdam: Van Gorcum, pp. 15–29.

COMAROFF, Jean (1985) *Body of Power: Spirit of Resistance: Culture and History of a South African People.* Chicago: University of Chicago Press.

COMAROFF, Jean, and John L. COMAROFF (1986) "Christianity and Colonialism in South Africa," 13 *American Ethnologist* 1.

COMAROFF, John L., and Simon ROBERTS (1981) *Rules and Processes.* Chicago: University of Chicago Press.

DIAMOND, Stanley (1973) "The Rule of Law versus the Order of Custom," in Donald Black and Maureen Mileski (eds.), *The Social Organization of Law,* New York: Seminar Press, Pp. 318–344. Reprinted from (1971) 38 *Social Research* 42.

EHRLICH, E. (1913) *Fundamental Principles of the Sociology of Law,* trans. W.L. Moll. Cambridge: Harvard University Press.

ENGEL, David M. (1987) "Law, Time, and Community," 21 *Law & Society Review* 605.

——— (1984) "The Oven Bird's Song: Insiders, Outsiders, and Personal Injuries in an American Community," 18 *Law & Society Review* 549.

——— (1980) "Legal Pluralism in an American Community: Perspectives on a Civil Trial Court," 3 *American Bar Foundation Research Journal* 425.

FITZPATRICK, Peter (1985) "Review Article: Is it Simple to be a Marxist in Legal Anthropology?," *Modern Law Review* 472.

——— (1984) "Law and Societies," 22 *Osgoode Hall Law Journal* 115.

——— (1983a) "Law, Plurality, and Underdevelopment," in D. Sugarman, (ed.), *Legality, Ideology, and the State.* London: Academic Press, pp. 159–183.

——— (1983b) "Marxism and Legal Pluralism," 1 *Australian Journal of Law and Society* 45.

——— (1980) *Law and State in Papua New Guinea.* London: Academic Press.

FORER, Norman (1979) "The Imposed Wardship of American Indian Tribes: A Case Study of the Prairie Band Potawatomi," in Sandra B. Burman and Barbara E. Harrell-Bond (eds.), *The Imposition of Law.* New York: Academic Press, pp. 89–114.

FOUCAULT, Michel (1979) *Discipline and Punish: The Birth of the Prison.* New York: Vintage.

FREEMAN, Alan (1986) "The Politics of Truth: On Sugarman's *Legality, Ideology, and the State,*" 1986 *American Bar Foundation Research Journal* 829.

GALANTER, Marc (1981) "Justice in Many Rooms: Courts, Private Ordering, and Indigenous Law," 19 *Journal of Legal Pluralism and Unofficial Law* 1.

GARDNER, James A. (1980) *Legal Imperialism: American Lawyers and Foreign Aid in Latin America.* Madison, Wis.: University of Wisconsin Press.

GEERTZ, Clifford (1983) *Local Knowledge: Further Essays in Interpretive Anthropology.* New York: Basic Books.

GORDON, Robert J., and Mervyn J. MEGGITT (1985) *Law and Order in the New Guinea Highlands: Encounters with Enga.* Hanover: University Press of New England (for University of Vermont).

GREENHOUSE, Carol (1982) "Nature is to Culture as Praying is to Suing: Legal Pluralism in an American Suburb," 20 *Journal of Legal Pluralism* 17.

GRIFFITHS, John (1986a) "What is Legal Pluralism?," 24 *Journal of Legal Pluralism* 1.

——— (1986b) "Recent Anthropology of Law in the Netherlands and its His-

894   LEGAL PLURALISM

torical Background," in Keebet von Benda-Beckman and Fons Strijbosch
(eds.), *Anthropology of Law in the Netherlands: Essays in Legal Pluralism*. Dordrecht and Cinnaminson: Foris.
——— (1985) "Introduction," A. Allott and G. Woodman (eds.), *People's Law
and State Law: The Bellagio Papers*. Dordrecht: Foris, pp. 13–20.
GURVITCH, Georges (1947) *The Sociology of Law*. London: Routledge and
Kegan Paul.
HARRINGTON, Christine (1985) *Shadow Justice: The Ideology and Institutionalization of Alternatives to Court*. Westport, Conn: Greenwood Press.
HARRINGTON, Christine, and Sally Engle MERRY (1988) "Ideological Production: The Making of Community Mediation," 22 *Law &Society Review*.
HAYDEN, Robert M. (1987) "Turn-taking, Overlap, and the Task at Hand:
Ordering Speaking Turns in Legal Settings," 14 *American Ethnologist* 251.
——— (1984) "A Note on Caste Panchayats and Government Courts in India:
Different Kinds of Stages for Different Kinds of Performances," 22 *Jour-
nal of Legal Pluralism* 43.
HENRY, Stuart (1987) "The Construction and Deconstruction of Social Con-
trol: Thoughts on the Discursive Production of State Law and Private
Justice," in J. Lowman, R. Menzies, and T. Palys (eds.), *Transcarceration*.
Farnborough: Gower.
——— (1985) "Community Justice, Capitalist Society, and Human Agency:
The Dialectics of Collective Law in the Cooperative," 19 *Law & Society
Review* 303.
——— (1983) *Private Justice*. Boston: Routledge and Kegan Paul.
HOLLEMAN, J.F. (1986) "Trouble-Cases and Trouble-Less Cases in the Study
of Customary Law and Legal Reform," in Keebet von Benda-Beckman
and Fons Strijbosch (eds.), *Anthropology of Law in the Netherlands: Es-
says in Legal Pluralism*. Dordrecht and Cinnaminson: Foris. Reprinted
from 7 *Law & Society Review* 585.
HOOKER, M.B. (1975) *Legal Pluralism: An Introduction to Colonial and Neo-
Colonial Laws*. Oxford: Clarendon Press.
IETSWAART, Heleen (1986) "Review of Keebet von Benda-Beckmann and
Fons Strijbosch (eds.) *Anthropology of Law in the Netherlands: Essays in
Legal Pluralism*," 24 *Journal of Legal Pluralism* 161.
JUST, Peter (1986) "Let the Evidence Fit the Crime: Evidence, Law, and Soci-
ological 'Truth' among the Dou Donggo," 13 *American Ethnologist* 43.
KIDDER, Robert L. (1979) "Toward an Integrated Theory of Imposed Law,"
in Sandra B. Burman and Barbara E. Harrell-Bond (eds.), *The Imposition
of Law*. New York: Academic Press, pp. 289–306.
——— (1974) "Formal Litigation and Professional Insecurity: Legal Entrepreneurship in South India," 9 *Law & Society Review* 11.
LAM, M. (1985) "The Imposition of Anglo-American Land Tenure Law on
Hawaiians," 23 *Journal of Legal Pluralism* 103.
LYNCH, Dennis O. (1983) "Hundred Months of Solitude: Myth and Reality in
Law and Development?," 1983 *American Bar Foundation Research Journal* 223.
MACAULAY, Stewart (1987) "Images of Law in Everyday Life: The Lessons
of School, Entertainment and Spectator Sports," 21 *Law & Society Review*
185.
——— (1986) "Private Government," Disputes Processing Research Program
Working Paper 1983–86. Madison, Wis.: University of Wisconsin Law
School. Reprinted in (1986) *Law and the Social Sciences*, ed. by Leon Lipson and Stanton Wheeler. New York: Russell Sage Foundation.
——— (1963) "Non-contractual Relations in Business: A Preliminary Study,"
28 *American Sociological Review* 55.
MALINOWSKI, Bronislaw (1926) *Crime and Custom in a Savage Society*.
Paterson, N.J.: Littlefield, Adams.
MARCUS, George E., and Michael M.J. FISHER (1986) *Anthropology as Cultural Critique: An Experimental Moment in the Human Sciences*. Chicago: University of Chicago Press.
MASSELL, Gregory (1968) "Law as an Instrument of Revolutionary Change
in a Traditional Milieu: The Case of Soviet Central Asia," 2 *Law & Society Review* 179.

MERRY, Sally Engle (1986) "Everyday Understandings of the Law in Working-class America," 13 *American Ethnologist* 253.
—— (1982) "The Articulation of Legal Spheres," in Margaret Jean Hay and Marcia Wright (eds.), *African Women and the Law: Historical Perspectives*. Boston: Boston University African Studies Center, pp. 68–89.
—— (1979) "Going to Court: Strategies of Dispute Management in an American Urban Neighborhood," 13 *Law & Society Review* 891.
MESCHIEVITZ, C.S., and Marc GALANTER (1982) "In Search of Nyaya Panchayats: The Politics of a Moribund Institution," in R. Abel (ed.), *The Politics of Informal Justice: Comparative Studies*. New York: Academic Press.
MESSICK, Brinkley (1986) "The Mufti, the Text, and the World: Legal Interpretation in Yemen," 21 *Man* n.s. 102.
MOORE, Sally Falk (1986a) *Social Facts and Fabrications: Customary Law on Kilimanjaro, 1880–1980*. Cambridge: Cambridge University Press.
—— (1986b) "Legal Systems of the World: An Introductory Guide to Classifications, Typological Interpretations, and Bibliographic Resources," in Leon Lipson and Stanton Wheeler (eds.). *Law and the Social Sciences*. New York: Russell Sage Foundation.
—— (1977) "Individual Interests and Organizational Structures: Dispute Settlements as 'Events of Articulation,' " in I. Hamnett (ed.), *Social Anthropology and Law*. New York: Academic Press.
—— (1973) "Law and Social Change: The Semi-Autonomous Social Field as an Appropriate Subject of Study," 7 *Law & Society Review*. 719.
NADER, Laura (ed.)(1980) *No Access to Law*. New York: Academic Press.
NADER, Laura (1984) "The Recurrent Dialectic Between Legality and Its Alternatives," 132 *University of Pennsylvania Law Review* 621.
NADER, Laura, and Harry F. TODD (eds.) (1978) *The Disputing Process–Law in Ten Societies*. New York: Columbia University Press.
NELKEN, David (1986) "Review Essay: Beyond the Study of 'Law and Society'? Henry's *Private Justice* and O'Hagen's *The End of the Law?*," 1986 *American Bar Foundation Research Journal* 323.
O'CONNOR, R.A. (1980) "Law as Indigenous Social Theory," 8 *American Ethnologist* 223.
OKOTH-OGENDO, H.W.O. (1979) "The Imposition of Property Law in Kenya," in Sandra B. Burman and Barbara E. Harrell-Bond (eds.), *The Imposition of Law*. New York: Academic Press, pp. 147–166.
POSPISIL, Leopold (1981) "Modern and Traditional Administration of Justice in New Guinea," 19 *Journal of Legal Pluralism* 93.
—— (1979) "Legally Induced Culture Change in New Guinea," in Sandra B. Burman and Barbara E. Harrell-Bond (eds.), *The Imposition of Law*. New York: Academic Press, pp. 127–146.
—— (1971) *The Anthropology of Law: A Comparative Theory of Law*. New York: Harper and Row.
PROVINE, Marie Doris (1986) *Judging Credentials: Non-lawyer Judges and the Politics of Professionalism*. Chicago: University of Chicago Press.
RANGER, Terence (1983) "The Invention of Tradition in Colonial Africa," in Eric Hobsbawm and Terence Ranger (eds.), *The Invention of Tradition*.
ROBERTS, Simon (1986) "Book Review: A.N. Allott and Gordon R. Woodman, *People's Law and State Law: The Bellagio Papers*," 24 *Journal of Legal Pluralism* 171.
ROSEN, Lawrence (1980–81) "Equity and Discretion in a Modern Islamic Legal System," 15 *Law & Society Review* 217.
RUFFINI, J.L. (1978) "Disputing over Livestock in Sardinia," in L. Nader and H. Todd (eds.), *The Disputing Process–Law in Ten Societies*. New York: Columbia University Press.
SALAMONE, Frank A. (1983) "The Clash Between Indigenous, Islamic, Colonial and Post-Colonial Law in Nigeria," 21 *Journal of Legal Pluralism* 15.
SALAS, Louis (1983) "The Emergence and Decline of the Cuban Popular Tribunals," 17 *Law & Society Review* 587.
SANTOS, Boaventura De Sousa (1987) "Law: A Map of Misreading; Toward a Postmodern Conception of Law," 14 *Journal of Law and Society* 279.
—— (1982) "Law and Community: The Changing Nature of State Power in

896   LEGAL PLURALISM

Late Capitalism," in Richard Abel. (ed.), *The Politics of Informal Justice*, Vol. I. New York: Academic Press.

——— (1977) "The Law of the Oppressed: The Construction and Reproduction of Legality in Pasagarda," 12 *Law & Society Review* 5.

SARAT, Austin (1988) "The 'New Formalism' in Disputing and Dispute Processing," 21 *Law & Society Review* 695.

SARAT, Austin, and William FELSTINER (1986) "Law and Strategy in the Divorce Lawyer's Office," 20 *Law & Society Review* 93.

SCHEINGOLD, Stuart A. (1974) *The Politics of Rights: Lawyers, Public Policy, and Political Change*. New Haven, Conn.: Yale University Press.

SILBEY, Susan S. (1980–81) "Case Processing: Consumer Protection in an Attorney General's Office," 15 *Law & Society Review* 849.

SILBEY, Susan S., and Egon BITTNER (1982) "The Availability of Law," 4 *Law and Policy* 399.

SILLIMAN, G. Sidney (1985) "A Political Analysis of the Philippines' Katarungang Pambarangay System of Informal Justice through Mediation," 19 *Law & Society Review* 279.

SNYDER, Francis G. (1981a) *Capitalism and Legal Change: An African Transformation*. New York: Academic Press.

——— (1981b) "Colonialism and Legal Form: The Creation of 'Customary Law' in Senegal," 19 *Journal of Legal Pluralism* 49.

——— (1980) "Law and Development in the Light of Dependency Theory," 14 *Law & Society Review* 723.

SPENCE, Jack (1978) "Institutionalizing Neighborhood Courts: Two Chilean Experiences," 13 *Law & Society Review* 139.

STARR, June (1978) *Dispute and Settlement in Rural Turkey* Leiden: E.J. Brill.

STARR, June, and Jane F. COLLIER (1989) *History and Power in the Study of Law: New Directions in Legal Anthropology*, Ithaca, N.Y.: Cornell University Press.

——— (1987) "Historical Studies of Legal Change," 28 *Current Anthropology* 367.

STARR, June, and Jonathan POOL (1974) "The Impact of a Legal Revolution in Rural Turkey," 8 *Law & Society Review* 533.

STRIJBOSCH, F. (1985) "The Concept of Pela and its Social Significance in the Community of Moluccan Immigrants in the Netherlands," 23 *Journal of Legal Pluralism* 177.

SUGARMAN, David (1983) "Law, Economy, and the State in England, 1750–1914: Some Major Issues," in David Sugarman (ed.), *Legality, Ideology and the State.* London and New York: Academic Press, pp. 213–267.

TRUBEK, David, and Marc GALANTER (1974) "Scholars in Self-Estrangement," 1974 *Wisconsin Law Review* 1062.

VAN DEN BERGH, G.C.J.J. et al. (1980) *Staphorst en zijn Gerichten* (Staphorst and its Popular Tribunals). Amsterdam: Boom Meppel.

WESTERMARK, George D. (1986) "Court is an Arrow: Legal Pluralism in Papua New Guinea," 25 *Ethnology* 131.

WOLF, Eric R. (1982) *Europe and the People Without History*. Berkeley: University of California Press.

WOODMAN, Gordon R. (1987–88) "What is the Commission About?," 14 *Newsletter of the Commission on Folk Law and Legal Pluralism* 3.

YNGVESSON, Barbara (1988) "Private Nuisance, Public Crime: The Clerk, the Court, and the Construction of Order in a New England Town," 22 *Law & Society Review.*

——— (1985) "Legal Ideology and Community Justice in the Clerk's Office," 9 *Legal Studies Forum* 71.

[9]

THE TWO FACES OF JANUS: RETHINKING LEGAL PLURALISM

Gunther Teubner*

Et enfin: les phrases de régime ou de genre hétérogène se 'rencontrent' sur les noms propres, dans les mondes déterminés par les réseaux de noms.[1]

I.

Postmodern jurists love legal pluralism. They do not care about the law of the centralized State with its universalist aspirations. It is the "asphalt law" of the Brasilian *favelas*, the informal counter-rules of the patchwork of minorities, the quasi-laws of dispersed ethnic, religious, and cultural groups, the disciplinary techniques of "private justice," the plurality of non-State laws in associations, formal organizations, and informal networks where they find the ingredients of postmodernity: the local, the plural, the subversive. The multitude of "fragmented discourses" which are hermetically closed to each other can be identified in numerous informal kinds of law that are generated quite independent of the State and that operate at various levels of formality. Looking to the "dark side" of the majestic rule of law, legal pluralism rediscovers the subversive power of suppressed discourses. Plural, informal, local quasi-laws are seen as the "supplement" of the official, formal centralism of the modern legal order.

It is the ambivalent, double-faced character of legal pluralism that is so attractive to postmodern jurists. Like the old Roman god Janus, guardian of gates and doors, beginnings and ends, with two faces, one on the front and the other at the back of his head, legal pluralism is at the same time both: social norms *and* legal rules, law *and* society, formal *and* informal, rule-oriented *and* spontaneous. And the relations between the legal and the social in legal pluralism are highly ambiguous, almost paradoxical: separate but intertwined, autonomous but interdependent, closed but open. Boaventura de

---

Professor of Private Law and Legal Sociology, Bremen and European University Institute at Florence. Dr. jur., Tübingen, 1970; Assessor, Stuttgart, 1971; M.A. (Law & Society), University of California at Berkeley, 1974; Habilitation, Tübingen, 1977.

[1] JEAN-FRANÇOIS LYOTARD, LE DIFFÉREND 51 (1983), *translated in* THE DIFFEREND: PHRASES IN DISPUTE [46 THEORY & HISTORY OF LITERATURE] 29 (Georges Van Den Abbeele trans., 1988) [hereinafter THE DIFFEREND] ("Finally: phrases from heterogeneous regimens or genres 'encounter' each other in proper names, in worlds determined by networks of names.").

Sousa Santos, one of the protagonists of postmodern legal style, declares the program:

> Legal pluralism is the key concept in a post-modern view of law. Not the legal pluralism of traditional legal anthropology in which the different legal orders are conceived as separate entities coexisting in the same political space, but rather the conception of different legal spaces superposed, interpenetrated and mixed in our minds as much as in our actions, in occasions of qualitative leaps or sweeping crises in our life trajectories as well as in the dull routine of eventless everyday life.[2]

The crucial question of how to reconstruct, in postmodern architecture, the connections between the social and the legal finds a highly vague answer: interpenetrating, intertwined, integral, superposed, mutually constitutive, dialectical . . . . We are left with ambiguity and confusion. After all, this is the very charm of postmodernism.

II.

Does autopoiesis lead us any further here? Can we better understand legal pluralism's interwovenness of the social and the legal via "operational closure and structural coupling"? Legal autopoiesis and postmodern jurisprudence have several things in common: the linguistic turn away from positivist sociology of law, the dissolution of social and legal realities into discursivity, the image of fragmentation and closure of multiple discourses, the nonfoundational character of legal reasoning, the decentering of the legal subject, the eclectic exploitation of diverse traditions in legal thought, the preference for difference, *différance and différends* over unity, and most important, the foundation of law on paradoxes, antinomies, and tautologies. But here the bifurcation begins. While postmodernists are obviously satisfied to deconstruct legal doctrine and are joyfully playing with antinomies and paradoxes, legal autopoiesis poses the somewhat sobering question: After the deconstruction?

Creative use of paradox is the message that moves autopoiesis beyond deconstructive analysis into reconstructive practice. It is the experience of real life, the experience that discursive practices "know" how to overcome the blockage of paradoxes and antinomies that does not allow autopoiesis theory to remain in the comforting twilight of closure and openness, separation and interwovenness, autonomy and interdependence in legal pluralism. Paradoxes, tautologies, contradictions, and ambiguities in discursive practice are not the end of auto-

---

[2] Boaventura de Sousa Santos, *Law: A Map of Misreading. Toward a Postmodern Conception of Law*, 14 J.L. & Soc'y 279, 293 (1987).

poietic analysis; they are seen as the starting point, as the very foundation of self-organizing social practices.

At the same time legal pluralism can be seen as a kind of test case for autopoiesis theory, since even for sympathizing observers this latter theory seems to have "tended towards a too radical separation between law and society."[3] Can a theory that stresses operational closure of social systems take sufficient account of intersecting bodies of expertise?[4] While it may be plausible to describe the official law of the centralized State as autonomous, self-referential, and self-productive, this becomes highly questionable in the "fleeting ambivalence" of legal pluralism[5] where the legal merges into the social and vice versa.

This problem has to do with autopoietics' own history. In regard to operational closure—which was the broadside on open systems theory—the theory is well developed. However, autopoietic theory is rather underdeveloped when it comes to spelling out the logics of informational openness and structural coupling. Until now, autopoietic theory has quite successfully transformed the theory of open systems into a theory of operationally closed systems without at the same time falling back into old ideas of a system without an environment.[6] Indeed, the reformulation of basic concepts of system theory from input-conversion-output into operational closure entails a full-fledged change of paradigm. System, function, structure, process, double contingency, communication, action, and, above all, meaning—all these notions find a new conceptualization in the world of autonomy and closure, self-reference and autopoiesis. However, this is the point where new problems emerge: How can one cope with the paradox that the closure of cognizing systems is the basis for their openness? How can one—on the basis of operative closure—construct an openness which is different from input-output relations? How does autopoiesis theory solve the self-imposed enigma: *"L'ouvert s'appuye sur le fermé"?*[7]

The metaphor is *order from noise.* Perturbation, structural coup-

[3] David Nelken, *Review Essay: Beyond the Study of "Law and Society"? Henry's "Private Justice" and O'Hagen's "The End of the Law"?*, 1986 AM. B. FOUND RES. J. 323, 338 (book reviews).

[4] Gunther Teubner, *How the Law Thinks: Toward a Constructivist Epistemology of Law*, 23 LAW & SOC'Y REV. 746 (1989).

[5] Stuart Henry, *The Construction and Deconstruction of Social Control: Thoughts on the Discursive Production of State Law and Private Justice*, in TRANSCARCERATION: ESSAYS IN THE SOCIOLOGY OF SOCIAL CONTROL 89, 93 (John Lowmann et al. eds., 1987).

[6] *See* NIKLAS LUHMANN, SOZIALE SYSTEME (1984).

[7] EDGAR MORIN, LA MÉTHODE III: LA CONNAISSANCE DE LA CONNAISSANCE/1, at 203 *passim* (1986).

ling, and coevolution are the key concepts.[8] This can be misunderstood as an easy compromise between operative closure and input-output-relations, a "middle path" between two extremes.[9] However, what it really does is to radicalize simultaneously both closure and openness. To make cognition possible at all, systems need to develop operative closure and at the same time open up toward their environment in a new and different way: not via input-output, but via perturbation and structural coupling. The difference is subtle but important. "Open systems" receive informational input from the environment and convert it through internal processes into informational output which may be used as new input in a feedback loop.[10] By contrast, an operationally closed system is structurally coupled to its niche when it uses events in the environment as perturbations in order to build or to change its internal structures. From external noise it creates internal order.[11] The contact between the system and its niche are real; however, the environmental constraints are not defined externally by spatio-temporal reality.[12] Rather, it is the system itself that defines its environmental constraints by projecting expectations on perturbating events. The perturbatory event then is interpreted as the expectation's fulfillment or its disappointment. And this bifurcation decides about the way in which internal operations will be continued. Thus, a system that disposes of the internal distinction between self-reference and hetero-reference makes itself dependent upon the environment using external events as conditions of its own operations, as irritations as well as opportunities for structural change.[13] The multiplication of such singular micro-synchronizations of system and niche then leads to a common path of development, to structural drift and coevolution.[14]

This seems a promising set of ideas to rethink the relations between the legal discourse and other social discourses, especially under the challenge of legal pluralism. It helps to understand the "relative

---

[8] HUMBERTO R. MATURANA & FRANCISCO J. VARELA, AUTOPOIESIS AND COGNITION: THE REALIZATION OF THE LIVING 102-11 (1980); HUMBERTO R. MATURANA & FRANCISCO J. VARELA, THE TREE OF KNOWLEDGE: THE BIOLOGICAL ROOTS OF HUMAN UNDERSTANDING ch. 6 (1987) [hereinafter TREE OF KNOWLEDGE]; HEINZ VON FÖRSTER, OBSERVING SYSTEMS 274-81 (1981); LUHMANN, *supra* note 6, at ch. 5.

[9] Francisco J. Varela, *Living Ways of Sense-Making: A Middle Path for Neuro-Science*, in DISORDER AND ORDER: PROCEEDINGS OF THE STANFORD INTERNATIONAL SYMPOSIUM (SEPT. 14-16, 1981) 208 (Paisley Livingston ed., 1984).

[10] *See, e.g.*, WALTER BUCKLEY, SOCIOLOGY AND MODERN SYSTEMS THEORY 34-35 (1967).

[11] FÖRSTER, *supra* note 8, at 15.

[12] MICHAEL A. ARBIB & MARY B. HESSE, THE CONSTRUCTION OF REALITY 3 (1986).

[13] NIKLAS LUHMANN, DIE WISSENSCHAFT DER GESELLSCHAFT 29-32, 163-66 (1990).

[14] TREE OF KNOWLEDGE, *supra* note 8, at ch. 5.

autonomy" of law better than the simple distinction of internal and external causes of legal change would permit.[15] It promises to clarify the obscure metaphor of *interwovenness* of the legal and the social and to replace it with a genuine theoretical construction that makes us see more clearly which aspects are responsible for the openness of law and which for closure, even in the twilight of legal pluralism.

However, in spite of all its innovative potential, the concept of structural coupling developed in General Systems Theory is not complex enough to cope with the special problems of law and society. After all, the relations between law and other social fields result from internal differentiation of one and only one society. Thus, in spite of all their autonomy, they belong to the same comprehensive social system and cannot simply be conceptualized according to the model of two independent autopoietic systems. The vexing conundrum of "autopoiesis within autopoiesis" which poses itself for autonomous sectors within society[16] presses for modifications of the general concept: Is not law, in relation to other cultural provinces like politics, science, economy, religion, culture, much more "open" than the general concept of structural coupling would permit? Is not "interdiscursivity"[17] in law and society much more dense than mere transitory perturbations could ever produce? And do we not find in the coevolution of law and society significantly more elective affinities than the mere coexistence of structural drift would provide for? To use our metaphor as a theme with variations: "order from music" instead of "order from noise"?

In order to do justice to interdiscursive relations in law and society I propose to modify the idea of structural coupling:

(1) *Productive misreading:* Since interdiscursivity means structural coupling in a situation of autopoiesis within autopoiesis, mere perturbation does not suffice to grasp the specific closure/openness of social subsystems. In the relations between social discourses, I suggest replacing perturbation with productive misreading. In legal pluralism the legal discourse is not only perturbated by processes of social self-production, but law productively misreads other social discourses as "sources" of norm production.

(2) *Linkage institutions:* Structural coupling depends on specific institutions of linkage that shape its duration, quality, and intensity.

---

15 Compare the debate between Richard Lempert in *The Autonomy of Law: Two Visions Compared*, in AUTOPOIETIC LAW: A NEW APPROACH TO LAW AND SOCIETY 152 (Gunther Teubner ed., 1988) [hereinafter AUTOPOIETIC LAW] and Niklas Luhmann in *Closure and Openness: On Reality in the World of Law*, in AUTOPOIETIC LAW, *supra*, at 335.

16 GUNTHER TEUBNER, LAW AS AN AUTOPOIETIC SYSTEM ch. 3 (forthcoming 1992).

17 BERNHARD S. JACKSON, LAW, FACT AND NORMATIVE COHERENCE (1988).

While in "old" legal pluralism the main institutional link was the legal formalization of diffuse social norms, the "new" legal pluralism is characterized by specialized institutions that bind law to a multitude of functional subsystems and formal organizations.

(3) *Responsiveness:* Coevolution leads to mere viability of internal constructs of law. In contrast, social responsiveness comes about when linkage institutions connect law more tightly to other autonomous social discourses. Legal pluralism makes law more responsive to society, not by increasing explicit social and economic knowledge of law, but by using the synchronicity of legal and social operations as the law's tacit knowledge.

III.

The new legal pluralism moves away from questions about the effect of law on society or even the effect of society on law toward conceptualizing a more complex and interactive relationship between official and unofficial forms of ordering. Instead of mutual influences between two separate entities, this perspective sees plural forms of ordering as participating in the same social field.[18]

Indeed, this new view—concisely conceptualized by John Griffiths[19]—means considerable progress, primarily as against a legalistic view of legal pluralism that defined it as a problem of State law's "recognition" of subordinate normative orders like regional or corporate regimes. It successfully moves away from hierarchical concepts of legal pluralism that tended to identify "legal levels" with a hierarchical stratified structure of society, ignoring legal phenomena outside the hierarchy.[20] And it liberates itself from the heritage of old-style institutionalism that "reified" the social locus of legal pluralism in formally structured institutions, corporations, and organizations.[21] The new legal pluralism is nonlegalistic, nonhierarchical, and noninstitutional. It focuses on the dynamic interaction of a multitude of "legal orders" within one social field.[22]

---

[18] Sally Engle Merry, *Legal Pluralism*, 22 LAW & SOC'Y REV. 869, 873 (1988).

[19] John Griffiths, *What is Legal Pluralism?*, 24 J. LEGAL PLURALISM 1 (1986).

[20] LEOPOLD POSPIŠIL, ANTHROPOLOGY OF LAW: A COMPARATIVE THEORY 125 (1971).

[21] MICHAEL G. SMITH, CORPORATIONS AND SOCIETY: THE SOCIAL ANTHROPOLOGY OF COLLECTIVE ACTION (1974).

[22] Sally Falk Moore, *Law and Social Change: The Semi-Autonomous Social Field as an Appropriate Subject of Study*, 7 LAW & SOC'Y REV. 719 (1973). *See also* Marc Galanter, *Justice in Many Rooms*, in ACCESS TO JUSTICE AND THE WELFARE STATE 147 (Mauro Cappelletti ed., 1981); Francis G. Snyder, *Colonialism and Legal Form: The Creation of "Customary Law" in Senegal*, 19 J. LEGAL PLURALISM & UNOFFICIAL L. 49, 79 (1981); Boaventura de Sousa Santos, *On Modes of Production of Law and Social Power*, 13 INT'L J. SOC. L. 299 (1985); de Sousa Santos, *supra* note 2; Peter Fitzpatrick, *Law and Societies*, 22 OSGOODE

There is a price to be paid for progress. As a consequence of its own construction, the new legal pluralism is confronted with the disquieting question: "Where do we stop speaking of law and find ourselves simply describing social life?"[23] Two things have been lost in the course of progress, in the move from spatial separation to discursive interwovenness: (1) the notion of what is distinctively "legal" in the new legal pluralism as well as (2) a clear-cut concept of the interrelations between the social and the legal.

If we take a concrete market as our "semi-autonomous social field,"[24] what counts as one among many legal "orders"? Antitrust rules, consumer protection laws, and the contract law of the courts are easy cases since they have the stamp of official law. The written agreements of the parties to the transaction and the rules of adhesion contracts clearly belong to the competing "private" legal orders as well as the unwritten customary rules of the trade and the disciplinary rules within a firm. But what about the demands required by informal exchange relations: the gifts, loans, and favors that dominate the day-to-day relations? What about the emerging habits in an ongoing contractual relationship, what about informal rules within the firms and their organizational patterns and routines, what about economic trust relations in the market? What about the exigencies of rational economic calculation? And what about power pressures from an oligopolist in the market or "tax" rules of a local mafia?

Structuralist solutions seem to me as unsatisfactory as functionalist ones. The usual structuralist solution is normativity; it includes within legal pluralism normative expectations of any kind, but excludes merely cognitive expectations as well as purely economic or political pressures. However, normative expectations as such (in a sociological, not in a legal sense, of course) are not sufficient to grasp the distinctively legal in legal pluralism. It is not only the age-old problem of how to delineate rules of non-State law from moral, social, and conventional norms, but also its inherently static, nondynamic, nonprocessual character that speaks against such a structuralist solution.

Therefore, new legal pluralists tend to replace "law" by social

---

HALL L.J. 115 (1984); STUART HENRY, PRIVATE JUSTICE: TOWARDS INTEGRATED THEORISING IN THE SOCIOLOGY OF LAW (1983); Stuart Henry, *Community Justice, Capitalist Society, and Human Agency: The Dialectics of Collective Law in the Cooperative*, 19 LAW & SOC'Y REV. 303 (1985) [hereinafter *Community Justice*]; Henry, *supra* note 5; Stewart Macaulay, *Private Government, in* LAW AND THE SOCIAL SCIENCES 445 (Leon Lipson & Stanton Wheeler eds., 1986); Griffiths, *supra* note 19; Merry, *supra* note 18.

[23] Merry, *supra* note 18, at 878.
[24] Moore, *supra* note 22, at 721.

control.[25] They would include all the phenomena mentioned in our example within legal pluralism, even purely economic exigencies and sheer power pressures. If legal pluralism entailed anything that serves the function of social control, it would be identical to a comprehensive pluralism of social constraints of any kind. Stanley Cohen probably exaggerates in calling social control a "Mickey Mouse concept, used to include all social processes ranging from infant socialisation to public execution, all social policies whether called health, education or welfare."[26] But he has a point. Why should it be just the function of "social control"[27] that defines law in legal pluralism and not the function of "conflict resolution," as theories of private justice would suggest?[28] But then we would have to include different social phenomena in legal pluralism and exclude others. Why could it not be the function of "coordinating behavior,"[29] the function of "securing expectations,"[30] or the function of "social regulation" which theories of private government would underline?[31] And why not "discipline and punish," which would tend to include any mechanism of disciplinary micro-power that permeates social life?[32] Each of these functions would bring rather diverse social mechanisms into the realm of legal pluralism.[33] Functional analysis of this kind, which occurs because of today's fashions in a hidden form rather than an overt one, is certainly fruitful in comparing functional equivalents of law. However, it is not at all suitable to provide criteria for the delineation of the legal and the nonlegal in legal pluralism.

Now, let us follow the linguistic turn. The decisive move—it seems to me—is from structure to process, from norm to action, from unity to difference, and, most important for the legal proprium, from

---

[25] *Id.* See explicitly Griffiths, *supra* note 19, at 50 n.41 ("more or less specialized social control").

[26] Stanley Cohen, *Social-Control Talk: Telling Stories about Correctional Change, in* THE POWER TO PUNISH: CONTEMPORARY PENALITY AND SOCIAL ANALYSIS 101, 101-02 (David Garland & Peter Young eds., 1983).

[27] Griffiths, *supra* note 19, at 50 n.41.

[28] Galanter, *supra* note 22; Henry, *Community Justice, supra* note 22.

[29] THEODOR GEIGER, VORSTUDIEN ZU EINER SOZIOLOGIE DES RECHTS 48 (4th ed. 1987).

[30] NIKLAS LUHMANN, A SOCIOLOGICAL THEORY OF LAW ch. II, § 2.6 (Martin Albrow ed., Elizabeth King & Martin Albrow trans., 1985).

[31] *See* Macaulay, *supra* note 22.

[32] MICHEL FOUCAULT, DISCIPLINE AND PUNISH: THE BIRTH OF THE PRISON (Alan Sheridan trans., Random House 1977) (1975); Peter Fitzpatrick, *"The Desperate Vacuum": Imperialism and Law in the Experience of Enlightenment*, 13 DROIT ET SOCIÉTÉ 347 (1989).

[33] *See* Joseph Raz, *On the Functions of Law, in* OXFORD ESSAYS IN JURISPRUDENCE (SECOND SERIES) 278 (A.W.B. Simpson ed., 1973); KLAUS F. RÖHL, RECHTSSOZIOLOGIE: EIN LEHRBUCH § 26.5 (1987); MICHEL VAN DE KERCHOVE & FRANCOIS OST, LE SYSTÈME JURIDIQUE ENTRE ORDRE ET DÉSORDRE 161-66 (1988).

function to code.[34] This move brings forward the dynamic processual character of legal pluralism, and at the same time delineates clearly the "legal" from other types of social action. *Legal pluralism is then defined no longer as a set of conflicting social norms in a given social field but as a multiplicity of diverse communicative processes that observe social action under the binary code of legal/illegal.* Purely economic calculations from our example are excluded from its ambit as are sheer pressures of power, merely conventional or moral norms, and organizational routines. But whenever such nonlegal phenomena are communicatively observed under the *distinction directrice* legal/illegal,[35] then they make part of the game of legal pluralism. It is the—implicit or explicit—invocation of the legal code which constitutes phenomena of legal pluralism, ranging from the official law of the State to the unofficial laws of markets and mafias.

To avoid misunderstanding, I should hasten to add: The binary code legal/illegal is not peculiar to the law of the State. This is not at all a view of "legal centralism."[36] It refutes categorically any hierarchically superior position of the official law of the State, but invokes rather the imagery of a heterarchy of diverse legal discourses. "Tax laws" of a local mafia that grants its "protection" to the merchants are the case in point. Clearly, in their "illegality," they are excluded from any "recognition" by the official law of the State. Nevertheless, mafia rules are an integral part of legal pluralism in our semiautonomous social field insofar as they use the binary code of legal communication. They belong to the multitude of fragmented legal discourses, be they State law, rules of private justice, regulations of private government, or outright "illegal" laws of underground organizations, that play a part in the dynamic process of mutual constitution of actions and structures in the social field. The multiple orders of legal pluralism always produce normative expectations in the sociological sense, excluding however merely social conventions and moral norms since they are not based on the binary code legal/illegal. And "law" in this broad sense may serve many functions (of the Mickey Mouse type): social control, conflict regulation, securing expectations, social regulation, coordination of behavior, or disciplining bodies and

---

[34] *See* Niklas Luhmann, *Operational Closure and Structural Coupling: The Differentiation of the Legal System*, 13 CARDOZO L. REV. 1419 (1992); TEUBNER, *supra* note 16, at ch. 3.

[35] Niklas Luhmann, *The Coding of the Legal System*, *in* STATE, LAW, ECONOMY AS AUTOPOIETIC SYSTEMS (Alberto Febbrajo & Gunther Teubner eds., forthcoming 1992).

[36] Griffiths, *supra* note 19, at 2-3; Franz von Benda-Beckmann, *Unterwerfung oder Distanz: Rechtssoziologie, Rechtsanthropologie und Rechtspluralismus aus rechtsanthropologischer Sicht*, 12 ZEITSCHRIFT FÜR RECHTSSOZIOLOGIE 97, 106 *passim* (1991).

souls. It is neither structure nor function but the binary code that defines what is *legal* in legal pluralism.

Why is it so important to be meticulous in defining the legal proprium? Should we not be more interested in a theory of law than in a mere concept of law?[37] And is the definition of law not something that varies according to the research interests involved? Surely, any observer may draw the lines between law and nonlaw according to the concrete cognitive interests. But there is one privileged delineation: this is the line that the discursive practice of law draws between itself and its environment. If we are interested in a theory of law as a self-organizing social practice, then it is not up to the arbitrary research interests to define the boundaries of law. Boundaries of law are one among many structures that law itself produces under the pressures of its social environment. And only a clear delineation of the self-produced boundaries of law can help to clarify the interrelations of law and other social practices.

IV.

If law and other discourses close their boundaries via the use of binary codes, how is "interdiscursivity"[38] nevertheless feasible? How does legal autopoiesis respond to Lyotard's challenge of fragmented discourses: "[I]l faut bien qu'elles aient ensemble des propriétés communes, et que la 'rencontre' ait lieu dans un même univers, sinon il n'y aurait pas de rencontre du tout!"[39]

In the case of legal pluralism, what about the relations between unofficial and official legal discourses? What about the relations between them and other social discourses? The formulas of neopluralism—interwoven, integral, dialectical, superimposed—are suggestive metaphors, but they lack analytical power.[40] "Mutually constitutive"[41] is by far the most powerful image, but how does mutual constitution work? Fitzpatrick explains what he calls *integral pluralism:* "Custom supports law, but law transforms the elements of custom that it appropriates into its own image and likeness. Law, in turn, supports other social forms, but becomes in the process part of the

---

[37] PHILIPPE NONET & PHILIP SELZNICK, LAW AND SOCIETY IN TRANSITION: TOWARD RESPONSIVE LAW 10-11 (1978).

[38] JACKSON, *supra* note 17.

[39] LYOTARD, *supra* note 1, at 50, *translated in* THE DIFFEREND, *supra* note 1, at 28 ("then they must have certain properties in common and their 'encounter' must take place within a single universe, otherwise there would be no encounter at all!").

[40] *Cf.* the critique by Nelken, *supra* note 3.

[41] Fitzpatrick, *supra* note 22, at 122.

other forms."[42] How separate are they in their interwovenness? After all, "talking of intertwining, interaction or mutual constitution presupposes distinguishing what is being intertwined."[43]

I propose to analyze "interdiscursivity" in terms of a clear-cut separation of autonomous (not semiautonomous) discourses and, at the same time, in terms of their structural coupling. In our example of market transactions, we have a simultaneous, but acausal parallel processing of diverse legal and nonlegal communicative chains that are operationally closed to each other. Each chain builds up structures of its own: concrete day-to-day interaction of the transacting parties, communication within formalized contracts and organizations, economic transactions as part of the larger economic system, and claims and counterclaims within diverse and competing legal discourses, both official and unofficial. All these discursive processes interfere in one and the same social situation. And each concrete communicative event will be processed in these different discourses which, in spite of this "overlapping membership" (of a communicative event, not of a person), remain closed to each other. Over time, these discourses coevolve in relations of structural coupling. They do not causally influence each other, rather they use each other as *chocs exogènes,*[44] as perturbations to build up their own internal structures.

This is the point where "productive misunderstanding" comes in to explain in more detail what could be meant by "mutually constitutive" relations between social and legal form and between different legal discourses.[45] In a firm, hierarchical patterns of decision making, roles of supervision and control, and rules of competence are law-free organizational routines that guide the self-production of ongoing social processes. Whenever the *quaestrio juris* is raised, for example in an internal disciplinary action, a subtle but decisive shift of meaning occurs. The firm's internal legal process, the system of "private justice"[46]—not the official law of the State—rereads, reinterprets, reconstructs, reobserves these routines under the code legal/illegal and constitutes them anew as integral part of intraorganizational law. This is a mere fiction because organizational routines were meant as something else. The intraorganizational legal discourse misreads or-

---

[42] *Id.*

[43] Franz von Benda-Beckmann, *Comment on Merry*, 22 LAW & SOC'Y REV. 897, 898 (1988).

[44] VAN DE KERCHOVE & OST, *supra* note 33, at 151.

[45] *See also* Gunther Teubner, *Autopoiesis and Steering: How Politics Profits From the Normative Surplus of Capital,* in AUTOPOIESIS AND CONFIGURATION THEORY: NEW APPROACHES TO SOCIETAL STEERING 127 (Roeland J. In't Veld et al. eds., 1991).

[46] HENRY, *supra* note 22.

ganizational self-production as norm production and thus invents a new and rich "source" of law. And it is the famous "legal affinity" of formal organizations[47] that supports law's subtle misreading of organization. Since organizational routines tend to be "formalized" (that is, they shift from a mix of cognitive and normative expectations to purely normative expectations), it needs only a minute shift of meaning to read them as legal norms that had already existed before.

Vice versa, a similar misreading occurs when the organization reincorporates legal rules developed and refined in the firm's disciplinary proceedings and makes use of them in order to restructure the firm's decision-making process. These originally legal norms are *decoded*. They are observed no longer under the code legal/illegal, stripped of their legal connotations of valid/nonvalid and of their structural context of disciplinary rules, and are reconstituted as power bases in the micropolitical games of the organization. The mutual constitution of law and organization turns out to be a mutual misreading, a reciprocal construction of fictitious realities, a mutual distortion which, however, works for practical purposes.

A similar constructive distortion takes place in the case of economic transactions. The structures of economic transactions are essentially nonlegal; they build on factual chances of action and create new chances of action or they build on trust in future changes of chances. In ongoing business relations it is wise to keep the lawyers out. They will distort business realities.[48] Why? They misread factual chances of action as legal "property," and they misunderstand mutual trust in future behavior as contractually binding "obligations," as "rights" and "duties." And if their rigid and formalist claims and counterclaims are reread in the ongoing transaction relation, they will destroy precarious trust relations. The difference between economic chances of action and legal property and between trust and obligations is again due to the difference in coding. The

---

[47] PHILIP SELZNICK, LAW, SOCIETY, AND INDUSTRIAL JUSTICE 32 *passim* (1969); Renate Mayntz, *Politische Steuerung und gesellschaftliche Steuerungsprobleme—Anmerkungen zu einem theoretischen Paradigma*, in 1 JAHRBUCH ZUR STAATS- UND VERWALTUNGSWISSEN-SCHAFT 89, 103 (Thomas Ellwein et al. eds., 1987); Fritz W. Scharpf, *Grenzen der institutionellen Reform*, in 1 JAHRBUCH, *supra*, at 111, 117-20; Fritz W. Scharpf, *Politische Steuerung und Politische Institutionen*. 30 POLITISCHE VIERTELJAHRESSCHRIFT 10, 16 (1989); Franz-Xaver Kaufmann, *Steuerung wohlfahrtsstaatlicher Abläufe durch Recht*, in GESETZGEBUNGSTHE-ORIE UND RECHTSPOLITIK [13 JARBUCH FÜR RECHTSSOZIOLOGIE UND RECHTSTHEORIE] 65, 82-85 (Dieter Grimm & Werner Maihofer eds., 1988); Lauren B. Edelman. *Legal Environments and Organizational Governance: The Expansion of Due Process in the American Workplace*, 95 AM. J. SOC. 1401, 1406-17, 1435-37 (1990).

[48] *See* STEWART MACAULAY, LAW AND THE BALANCE OF POWER: THE AUTOMOBILE MANUFACTURERS AND THEIR DEALERS (1966).

lawyers observe economic action under the code legal/illegal and misread economic processes and structures as sources of law. Conversely, clever economic actors misread legal norms under the economic code as bargaining chips, as new opportunities for profit-making. Again, we have a symbiosis of mutual distortion. In Lyotard's words, the isolated discourses which are not translatable into each other "meet" in the *"reseaux de noms."*[49]

Note that in both our examples the State and its official law did not enter our consideration. The juridification of social phenomena, or, in our words, the legal distortion of social realities, happens independently of the "recognition" of this law through the State and the courts. Within the regimes of "private government,"[50] "private justice,"[51] and "private regulation,"[52] one should distinguish carefully between (1) phenomena like micropolitical power structures and economic exigencies and moral or social conventional expectations, which are essentially nonlegal, (2) their reconstruction within genuinely legal processes of non-State character like private agreements, intraorganizational disciplinary procedures, interorganizational regimes of oligopolist market regulations, and (3) their legislative, administrative, or judicial "recognition" which produces new rules of State law. Thus, interdiscursivity occurs in two diverse forms: between legal discourses (State law versus "private law" and mafia law) and between legal and nonlegal discourses (legal versus moral, economic, political phenomena). This is due to the difference between *binary codes,* which are stable, and *programs,* which are historically contingent.[53] In both cases, one can speak about recontextualization, in the first case between legal and nonlegal discourses as decoding and recoding, in the second case between different legal discourses as deprogramming and reprogramming. But one has to free one's mind of any idea of information transportation.[54] After all these distortions, the original normative meaning will not be recognizable any more.

In any case, interdiscursivity in legal pluralism is a conspicuous case of systematically distorted communication. One cannot simply

---

[49] LYOTARD, *supra* note 1, at 10, 51, *translated in* THE DIFFEREND, *supra* note 1, at xii, 29.

[50] Macaulay, *supra* note 22.

[51] HENRY, PRIVATE JUSTICE, *supra* note 22.

[52] Brian Bercusson, *Juridification and Disorder, in* JURIDIFICATION OF SOCIAL SPHERES 49 (Gunther Teubner ed., 1987).

[53] For this distinction, see Luhmann, *supra* note 35.

[54] *See* Klaus Krippendorff, *Eine häretische Kommunikation über Kommunikation über Kommunikation über Realität,* 13 DELFIN 52 (1990).

speak of a "transfer" of constructs from one normative order to the other as older theories of legal pluralism had it. Neither is "interaction," "negotiation," or "interpenetration" of diverse legal orders the adequate metaphor. "Mutual constitution" comes close, however, only under three conditions. First, against all recent assertions on blurring the "law/society" distinction,[55] the boundaries of meaning that separate closed discourses need to be recognized.[56] Second, mutual constitution cannot be understood as a transfer of meaning from one field to the other but needs to be seen as an internal reconstruction process. Third, the internal constraints that render the mutual constitution highly selective must be taken seriously. The constraints that are responsible for systematic distortion are not something that could be avoided by rational argument. It is not just the local specialties of the diverse discourses involved, but basic requirements of their self-reproduction, including the resistance of presently existing structures, that lead with necessity to mutual misreading of discourses.

Unavoidably, this leads us back to closure, to the separation of intertwined systems, to the *différend* of heterogenous discourses, to the "necessarily unbridgeable gaps [sic!] between law and other social forms."[57] The dynamics of legal pluralism cannot be understood by a common logics of the discourses involved, be it the transaction economics of law and organization, the politics of omnipresent micro-power, the socio-logics of social control, or yesterday's political economy. Rather, it is the radical diversity of discourses—the internal rationality of the organization, the exigencies of the market, the idiosyncracies of personal interaction, and the intrinsic logics of diverse public and "private" legal orders—that are responsible for distorted communication in legal pluralism.

V.

The shift from old to new legal pluralism is often described as a conceptual expansion from colonial domination of the indigenous population to the modern State's domination of a variety of groups.

> Legal pluralism has expanded from a concept that refers to the relations between colonized and colonizer to relations between dominant groups and subordinate groups, such as religious, ethnic, or cultural minorities, immigrant groups, and unofficial forms of ordering located in social networks or institutions.[58]

---

55 Robert W. Gordon, *Critical Legal Histories*, 36 STAN. L. REV. 57, 102-09. (1984).
56 LYOTARD, *supra* note 1, at 24-25, *translated in* THE DIFFEREND, *supra* note 1, at 9-10.
57 Fitzpatrick, *supra* note 22, at 128.
58 Merry, *supra* note 18, at 872-73.

In my view, such a perspective of "internal colonialism" that focuses on the modern State dominating the "laws" of diverse groups, misses crucial aspects of modernity. As a consequence, it unduly restricts the scope of the new legal pluralism. "Old" legal pluralism, be it in Europe or be it in the colonies, had to do with the legal formalization of social norms that were the product of general coordination of behavior in diffuse processes of social reproduction. *The "new" legal pluralism needs to shift emphasis and focus on the fragmentation of social self-production in a multiplicity of closed discourses.* "Standard setting" is the new paradigm supplanting "social customs"! Today we face an immense pluralization of legal pluralism which is due not just to the pluralization of groups and communities, but to the fragmentation of social discourses. There is a danger that legal pluralism will be marginalized if the idea of internal colonialism draws attention only to diverse groups, communities, and networks and their social norms, instead of looking to social discourses and their diverse rationalities.

Ubi societas, ibi ius. This old juridical wisdom has undergone a dramatic shift of meaning. In traditional societies it meant the emergence of legal phenomena in different clans, groups, casts, strata, or classes according to the prevailing principle of differentiation.[59] In modern societies it means the emergence of legal phenomena in the context of highly specialized discourses that are the new sources of social self-reproduction which the law then misreads as sources of norm production. This process changes the character of legal pluralism, its content, and its dynamics. To use Gurvitch's imagery of "vertical" and "horizontal" relations between law and society,[60] the main question for legal pluralism is no longer how, in the vertical dimension of law and society, informal and diffuse social norms are gradually formalized into more specific legal norms. Rather, it is in the horizontal dimension, in the relation of law to a variety of other language games, that we today observe pluralist norm production processes. The problem has changed from a translation of social norms of group into legal norms to the recoding of a bewildering multitude of otherwise coded communication in the code of the law. And in this process, I submit, the linkage institutions of legal pluralism have also changed their character; they change from concept and structure to process and transformation.

What are linkage institutions? I propose to distinguish between

---

[59] OTTO GIERKE, DIE GENOSSENSCHAFTSTHEORIE UND DIE DEUTSCHE RECHTSPRECHUNG (Weidmann 1963) (1887).

[60] GEORGES GURVITCH, THE SOCIOLOGY OF LAW 181 (1942).

structural coupling and linkage institutions.[61] Structural coupling as such leads only to transitory structural changes. Legal misreading of other discourses occurs only randomly—as tangential responses, as it were—whenever social communications are observed under the code legal/illegal. The misreading becomes epidemic when linkage institutions are evolving that are responsible for the duration, intensity, and quality of structural coupling. Not only Roman law's *boni mores,* but also classical formulas of *bona fides* and *bonus pater familias*, are the paradigms of the legal tradition. It is their very ambiguity that makes them the institutional links between legal and social processes. They represent, at the same time, social norms and legal norms, "standards" as well as "directives."[62] Like the ancient Roman god Janus, they have a double-faced character. While the concept is identical in law and in society, it is nevertheless different; if you look at it from society "outside" it is different from what you see if you look at it from law "inside."

In modern terminology, the old *boni mores* and other institutional links between law and society would have to be called "essentially contested concepts."[63] They have no fixed reference and take on a different meaning according to the context of the relevant discourse. They have no determined content but are loci for the socio-legal debate. These concepts are "essential" because they reflect the very intrinsic logic of the discourses involved. And they are "contested" because they reflect the basic discursive differences. They do not create a new unity of the separate discourses involved, they only link them transcending the boundaries but respecting, even reaffirming them. In spite of their identical *nom propre* they are purely internal constructs of each discourse involved. Linking institutions do not have an interdiscursive common meaning, they are internal constructs, separate but complementary. "Et enfin: les phrases de régime ou de genre hétérogène se 'rencontrent' sur les noms propres, dans les mondes déterminés par les réseaux de noms."[64]

Now, if it is true that the new legal pluralism "juridifies" specialized discourses instead of diffuse social norms in the lifeworld of groups and communities, then we should also expect the linkage institutions to change. Indeed, in relation to economic processes "con-

---

[61] For details see Teubner, *supra* note 45.

[62] GUNTHER TEUBNER, STANDARDS UND DIREKTIVEN IN GENERALKLAUSELN: MÖGLICHKEITEN UND GRENZEN DER EMPIRISCHEN SOZIALFORSCHUNG BEI DER PRÄZISIERUNG DER GUTE-SITTEN-KLAUSELN IM PRIVATRECHT (1971).

[63] WILLIAM E. CONNOLLY, THE TERMS OF POLITICAL DISCOURSE (2d ed. 1983).

[64] LYOTARD, *supra* note 1, at 51, *translated in* THE DIFFEREND, *supra* note 1, at 29.

tracting" has emerged as the modern linkage institution,[65] in relation to technical, scientific and medical processes "standard setting."[66] The legal discourse, including "private government," "private justice," and "private regulation," constructively misreads economic or technical processes of social reproduction and turns them into new and rich "sources" of law. Certainly, one could interpret this as a specialization of institutional links and still adhere to the model of *boni mores*, the only difference being that their content varies from field to field. But there is more to it. Our "essentially contested concepts" have become "essentially contested processes." The legal discourse no longer "incorporates" results by misreading social norms as legal norms; today it "incorporates" processes misreading economic or technical production as law production.

VI.

We can now see more clearly why legal pluralism represents the "openness" of the law toward society. The legal system's boundaries, to repeat, are not defined by the official law of the State. Rather, any communication that observes action under the legal code constitutes an integral part of the legal discourse, including communication among lay people who invoke claims against one another. It is not the distinction legal/illegal that separates the State's law from the "law" of organizations and groups, but the different use of the operative symbol of "validity." And it is within the overarching legal discourse that we can observe secondary differentiation processes that separate center and periphery.[67] The center is not—as one would expect in old European traditions of thought—political legislation. Legislative law is peripheral law! Rather, the center is represented in the hierarchy of courts. Courts generate law in its most autonomous form. They celebrate the central function of law: using the occasion of conflicts to create congruently generalized expectation. Contemporary law's real dynamism, however, takes place in the "legal peripheries" like the dynamism of social life in the peripheries of the grand

---

65 Teubner, *supra* note 45.

66 *Cf.* Giandomenico Majone, *Science and Trans-Science in Standard Setting*, 9 Sci., Tech. & Hum. Values 15 (1984); Giandomenico Majone, Evidence, Argument and Persuasion in the Policy Process (1989); Liora Salter, *Science and Peer Review: The Canadian Standard-Setting Experience*, 10 Sci., Tech. & Hum. Values 37 (1985); Christian Joerges, *Quality Regulation in Consumer Goods Markets: Theoretical Concepts and Practical Examples*, *in* Contract and Organisation 142 (Terence Daintith & Gunther Teubner eds., 1986).

67 Niklas Luhmann, *Die Stellung der Gerichte im Rechtssystem*, 21 Rechtstheorie 459, 466-69 (1990).

metropolis. Peripheral law is that part of official and unofficial law that is structurally coupled to other social discourses. Here, we find the linkage institutions that participate in legal processes as well as in economic, technical, scientific, and cultural processes. Thus, legal pluralism makes the law "responsive" toward society by transforming social self-production processes into sources of law production.

Responsiveness is not identical to viability. The distinction coupling/binding forces us to distinguish between the mere viability of social structures (knowledge, law, policies) and their responsiveness. Viability means survival of structures under conditions of "structural drift."[68] Indeed, if social systems coevolve under conditions of transitory structural coupling, the result is mere survival of certain structures which have proved resistant to environmental perturbations. Of course, this provides the system with a certainty of reality. If the system is capable of maintaining its own autopoiesis via highly specified structures, then it disposes of an internal indication that it is "on the right track, even without knowing where and how."[69] Viability, however, has two problems. First, there will usually be a whole variety of similarly viable solutions presenting the question of how to select among them. Second, mere viability says nothing about ecological compatibility, about the suitability with social, psychic, and natural environments. Usually, there are more or less ecologically suitable solutions.

Thus, mere viability of systemic eigenvalues does not tell very much about their responsiveness. It is the introduction of linkage institutions that changes the situation drastically. If such institutions permanently link parallel processes of social self-reproduction to each other, the number of possible viable eigenvalues will decrease since they are exposed to increased perturbation under which they have to endure. But at the same time their ecological responsiveness is increasing. Such a responsiveness may become stable if linkage institutions squeeze structural coupling into a direction that prompts systems to act on each other in a cyclical fashion. We then have the interesting case in which processes of self-reproduction would, without the systems involved losing their autopoietic closure, operate outside the boundaries of autopoietic systems. This would be the case of ecological (not systemic!) recursiveness. The autopoiesis of the sys-

---

[68] ERNST VON GLASERSFELD, WISSEN, SPRACHE UND WIRKLICHKEIT: ARBEITEN ZUM RADIKALEN KONSTRUKTIVISMUS (1987); Ernst von Glasersfeld, *An Epistemology for Cognitive Systems, in* SELF-ORGANIZING SYSTEMS: AN INTERDISCIPLINARY APPROACH 121 (Gerhard Roth & Helmut Schwegler eds., 1981).

[69] LUHMANN, *supra* note 13, at 317.

tems involved is not impaired; instead, it is being exploited to build up ecological cycles respecting system boundaries, even though crossing them.

This would indicate the direction in which we would have to search for "responsive law."[70] The usual recommendation is: Politicize formal law! The open acknowledgment of the political character of law and the change of its conceptual apparatus in the political direction, the governance of "purpose," "policies," and "interests"—all this would make the law more responsive to political needs. This is the message of "political jurisprudence" from Jhering to Habermas. To be sure, this strategy has made law more responsive to the political process as such. However, at the same time it has subordinated law to the constructs of political reality. This raises the question of whether such a politicization would not remove law even further away from other social discourses instead of bringing it closer to them.

Importing social science knowledge into law is the other recommendation for making law more responsive. Instead of using the artificial reasoning of law, we should use theoretical insights, empirical experience, and policy recommendations of the social sciences. But again: What reassures us that scientific constructs make law more responsive to social needs?

Legal pluralism—as understood in this text—may be more promising. Linkage institutions that bind law to diverse social discourses much more closely than politics or social science suggest a "resonance" of law with civil society. The institutions of legal pluralism may become a source for the law's "tacit knowledge"[71] about its social ecology. Rethinking legal pluralism in the end could open an "ecological approach" to law and legal intervention.[72] Indeed, the intellectual tradition of "private law" which paved the way for law's historical extraordinary responsiveness to the economic system via the institutions of property, contract, and organization needs to be generalized. Social autonomy is the key word:

Taking autonomy seriously means to rely on self-determination and at the same time on inevitable externalization (outside con-

---

[70] NONET & SELZNICK, *supra* note 37, at 73 *passim*.

[71] MICHAEL POLANYI, PERSONAL KNOWLEDGE: TOWARD A POST-CRITICAL PHILOSOPHY 69 *passim* (1958).

[72] Karl-Heinz Ladeur, *Flexibilisierungsstrategien—Alternativen zum "Steuerungsstaat"—"Reflexives Recht"—"Prozeduralisierung"—"Ökologisches Recht,"* in WORKSHOP ZU KONZEPTEN DES POSTINTERVENTIONISTISCHENRECHTS 311 (Gert Brüggemeier & Christian Joerges eds., 1984); Karl-Heinz Ladeur, *The Law of Uncertainty, in* CRITICAL LEGAL THOUGHT: AN AMERICAN-GERMAN DEBATE 567 (Christian Joerges & David Trubek eds., 1989); David Nelken, *Law in Action or Living Law? Back to the Beginning in Sociology of Law,* 4 LEGAL STUD. 157, 171-74 & n.54 (1984).

trol), not understood as hetero-determination but as a potential outside support in situations of impossible self-help. It would be similar to therapeutical help and to supportive structures outside of the law.[73]

If private law's reliance on social autonomy and structural coupling is applied not only to the economic system but also to the multiplicity of social discourses,[74] it may become a model for new ways in which law, instead of relying solely on its political legitimation and its economic efficiency, opens up to the dynamics of "civil society."

---

[73] Rudolf Wiethölter, *Zum Fortbildungsrecht der (richterlichen) Rechtsfortbildung: Fragen eines lesenden Recht-Fertigungslehrers*, 3 KRITISCHE VIERTELJAHRESZEITSCHRIFT FÜR GESETZGEBUNG UND RECHTSWISSENSCHAFT 1, 27-28 (1988) (author's translation).

[74] Rudolf Wiethölter, *Zur Regelbildung in der Dogmatik des Zivilrechts*, 78 ARCHIV FÜR RECHTS- UND SOZIALPHILOSOPHIE. BEIHEFT 44 (forthcoming 1992).

Part III
Normative Social Control Inside and Outside the State

[10]

COMMENTS

Community Courts: An Alternative To Conventional Criminal Adjudication

INTRODUCTION

A major thrust of modern criminal law reform is to increase community involvement in both the prevention of crime and the treatment of criminal offenders. Many authorities have come to the conclusion that only people who are involved in and are aware of the community can act as effective forces in crime prevention, and that simply increasing police and court capacity will not solve the problems presently plaguing the criminal justice system.[1] This comment will explore the utilization of one proposed alternative to conventional adjudication in the criminal context—a "community court" for selected groups of offenses and offenders.

For the purposes of this discussion, community court will be defined as a lay body dealing with a population that has objective features in common, with jurisdiction over offenses otherwise criminal, and with the power to impose meaningful sanctions. Besides an emphasis on informality and use of community members, a community court as conceived in this comment would perform an adjudicatory as well as a conciliatory function. In this context, "community" is not meant merely to denote "territoriality," but to

---

1. *See generally* NAT'L ADVISORY COMM'N ON CRIMINAL JUSTICE STANDARDS AND GOALS, U.S. DEP'T OF JUSTICE, COMMUNITY CRIME PREVENTION (1973) [hereinafter cited as COMMUNITY CRIME PREVENTION].

> Community crime prevention is based on the premise that the principal and direct responsibility for crime prevention rests with the total community—the private as well as the official sectors. Government and society must join in this effort.

Id. at 281.

See also PRESIDENT'S COMM'N ON LAW ENFORCEMENT AND ADMINISTRATION OF JUSTICE, THE CHALLENGE OF CRIME IN A FREE SOCIETY 288 (1967); PRESIDENT'S COMM'N ON LAW ENFORCEMENT AND ADMINISTRATION OF JUSTICE, TASK FORCE REPORT: THE POLICE 221, 228 (1967).

> Government programs for the control of crime are unlikely to succeed all alone. Informed private citizens, playing a variety of roles, can make a decisive difference in the prevention, detection and prosecution of crime, the fair administration of justice, and the restoration of offenders to the community.

COMMUNITY CRIME PREVENTION, *supra* at 7, *quoting* J. CAMPBELL, J. SAHID & D. STANG, LAW AND ORDER RECONSIDERED 278 (1969) (staff report to the Nat'l Comm'n on the Causes and Prevention of Violence).

describe a group of people living or working in the same locality, supporting common goals, and subject to the same laws or regulations.[2]

Community courts are in many ways similar to the informal courts relied upon to a great extent in most socialist countries.[3] However, in the west, and especially in the United States, the closest examples are found only in special settings such as universities, labor unions, and prisons.[4] Following a description of recent crimi-

---

2. One sociologist has defined "community" as "a social organization that is territorially localized and through which its members satisfy most of their daily needs and deal with most of their common problems." M. OLSEN, THE PROCESS OF SOCIAL ORGANIZATION 91 (1968) (emphasis omitted). However, for the purpose of discussing community courts a better definition of community would seem to be one which encompasses the following terms:

[I]n its ordinary or popular sense [community] does not signify township . . . . [or] connote a large geographical area with widely diverse interests.

The better and more generally accepted signification of the term is a number of people associated in the same locality having common interests or privileges and subject to the same laws or regulations. . . .

15A C.J.S. *Community* at 89 (1955) (footnotes omitted).

The National Advisory Commission on Criminal Justice Standards and Goals also discusses the current use of the term:

Traditionally the term community has denoted territoriality. The community was the place where the householder lived and worked, raised children, and attended church. Today, the meaning of community has changed.

As the population has increased and more people have moved to the cities, the old sense of community has been lost. Today places of living and working often are separated. In large cities, the sense of being part of a neighborhood community has disappeared. Community has come to mean, not a neighborhood, but shared values or a common interest, which may or may not have to do with where one lives. Community then refers to two distinct concepts: in the older sense it is a geographical area, while today it often implies support of common goals.

COMMUNITY CRIME PREVENTION, *supra* note 1, at 280.

3. One American authority discussing the community court concept in relation to the experience in socialist countries is Danzig, *Toward the Creation of a Complementary, Decentralized System of Criminal Justice,* 26 STAN. L. REV. 1 (1973) [hereinafter cited as Danzig]. He proposes a "community moot" which he distinguishes from the socialist informal courts "because of [the latter's] coercive power (either through punishment or recordkeeping), their adjudicative emphasis (guilt or innocence determined by a tribunal of judges), and their link with the centralized state machinery." *Id.* at 42 n.118.

Several names given to these informal courts in socialist countries are: Comrades' Courts in the Soviet Union, Popular Tribunals in Cuba, Mediation Committees in the People's Republic of China, and Disputes Commissions in the German Democratic Republic. For a discussion of each of these courts see notes 97—150 & accompanying text *infra.*

4. *See* notes 28—96 & accompanying text *infra.*

nal law reform projects in the United States,[5] this comment will examine the tribunals found in these special settings. The foreign experience with informal courts will also be analyzed. Finally the likelihood of acceptance of the community court concept in this country will be discussed and a model community court proposed.[6]

I. DOMESTIC EXAMPLES

A. Arbitration Programs Approaching the Community Court Concept

Among the many criminal reform programs involving citizen participation instituted in the United States, those stressing the process of arbitration come closest to the community court concept. Non-professionals may be employed as arbitrators in these programs, but their primary function is that of conciliation, with little, if any, ability to adjudicate disputes. Rarely is guilt or innocence determined, and the only meaningful sanction available is referral of the case back to the formal criminal justice system in the event of non-compliance with the arbitrator's decision. The domestic arbitration programs focus upon conciliation of the parties and may be an alternative to the formal criminal justice system only in some instances, while a true community court is designed to be an alternative to conventional criminal adjudication. Moreover, while an arbitration program relies on the courts or prosecutors for case referrals, a community court would exercise exclusive jurisdiction over a finite variety of offenses. Despite the dissimilarities between the domestic arbitration examples and a community court, a brief look at the more successful arbitration programs should be of value as they demonstrate the use of many of the elements in a community court.

The Night Prosecutor Program in Columbus, Ohio[7] is an example of a domestic arbitration program. This is an attempt to divert petty criminal cases from the formal judicial system. Minor criminal complaints are referred to the program by the police department, by the clerk of courts, or through calls from aggrieved citizens.[8] Following

---

5. See notes 7—27 & accompanying text infra.

6. See notes 160—72 & accompanying text infra.

7. See generally Law Enforcement Assistance Administration, Nat'l Institute of Law Enforcement and Criminal Justice, U.S. Dep't of Justice, Citizen Dispute Settlement: The Night Prosecutor Program of Columbus, Ohio (undated) [hereinafter cited as Citizen Dispute Settlement].

8. G.R. Smith, The Night Prosecutor Program: A very special experiment 7—8 (undated) (report prepared as part of a study of alternatives to conventional adju-

1256   *THE AMERICAN UNIVERSITY LAW REVIEW*   [Vol. 24:1253

an initial interview by a law student-clerk on duty in the prosecutor's office, either a hearing is scheduled or the complainant is referred to another agency.[9] The hearings are conducted informally by a panel of law students, and an attempt is made to conciliate the parties at that time. The panel can merely give advisory opinions, however, and it is without the power to impose meaningful sanctions. If conciliation is not reached, the hearing officers can do little else than suggest a solution or compromise, and, failing that, the final alternative is referral back to the formal criminal justice system. Clearly, reconciliation or mediation is the basic goal of the program, not adjudication.[10]

There are several other "neighborhood arbitration" programs in effect in the United States.[11] Although the power to impose minor sanctions exists under many of these programs, enforcement must generally take place in the courts since the "neighborhood arbitration" programs do not have enforcement powers. Trained arbitrators, usually attorneys, act as the mediators in these programs which are generally dependent on the formal criminal justice system for referrals. In addition, the "neighborhood arbitration" process often depends on voluntary submission to the program by both the complainant and respondent.[12]

The National Center for Dispute Settlement (NCDS) of the American Arbitration Association, under its initial 4-A program in Philadelphia, sought to reduce much of the congestion in the courts by use of arbitration.[13] In the event the parties to a dispute cannot

---

dicative practices by the American University Institute for Studies in Justice and Social Behavior) [hereinafter cited as The Night Prosecutor Program].

9. If the law student clerks decide that the charge is unacceptable for the Program they can refer complainants to either the Detective Bureau if the charge is a serious felony, or to a community service agency in cases that involve minor social problems. Citizen Dispute Settlement, *supra* note 7, at The Diversion and Hearing Process.

10. The Night Prosecutor Program, *supra* note 8, at 8.

11. The Philadelphia 4-A Program of the National Center for Dispute Settlement of the American Arbitration Association was considered successful, and as a result 4-A projects were started in East Cleveland and Akron, Ohio, and Rochester, New York. For a discussion of these programs see B. Hoff & J. Stein, Interim Evaluation Report: Philadelphia 4-A Project, Arbitration as an Alternative to Criminal Courts (Dec. 15, 1973) [hereinafter cited as B. Hoff & J. Stein].

12. *See* NAT'L CENTER FOR DISPUTE SETTLEMENT OF THE AMERICAN ARBITRATION ASS'N, THE 4-A PROGRAM: ARBITRATION AS AN ALTERNATIVE TO THE PRIVATE CRIMINAL WARRANT AND OTHER CRIMINAL PROCESSES 4 (rev. report 1972) [hereinafter cited as ARBITRATION AS AN ALTERNATIVE].

13. *Id.* at 1—2.

The National Center for Dispute Settlement's Philadelphia 4-A Project

reach an agreement through mediation efforts, an arbitrator in the 4-A program renders a decision based on the facts presented. If the respondent fails to comply with the decision and does not contact 4-A within the time prescribed for response, the case is referred back to the courts. "Depending on what has been designed, the court may re-issue the old warrant and/or may use its contempt powers to enforce the agreement or award."[14]

In the next two examples, the Community Youth Responsibility Program (CYRP) and the Neighborhood Youth Diversion Program (NYDP), the community-based adjudicatory role envisaged for a community court is more closely approached, although available only to juvenile offenders.[15] These two programs are dependent upon the police, social service agencies, parents, and neighbors for case referrals. Following an investigation by project staff members, the disputes are heard by community members trained by the program.[16]

Operating in the predominantly black community of East Palo Alto, California, CYRP offers an "alternative to the traditional system of preventing and treating juvenile delinquency and crime."[17] Its most innovative feature is a trained panel of residents of the community, including youth, which holds a hearing that results in a recommended disposition of the case.[18]

Similarly, the NYDP in East Bronx, New York, also includes a community forum for juveniles in trouble with the law.[19] The

seeks to apply arbitration and mediation techniques long successful in resolving labor difficulties, and more lately disputes between groups or factions in the community, to private criminal complaints. A significant portion of the cases arise from long-standing disputes between neighbors or acquaintances.
B. Hoff & J. Stein, *supra* note 11, at i.

[P]arties to 4-A project arbitration stand as persons seeking arbitration of a controversy or quarrel not yet in litigation. . . .

Thus, this Project is better viewed as a form of diversion from the criminal justice system, rather than an alternative criminal forum.
Id. at 58—59.

14. ARBITRATION AS AN ALTERNATIVE, *supra* note 12, at 50.

15. Both of these programs are considered alternatives to the juvenile justice system. *See* Urban and Rural Systems Associates, East Palo Alto Community Youth Responsibility Program, Evaluation of the Community Youth Responsibility Program (undated) [hereinafter cited as U.R.S.A. Report]; J. Jones & L. Bailey, Center for Research & Demonstration, The Columbia University School of Social Work, Second Year Evaluation Report of the Neighborhood Youth Diversion Program (1973) [hereinafter cited as J. Jones & L. Bailey].

16. B. Hoff & J. Stein, *supra* note 11, at 50.

17. U.R.S.A. Report, *supra* note 15, at 4.

18. *Id.*

19. W. Williams, Neighborhood Youth Diversion Program, Bronx, N.Y., Pro-

"forum" in this program is staffed by trained community volunteers, who work in panels of two and three, but again, the prime objective is mediation and panel members are limited to recommendations at dispositional hearings. This program, as well as the other arbitration programs previously discussed, depends on referrals from the formal criminal justice system for its cases.[20] Although the "forum" has the power to determine "whether the participant will continue in the program, and, if so, under what terms and conditions,"[21] as of 1973 it has been viewed by NYDP as a family service.[22] Generally, no judgments and rulings are made, as the mediator attempts to bring the disputing parties together by listening, asking questions, and offering suggestions and ideas. No sanctions are applied in an effort to resolve the difficulties without reference to the formal criminal justice system.[23]

The various arbitration programs increase community involvement and have produced lasting results,[24] although a few have higher costs per case than in the formal system.[25] Because the regu-

gram Description 1 (1974) (report prepared as part of a study of alternatives to conventional adjudicative practices by the American University Institute for Studies in Justice and Social Behavior) [hereinafter cited as W. Williams].

20. The "forum," in NYDP, has cases referred to it only from the office of probation, the family court, or the police department. Neighborhood Youth Diversion Program, Bronx, N.Y., Annual Report, Dec. 1, 1971—Nov. 30, 1972, at 2 (undated).

21. *Id.* at 5—6.

22. J. Jones & L. Bailey, *supra* note 15, at 115. A Family Court Predisposition Panel was proposed as an addition to this program in January, 1973, but this would be even less like a community court. Its powers would be limited to making recommendations to the office of probation on predisposition of juvenile cases. *See* Neighborhood Youth Diversion Program, Bronx, N.Y., A Proposal: Family Court Predisposition Panel (Jan. 1973).

23. *See* W. Williams, *supra* note 19, at 1; Vera Institute Report, 1961—1971, Expanding the Diversion Idea, 106—07 (undated).

The life of the Forum is totally dependent on the genuine consent of everyone involved. This very absence of coercion, however, is the principal foundation for the Forum's technique of conflict resolution. Only within a voluntary environment can reconciliation occur.

Statsky, *Community Courts: Decentralizing Juvenile Jurisprudence*, 3 CAPITAL U.L. REV. 1, 26 (1974) [hereinafter cited as Statsky].

24. The incidence of recidivism—cases in which an individual involved in the mediation later returns to court on an additional charge—has been reduced in cases resolved through these arbitration programs. However, it must be noted that only those cases with the potential for resolution through mediation efforts are referred to the program in the first instance. *See* B. Hoff & J. Stein, *supra* note 11, at 33—36.

25. Although the estimated cost per case is only $126 for the 4-A project, as

lar courts are still relied upon to deal with any disputes that are not resolved through mediation, there is often duplication of effort in handling many of the cases which initially enter the arbitration programs, thereby increasing overall costs. In contrast, an ideal community court would have exclusive jurisdiction, thus avoiding duplication of cost and effort.

In addition, the arbitration programs have tenuous jurisdictional status, as the prosecutor retains control of the case until a settlement is reached. In the event an agreement cannot be reached or that a party fails to comply with any arbitral decision, jurisdiction reverts back to the prosecutor to decide whether to sanction through the formal criminal justice system. A true community court should have a delineated area of exclusive jurisdiction and greater control over decisions affecting retention of jurisdiction. Despite the fact these domestic arbitration programs do not closely approach the community court model in terms of structure or function,[26] the arbitration programs are a step towards a solution to many of the problems plaguing the courts.[27]

B. Specialized Community Courts

In addition to the arbitration programs another type of tribunal that can be compared to the community court concept is found in a few special communities. Although limited to handling primarily disciplinary matters within their own institutions, these tribunals provide a useful working example with which to contrast a model

---

opposed to an estimated $144 for direct costs of an average case taken through the formal criminal courts, the estimated cost per case for CYRP is $328 and $639 for an average NYDP settlement. *Id.* at 36—44. However, as has been pointed out:

These two community forum projects [NYDP and CYPR] have a much more clear community focus than the Philadelphia 4-A Project, in terms of physical location and background of the hearing officers. . . . [T]hese projects can adjudicate a broader range of serious and difficult problems than those resolved by the 4-A Project.

. . . Both handle relatively small numbers of cases, at a rather high cost-per-case.

Id. at 52—53.

26. Whereas the arbitration programs outlined are limited to conciliation of the parties, a community court should function in both a conciliatory and adjudicatory capacity.

27. One expressed goal of the Philadelphia 4-A Program "is to provide a more lasting resolution of private criminal complaint cases, through means which are less costly and more swift than Municipal Court processing." *Id.* at 33. Cost and time factors could be greatly reduced through the use of community courts as well as these various arbitration techniques.

community court.

The closest approximations in this country of community courts, as previously defined, are found in very limited and unique communities. Many universities,[28] most labor unions,[29] and most prisons[30] have recognized procedures for deciding disciplinary problems within their respective communities. Often a tribunal of community residents is utilized to adjudge the guilt or innocence of the alleged offenders. These "disciplinary hearing boards" adjudicate many cases arising in the community, and they impose sanctions which have a meaningful impact on the community members penalized. While these tribunals are usually restricted to hearing cases involving only violations of the particular organization's regulations, many of these breaches also constitute bona fide criminal activity. The communities involved usually decide to handle these problems without recourse to the formal criminal justice system, although concurrent jurisdiction with the possible imposition of sanctions by both the special and formal courts has been recognized as permissible.[31]

1. University courts

The disciplinary system employed at Boston University is a good example of the type of community court used on many college campuses today. Not only will it provide a good basis for theory, but because of the recent test to which that school's particular alternative process was put, it should provide some useful insights into how well it actually works in practice.

In the spring of 1973, following a series of campus demonstrations resulting in several arrests, the Boston University community, through the efforts of the Faculty Senate and Student Union, approved a Provisional Student Code and a Provisional Faculty Code on April 20, 1973. Although the Codes were meant to be provisional only, they were called into use the following fall when several of the

---

28. "Almost all authors agree that the university is a 'special' rather than a 'general' purpose community." T. Fischer, Due Process in the Student-Institutional Relationship, A White Paper on Procedural Due Process for Public College Presidents, Administrators and Student Leaders 7 (1970) (prepared for the American Ass'n of State Colleges and Universities) [hereinafter cited as T. Fischer]. *See also* Comment, 45 DENVER L.J. 663, 665 (1968); N.Y.U. School of Law, Student Conduct and Discipline Proceedings in a University Setting 1, 5 (1968) [hereinafter cited as N.Y.U. Student Conduct].

29. *See* notes 88—96 & accompanying text *infra.*

30. *See* notes 67—87 & accompanying text *infra.*

31. *See* notes 64, 65 & accompanying text *infra.*

demonstrators were brought before the tribunals created by the Codes.

The University imposes discipline for a variety of offenses,[32] such as damaging university property and obstructing university activities, as well as academic misconduct on the part of faculty.[33] Both the student and faculty Codes also contain a "blanket provision" to encompass any and all "officially promulgated [pre-existing] rules and regulations of the university."[34] The Codes provide for the imposition of various sanctions[35] ranging from permanent expulsion to reprimand and warning, with the proviso that, for faculty members, instead of outright expulsion, only termination can be recommended.[36] Furthermore, administration of the Code is the primary responsibility of the Director of Student Academic Support Services, in cases involving students,[37] and of the Dean of the respective

---

32. The types of offenses for which the University will impose discipline under these Codes consist of:

    1.) conduct that seriously damages or destroys University property or property in the care, custody and control of the University;

    2.) conduct that indicates a serious continuing danger to the personal safety of other members of the University community;

    3.) conduct that obstructs or seriously impairs University-run or University-authorized activities on the campus . . . .

Boston University, Provisional Student Code, ch. II, at 3 (1973) [hereinafter cited as Student Code].

33. In the Faculty Code, "academic misconduct" is described as including "neglect, disregard, or dereliction of professional duties, tasks, and assignments which are explicit or implicit in a faculty member's letter of appointment." Boston University, Provisional Faculty Code, ch. II, at 3 (1973) [hereinafter cited as Faculty Code].

34. *Id.* ch. II(4), at 3; Student Code, *supra* note 32, ch. II(3), at 3.

35. The Codes provide several sanctions to be imposed upon a student or faculty member found guilty of conduct punishable under chapter II:

    1.) serious disciplinary sanctions

    a.) separation—the permanent expulsion and severance of a student from the University . . .;

    b.) suspension . . .;

    2.) minor disciplinary sanctions

    a.) suspension of eligibility for official athletic or non-athletic extra curricular activities . . .;

    b.) restitution . . .;

    c.) continuance without a finding . . .;

    d.) suspended sanction . . .;

    e.) reprimand and warning . . . .

Student Code, *supra* note 32, ch. III, at 3.

36. Faculty Code, *supra* note 33, ch. III(1)(a), at 3.

37. Student Code, *supra* note 32, ch. IV, at 3—4.

college of the university for faculty.[38]

Recognizing that the procedures enunciated by the Codes are not overly formal, a study of the accounts of the disciplinary proceedings that did take place reveals that even these procedures were not taken seriously. The students eventually brought before the disciplinary panel had initially been arrested by the police and charged with criminal conduct through the traditional criminal justice system. Although the criminal charges were dropped,[39] each student was "tried" before a Judicial Committee consisting of three community members—a student, a faculty member, and an administrator—empaneled by an Advisory Judicial Council selected by the president of the university.[40]

The Codes provide that "technical rules of procedure" and evidence will not govern, and that the hearings will be closed to the public.[41] In addition, although the "three members of each Judicial Committee are the sole and final arbiters of the weight of the evidence, guilt or innocence of the student and the appropriateness of any sanctions imposed,"[42] there is provision made for appeal to the president of the university.[43] The university Codes also ensure many

---

38. Faculty Code, *supra* note 33, ch. IV, at 3.

39. After numerous trips to court by the University and the defendants the judge finally dismissed the case. [The court] ruled . . . that although there was a violation of a court restraining order on demonstrating, it could not be proven that the defendants were the violators.

The Daily Free Press, Oct. 17, 1973, at 6, col. 4. (Boston University daily student newspaper).

40. The President will select an Advisory Judicial Council of three members to empanel Judicial Committees. The President will select one member each from the general faculty, student body, and administration.

Student Code, *supra* note 32, ch. VII, at 4.

Hearings conducted before the Judicial Committees are presided over by a Hearing Examiner, appointed by the President of the University. This "Hearing Examiner will be an attorney duly licensed to practice law in the courts of one of the fifty states." *Id.* ch. VIII, at 4. The Faculty Code, note 33 *supra*, contains procedures identical to those found in the Student Code. Therefore, only the Student Code will be cited hereinafter.

41. Student Code, *supra* note 32, ch. XII, at 5.

42. *Id.* ch. XIII, at 5.

43. In regard to appeal from the decision of a Judicial Committee, the Codes provide:

The President (of the university) has discretion to:
   a.) affirm the finding of guilt and imposition of sanction;
   b.) affirm the finding of guilt and reduce the sanction imposed;
   c.) set aside the finding of guilt and imposition of sanction and remand the case to the Judicial Committee for further proceedings; or
   d.) set aside the finding of guilt and imposition of sanction and dismiss

of the customary "protections of due process,"[44] such as the right to counsel, the right to notice of the alleged offense, the right to an impartial judicial body, the right to cross-examine witnesses, the right to remain silent, the right to a written decision,[45] and several others.[46]

Only three students eventually went through the entire disciplinary process. One student was found innocent by one judicial committee, another was found guilty and given a suspension by a different committee, and the third pleaded guilty and accepted the same sentence after a 45-minute conference between the prosecution and the defense.[47]

Significantly, it appears from campus newspaper accounts of the trials that the university considered the cases to be "internal private matters,"[48] and the president of the university was quoted as saying

---

the case against the student.
Id. ch. XVI, at 6.

44. The modern trend has been for the court to scrutinize increasingly these informal proceedings to insure that "limited" procedural rights are provided. For a more detailed discussion of the development of the courts' enforcement of due process in this area see notes 55—63 & accompanying text *infra.*

45. This author was told in an interview with Daniel J. Finn, Vice President for Operations, Boston University, in Boston, Massachusetts in June of 1974, that no decisions were written under the Boston University Codes, although in fact three were eventually made. This would seem to suggest that these procedural rights were not strictly enforced, or that the defendants did not find it necessary to request a written decision.

46. The Boston University Codes ensure the following "protections of due process":

1.) notice of his alleged offense with adequate clarity and sufficiently in advance of the date of his hearing to enable him to prepare his defense;

2.) the right to be represented at the hearing by legal counsel or an advisor of his own choosing;

3.) the right to have his case decided by an impartial judicial body;

4.) the right to confront and cross examine any witnesses who testify against him at the hearing;

5.) the right to call witnesses and introduce evidence in his own behalf at the hearing;

6.) the right to remain silent at the hearing;

7.) the right to have the hearing recorded at the University's expense, and the right to a copy of said recording at the student's expense;

8.) the right to a written decision setting forth all findings of guilt or innocence and any sanctions imposed;

9.) the right to appeal to the President of the University in cases involving major sanctions.

Student Code, *supra* note 32, ch. XI, at 5.

47. The Daily Free Press, Oct. 25, 1973, at 1, col. 3.

48. *Id.*, Sept. 6, 1973, at 5, col. 4.

that "the code was not designed to be an alternative to the federal judiciary or the state courts."[49] This would appear to leave open the possibility of criminal sanctions also being applied, a suggestion made by a number of commentators.[50] A true community court, on the other hand, would be most effective if it could escape this concurrent jurisdiction of the courts and obtain exclusive jurisdiction over a statutorily defined group of offenses.[51]

In addition to this all-university hearing procedure, several of the large dormitories at Boston University also enacted their own judicial systems. The only real differences are in the offenses punishable, the sanctions available, and the lessened emphasis on formality. A report was written on the cases heard in one of the large dormitories and it was found that "157 or about 10% of the student population, taking into account repeated violations by some individuals" were sanctioned with either a warning, probation, or expulsion.[52] The inability to impose any such meaningful sanctions is the primary deficiency of the previously discussed arbitration programs; the power to impose real sanctions is an essential aspect of a viable community court concept.

Several authors have suggested model disciplinary codes,[53] similar to the Boston University system, but the dispute among academic circles in this field appears to be over how much due process is proper in these disciplinary proceedings.[54] In the past, the courts

---

49. During an interview with the campus daily newspaper, President Silber of Boston University stated that the Code was not meant to be the "equivalent of a judicial system," that it was "only a hearing procedure which enables the administration to get on with its job of managing, to some extent, the affairs of the University . . . ." *Id.*, Oct. 9, 1973, at 1, col.1.

50. *See* notes 64—66 & accompanying text *infra.*

51. *See* note 166 & accompanying text *infra.*

52. Office of Student Life, Boston Univ., Boston University Disciplinary Report 1 (June 3, 1974)(on file at the offices of the American University Law Review).

53. *See, e.g.*, Address by C. Blocker, Annual Convention of the American Ass'n of Junior Colleges, Atlanta, Ga., March, 1969 (Dissent and the College Student in Revolt, Appendix—Student Disciplinary Procedure); N.Y.U. Student Conduct, note 28 *supra*; T. Fischer, note 28 *supra*. Most institutions of higher education have established student discipline systems. In varying degrees, these systems consist of regulations circumscribing and proscribing certain types of behavior deemed to be inimical to the learning environment, and penalties that can accrue to behavior in breach of the regulations.
S. Cazier, Student Discipline Systems in Higher Education 1 (Educational Resources Information Center, Nat'l Institute of Educ., U.S. Dep't of Health, Educ. & Welfare, Rep. No. ERIC-HE-RR-7, 1973) [hereinafter cited as S. Cazier].

54. [I]nternal adjudicatory system[s], aimed at dealing promptly with internal disciplinary problems [must guarantee] at the same time "fair

have had a hands-off policy with respect to disciplinary hearings within the context of educational institutions.[55] However, the Fifth Circuit Court of Appeals in *Dixon v. Alabama State Board of Education*[56] initiated the drive for due process in disciplinary hearings of this nature. The court determined that several, but not all, of the elements of due process recognized in criminal courts were applicable to such hearings. The elements mandated include: notice of specific charges, a hearing, the opportunity for the student to prepare and present his own defense, confrontation and cross-examination of adverse witnesses, and the right to a report on the results and findings.[57]

---

play" and "the rudiments of 'due process' to the student accused." This system should be called into use whenever it is necessary to review an alleged violation of the student codes; that is, whenever "student misconduct [has] distinctly and adversely affect[ed] the university's pursuit of its recognized educational purposes."

T. Fischer, *supra* note 28, at 11, *citing* N.Y.U. Student Conduct, *supra* note 28, at 7 (footnotes omitted).

For a discussion of due process in prison and labor disciplinary hearings see notes 73, 93 & accompanying text *infra*.

55. *See, e.g.,* State *ex rel.* Sherman v. Hyman, 180 Tenn. 99, 171 S.W.2d 822, *cert. denied,* 319 U.S. 748 (1942) (writ of mandamus to compel reinstatement of student expelled for alleged sale of exam papers dismissed).

[C]ourts will not interfere with the discretion of school officials in matters affecting discipline of students unless there is a manifest abuse of discretion or where their action has been arbitrary or unlawful.

Id. at 113, 171 S.W.2d at 827—28.

Accord, Cornette v. Aldridge, 408 S.W.2d 935 (Tex. Civ. App. 1966). *Cf.* Annot., 58 A.L.R.2d 903 (1958) (collection of precedents regarding public schools and the right of a student to a hearing before suspension). *See also* notes 74—75 & accompanying text *infra* for a discussion of this hands-off attitude by courts in reviewing prison disciplinary hearings.

56. 294 F.2d 150 (5th Cir., *cert. denied,* 368 U.S. 930 (1961). In this case the circuit court held that due process requires notice and some opportunity for a hearing before students in tax-supported colleges could be expelled for misconduct. This holding "had an impact on student discipline of the same dimension as the Brown decision on school desegregation." S. Cazier, *supra* note 53, at 3.

See also Pervis v. LaMarque Independent School Dist., 466 F.2d 1054 (5th Cir. 1972). In this case the court concluded that where students were improperly suspended without a hearing, a subsequent hearing, even if valid, would not cure the initial deprivation of due process.

57. 294 F.2d at 158—159. *Cf.* Barker v. Hardway, 283 F. Supp. 228, 237 (S.D.W. Va.), *aff'd per curiam,* 399 F.2d 638 (4th Cir. 1968) (circumstances of each case control what due process rights should be accorded but disciplinary hearings need not be full-dress judicial hearings). *But see* Esteban v. Central Missouri State College, 415 F.2d 1077 (8th Cir. 1969), *cert. denied,* 398 U.S. 965 (1970) (no failure to accord due process to college students suspended without notice and hearing).

More recently, the Supreme Court in *Goss v. Lopez*[58] ruled that suspension from a public school was sufficient interference with a protected property interest to warrant review by the courts to insure that "[a]t the very minimum . . . *some* kind of notice and . . . *some* kind of hearing" be afforded.[59] The Court held that in cases where the deprivation was a suspension of ten days or less, due process required only notice of the charges against the student and an opportunity to be heard.[60] Although many due process safeguards, such as the right to confront witnesses and secure counsel, were not made applicable to temporary suspensions,[61] the Court left open the possibility that more stringent due process standards would be demanded if a greater penalty was to be imposed.[62] *Goss* appears to be the latest Supreme Court decision indicative of a trend in which the Court seems to be willing to scrutinize specialized community courts to insure that due process safeguards are provided.[63]

Most university tribunals deal primarily with disciplinary prob-

---

The *Dixon* decision was based on the due process clause of the fourteenth amendment and, therefore, is applicable only to state action. Many private institutions, however, have been held within its mandate through numerous judicial theories. For a general discussion of this aspect of the problem of requiring due process in the educational setting see Thiegpien, *An Overview of the Interaction*, in LAW AND HIGHER EDUCATION 2 (T. Diener ed. 1971).

58. 95 S.Ct. 729 (1975).

59. *Id.* at 738.

60. Students facing temporary suspension have interests qualifying for protection of the Due Process Clause and due process requires, in connection with a suspension of 10 days or less, that the student be given oral or written notice of the charges against him, and if he denies them, an explanation of the evidence that the authorities have and an opportunity to present his side of the story. The clause requires at least these rudimentary precautions against unfair or mistaken findings of misconduct and arbitrary exclusion from school.

Id. at 740 (footnote omitted).

61. The Court did not require that the right "to secure counsel, to confront and cross-examine witnesses supporting the charge or to call his own witnesses to verify his version of the incident," be afforded a student where the penalty to be imposed was only a temporary suspension. *Id.*

62. *Id.* at 741. *But see* D. Young, *Student Rights and Responsibilities*, in LAW AND HIGHER EDUCATION 16 (T. Diener ed. 1971).

Student disciplinary proceedings have been held to be civil and not criminal proceedings and therefore do not necessarily require all of the judicial safeguards and rights accorded to criminal proceedings.

Id.

63. For another example of the Court's recent activity in this area see the discussion of Wolff v. McDonnel, 418 U.S. 539 (1974), in note 81 & accompanying text *infra.*

lems, but some criminal conduct is also handled. Where criminal conduct is involved, formal criminal charges may be brought in addition to the particular organization's hearings. This idea of concurrent jurisdiction has been advocated by several authorities[64] who feel that if student conduct is in violation of the criminal law it should be subject to the regular criminal process. In other words, "[u]niversity discipline [should be] an administrative matter entirely separate from the criminal law. Disciplinary sanctions should be independent of any criminal sanctions."[65]

These authorities contend that students should be subject to sanctions by all the communities which they offend by their actions. One study even concluded that law breakers should go to the courts exclusively and not university tribunals as only disciplinary matters are appropriate for action by these tribunals.[66] This would severely limit the scope of the university court, in direct contrast to the concept of creating community courts with a wide range of authority and power.

2. Prison disciplinary hearings

The university is not the only specialized community to develop "disciplinary hearing panels." Many prisons utilize informal systems to ensure that their rules and regulations are followed. A Policy Statement on Inmate Discipline from the Bureau of Prisons of the Department of Justice outlines the disciplinary procedures employed in federal penal institutions.[67] Federal prisons are perhaps

---

64. The university hearing system is not set up to enforce the criminal or civil laws of the community in which the university is located . . . .

[U]niversity disciplinary proceedings should be "limited to instances of student misconduct which distinctly and adversely affect the university's pursuit of its recognized educational purposes."
T. Fischer, *supra* note 28, at 21 (footnote omitted).

[I]t would be unreasonable to suggest that a wrongful act, committed on or off campus, which violated both university codes and criminal statutes, and damaged private property, could not be punished by all injured parties: the university, the public, and the property owner.
Id. at 22, *citing* N.Y.U. Student Conduct, *supra* note 28, at 17.

65. Ohio House of Representatives, Interim Report of the Select Comm. to Investigate Campus Disturbances to the 108th Ohio Gen. Assembly 9 (1971). *See also* N.Y.U. Student Conduct, *supra* note 28, at 7; T. Fischer, *supra* note 28, at 11; S. CAZIER, *supra* note 53, at 40.

66. S. Cazier, *supra* note 53, at 40, *citing* THE CARNEGIE COMM'N ON HIGHER EDUC., DISSENT AND DISRUPTION: PROPOSAL FOR A CONSIDERATION BY THE CAMPUS 95 (1971).

67. BUREAU OF PRISONS, U.S. DEP'T OF JUSTICE, No. 7400.5B, POLICY STATEMENT:

more liberal than most state penal institutions, and, therefore, this quasi-judicial system is likely to be more the exception than the rule in state and local prison facilities.

In the federal system, the name given to the body which determines the disciplinary measures to be taken against an inmate is the "Adjustment Committee." The Policy Statement, in addition to describing the composition of that Committee (which does not contain prisoners), outlines its function and authority.[68] The Committee receives reports of misconduct, conducts hearings, makes findings, and imposes disciplinary actions. In addition, over 60 specific acts are listed as prohibited in federal penal and correctional institutions. They range in degree from killing and escape to tattooing.[69] Furthermore, rules of evidence and trial procedure are not applied to the hearing.[70] Provision is made, however, for many procedural rights. Of the most importance are: notice of the charges, a hearing before an impartial tribunal, a review of the case every 30 days that the inmate remains in segregation, and a written decision by the adjustment committee.[71] Various sanctions are available to the Ad-

---

INMATE DISCIPLINE (June 1972) [hereinafter cited as POLICY STATEMENT].

68. The Committee shall consist of at least three members appointed by the head of the institution. . . . [These] personnel [must be] competent and . . . broadly represent the primary areas of correctional treatment. . . .
      . . . The Adjustment Committee . . . shall receive reports of misconduct, conduct hearings, make findings, and impose disciplinary actions. The Committee shall, where indicated, refer violators for diagnosis or special handling.
Id. at 7.

69. For example, killing, assaulting any person, extortion, indecent exposure, escape, stealing, rioting, being in an unauthorized area, gambling, and tattooing or self-mutilation are all proscribed by the federal disciplinary code. *See id.* at 4—6.

70. BUREAU OF PRISONS, U.S. DEP'T OF JUSTICE, No. 7400.6A, POLICY STATEMENT: WITHHOLDING, FORFEITURE, AND RESTORATION OF GOOD TIME (Aug. 1971).

71. The Adjustment Committee . . . handling inmate discipline will adopt the following practices:

(1) All inmates charged with misconduct or violation of a rule or regulation of the institution will be informed of the specific charges and will be given an opportunity to answer. The investigation of the charges and written notification to the inmate of the charges must be done within 24 hours of placement in segregation. The investigation shall be conducted by a member of the staff other than the reporting officer. Neither the reporting or the investigating officer shall be a member of the Adjustment Committee.

. . . .

(3) Every inmate who spends over ten continuous days in segregation status will have his case formally reviewed by the Committee a second time and this review will be repeated at least every 30 days thereafter that the inmate remains in segregation. . . .

justment Committee.[72] As these sanctions can be quite substantial—for example, restriction and segregation—the courts have begun to review prison disciplinary hearings to ensure that some measure of due process is afforded in this special community setting.[73]

This was not always the case, however, as an early decision by the Second Circuit Court of Appeals, *Henson v. Welsh*,[74] held that courts have no power to review disciplinary action taken against prisoners in federal prison for alleged breach of prison discipline. The court concluded that, by statute, "the prison system of the United States is entrusted to the Bureau of Prisons under the direction of the Attorney General."[75]

In contrast to the *Henson* court's view, a federal district court in

---

The 10 day and 30 day reviews will be documented along with the Committee findings or decisions and will be sent to the next highest authority for review. . . .

. . . .

(5) . . . The inmate will be advised in writing of the Committee's decision. . . .

POLICY STATEMENT, *supra* note 67, at 7—8.

72. Several of the sanctions available to the Adjustment Committee as a result of violation of the rules of the institution may include referral to various institutional programs and resources, reprimand, restrictions of various kinds, segregation and recommending the withholding or forfeiture of good time.

Id. at 6.

73. *See, e.g.*, Johnson v. Avery, 393 U.S. 483 (1969). This case signalled a shift from the hands-off policy previously followed by federal courts in reviewing prison disciplinary hearings. The Supreme Court in *Johnson* allowed judicial intervention in the area of executive responsibility where prison regulations infringed on constitutional rights of persons. Gray v. Creamer, 465 F.2d 179 (3d Cir. 1972), held that transfer of state prison inmates from the general prison population to solitary confinement without either notice of charges or a hearing is a violation of minimal due process requirements. *See generally* Millemann, *Prison Disciplinary Hearings and Procedural Due Process—The Requirements of a Full Administrative Hearing*, 31 MD. L. REV. 27 (1971).

74. 199 F.2d 367 (4th Cir. 1952).

75. *Id.* at 368, *citing* 18 U.S.C. § 4042 (1946). This section describes the duties of the Bureau of Prisons and remains unchanged in the present Code. *Accord*, Haynes v. Harris, 344 F.2d 463 (8th Cir. 1965) (enforcement of discipline and supervision of inmates are exclusive prerogatives of administrative authorities and federal courts will not intervene in absence of unusual or exceptional circumstances), *citing* Harris v. Settle, 322 F.2d 908 (8th Cir. 1963). *Cf.* Roberts v. Pegelow, 313 F.2d 548 (4th Cir. 1963).

[T]he Executive Department is solely responsible . . . and . . . must be allowed to exercise a largely unfettered discretion in deciding . . . what relative freedom [each prisoner] safely may be allowed.

Id. at 550.

Braxton v. Carlson[76] found that, in disciplinary proceedings, prisoners should not be condemned to suffer "grievous loss" of privileges without some due process safeguards. However, the *Braxton* court felt that the procedures provided by the prison authorities were adequate.[77] The prisoners were given adequate notice of the charges, informed of the substance of the evidence against them, given an opportunity to respond, and a reasonable investigation into the facts was made before the disciplinary committee acted.[78] The court in *Braxton* further noted that prison authorities need not afford inmates all the constitutional rights granted defendants in a criminal case.[79]

Some of these due process issues[80] were resolved recently by the Supreme Court in *Wolff v. McDonnell*,[81] where it was held that "some but not all"[82] of the due process safeguards the Court has guaranteed in criminal cases must be afforded a prison inmate when disciplinary action could prolong confinement. The safeguards which the Court found to be required were: 1) advance written notice of the claimed violation;[83] 2) a written statement of the findings as to the evidence relied upon and the reasons for the disciplinary action taken;[84] and 3) "[t]he inmate facing disciplinary proceed-

---

76. 340 F. Supp. 999 (M.D. Pa. 1972).

77. *Id.* at 1003.

78. *Id.* at 1002.

79. The court in *Braxton* concluded that prisoners claiming deprivation of constitutional rights at federal prison disciplinary hearing are not entitled to such due process safeguards as confrontation and cross-examination of witnesses, representation of counsel or lay substitutes, presentation of witnesses in their own behalf, written notice of charge, or written notice of the disciplinary authorities' determinations. *Id.* at 1003.

80. Several courts have discussed the due process issues involved in the prison setting. *See, e.g.*, Sostre v. McGinnis, 442 F.2d 178 (2d Cir. 1971), *cert. denied*, 404 U.S. 1049 (1972) (confining prisoners to punitive segregation for indefinite period of time can amount to cruel and unusual punishment and the hearing panel must observe basic procedural safeguards); Landman v. Royster, 333 F. Supp. 621, 653 (E.D. Va. 1971) (prisoners granted relief because they were denied due process safeguards, but all the due process safeguards required in regular criminal courts are not necessary); Bundy v. Cannon, 328 F. Supp. 165 (D. Md. 1971). The court in *Bundy* reasoned that some due process rights are guaranteed to prisoners. For example, adequate notice of charges and a hearing before an impartial tribunal would be necessary if punishment was "sufficiently severe to require minimum due process safeguards." *Id.* at 173.

81. 418 U.S. 539 (1974).

82. *Id.* at 571.

83. *Id.* at 563—64.

84. *Id.* at 564—65.

ings should be allowed to call witnesses and present documentary evidence in his defense when permitting him to do so will not be unduly hazardous to institutional safety or correctional goals."[85] However, confrontation and cross-examination of witnesses were listed as discretionary with prison authorities,[86] and the right to counsel was denied although some assistance is permissible if the inmate is incompetent to prepare his own defense.[87]

This "special community court" of prison disciplinary hearings can be distinguished from the ideal community court by the fact that jurisdiction is not exclusive. Many of the cases dealt with by the prison disciplinary tribunals are also violations of the criminal law and the formal criminal courts can, and sometimes do, exercise jurisdiction. Although this legal right to exercise jurisdiction is more often ignored—due to the formal courts' reluctance to deal with intra-prison behavior—it would be preferable for an ideal community court to have exclusive jurisdiction. Moreover, the prison tribunals rarely allow for prisoner participation thereby raising doubts as to whether the "judges" are really "community" members.

3. Labor union disciplinary hearings

Most labor unions have procedures for hearing disciplinary actions by specialized community courts.[88] Following a finding of culpability on a number of different charges,[89] a variety of penalties may

---

85. *Id.* at 566.

86. *Id.* at 569.

87. *Id.* at 570.

88. A study of the various disciplinary systems common in many labor unions conducted in 1955 found that

of the 194 Union constitutions in this study . . . 170 of them contain provisions which lay down the procedures by which a member may be expelled or otherwise disciplined.

HANDBOOK OF UNION GOVERNMENT 65 (1955) (available from the AFL-CIO Library in Washington, D.C.) [hereinafter cited as HANDBOOK].

89. Although the union study was undertaken in 1955, current union constitutions have changed little since that time, and the data compiled at that time is still useful in describing the scope of the authority exercised by these "specialized community courts." From that study it is apparent that the charges which may be made against a union member vary considerably.

The most common grounds for discipline are violations of any provision of the international constitution or the local union constitution, strikebreaking, slander of fellow members or officers, "dual unionism" . . . , violating "trade rules" . . . , "secessionism" . . . , and being a member of the Communist party or participation in other subversive activities.

Id.

be imposed.[90] As union constitutions are not usually lengthy documents, however, a single sentence on trial procedure and a statement of the grounds for expulsion or other punishment may be all that is provided in the constitution concerning discipline.[91] The one common element appears to be that the investigation of charges and the holding of a hearing is done by a committee of union members.[92]

Significantly, there has been a recent tendency to put more procedural due process safeguards into union constitutions,[93] although a

---

90. In the great majority of the unions covered by this study, any one of several penalties may be imposed, depending on the seriousness of the offense:
- Reprimand: (the convicted member is brought before a union meeting and formally denounced for his conduct);
- Fine;
- Suspension from membership for a definitely stated period of time;
- Expulsion from membership.
    . . . In a few constitutions, it also includes two other kinds of penalties: (1) disqualification to run for elective office in the union, and (2) removal from his union job if the member happens to be a salaried employee of the union.
Id.

91. *Id.* at 67.

92. |Very few of the constitutions studied in 1955 provided| that the member be tried and punished by a local union membership meeting. A much more common system is to turn the investigation of charges and the holding of a hearing over to a committee of members. . . . [Very often the local union membership will vote on the decision reached] on the basis of the committee's report . . . .
    . . . The members of the committee may be elected from among the local's membership, chosen by lot, or appointed by the local's officers.
Id. at 68.

Almost all the union constitutions which contain disciplinary provisions also provide for appeals by members dissatisfied with the local union verdict. . . .

The appeals procedure laid down in most union constitutions guarantees international control over local disciplinary power. . . . The international may set aside the local's decision, reverse it, alter the penalty, dismiss the case, or take any other action it feels is necessary.
Id. at 70.

93. *See, e.g.*, Constitution and Laws of the United Brotherhood of Carpenters and Joiners of America 53—60 (as amended 1971).
    J) The following trial procedures shall be observed:
    (1) The Chairman shall read the charges . . . .
    (2) The accuser or his counsel, shall present his case first.
    (3) Witnesses shall be called into the trial room one at a time, and will leave upon completing their testimony, subject to recall by either the Trial Committee or any of the parties.
    (4) The accuser's witnesses shall be called first.

recent study shows "that procedural requirements still appear in only a minority of them."[94] Congress provided the impetus to requiring due process in union discipline actions with the enactment of the Labor-Management Reporting and Disclosure Act of 1959.[95] Thus, some due process is required in all labor union disciplinary actions, suggesting that some minimum safeguards would also be required for more general community courts.[96]

(5)   Each party or his counsel shall have the right to cross-examine witnesses presented by the other party.

(6)   Before the Trial Committee shall begin their deliberations, all other persons shall leave the trial room.

K)   When the committee has come to a decision in the case, the chairman of said committee shall, at the next regular meeting thereafter, submit a full report of the case with their verdict and the evidence in writing to the Local Union or District Council. The Local Union to which the member belongs shall be notified of the verdict and the penalty.

Id. §§ 56(J), (K), at 57.

See also The Constitution and By-Laws of the International Association of Marble Slate and Stone Polishers, art. XII, at 55—58 (1967).

94. Disciplinary Power and Procedures in Union Constitutions 92 n.6 (U.S. Dep't of Labor Bulletin No. 1350, 1963). *Cf.* Smythe, Schwab & Madigan, *Individuals' Procedural Rights in Union Disciplinary Actions*, 17 LAB. L. J. 226, 228 nn.6 & 7 (1966) [hereinafter cited as Smythe].

95. Labor Management Reporting and Disclosure Act of 1959, 29 U.S.C. §§ 401—531 (1970) [hereinafter cited as LMRDA]. Section 101(a)(5) of LMRDA, the so-called "due process" provision, provides that any member to be disciplined must be: 1) served with written specific charges; 2) given a reasonable time to prepare a defense; and 3) afforded a full and fair hearing. 29 U.S.C. § 411(a) (5) (1970).

One commentator, while analyzing the public policy expressed in Congress' enactment of LMRDA, examined the judicial interpretation of section 101(a)(5) of the Act, and concluded that "[t]he federal courts, in defining § 101(a)(5), have relied heavily on state precedents." Smythe, *supra* note 94, at 227, *citing* Parks v. International Bhd. of Elec. Workers, 314 F.2d 886 (4th Cir.), *cert. denied*, 372 U.S. 976 (1963). This case held that revocation by the International Union of the local union's charter did not violate rights of local members protected by the Labor-Management Reporting and Disclosure Act.

[I]t is appropriate for federal courts, relatively inexperienced in handling internal union cases, to look to existing state law concepts in applying the new provisions of the LMRDA.

314 F.2d at 904 (footnote omitted).

The authors also feel that the federal courts are empowered under section 101(a)(5) to intervene when the specified procedural rights of union members are endangered. Smythe, *supra* note 94, at 228. *See also* Detroy v. American Guild of Variety Artists, 286 F.2d 75, 78—79 (2d Cir.), *cert. denied*, 366 U.S. 929 (1961) (union members granted relief against the union for its failure to provide a hearing before disciplinary action against a member as provided in the LMRDA).

96. Court martial proceedings can also be likened to a "specialized" community court. The Supreme Court has not as yet "clearly settled to what extent the Bill

Labor union disciplinary panels resemble more the university courts than the prison tribunals. Labor panel members are chosen by the union to decide cases which, although occasionally involving minor criminal law violations, are primarily concerned with internal disciplinary matters. Should a case involving a criminal act come before the union tribunal, the same problem seen in the discussion of the university and prison experiences would arise concerning the exercise of concurrent jurisdiction by the formal courts. An ideal community court would require exclusive jurisdiction. This jurisdiction might arise de facto, as is the case in some specialized community courts, due to the formal courts' reluctance to handle certain matters. However, de jure jurisdiction through legislative enactment would be a preferable approach. A legislative act could ensure that these community courts provide the due process safeguards required in the formal legal system while also ensuring that the community courts would have sufficient authority to impose meaningful sanctions.

---

of Rights and other protective parts of the Constitution apply to military trials." Reid v. Covert, 354 U.S. 1, 37 (1957) (footnote omitted). However, the Court has held that the military courts are responsible to protect members of the armed forces from a violation of their constitutional rights. Burns v. Wilson, 346 U.S. 137, 142 (1953).

[11]

CONTRABAND
The Basis for Legitimate Power in a Prison Social System

DAVID B. KALINICH
Michigan State University

STAN STOJKOVIC
University of Wisconsin—Milwaukee

Much of the past literature on inmate socialization and social control in prison organizations has focused on the reciprocal relationships between key inmate leaders and members of the custodial staff. In addition, the literature is replete with examples of how prisoners adapt to their incarceration, in part, through the sub-rosa market system. However, what has not been systematically examined is the relationship between contraband activity and stability in the prison environment. This article explores the role of the contraband market in developing control and legitimate power in a prison social system, with suggested implications on how proper and improper manipulations of the illegal market perpetuate stability or instability in the prison setting. Finally, how other strategies may be employed by correctional administrators to control their environments are discussed.

The traditional approach to prison organization and management has been the application of bureaucratic authority over guards and inmates. Control over inmates is based on a lengthy set of institutional rules and regulations. Threats of

Authors' Note: *A version of this article was originally presented at the Midwestern Criminal Justice Association Annual Meeting, Chicago, 1983. We appreciate the substantive comments made by Carl Pope, and John Conley, and two anonymous reviewers.*

CRIMINAL JUSTICE AND BEHAVIOR, Vol. 12 No. 4, December 1985 435-451
© 1985 American Association of Correctional Psychologists

coercion are used for noncompliance, with institutional rules and rewards, such as "good time," being offered to inmates for conformance. The preponderance of research literature on prison organizations points out, however, that a great deal of leakage of administrative control exists, and prison rules and regulations are readily circumvented both by guards and inmates (Sykes, 1958; Sykes & Messinger, 1960; Cloward, 1960). This understanding of prison organizations is supported by literature and research in organizational theory, which suggests that control over subordinates, especially in large bureaucratic agencies, is difficult to achieve, and leakage of control is normal for such organizations (Downs, 1966; Warwick, 1975). Yet prisons are relatively stable, with disturbances and rioting occurring with no more frequency than civil disturbances and rioting.

The popular question posed after a riot or disturbance is, "why do prisoners riot?" This question is ultimately posed visibly after a prison riot by the establishment of a blue ribbon committee appointed by the executive branch of the government empaneled to investigate the causes of the riot. Given that the traditional bureaucratic approach to prison is a weak form of management fraught with leakages of control and inmates seemingly without a normative commitment to the system to which they are are unwilling subordinates, the more perplexing question that should be addressed is why prisons are relatively stable. It seems that addressing this question will provide insights into periods of instability. The purpose of this article is to examine the phenomenon of stability in prison organizations, and how this is augmented, in part, by the prison contraband marketplace.

Stability in a prison environment is dependent to a great extent upon the need most inmates have for stability, certainty, and safety. Most inmates attempt to find a niche in the prison community, serve their time unobtrusively, and earn their release at the earliest possible time (Toch, 1977). Prison guards similarly desire certainty, stability, and safety. Guards attempt to establish a working relationship with inmates by using their discretion in enforcing rules, which becomes the basis for cooperation with the inmates, as well as providing the guards with a reputation among inmates as being fair (Lombardo, 1981). It is these interactions between officers and inmates that help ameliorate the stressful conditions of prison life. As described by Lombardo (1982), when adaptation by inmates to the stress-producing situations of prison is unsuccessful, then individual and collective violence supersede control and stability as predominant elements in the prison social setting.

The literature on informal prison social structure suggests that order and stability in prison are provided through accommodative and exchange relationships between inmates and custodial staff. Sykes (1958) provides the earliest systematic analysis of the leakage of formal control over the prison environment and the development of the informal social system based on the accommodation of inmate needs. He suggests that the systematic deprivation that inmates suffer provides them with the incentive to develop an identifiable social system that provides mechanisms that help alleviate the pains of imprisonment. The inmate social system includes the development and selection of leaders who facilitate and support the inmate culture.

The leaders are appropriately referred to as "politicians" in prison jargon as they are capable of developing favorable interpersonal relationships with inmates, guards, and treatment personnel and gaining the trust of individuals with whom they deal. Leaders are typically older than other inmates, have spent considerable time in the institution, and are serving long sentences. They have usually been involved in criminal behavior that gives them status with their peers, and sometimes they have been important members of criminal gangs or organizations on the outside (Irwin, 1970). By and large, inmate leaders hold key administrative or clerical positions and have access to avenues of communication and influence in administrative decision making through relationships of trust and the power of persuasion (McCleery, 1960).

Inmate leaders and guards form exchange relationships and share a common concern for a smoothly running prison. Inmate leaders, who gain relatively more from the informal social system, have a vested interest in a status quo posture within the prison environment, and will assist guards in keeping an orderly and smooth-running cell block by exerting influence and pressure on potentially disruptive inmates. As a result, inmate leaders and prison administrators share the goal of maintaining an orderly institution (Cloward, 1960). It is at this focal point where guards and inmate leaders develop compromises that the formal system interacts with, and that facilitates the informal power structure, as both systems have the same organizational objectives—order maintenance and social control in the environment.

It has been pointed out that guards could not control the inmate population and keep order (the criteria by which they are ultimately judged) without the assistance of key inmate leaders (McCorkle & Korn, 1954; McCleery, 1960). However, there is a cost to the institution for assistance from inmates in maintaining its system. The basis of power wielded by influential inmates who facilitate order maintenance is their ability to alleviate the systematic pains of imprisonment imposed upon their fellow inmates. To allow inmate leaders to maintain their leadership and influence roles, the prison staff must give inmate leaders autonomy to circumvent and manipulate the formal oppressive system of control and operate a system that minimizes inmate deprivations. A major facet of that informal system is the contraband market, which provides (a) material goods and services to inmates that they otherwise would not have access to, and (b) a sense of psychological satisfaction, both from seeing the formal system "beat" and from feeling they have at least some control over their lives. In effect, inmates have created their own system of governance, one that they accept and legitimize at the informal level.

In this informal social system, rules and norms are promulgated and imposed, at least through influence, by inmate leaders. These rules can provide the basis for a stable environment—an output that administrators can accept. What is developed at the informal level is a legitimate form of governance for inmates that is based, in part, on the contraband marketplace and, as such, is at odds with bureaucratic prison authority. It is this legitimate form of governance, we posit, that ultimately enhances stability in prisons. Ironically, this form of legitimate governance evolves naturally out of the contradiction between the rigid control orientation of prison and the inherent inability of the traditional bureaucratic system to achieve control. Therefore, the stability of a prison is contingent upon the strength of the informal inmate social system, which is linked inexorably to the contraband market system.

The social system within prisons is defined relative to the patterns of social interactions of inmates (Sykes, 1958). These interactions are predicated on a separate system of values, beliefs, and attitudes among inmates. These attributes promulgate an informal hierarchy, with the presence of specific roles by inmates, including leaders within the inmate corp. Strength within an inmate social system is defined as the degree of consensus, commitment, and acquiescence on the part of inmates to the rules of the informal system and to those who are given leadership roles—in other words, the formation of a legitimate form of governance.

Current literature suggests that a cohesive inmate social system does not exist to any great extent in contemporary prisons, as some prison societies are divided by race (Carroll, 1974), dominated by "supergangs" (Jacobs, 1977), organized along loosely connected cliques (Irwin, 1980), and are torn internally because of the rising politicalization of the typical inmate (Stastny and Tyrnaurer, 1982). The heterogeneity of the prison society clearly is an impediment to the development of a universally accepted informal inmate social structure, and, as such, limits the development of an informal form of legitimate governance; this creates the potential for instability (Lombardo, 1982). In fact, conflict between inmates or groups of inmates is sometimes based on feuds over marketing territories and rights of more profitable forms of contraband (Davidson, 1977). However, coalitions are formed, and compromises are often struck in deference to the survival of the marketplace and the individual buyers and sellers involved.

THE CONTRABAND MARKETPLACE:
THE BASIS OF THE INFORMAL SOCIAL SYSTEM AND
INFORMAL LEGITIMATE GOVERNANCE

The position of this article is that the contraband marketplace is a factor that is instrumental to the development of a legitimate form of inmate governance.[1] Contraband is defined as materials that are unauthorized by the formal prison administration. Common examples of contraband are the following: drugs, alcohol, gambling and gambling paraphernalia, real money, and a host of other assorted commodities and services. The demand for contraband is created by the institution's formal goals: the control and punishment of inmates. The supply of contraband products comes about due to the inability of the organization to achieve its primary goal.

The organization cannot totally control its inmate body for a variety of reasons: low officer-to-inmate ratio, lack of normative commitment to the organizational rules by inmates, and the inability to implement an efficient reward/punishment system to gain compliance among inmates. Thus administrators emphasize that which is obtainable: relatively quiet and clean cell blocks that are free of visible violence. This obtainable goal is achieved through a series of relationships developed between guards and influential leaders. It is at this focal point that the formal system erodes and the inmate social structure begins.

Much activity in the inmate social structure evolves around the maintenance of the contraband marketplace. A vast amount of inmate time is dedicated to the contraband marketplace; inmates are dependent upon the marketplace for material and psychological well-being, and inmates who are influential and are cast in leadership roles are those who contribute to the maintenance of the contraband marketplace (Kalinich, 1980; Stojkovic, 1984).

One of the earliest works on the black market in prison was written about a prisoner of war (POW) camp for American soldiers in Germany during World War II; the work described a flourishing contraband system that included a system of trade between prison camps (Radford, 1945). Since then, a great deal has been written about prisons, particularly in relation to the informal inmate social structure. Although most of the literature does not focus on the contraband marketplace, almost all of it makes reference to contraband flow, with some of the literature describing that phenomenon in detail. McCleery (1960) and Davison (1977) describe active and prosperous contraband market systems that were controlled by powerful inmate leaders. Irwin (1970) depicts the links between inmates' street behaviors and their behaviors in the prison contraband market and the tenuous connection contraband provides among prison gangs. As a result of his research in a Federal Prison, Guenther (1975) concluded that contraband was rather common, and guards attempted to control dangerous contraband (weapons, escape equipment) whereas they, in effect, turned their backs on contraband that was considered a nuisance (drugs, gambling material, homemade alcohol). Shoblad (1972), describing his life as an inmate, discusses with some detail the sophisticated nature of the contraband marketplace and the ease with which inmates provided unauthorized goods and services to the prison population.

Research focusing on the contraband marketplace in a maximum security prison described the existence of a thriving marketplace in which most inmates participated with a great deal of frequency and with an array of goods and services available to them (Kalinich, 1980). The major categories of goods and services available were the following: drugs, alcoholic beverages, gambling, appliances (TV sets, hot plates, radios, and so on), clothing, buying of institutional privileges and reports, weapons, food and snack services, and prostitution. Each of these categories included a number of subcomponents, with complex or simple interactions, and the system was found to be based on a complex monetary operation that included the use of a regular banking system, organized loan sharking in the institution, inmates' prison accounts, inmate script, and real money—"green"—and cigarettes. Similar to Guenther's (1975) research, this study showed that some forms of contraband were considered dangerous by guards—and inmates—such as weapons, whereas much of the contraband was considered a thorn in the side of guards. However, this study found that certain forms of contraband were considered beneficial by custodial staff and were allowed to exist with the tacit but rather open approval of the majority of the staff.

A common and approved contraband service was the "inmate store." Each cell block had one or two inmates who kept a large stock of snacks, pop, instant coffee, and so on, that they purchased at the inmate commissary—the authorized outlet— and resold to inmates in the evenings after the commissary was closed. This form of "convenience store" was found beneficial by the custodial staff as it gave the inmates a method to help structure their free evening time. This was harmless though unauthorized and added to the smooth running of the cell block. Guards' views on drug use by inmates were mixed, even though administrators saw drugs as a definite threat to the security of the institution. Whereas older guards viewed drugs as dangerous, but alcoholic beverages brewed in the institution harmless, younger guards viewed marijuana use as a method of pacifying inmates (Kalinich, 1980).

Other research in a maximum security prison has concluded that narcotics and its distribution are extremely important in controlling the institutional environment (Stojkovic, 1984). When inmates were asked to describe the influence of drugs within the facility, they stated the importance of the sub-rosa drug market in stabilizing the environment. The consensus among inmates was that the providing of illegal goods and services by pivotal inmates in the inmate social system provided control for correctional officers and comfort to inmates in coping with their incarceration. In effect, the distribution of specific contraband items—differing types of narcotics—was essential for both custodial staff and key inmates in the control of the environment.

What was produced was a situation in which institutional capital was concentrated and power centralized with a few inmates. The short-term effect was that the inmate society was pacified until the next supply of drugs was delivered. In the interim, inmates attempted to cope with imprisonment using illegal means. It was at this juncture that inmate violence, assaults, and robberies surfaced. More important, this is where the value of inmate leaders is pivotal. When institutional violence surfaces, it becomes incumbent upon these leaders to develop compromises among the warring factions to ensure "domestic tranquility." In this way, not only is the institution stabilized through the influence of inmate politicians but the market structure remains intact.

Thus it becomes clear that the contraband markeplace is an important focal point for inmates, around which they focus a great deal of their activities as well as structure their behaviors and interactions with each other and the prison staff, especially custodial staff.

POWER OF INMATE LEADERS, LEGITIMACY, AND STABILITY

The link between inmates and staff is through the inmate leaders. One of the major roles of inmate leaders is to facilitate the flow of contraband. In doing so, they gain the backing and support of those inmates who value contraband and, thus, can influence them and their behaviors.

The use of formal rewards and punishments to control inmates' behavior is limited. Guards often overlook rule violations by inmates who are not troublemakers and tend to be cooperative over all. As stated earlier, guards depend on more influential inmates' cooperation in keeping the cell blocks clean and relatively peaceful. In return for their cooperation, guards will overlook the manipulations of the influential inmates as long as the order of the cell block is facilitated and not disrupted by those manipulations.

There are three elements that are common to inmate leaders. First, they have had extensive knowledge of the informal institutional structure from past experience and are serving long sentences. Second, they have jobs that permit freedom of movement from one area within the institution to another. Third, they have a large number of contacts with fellow inmates who will work for or with them, and some may have criminal contacts outside the institution that can help coordinate the inflow of contraband into the prison black market (Kalinich, 1980). In addition, they are skillful at developing good relationships with inmates and guards. They can usually gain a relationship of trust with inmates and guards, giving both groups the appearance of allegiance to them. In most cases, the inmate leaders have a vested interest in the status quo and the stability of the institution (Cloward, 1960) and, therefore, share the guards' interest in an orderly cell block. They have resources, "business" expertise, are sensitive to the needs of both inmates and prison staff, and can negotiate with the two groups who may otherwise be in constant conflict. In effect, they can contribute to the sense of control and order of the custodial staff, and they can control their constituents—the inmates—through overt and covert means and help keep order in the prison community.

It was found to be a common practice for inmates who were politicians to be selected by prison staff for work assignments, involving some responsibility and trust, such as clerical position working under a supervisor or counselor. The selection is made on the inmate's potential as a "politician" as staff look for inmates who "know how the prison really works." These inmates, though not expected to be informants, have their finger on the pulse of activities in the institution, and can help legitimize the authority of the staff member they are working for through their influence over other inmates. Staff members enter this employment relationship usually knowing the inmate will use the position for his own benefit. The trade-off of bureaucratic control for stability is considered a rational choice at the operational level (Kalinich, 1980).

The label "politician" suggests that inmate leaders hold legitimate power over their fellow inmates. Their ability to supply contraband goods and services directly and facilitate the behavior of others who are active in the contraband marketplace provides them with the ability to influence and lead their fellow inmates. They nurture and sustain a system that inmates have a normative commitment to in that it concurs with their values, and it provides a material and psychological payoff. Thus a system exists upon which a set of acceptable rules are readily promulgated that reify the system. Inmate leaders are expected to support the rules and system developed at the sub-rosa level and to enforce the rules when necessary and possible. Inmates who inadvertently fall into positions of potential influence with the staff through job assignments or personal interactive skills are expected to become politicians and support the sub-rosa system by facilitating the contraband flow. If they do not take on politician roles and leadership responsibilities as defined by the inmate subculture, other inmates will bring pressures to bear to influence that inmate into accepting at least a partial role as a politician, or will manipulate that person out of the position (Kalinich, 1980). Within this framework of legitimacy, inmate leaders have access to specific forms of power to influence inmate behaviors.

These kinds of power are everchanging within the prison environment. These forms of power vary depending upon the individual and the situation. Past research has suggested that inmate leaders express these disparate forms of power dependent upon how well they influence their peers (Stojkovic, 1984). Accordingly, there are five types of power exercised by politicians: coercive, referent, providing of resources, expert, and legitimate.

Coercive power is defined as the threat of force or the actual application of punishment to gain conformity among inmates. This type of power has been documented as the primary method inmate leaders employs as a control strategy (Jacobs, 1977; Irwin, 1980). Referent power can be defined as the identification inmates have with a group or gang, and conformity is achieved through a commitment to group norms. This, too, is quite common in our prisons and usually is advanced by various religious groups and "super gangs" in the institution.

Third, providing resources is a particularly important form of power. This kind of power is predicated on the ability of the leader to access goods and services. This type of power is the most relevant to the contraband system. Fourth, expert power is rooted in the knowledge an individual possesses. Typically, leaders who understand the legal system are able to gain much power in the inmate social world and can influence many other prisoners. Finally, legitimate power can be identified; this power base is dependent upon an internalization process, where inmates follow the rules and regulations prescribed by leaders because they perceive them as as justified and in the best interest of inmates. We found that those inmate leaders who focused their efforts on facilitating the flow of contraband had access to all of the above-mentioned social bases of power and were the strongest stabilizing force within the informal system. Therefore, conformity is accomplished through a consensus among inmates that adherence to the rules furthers the inmates' needs vis-à-vis the formal administration (Stojkovic, 1984).

Therefore, a loosely defined but strong form of governance develops at the informal level. This promotes stability in that a set of rules is created that inmates can accept; leadership is denied by inmate values, and leaders will develop who contribute to the maintenance of the accepted system. Disturbances in the contraband marketplace will cause similar disturbances in the inmate legitimate governance system. If the contraband system is suppressed through tightening of administrative controls, the basis of legitimate governance is also suppressed. This will, in turn, disrupt the basis for stability in the prison environment.

IMPLICATIONS

What we have attempted to convey is that contraband market systems in our prison environments establish legitimacy among often alienated bodies of inmates. In this way inmates tacitly approve of the social organization of the prison through a shared and agreed upon operation of prescribed rules and regulations. Furthermore, these separate and identifiable roles played by inmate politicians foster a subtle form of control, which ironically stabilizes the prison setting. However, if legitimacy is sought after as an end by prison officials, fostering illegal contraband markets among prisoners only further separates keepers from kept. The pivotal question, therefore, becomes the following: Can a formal sense of legitimacy be developed among antagonistic groups of inmates in our prisons by administrators?

Irwin (1980) states: "Thus, in order for these organizations to obtain and hold the commitment of a number of leaders and

thereby to begin supplanting the violent, rapacious group structures, they will have to have some power in decision making."
Fogel (1975) arrives at the same conclusion when he suggests that
prisoners should be allowed to "wield lawful power" within the
institutional environment. Other writers have suggested this
approach through the development of participatory models of
management within prison settings (Baker, 1977; Baunach, 1981).

As described by Stastny and Tyrnauer (1982), however, the
movement for more inmate self-governance has been ineffective
in reorganizing the internal structure of our prisons. They state
that "the trend toward a less isolated prison milieu, toward the
detotalization of the prison culture, which had its beginnings in a
very different era, appears to be inching slowly forward."
Although movement in the direction of more inmate input into
the day-to-day operations of the prison remains slow, it is still
essential in trying to form a consensus among inmates that their
incarceration is justified.

What we have shown is that there is agreement among
prisoners today, and that it is contingent upon, in part, the
contraband market. Although prison social groupings are not as
integrated and cohesively bound today as in the past, what we are
suggesting is that the violence and fragmentation of the more
modern inmate social milieu is relative to the operation and
control of sub-rosa activities. As mentioned by Jacobs (1977), the
old, traditionally oriented con power structure was replaced by
more violent and racially motivated gangs. He describes the role
these gangs play in the distribution of goods and services:

> The gang in prison serves important economic and psychological
> functions. To some degree the gang functions as a buffer against
> poverty. Each organization has a poor box. Each of the six cell-
> house chiefs in each gang collects cigarettes from his members and
> stores them for those who are needy. When a member makes a
> particularly good "score," he is expected to share some of the
> bounty with the leaders and donate to the poor box.

The gang or group in the contemporary prison serves the same
purpose as the old inmate organization: the fulfillment of

psychological and physical needs and desires. In this way, the gang develops normative symbols, rules, and regulations that support the structure of the gang, while fulfilling the basic needs of its members. Thus the strong identification of members is what binds individuals to the group and, at the same time, the unifying theme of the gang is the collection and distribution of contraband items. It is at this focal point that violence reaches its zenith; each gang competes for scarce resources, which helps the individual collective cope with incarceration process. This provides material comfort and status to the group. Therefore, the group's physical and psychological needs are met by the informal contraband market operation.

However, this process promotes more manipulation and dishonesty among prisoners and staff, causing a situation in which stability is dependent upon informalities and illegalities within the prison environment. In addition, the contraband market system may lead to direct violence and hidden hostilities. The most salient problem is the use of individual or gang violence to take over lucrative contraband markets. Recently in the Michigan system, a drug dealer was burned to death by a competitor who resented the victim's intrusion into his territory. (The gasoline used in the murder was purchased as contraband.) In a flourishing prison contraband market system, an economic class structure emerges, with those willing and able to participate as dealers gaining relatively greater wealth and status than other inmates.

It is not uncommon for inmates with relatively limited wealth to feel even more alienated and deprived within the system than they otherwise might feel. Inmates in the "low economic class" found the class difference a ready rationalization to steal from fellow inmates who had accumulated some material wealth, whether the accumulation was from contraband dealing or legal sources (Kalinich, 1980). Finally, the opportunity and temptation for staff to become corrupted exists in the delivery of contraband goods that are highly profitable. It would seem demoralizing to conscious staff to think certain inmates are making large sums of money by continuing their criminal careers while in prison. Although contraband organization and distribution enhances a tenuous form of stability, what is required is more formalized sense of legitimacy among inmates. It is our contention that this could be accomplished through a more direct relationship between inmate bodies and the prison hierarchy in the decision-making processes of the organization.

As posited by Baunach (1981), although participatory approaches have been implemented in various prisons throughout the country over the years, there has been no long-term incorporation of the concept within our correctional institutions. What we are suggesting is that the operation of our prisons requires some form of legitimacy among those being incarcerated; at present, that is being provided by the supply of goods and services via the sub-rosa market structure. The power that such a system exhibits is tremendous, and if administrators would seek more control over their institutions, they need to alter the structural arrangements within the environment to promote more legitimate forms of power among inmates. If not, they will continue to operate on the symbiotic relationships endemic to the contraband system and be subject to its many uncertainties. Having looked at contraband as a major determinant of stability, we need to return briefly to the more popular question of what causes prison riots. Factors that disrupt the contraband economic system will destabilize the normative system developed by inmates. One observable factor that can disrupt the delicate economic system is an aggressive prison administration that on occasion may impose its goal of bureaucratic control effectively and interfere with the contraband flow. Ironically, effective administration of a prison in the classic bureaucratic sense may cause prisoners to riot.

NOTE

1. In the way we are employing this term, we mean "legitimate" as something that is accepted and agreed upon by a majority of inmates. On the other hand, we do not intend the reader to perceive "legitimate" as something that is "legal" and formal in nature, such as the rules and regulations of the institution. See French and Raven (1968) for a further discussion and clarification of legitimate power.

REFERENCES

Baker, J. E. (1977). Inmate self-government and the right to participate. In R. M. Carter et al. (Eds.), *Correctional institutions* (2nd ed.). Philadelphia: J. B. Lippincott.

Baunach, P. J. (1981). Participatory management: Restructuring the prison environment. In D. Fogel & J. Hudson (Eds.), *Justice as fairness: Perspectives on the justice model.* Cincinnati, OH: Anderson.

Carroll, L. (1974). *Hacks, blacks, and cons.* Lexington, MA: D. C. Heath.

Cloward, R. A. (1960). Social control in prison. In L. Hazelrigg (Ed.), *Prison within society.* New York: Doubleday.

Davidson, R. T. (1977). The prisoner economy. In R. M. Carter et al. (Eds.), *Correctional institutions* (2nd ed.). Philadelphia: J. B. Lippincott.

Downs, A. (1967). *Inside bureaucracy.* Boston, MA: Little, Brown.

Fogel, D. (1975). *We are the living proof.* Cincinnati, OH: Anderson.

French, J.R.P., & Raven, B. (1968). The bases of social power. In D. Cartwright & A. Zander (Eds.), *Group dynamics* (3rd ed.). New York: Harper & Row.

Guenther, A. L. (1975). Compensations in a total institution: The forms and functions of contraband. *Crime & Delinquency, 21*, 243-254.

Irwin, J. (1970). *The felon.* Englewood Cliffs, NJ: Prentice-Hall.

Irwin, J. (1980). *Prison in turmoil.* Boston, MA: Little, Brown.

Jacobs, J. B. (1977). *Stateville: The penitentiary in mass society.* Chicago: University of Chicago Press.

Kalinich, D. B. (1980). *The inmate economy.* Lexington, MA: D. C. Heath.

Lombardo, L. X. (1981). *Guards imprisoned: Correctional officers at work.* New York: Elsevier.

Lombardo, L. X. (1982). Stress, change, and collective violence in prison. In H. Toch & R. Johnson (Eds.), *The pains of imprisonment.* Beverly Hills, CA: Sage.

McCleery, R. (1960). Communication patterns as bases of systems of authority and power. In *Studies in social organization of the prison* (pp. 49-77). New York: Social Sciences Research Council.

McCorkle, L., & Korn, R. (1954). Resocialization within the walls. In S. Johnson & Wolfgang (Eds.), *The sociology of punishment and corrections.* New York: John Wiley.

Radford, R. A. (1945). The economic organization of a prisoner of war camp. *Economics, 12,* 258-280.

Shoblad, R. (1972). *Doing my own time.* Garden City, NY: Doubleday.

Stastny, C., & Tyrnauer, G. (1982). *Who rules the joint: The changing political culture of maximum-security prisons in America.* Lexington, MA: D. C. Heath.

Stojkovic, S. (1982). *Social bases of power in a maximum-security prison. A study of the erosion of traditional authority.* Unpublished doctoral dissertation, Michigan State University.

Sykes, G. (1958). *Society of captives.* Princeton, NJ: Princeton University Press.

Sykes, G., & Messinger, S. L. (1960). The inmate social system. In R. Cloward et al. (Eds.), *Theoretical studies in social organization of the prison* (pp. 5-19). New York: Social Science Research Council.

Toch, H. (1977). *Living in prison: The ecology of survival.* New York: Free Press.

Warwick, D. P. (1975). *A theory of public bureaucracy: Politics, personality, and organization in the state department.* Cambridge, MA: Harvard University Press.

David B. Kalinich is Associate Professor of Criminal Justice at Michigan State University. His research emphases are in correctional administration and management, inmate subcultures, and prisoner economics. At present, he is developing a text in the training of correctional officers at the front-line level.

Stan Stojkovic is Assistant Professor of Criminal Justice at the University of Wisconsin—Milwaukee. His interests are in the analysis of forms of power in prison among administrators, officers, and inmates, and he is currently developing empirical measures to assess the quantity and quality of goods and services in differing prison contraband systems.

[12]

SOCIAL PROBLEMS, Vol. 30, No. 5, June 1983

PRIVATE SECURITY: IMPLICATIONS FOR SOCIAL CONTROL*

CLIFFORD D. SHEARING
PHILIP C. STENNING
University of Toronto

Private security has become a pervasive feature of modern North American policing, both because of its rapid growth since 1960 and because it has invaded the traditional domain of the public police. Because this development has been viewed as an addendum to the criminal justice system, its significance for social control has not been recognized. This paper traces the development of private security in Canada and the United States since 1960, examines the reasons for its present pervasiveness, and explores its essential features: it is non-specialized, victim-oriented, and relies on organizational resources as sanctions. We conclude that private security is having a major impact on the nature of social control.

One of the most striking features of social control in North America is the pervasive presence of private security, which embraces a wide variety of services from security guards to computer fraud investigators, from home burglar alarms to sophisticated industrial and commercial surveillance systems, from anti-bugging devices to anti-terrorist "executive protection" courses. Private security offers protection for both persons and property which is often more comprehensive than that provided by public police forces. Internal security — so-called "in-house security" — has traditionally been provided by "corporate entities" (Coleman, 1974) such as profit-making corporations, and public institutions such as schools. Since the early 1960s there has been an enormous growth in "contract security," which provides police services on a fee-for-service basis to anyone willing to pay.

Private security is not a new phenomenon. Self-help and the sale of protection as a commodity have a long history (Becker, 1974; Radzinowicz, 1956). Even after the state sought to monopolize public protection through the establishment of public police forces in the 19th century, private interests continued to provide additional protection for themselves through private security (Spitzer and Scull, 1977). What is new about modern private security is its pervasiveness and the extent to which its activities have expanded into public, rather than purely private, places. In urban environments at least, private security is now ubiquitous and is likely to be encountered by city dwellers at home (especially if they live in an apartment building or on a condominium estate), at work, when shopping or banking, when using public transit, or when going to a sports stadium, university, or hospital.

In this paper we consider the extent and nature of modern private security in Canada and the United States and its implications for social control. In doing so, we draw on the findings of research which we and our colleagues have undertaken since the early 1970s in Canada. This has included a series of studies of the legal context within which private security operates (Freedman and Stenning, 1977; Stenning, 1981; Stenning and Cornish, 1975; Stenning and Shearing, 1979); a major survey of the contract security industry — guard and investigative agencies — in the province of Ontario during 1976, which involved interviews with security agency executives and the administration of a questionaire to their employees (Shearing et al., 1980); a similar, but less extensive, survey of "in-house" security organizations in Ontario in 1974 (Jeffries, 1977); an examination of the available national statistics on the size and growth of private security in

---

* This is a revised version of a paper presented at the 33rd annual meeting of the American Society of Criminology in Washington, D.C., November, 1981. The authors thank John Gilmore and the anonymous *Social Problems* reviewers for their comments. Correspondence to: Centre of Criminology, University of Toronto, 8th Floor, John Robarts Library, 130 St. George Street, Toronto, Ontario M5S 1A1, Canada.

Canada between 1961 and 1971 (Farnell and Shearing, 1977); and three related studies of police, client, and public perceptions of private security, focussing primarily on the province of Ontario, using both interviews and questionaires during 1982.

Most studies of formal social control within sociology have focused on systems of state control. They view law, justice, and the maintenance of public order as having been virtual state monopolies since early in the 19th century. Even those studies focusing on private forms have typically examined those instances in which state functions have been contracted out to private organizations (Scull, 1977), thus implicitly reinforcing the notion of a state monopoly over such functions (Cohen, 1979).[1]

The few sociologists who have studied the modern development of private security (Becker, 1974; Bunyan, 1977; Kakalik and Wildhorn, 1977) have, with few exceptions (Spitzer and Scull, 1977), broadly followed this tradition and have treated private security as little more than a private adjunct to the public criminal justice system. They assume that private security is essentially a private form of public policing, and that it can be understood in the same way as the public police.

We argue that this approach to understanding private security is inadequate because it fails to account for some of the most important differences between private security and public police and, more importantly, between the contexts within which each operates. The context in which private security functions is not public law and the criminal justice system, but what Henry (1978:123) has called "private justice." We follow the view of legal pluralists who maintain that "in any given society there will be as many legal systems as there are functioning social units" (Pospisil, 1967:24).

We begin by examining the size and growth of private security in Canada and the United States. Then we look at changes in the urban environment which have been associated with the involvement of private security in maintaining public order. Finally we consider various features of private security: who supports it, its authority, its organizational features, and its relationship to the public police.

THE SIZE AND GROWTH OF PRIVATE SECURITY[2]

While private security has probably existed in one form or another in North America since the continent was first settled by Europeans, little is known about its practice prior to the mid-19th century. Older accounts contain no reliable information about the size and growth of private security (Horan, 1967; Johnson, 1976; Lipson, 1975.) It was not until 1969 that the first major study of contract security was undertaken in the United States (Kakalik and Wildhorn, 1971), and not until these researchers revised their findings in 1977, in the light of 1970 census data, that a reasonably complete picture of size and growth trends became available. For Canada, the available statistical information is even less adequate.

Table 1 provides a summary of the statistics available for the United States and Canada respectively. We emphasize, however, that because of definitional difficulties and unreliable record-keeping practices, these figures are at best approximate. Table 1 shows that in the United States in 1960, private security almost equalled the public police in number. By 1970, both sectors had experienced substantial growth, with public police outdistancing private security. The early 1970s show a significant slowdown in the growth of public police, but a continued escalation in the growth of private security, especially in the contract security sector; by 1975,

---

1. An exception to this is the research on dispute resolution, especially that done by anthropologists (Nader, 1980; Pospisil, 1978; Snyder, 1981).
2. For a more detailed analysis of current statistics on the size and growth of private security see Shearing and Stenning (1981:198).

TABLE 1

Public Police and Private Security Personnel, in Thousands (Rounded)

	Police		Security						Ratio of Police to Security	Ratio of In-house to Contract
		% Increase	In-house	% Increase	Contract	% Increase	Total	% Increase		
				UNITED STATES						
1960[a]	258		192		30		222		1.2:1	6:1
		51		15		103		27		
1970[a]	390		220		61		281		1.4:1	3.5:1
		5		18		187		55		
1975[b]	411		260		175		435		0.9:1	1.5:1
				CANADA						
1971[c]	40		25		11.5		36.5		1.1:1	2.2:1
		30		14		65		32		
1975[d]	51		29		19		48		1.1:1	1.5:1

Sources:
a. Adapted from table 2.11 "Security Employment Trends by Type of Employer" (Kakalik and Wildhorn, 1977:43).
b. Police strength figure derived from U.S. Department of Justice, Federal Bureau of Investigation (1976:26). Private security figures, which are estimates only, adapted from Predicasts, Inc. (1974:26).
c. Adapted from Farnell and Shearing (1977).
d. Adapted from Friendly (1980).

private security outnumbered public police. Between 1960 and 1975 the ratio of in-house to contract security diminished from 6:1 to 1.5:1, indicating a major restructuring of the organization of private security.[3]

Directly comparable data on the growth of private security in Canada from 1960 to 1970 are not available.[4] Census data suggest, however, that growth rates within the contract security sector may have been as high as 700 percent (Farnell and Shearing, 1977:113). By 1971, however, there were almost as many private security as public police in Canada, but in-house personnel still outnumbered contract security by more than 2 to 1. Within the next four years, both public police and private security personnel continued to increase, at approximately the same rate (30 percent). Within private security, however, contract security increased 65 percent, a rate almost five times that of the rate of growth of in-house security.

While reliable national statistics since 1975 are not available, statistics for the province of Ontario (which have in the past proved a good indicator of national trends) indicate a levelling off of contract security growth during the latter half of the 1970s. Overall, contract security in Ontario appears to have increased 90 percent from 1971 to 1980, while the growth rate of public police during the same period was 29 percent (Waldie *et al.*, 1982:8). Assuming that there has been no absolute numerical decline in in-house security, this almost certainly means that in Ontario (and probably the rest of Canada) private security now outnumbers the public police. Furthermore, contract security alone now rivals the public police numerically. In Ontario, by 1980, there were three contract security personnel for every four public police officers -- 15,000 contract security, and just under 20,000 public police officers (Waldie *et al.*, 1982:9).

3. Reliable data for the United States since 1975 are not yet available.
4. Although 1961 and 1971 census data are available they cannot be compared to establish growth rates due to changes in category definitions (Farnell and Shearing, 1977:39).

496   SHEARING AND STENNING

These findings indicate that in Canada and the United States the public police have for some time shared the task of policing with private organizations, and that private security probably now outnumber public police in both countries. The major change has been the rapid growth, since the early 1960s, of policing provided on a contract basis, for profit, by private enterprise (Spitzer and Scull, 1977). This has established private security as a readily available alternative to public police for those with the means to afford it, and has made private security a much more visible contributor to policing than it has been hitherto. The result has been an unobtrusive but significant restructuring of our institutions for the maintenance of order, and a substantial erosion by the private sector of the state's assumed monopoly over policing and, by implication, justice.

MASS PRIVATE PROPERTY

To understand the locus of private security it is necessary to examine the changes that have taken place, particularly since the early 1950s, in the organization of private property and public space. In North America many public activities now take place within huge, privately owned facilities, which we call "mass private property." Examples include shopping centers with hundreds of individual retail establishments, enormous residential estates with hundreds, if not thousands, of housing units, equally large office, recreational, industrial, and manufacturing complexes, and many university campuses. While evidence of these developments surrounds every city dweller, there is little data on how much public space in urban areas is under private control (Bourne and Harper, 1974:213, Lorimer, 1972:21). However, the available data does indicate an enormous increase in mass private property.

Spurr (1975:18) surveyed 60 major companies producing new urban residential accommodation in 24 Canadian metropolitan centers:

> Forty-seven firms hold 119,192 acres (186 square miles) of land, including 34 firms which each own more than one square mile. . . . Forty-two firms hold 95,174 apartment units including 13 firms with 123 apartment buildings. Twenty-nine firms have 223 office and other commercial buildings, while 23 firms have nearly 26,000,000 square feet of commercial space. While these commercial and apartment figures may appear large, the survey is particularly incomplete in these areas. Finally, twenty-seven firms have 185 shopping centres and sixteen firms own 38 hotels.

Gertler and Crowley (1977:289) used data collected by Punter (1974) to study four townships within 40 miles of Toronto, from 1954 to 1971. They identified

> . . . two striking changes in the ownership patterns. Absentee ownership by individuals increased from less than 5 per cent of total area to about 20 per cent; and corporate ownership of the land which was negligible in 1954 increased to more than 20 per cent in 1971, with increases occurring particularly in the investment-developer category.

Martin (1975:21), in a study of the north-east Toronto fringe, found that corporations represented 22 per cent of all buyers and 16 per cent of all sellers. He argued that these transactions represented "the nucleus of land dealer activities in the study area between 1968 and 1974" (1975:27). Gertler and Crowley (1977:290) comment on these findings:

> Land development has changed from an activity carried out by a large number of small builder/developers in the 1950s to a process in the seventies which is increasingly shaped by large public companies. These firms are vertically integrated, that is, organized to handle the entire development package from land assembly to planning and design, construction, property management, and marketing.

The modern development of mass private property has meant that more and more public life now takes place on property which is privately owned. Yet the policing needs of such privately owned public places have not been met by the public police for two reasons. First, the routine "beat" of the public police has traditionally been confined to publicly owned property such as streets and parks (Stinchcombe, 1963). Therefore, even when they have had the resources to police privately owned public places — and typically they have not — they have been philosophically disinclined to do so. Second, those who own and control mass private property have commonly preferred to retain and exercise their traditional right to preserve order on their own property and to maintain control over the policing of it, rather than calling upon the public police to perform this function.

Because more and more public places are now located on private property, the protection of property — which lies at the heart of private security's function — has increasingly come to include the maintenance of public order, a matter which was, hitherto, regarded as the more or less exclusive prerogative of the public police. With the growth of mass private property, private security has been steadily encroaching upon the traditional beat of the public police. In so doing, it has brought areas of public life that were formerly under state control under the control of private corporations.

LEGITIMATION OF PRIVATE SECURITY AUTHORITY

The close association between private security and private property provides its most important source of social legitimation as an alternative to systems of public justice, and helps to explain why its development has proceeded with so little opposition. Because the development of modern institutions of public justice (during the early 19th century) necessarily involved the conferring of exceptional authority, such as police powers, on public officials, it has required legislative action and all the public debate which that engenders (Baldwin and Kinsey, 1980). By contrast, the development of private security has required virtually no legislation and has generated little public interest. This is because the authority of private security derives not so much from exceptional powers as from the ordinary powers and privileges of private property owners to control access to, use of, and conduct on, their property. While modern private security guards enjoy few or no exceptional law enforcement powers, their status as agents of property allows them to exercise a degree of legal authority which in practice far exceeds that of their counterparts in the public police. They may insist that persons submit to random searches of their property or persons as a condition of entry to, or exit from, the premises. They may even require clients to surrender their property while remaining on the premises, and during this time they may lawfully keep them under more or less constant visual or electronic surveillance. Before allowing clients to use the premises (or property such as a credit card) they may insist that clients provide detailed information about themselves, and authorize them to seek personal information from others with whom they have dealings. Private security may use such information for almost any purpose, and even pass it on, or sell it, to others.

In theory, the public can avoid the exercise of such private security authority by declining to use the facilities, as either customers or employees. In practice, however, realistic alternatives are often not available; for example, airport security applies to all airlines. This is a function of both the modern trend toward mass private property, and the fact that more and more public places are now situated on private property. Between them, these trends result in a situation in which the choices available to consumers are often severely limited. Employees and customers alike must submit to the authority of property owners and their agents as a condition of use. Thus, because private security is so pervasive, and because it is found in so many services and facilities essential to modern living (employment, credit, accommodation, education, health, transportation), it is practically impossible to avoid.

The fact that private security derives so much of its legitimacy from the institution of private property involves a profound historical irony. In the United States and Canada, state power has historically been perceived as posing the greatest threat to individual liberty. The legal institutions of private property and privacy arguably evolved as a means of guaranteeing individuals a measure of security against external intrusions, especially intrusions by the state (Reich, 1964; Stinchcombe, 1963). These institutions defined an area of privacy to which the state was denied access without consent, other than in exceptional circumstances. On private property, therefore, the authority of the property owner was recognized as being paramount — a philosophy most clearly reflected in the adage, "a man's home is his castle."

The validity of this notion, however, requires a reasonable congruence between private property and private places: a man's home was his castle, not because it was private property as such, but because it was a private place. However, as more and more private property has become, in effect, public, this congruence has been eroded. The emergence of mass private property, in fact, has given to private corporations a sphere of independence and authority which in practice has been far greater than that enjoyed by individual citizens and which has rivaled that of the state. The legal authority originally conceded to private property owners has increasingly become the authority for massive and continuous intrusions upon the privacy of citizens (as customers and employees) by those who own and control the mass private property on which so much public life takes place. Nevertheless, the traditional association between the institution of private property and the protection of liberty has historically been such a powerful source of legitimacy that, despite these important changes in the nature of private property, the exercise of private security authority is rarely questioned or challenged.

What little resistance has occured has been mainly in the workplace, and has taken one or both of two forms — one an "underground" movement, and the other a more open and organized phenomenon. The underground movment is apparent in a "hidden economy" (Henry, 1978) of systematic pilfering, unofficial "perks," "padding" of claims for sickness benefits and other forms of compensation, as means of circumventing the formal structures and procedures established to protect corporate assets and profits. While such resistance sometimes occurs on a grand scale, it is mostly informal and individualistic.

Labor unions have posed a more formal and openly organized challenge to the unrestricted exercise of private security authority. They have fought private security processes and procedures through industrial action, collective bargaining, and arbitration. For example, in our research we have encountered collective agreements containing clauses specifying in detail the occasions on which employees may be searched, the procedures to be used in such searches, and the processes to be followed in the event that employees come under suspicion (Stenning and Shearing, 1979:179). Indeed, the growing body of so-called "arbitral jurisprudence" suggests there may be a trend toward a greater degree of accountability within private justice in the industrial and commercial sectors, just as the growing body of administrative law suggests a similar trend in the public domain (Arthurs, 1979).

To regard such developments simply as resistance to the growth of private security, however, is obviously overly simplistic, since in an important way they serve to institutionalize and legitimate it. When private security has been negotiated rather than imposed, its legitimacy is enhanced, co-opting the unions in the process. Furthermore, as private security procedures become more formalized and institutionalized they are often abandoned in favour of newer, less formal, and more flexible ones. An example of this is the replacement of formal arbitration by informal on-site mediation processes. Other researchers have noted similar reactions in the fields of administrative and labor law (Arthurs, 1980; Zack, 1978).

THE NATURE OF PRIVATE SECURITY

Three characteristics of private security reveal its essential nature: (1) its non-specialized character; (2) its client-defined mandate; and (3) the character of the sanctions it employs. We discuss each of these in turn.

Non-Specialized Character

The criminal justice system is divided into many specialized divisions and employs people in distinct roles, such as police, prosecutors, defence counsel, judiciary, and correctional officers. In contrast, we have found that private security is often integrated with other organizational functions, as the following example illustrates.

One of the companies which we studied operated a chain of retain outlets selling fashionable clothing for teenagers and young adults. Officials of the company emphasized that security was one of their principal concerns, because the company operated in a competitive market with slender profit margins. The company tried to improve its competitive position by reducing its losses, and boasted that it had one of the lowest loss-to-sales ratios in the industry. In accounting for this, officials pointed to the success of their security measures. Yet the company employed only one specialized security officer; security was not organizationally separated into discrete occupational roles. Rather, officials attributed responsibility for security to every employee. Moreover, employees typically did not undertake security activities distinct from their other occupational activities. Security functions were regarded as most effective when they were embedded in other functions. For example, officials believed that good sales strategies made good security strategies: if sales persons were properly attentive to customers, they would not only advance sales but simultaneously limit opportunities for theft. The security function was thus seen as embedded in the sales function.

What, then, is the role of specialized persons such as security guards? Our survey of contract security guards indicated that, while they frequently engaged in such specialized security functions as controlling access to commercial facilities (26 percent), they were employed mainly to supervise the performance of security functions by non-specialized personnel (Shearing *et al.*, 1980). Thus 48 percent reported that the problem most frequently encountered was the carelessness of other employees. An important element of the security function, therefore, was to check on employees after hours, to see whether they had kept up with their security responsibilities by seeing whether doors had been left unlocked or valuable goods or confidential papers had been left in the open. When they discovered such failings, security guards would inform the employee's supervisor, using strategies such as the one described by Luzon (1978:41):

> In support of the project drive for theft reduction, Atlantic Richfield security instituted an evening patrol, still in effect. For each risk found, the patrolling officer fills out and leaves a courteous form, called a "snowflake," which gives the particular insecure condition found, such as personal valuable property left out, unlocked doors, and valuable portable calculators on desks. A duplicate of each snowflake is filed by floor and location, and habitual violators are interviewed. As a last resort, compliance is sought through the violator's department manager.

This feature of private security is reminiscent of the pre-industrial, feudal policing system in Britain known as "frankpledge," in which policing was the responsibility of all community members, was integrated with their other functions, and was supervised by a small number of specialized security persons—sheriffs and constables—designated to ensure that community members were exercising their security responsibilities properly (Critchley, 1978). This non-specialized character of private security, however, creates particular difficulties in numerically comparing private security with public police and in attempting to measure the extent of the shift in policing from public to private hands.

Client-Defined Mandate

The mandate and objectives of private security, we found, were typically defined in terms of the particular interests and objectives of those who employed them. Table 2 presents results from our study of contract security in Ontario, which show that the employers of private security are

500   SHEARING AND STENNING

TABLE 2

Classification of Five Largest Clients

| | Type of Contract Security Agency | | | | | |
| | Guard (N = 19) | | Investigator (N = 26) | | G. & I. (N = 47) | |
Client	%[a]	Rank	%[a]	Rank	%[a]	Rank
Industrial	42	1	31	5	70	1
Lawyers	5	c	92	1	28	c
Construction	32	2	b		55	2
Shopping Mall	21	5	35	4	36	4
Offices	32	2	b		45	3
Hospitals	10	c	b		30	5
Education	32	2	b		21	c
Insurance	b		69	2	17	c
Citizens	5	c	54	3	19	c
Government	21	5	15	c	28	c

Notes:

a. As a result of multiple responses, percentages do not total 100.

b. Client type not mentioned.

c. Client type mentioned but not ranked within first five.

Source:

Adapted from Shearing *et al.*, (1980).

most commonly private industrial and commercial corporations. Furthermore, we found that contract security agencies, in their advertising, appeared to assume that their major audience was made up of executives of private corporations, and that they typically promoted their services on the basis that they would increase profits by reducing losses (Shearing, *et al.*, 1980:163). While we do not have exactly comparable data revealing the distribution of in-house security, there is every reason to believe that here too private industrial and commercial corporations are the major users.

Private security is most typically a form of "policing for profit" (Spitzer and Scull, 1977:27) — that is, policing which is tailored to the profit-making objectives and its corporate clients. In those cases in which the principal objective of the clients is not the making of profit (e.g. where the client's principal objective is to provide health services, education, or entertainment) it will be that objective which will shape and determine the mandate and activities of private security.

This client orientation has important implications for the nature of policing undertaken by private security, and serves to distinguish it from public policing. In the criminal justice system, the state is nominally impartial and individuals are judged in terms of crimes against the public interest. By contrast, private security defines problems in purely instrumental terms; behavior is judged not according to whether it offends some externally defined moral standards, but whether it threatens the interests (whatever they may be) of the client. This establishes a definition of social order which is both more extensive and more limited than that defined by the state; more extensive because it is concerned with matters such as absenteeism or breaches of confidentiality (Gorrill, 1974:98) which may threaten the interests of the client but are not violations of the law; more limited because it is not normally concerned with violations of the law — such as some victimless crimes — which are not perceived as threatening the interests of the client.

In this sense, policing by private security is essentially victim-controlled policing. Corporate victims can maintain order without having to rely exclusively, or even primarily, on the criminal justice system. By establishing their own private security organizations directed to maintaining their own definitions of social order, corporate landlords and entrepreneurs not only ensure that their interests as potential victims are given priority in policing, but also avoid "the difficulty of proving matters in a formal system of justice arising from the extension of individual rights (Reiss, forthcoming). With private security, conflict remains the property of victims (Christie, 1977). As one of the security managers we interviewed put it:

> See those *Criminal Codes*? I got a whole set of them, updated every year. I've never used one. I could fire the whole set in the garbage, all of them. Security is prevention; you look at the entire operation and you see the natural choke points to apply the rules and regulations. The police, they don't understand the operation of a business. They don't come on the property unless we invite them.

Just as the social order enforced by private security is defined in terms of the interests of the client, so are the resources which are allocated for enforcement and the means which are employed. Thus, a retail organization which sells clothes will usually not install surveillance systems in changing rooms; this is not because such systems are ineffective in catching thieves, but because they might deter too many honest shoppers. The inevitable result of such instrumental policing is, of course, that a certain amount of known or suspected deviance will often be tolerated because the costs or the means of controlling it would threaten the interests of the client more than the deviance itself. There is little room for retribution within this instrumental approach. Social control exists solely to reduce threats to the interests of the client and the focus of attention shifts from discovering and blaming wrongdoers to eliminating sources of such threats in the future. This shifts the emphasis of social control from a judicial to a police function, and from detection to prevention. As one steel company security director expressed it:

> . . . The name of the game is steel. We don't want to be robbed blind, but we aren't interested in hammering people. . . . I'm not responsible for enforcing the *Criminal Code*; my basic responsibility is to reduce theft, minimize disruption to the orderly operation of the plant.

In our study of contract security we found that both security guards and private investigators focused attention primarily on identifying and rectifying security loopholes rather than on apprehending or punishing individuals who actually stole goods (Shearing *et al.*, 1980:178). This focus generates a new class of "offenders"—those who create opportunities for threats against the interests of the client. For example, a major Canadian bank launched an internal investigation into the loss of several thousands of dollars from one of its branches. The emphasis of the investigation was not on identifying the thief, but on discovering what breach of security had allowed the loss to occur and who was responsible for this breach, so that steps could be taken to reduce the risk of it recurring. The police were not involved in the investigation, despite the obvious suspicions of theft, and its results were the tightening up of security rules within the branch and the disciplining of the head teller who had breached them (*Freeborn v. Canadian Imperial Bank of Commerce*, 1981).

Even when a traditional offender is caught by private security, the client's best interest will often dictate a course of action other than invoking the criminal justice system. In 1982 in Calgary, Alberta, a bank succeeded in tracking down someone who had stolen over $14,000 from its automatic tellers. Instead of calling the police, the bank tried to persuade the offender to sign for the amount as a loan. Only when he refused to agree to this resolution of the matter was the case turned over to the police (*Globe and Mail*, 1982).

The Character of Sanctions

The fact that private security emphasizes loss prevention rather than retribution does not mean that sanctions are never employed. When they are invoked, however, they usually draw on private and corporate power, rather than state power.

The sanctions available within the criminal justice system rest ultimately on the state's access to physical force, over which it has a legal monopoly (Bittner, 1970). Private security's use of force is legally limited to cases in which they act as agents of the state, using citizen powers of arrest, detention, and search (Stenning and Shearing, 1979). This does not mean that private security lacks powerful sanctions; on the contrary, as the agents of private authorities they have available a range of sanctions which are in many respects more potent than those of the criminal justice system, and which they perceive as being far more effective (Scott and McPherson, 1971: 272; Shearing *et al.*, 1980:232). One of the corporate security executives whom we interviewed said:

> [In a court] a different degree of proof is required; if the judge decides that there is insufficient evidence, you might be reinstated, because of some *legal* reason; in the disciplining process, I can get rid of you. If he's charged, we may have to continue him with benefits. To charge a person is a very serious thing, a very complicated process. We have to ask ourselves, do we just want to get rid of him, or do we want to throw the book at him? Maybe he's not a crook, he's just a dope.

As this example illustrates, foremost among the sanctions available to private security is the ability of corporations to restrict access to private property and to deny the resources which such access provides. Thus, private security can deny persons access to recreational and shopping facilities, housing, employment, and credit.

The essentially economic character of private security's sanctions does not mean that physical force has no bearing on what happens. When organizations want a legally imposed resolution to their problem, they can involve the police or initiate a civil suit. In drawing upon state power to support their legal rights to control access to property, organizations effectively expand the range of sanctions available to them.

PRIVATE SECURITY AND THE CRIMINAL JUSTICE SYSTEM

While many writers have suggested that private security is a mere adjunct to the criminal justice system—the so-called "junior partner" theory (Kakalik and Wildhorn, 1977)—our research suggests that many of those who control private security view the relationship quite differently. They saw the criminal justice system as an adjunct to their own private systems, and reported invoking the former only when the latter were incapable of resolving problems in a way which suited their interests.

Nevertheless, private security executives as well as senior public police officers preferred in public statements to characterize private security as the "junior partner" of the criminal justice system. For private security, this characterization minimized public fears that private security was "taking over" and that "private armies" were being created. It also carried the welcome implication that private security shared in the legitimacy and accepted status of the public police. The "junior partner" theory was attractive to the public police because it downplayed suggestions that they were losing their dominant role, while allowing them to take advantage of the interdependence of the private and public security systems.

The "junior partner" theory significantly distorts the relationship between the public police and private security in at least three ways. First, the theory implies that private security is concerned only with minor cases, thereby freeing the public police to deal with more serious matters (Harrington, 1982). Yet this proved to be *not* true for property "crime"; in fact, the reverse was probably the case. Private security routinely dealt with almost all employee theft, even those cases involving hundreds of thousands of dollars. Security directors told us that they typically reported only relatively petty cases of theft to the public police and one Canadian automotive manufacturer reported that it was their policy never to refer employee theft to the public police. Even serious assaults, such as employee fights involving personal injury, were sometimes handled internally. Furthermore, while most serious personal injuries resulting from crimes were reported to the police, most so-called "industrial accidents" were dealt with internally (Carson, 1981).

A second, unfounded implication of the "junior partner" theory is that the public police direct the operations of private security. While the public police sometimes attempt such direction by establishing crime prevention squads and acting as consultants, private security personnel often mocked what they saw as presumptuous police officials who set themselves up as "crime prevention experts." Furthermore, because private security are usually the first to encounter a problem, they effectively direct the police by determining what will and what will not be brought to their attention (Black, 1980:52; Feuerverger and Shearing, 1982). On those occasions where the public police and private security work together—for example, police fraud squads with bank security personnel—it cannot be assumed that the public police play the leading role, either in terms of investigative expertise or in terms of direction of the investigation.

Third, private security is by no means a "junior partner" to the public police in the resources it draws upon, such as mechanical hardware or information systems. Private security not only frequently has access to sophisticated weapons and electronic surveillance systems, but is well equipped with standard security hardware including patrol cars and armored vehicles (Hougan, 1978; Scott and McPherson, 1971).

What, then, is the relationship between the public police and private security? Our research left little doubt that it was a co-operative one, based principally on the exchange of information and services. This was facilitated by the movement of personnel from public police to private security (Shearing *et al.*, 1980:195). This movement was particularly prevalent at the management level. Thirty-eight percent of the contract security executives we interviewed (Shearing *et al.*, 1980:118) and 32 percent of the in-house executives (Jeffries, 1977:38) were ex-police officers. Furthermore, many organizations reported relying on ex-police officers to gain access, through the "old boy network," to confidential police information. This was particularly common within private investigation agencies (Ontario Royal Commission, 1980:166). A private investigator summed up the exchange of information between private investigators and the public police this way:

> There are approximately a hundred private investigators in Toronto who can literally get any information they want whether it is from the Police Department, Workmen's Compensation records, O.H.I.P. [Ontario Health Insurance Plan], insurance records, or whatever. In the space of a ten-minute telephone conversation I can get what it would take me perhaps three weeks to discover. With experience and contacts, a well-established investigator can provide a better quality of information and can do so at a much lower cost to his client even though his hourly rates might be twice as much as a new investigator might charge.

The extent of this cooperation with the public police was summed up by the director of security we interviewed at a large commercial shopping mall in Toronto. After noting how easy it was for him to obtain the support of the local public police, he described his relationship with them as "one big police force." Yet there was no doubt in his mind that it was *he* who effectively controlled this force, through his control over access to the private property under his jurisdiction.

SUMMARY AND CONCLUSIONS

Private organizations, and in particular large corporations, have since 1960, and probably earlier, exercised direct power over policing the public through systems of private security. The growth of mass private property has facilitated an ongoing privatization of social control characterized by non-specialized security. As a result, North America is experiencing a "new feudalism": huge tracts of property and associated public spaces are controlled—and policed—by private corporations. To undertake this responsibility, these corporations have developed an extensive security apparatus, of which uniformed security personnel are only the supervisory tip of the iceberg.

The shift from public to private systems of policing has brought with it a shift in the character of social control. First, private security defines deviance in instrumental rather than moral terms: protecting corporate interests becomes more important than fighting crime, and sanctions are applied more often against those who create opportunities for loss rather than those who

504   SHEARING AND STENNING

capitalize on the opportunity—the traditional offenders. Thus, the reach of social control has been extended. Second, in the private realm, policing has largely disappeared from view as it has become integrated with other organizational functions and goals, at both the conceptual and behavioral levels. With private security, control is not an external force acting on individuals; now it operates from within the fabric of social interaction, and members of the communities in which it operates are simultaneously watchers and the watched. They are the bearers of their own control. Third, this integration is expressed in the sanctioning system, in which private security draws upon organizational resources to enforce compliance. Together these three features of private security create a form of social control that Foucault (1977) has termed discipline: control is at once pervasive and minute; it takes the form of small, seemingly insignificant observations and remedies that take place everywhere (Melossi, 1979:91; Shearing and Stenning, 1982).

Is private security here to stay? We think this depends less on the fiscal resources of the state, as some writers have suggested (Kakalik and Wildhorn, 1977), and more on the future structure of property ownership and the law related to it. There is little reason to believe that mass private property will not continue to develop, thereby permitting corporations to secure control over "relationships that were once exclusively in the public realm" (Spitzer and Scull, 1977:25). Thus, we believe private security will continue to develop as an increasingly significant feature of North American social life.

To the extent that control over policing is an essential component of sovereignty (Gerth and Mills, 1958:78), the development of modern private security raises the possibility of sovereignty shifting from the state directly to private corporations in both their national and, more significantly, their international guises. This in turn raises questions about the limitations of state control over private security and the validity of claims that the state is becoming more dominant in capitalistic societies (Boehringer, 1982; Cohen, 1979). Indeed, the evidence of direct control by capital over important aspects of policing points to the necessity of a thorough re-examination of conventional theoretical statements—be they instrumentalist or structural (Beirne, 1979)—about the relationship between the state and capital under modern capitalism.

REFERENCES

Arthurs, Harry W.
   1979   "Rethinking administrative law: A slightly dicey business." Osgoode Hall Law Journal 17(1):1–45.
   1980   "Jonah and the whale: The appearance, disappearance, and reappearance of administrative law." University of Toronto Law Journal 30:225–239.
Baldwin, Robert, and Richard Kinsey
   1980   "Behind the politics of police powers." British Journal of Law and Society 7(2):242–265.
Becker, Theodore M.
   1974   "The place of private police in society. An area of research for the social sciences." Social Problems 21(3):438–453.
Beirne, Piers
   1979   "Empiricism and the critique of Marxism on law and crime." Social Problems 26(4):273–385.
Bittner, Egon
   1970   The Functions of the Police in Modern Society. Chevy Chase, Maryland: National Institute of Mental Health, Centre for Studies in Crime and Delinquency.
Black, Donald
   1980   The Manners and Customs of the Police. New York: Academic Press.
Boehringer, Gill
   1982   "The strong state and the surveillance society: Changing modes of control." Paper presented at the Australian and New Zealand Association for the Advancement of Science Congress, Macquarie University, New South Wales, Australia, May 1982.
Bourne, Larry S., and Peter D. Harper
   1974   "Trends in future urban land use." Pp. 213–236 in Larry S. Bourne, Ross D. MacKinnon, Jay Siegel, and James W. Simmons (eds.), Urban Futures for Central Canada: Perspectives on Forecasting Urban Growth and Form. Toronto: University of Toronto Press.
Bunyan, Tony
   1977   The History and Practice of Political Police in Britain. London: Quartet Books.

Carson, W.G.
1981   The Other Price of Britain's Oil: Safety and Control in the North Sea. Oxford: Martin Robertson.
Christie, Nils
1977   "Conflicts as property." British Journal of Criminology 17(1):1–15.
Cohen, Stanley
1979   "The punitive city: Notes on the dispersal of social control." Contemporary Crisis 3(4):339–364.
Coleman, James
1974   Power and the Structure of Society. New York: Norton.
Critchley, Thomas A.
1978   A History of Police in England and Wales: 900–1966. London: Constable.
Farnell, Margaret B., and Clifford D. Shearing
1977   Private Security: An Examination of Canadian Statistics, 1961–1971. Toronto: Centre of Criminology, University of Toronto.
Feuerverger, Andrey, and Clifford D. Shearing
1982   "An Analysis of the Prosecution of Shoplifters." Criminology 20(2):273–289.
Foucault, Michel
1977   Discipline and Punish: The Birth of the Prison. New York: Pantheon Books.
Freedman, David J., and Philip C. Stenning
1977   Private Security, Police, and the Law in Canada. Toronto: Centre of Criminology, University of Toronto.
Friendly, John Ashley
1980   "Harbinger." Unpublished paper. Osgoode Hall Law School, Toronto.
Gerth, Hans H., and C. Wright Mills (eds.)
1958   From Max Weber: Essays in Sociology. New York: Oxford University Press.
Gertler, Leonard O., and Ronald W. Crowley
1977   Changing Canadian Cities: The Next Twenty-Five Years. Toronto: McClelland and Stewart.
Globe and Mail (Toronto)
1982   "Bank scolded over theft." October 16:11.
Gorrill, B. E.
1974   Effective Personnel Security Procedures. Homewood, Illinois: Dow Jones-Irwin.
Harrington, Christine B.
1982   "Delegalization reform movements: A historical analysis." Pp. 35–71 in Richard L. Abel (ed.), The Politics of Informal Justice. Volume 2. New York: Academic Press.
Henry, Stuart
1978   The Hidden Economy: The Context and Control of Borderline Crime. London: Martin Robertson.
Horan, James D.
1967   The Pinkertons: The Detective Dynasty that Made History. New York: Crown Publishers.
Hougan, Jim
1978   Spooks: The Haunting of America: The Private Use of Secret Agents. New York: Bantam.
Jeffries, Fern
1977   Private Policing: An Examination of In-House Security Operations. Toronto: Centre of Criminology, University of Toronto.
Johnson, Bruce C.
1976   "Taking care of labor: The police in American politics." Theory and Society 3(1):89–117.
Kakalik, James S., and Sorrel Wildhorn
1971   Private Policing in the United States. Five volumes. Santa Monica, Calif.: Rand Corporation.
1977   The Private Police: Security and Danger. New York: Crone Russak.
Lipson, Milton
1975   On Guard: The Business of Private Security. New York: Quandrangle/New York Times Book Co.
Lorimer, James
1972   A Citizen's Guide to City Politics. Toronto: James Lewis and Samuel.
Luzon, Jack
1978   "Corporate headquarters security." The Police Chief 45(6):39–42.
Martin, Larry R.G.
1975   "Structure, conduct, and performance of land dealers and land developers in the land industry." Mimeographed. School of Urban and Regional Planning, University of Waterloo.
Melossi, Dario
1979   "Institutions of control and the capitalist organization of work." Pp. 90–99 in Bob Fine, Richard Kinsey, John Lea, Sol Picciotto, and Jock Young (eds.), Capitalism and the Rule of Law: From Deviance Theory to Marxism. London: Hutchinson.
Nader, Laura
1980   No Access to Law: Alternatives to the American Judicial System. New York: Academic Press.
Ontario Royal Commission of Inquiry into the Confidentiality of Health Records in Ontario
1980   Report of the Commission of Inquiry into the Confidentiality of Health Information. Volume 1. Toronto: Queen's Printer.

506 SHEARING AND STENNING

Pospisil, Leopold
   1967   "Legal levels and the multiplicity of legal systems in human societies." Journal of Conflict Resolution 11(1):2–26.
   1978   The Ethnology of Law. Menlo Park, Ca.: Cummings.
Predicasts, Inc.
   1974   Private Security Systems. Cleveland, Ohio: Predicasts Inc.
Punter, John V.
   1974   The Impact of Ex-Urban Development on Land and Landscapes in the Toronto Central Region, 1954–1971. Ottawa: Central Mortgage and Housing Corporation.
Radzinowicz, Leon A.
   1956   A History of English Law and Its Administration from 1750: The Clash Between Private Initiatives and Public Interest in the Enforcement of the Law. Volume 2. London: Stevens and Sons, Ltd.
Reich, Charles A.
   1964   "The new property." Yale Law Journal 73(5):733–787.
Reiss, Albert J.
   forth   "Selecting strategies of control over organizational life." In Keith Hawkins and John Thomas (eds.),
   coming   Enforcing Regulation. Boston: Kluwer-Nijhoff.
Scott, Thomas M., and Marlys McPherson
   1971   "The development of the private sector of the criminal justice system." Law and Society Review 6(2):267–288.
Scull, Andrew T.
   1977   Decarceration: Community Treatment and the Deviant—A Radical View. Englewood Cliffs, N.J.: Prentice Hall.
Shearing, Clifford D., and Philip C. Stenning
   1981   "Private security: Its growth and implications." Pp. 193–245 in Michael Tonry and Norval Morris (eds.), Crime and Justice—An Annual Review of Research. Volume 3. Chicago: University of Chicago Press.
   1982   "Snowflakes or good pinches? Private security's contribution to modern policing," Pp. 96–105 in Rita Donelan (ed.), The Maintenance of Order in Society. Ottawa: Canadian Police College.
Shearing, Clifford D., Margaret Farnell, and Philip C. Stenning
   1980   Contract Security in Ontario. Toronto: Centre of Criminology, University of Toronto.
Snyder, Francis G.
   1981   "Anthropology, dispute processes, and law: A critical introduction." British Journal of Law and Society 8(2):141–180.
Spitzer, Stephen, and Andrew T. Scull
   1977   "Privatization and capitalist development: The case of the private police." Social Problems 25(1):18–29.
Spurr, Peter
   1975   "Urban land monopoly." City Magazine (Toronto) 1:17–31.
Stenning, Philip C.
   1981   Postal Security and Mail Opening: A Review of the Law. Toronto: Centre of Criminology, University of Toronto.
Stenning, Philip C., and Mary F. Cornish
   1975   The Legal Regulation and Control of Private Policing in Canada. Toronto: Centre of Criminology, University of Toronto.
Stenning, Philip C., and Clifford D. Shearing
   1979   "Search and seizure: Powers of private security personnel." Study paper prepared for the Law Reform Commission of Canada. Ministry of Supply and Services Canada, Ottawa.
Stinchcombe, Arthur L.
   1963   "Institutions of privacy in the determination of police administrative practice." American Journal of Sociology 69:150–160.
U.S. Department of Justice, Federal Bureau of Investigation
   1976   Uniform Crime Reports for the United States: 1975. Washington, D.C.: U.S. Government Printing Office.
Waldie, Brennan, and Associates
   1982   "Beyond the law: The strikebreaking industry in Ontario—Report to the Director, District 6, United Steelworkers of America." Mimeographed. United Steel Workers of America, Toronto.
Zack, Arnold M.
   1978   "Suggested new approaches to grievance arbitration." Pp. 105–117 in Arbitration—1977. Proceedings of the 30th annual meeting of the National Academy of Arbitrators. Washington, D.C.: Bureau of National Affairs, Inc.

Case Cited

Freeborn v. Canadian Imperial Bank of Commerce, 5(9) Arbitration Services Reporter 1 (Baum), 1981.

[13]

DISPUTE SETTLEMENT IN AN AMERICAN SUPERMARKET
A Preliminary View

Spencer MacCallum

A N IMPRESSIVE development in modern American land tenure has been the postwar rise of professional property management. Besides this, there has been a proliferation of new forms and functions of the multiple-tenant income property. Types of the latter that have become familiar in the landscape since the War include shopping centers, marinas, industrial and research parks, medical clinics, professional and office centers, mobile-home parks, real-estate complexes for which Rockefeller Center was an early prototype, and some of the new "planned communities."

As a landlord-tenant arrangement, the multiple-tenant income property represents a land-tenure pattern of a kind we are used to thinking of in terms of peasants and feudal institutions and of absentee aristocracy battening on the land. But in the present case, the landlords are modern, efficient firms specializing in property management for income on invested capital. From a structural viewpoint, nevertheless, these organizations are indeed akin to the landed estates and manorial organizations of antiquity, in which the internal public authority derived mainly from the proprietary land authority. They are truly "little communities" in modern garb, for to some extent they are modern counterparts

This paper is based on research by the writer which included a preliminary field survey of 35 shopping centers in California in 1962 under an NIH grant through the Department of Anthropology of the University of Chicago. The appended cases are taken from a group of 45 cases collected at the time.

also of village communities organized on the kinship tie, in which
the land-distributive function was an attribute of the public authority, such as there was, vested in the chief or headman of the
group.

The point I wish to make in this paper is simply that the
multiple-tenant income property can be viewed in its internal organization as a community of landlord and tenants. Of the many
forms, the shopping center is sociologically most interesting because of the complex relations among its members. This complexity derives especially, but not by any means solely, from the
need for joint promotions on which the center characteristically
depends because of its locations away from downtown where
there is sufficient "natural traffic" to sustain the stores. While
neighborhood centers are narrowly specialized, the larger shopping centers—containing from 50 to 200 merchant tenants and a
mixed composition of land uses, including professional and office
buildings and even motels and apartments in the same plan of
development—begin to resemble communities as we are accus-
tomed to thinking of them.

Pospisil (1958: 274) has pointed out that we need not think
of there being one system of law in a given society, but that each
subgroup has its own.[1] Following this idea and inquiring into the
law of the shopping center as a community of landlord and
merchant tenants, we find an intriguing situation: The legal system of a shopping center is composed of two parts, a written part
and an unwritten part. For the totality of the leases in effect at
any given moment in time is the written, formal law which defines the respective rights and duties of all parties, merchants and
landlord alike. The employed personnel of the individual busi-

---

[1] "Many ethnographers assume that a given society has a single legal system. They either neglect legal phenomena on the subgroup levels or project
these phenomena into the top society level and make them consistent with
it. Instead of accepting this smoothed-out picture of a single legal system in
a society, the writer suggests recognition of the fact that there are as many
such systems as there are functional groups. The legal systems of families,
clans, and communities, for example, form a hierarchy of what we may call
legal levels, according to the inclusiveness of the respective groups."

ness firms within the center do not come directly under this jurisdiction, but are subject to the rules of their respective organizations. They belong to the shopping center community not in their
own right, but through their respective employers, as the members
of the domestic groups making up a village community might be
related to the polity through their respective "patresfamilias" and
not in their individual rights. Case 3 below illustrates an appeal
to lease law, and Case 4, the hierarchy of legal levels in the
center.

The informal law on the other hand develops outside of the
leases and consists of a body of rules and understandings, bylaws
as it were, governing behavior in the center. Case 5 suggests one
of the ways in which such law may develop, as does Case 4.

An important problem of shopping-center administration is
writing effective leases. One of the requirements of an effective
lease is that it consist with the existing leases—the rest of the
body of written law—and also with the unwritten law of the center.
A general development in the shopping-center lease has been a
movement away from the traditional form of lease which defined
a narrow dyadic relationship, specifying what the two parties
would do for one another and leaving it at that, toward the lease
becoming a conscious instrument of social policy in the shopping
center as a community of merchants. Increasingly, it has been developing lateral extensions, as it were, citing positive obligations
of the lessee not only to the landlord but also to the other
merchants in the center. Clauses requiring tenants to participate
in the merchants' council, spend a minimum percentage of gross
income on advertising and a portion of this in council-sponsored
media, coordinate his minimum opening hours with those of other
merchants, enforce the center parking rules among his own employees, and so forth, are becoming standard items in shopping-
center leases.

If the shopping center is thought of in this way as an autonomous community of landlord and merchant tenants, then many
suggestive parallels come to mind between its law and the law of
primitive communities. The emphasis in both is toward resolving

differences and preserving social relations, and neither is fundamentally concerned with rules and penalties.

One of the most fruitful areas for study, however, may be the problem of writing effective leases, since it is here that we confront the problem of the relation between written and unwritten law, and perhaps also the problem of boundaries between law and custom, on a manageable scale and, incidentally, without a language barrier. Moreover, the recent growth of these new forms of organization on the land—truly estate forms of urban land tenure —appearing *de novo* in the bare space of twenty years, affords unusual conditions for studying institutional emergence and change. For the anthropologist, moreover, it offers a natural opening to the study of contemporary society.

CASES

CASE 1   THE CASE THAT TURNED AROUND

Informants: Shopping-center manager; former promotion director; succeeding promotion director; consultant from an outside promotion firm who attended meetings of the board of directors of the merchants' council after the resignation of the promotion director.

Facts: Each year the baker had made a 500-pound cake for the center's Birthday Anniversary Sale. The new promotion director thought the baker charged the merchants' council too much for his cake. He told the baker that and asked for a specific bid on the following year's cake. When the baker failed to give a price, the promotion director obtained a cake at a low price from a baker firm in another city that operated a chain outlet for ready-baked goods as a concession in the supermarket in the center. At a council meeting after the Anniversary Sale, the baker was irate. He said the arrangement had been "rigged" and that he had been unjustly accused of charging too much for his cake. He said his cake was better quality. He charged that the promotion director had been disloyal to the merchants in the center by going "off the mall."

Dispute Settlement in an American Supermarket 295

Outcome: The promotion director publicly asked the baker for his friendship and was refused. The baker withdrew from the council and stopped paying dues. Within a year, the promotion director had resigned under diffuse pressure from the council. The baker still did not return. Shortly afterward, the council directors decided to feature a cake again at the next Birthday Anniversary Sale and to ask the baker to provide it.

Comment: The former promotion director's account differed from the other accounts on the point of whether he had "gone off the mall" or whether there were, as he recounted it, "two bakers in the center." (E.g., the center manager's story: "We went outside and got another baker . . .") He thus contrived to avoid the issue of disloyalty on a technicality and cited more fundamental reasons for his inability to get along with the merchants, of which he said the baker's withdrawal and refusal to pay dues was only a symptom and a further aggravation. Among his reasons, he cited (1) tension in the center over a leveling off of volume gains over the past year due to new discount stores in the area and a natural tendency for a center's growth to slow around its seventh year, (2) the structural problem of his being employed directly by the council instead of by the landlord, so that every merchant felt he "owned a piece of" the promotion director, and (3) that he was not temperamentally suited to the job.

He predicted the problem with the baker would be settled by a delegation from the promotion committee of the council going to him and saying, "Frank, we like your cake best and want to have it, to hell with the cost. Will you make it?" And Frank would say, "Well, I'll think it over." Two months later, just prior to the writer leaving the field, this seemed to be the way events were developing; the promotion committee had decided to ask the baker to bake the cake, without making a point of price.

The succeeding promotion director suggested a further element in the baker's stand may have been that it gave him a chance not to pay dues. He quoted the baker as once having said to him, "Promotions don't help bakers."

296   *Law and Warfare*

CASE 2   THE CASE OF THE SHOPPING CARTS

Informant: Shopping center manager.

Facts: A supermarket's checkout area faced onto an arcade of shops. On more than one occasion, boys bringing in shopping carts from the parking lots made up lines of carts that partly blocked access to shops in the arcade. Several of the merchants spoke to the manager of the center about it.

Outcome: The manager took the problem to the food-store manager and questioned him in detail about what could be done. Together, they worked out a different system of stacking the carts and decided upon various areas of the store where excess carts would be stored when not in use. The manager of the center then spoke to the other merchants, telling them something had been worked out, and suggesting they be lenient with the food-store manager, pointing out that often it is not the manager but employees who make the difficulties.

Comment: The center manager emphasized that problems are handled in a face-to-face manner when they are still small. He said the management could do this because they spent so much time with the tenants that they learned the characteristics of each person. He said, "Just so they know you're doing something, it doesn't matter what you do. The merchants have got to feel that their interests are being looked out for."

CASE 3   THE CASE OF THE WINDOW FULL OF SLIPPERS

Informants: Shopping-center manager; promotion director.

Facts: A shoe store had an exclusive to sell shoes in the center. The ready-to-wear shop therefore had an express clause in its lease forbidding sale of shoes. The shop bought a lot of colorful, mule-type slippers of many different kinds and filled a window full of them. The shoe-store man did not make a point of going to the manager of the center, but he met him on the street, walking casually, and said, "I see they're selling shoes next door. I didn't think they were supposed to do that." The manager said, "I'll chase the lease up and see what I can find out." He talked to the manager of the ready-to-wear shop, who said, "Oh no, these aren't shoes. They're boutique." The center manager went to his office and "let it cool off a bit . . . probably it was two hours." In the meantime, he looked for *boutique* in the dictionary and did not find it. He went to the shoe store, then back once more to the ready-to-wear shop, talking the thing down, rather than inflaming it. The ready-to-wear man, appealing to the professionalism that is stressed in the shoe business, said it really was not a shoe because it did not have to be fitted. It was not customized. He said, moreover, that he had a tremendous stock.

Outcome: The center manager went to his office, and then, after a while, went back to the manager of the ready-to-wear shop and "just sat down with him." He said, "This is a borderline case; you're asking me to define something the dictionary hasn't defined. I think the thing to do on this is to compromise. Instead of filling the window and making a specialty item of it, just put two or three pairs in the window as you would an accessory. Then you won't look like a shoe store." He allowed him to keep his stock and sell it.

Comment: The center manager said, "We don't let those things go quickly. We let them cool, go slowly on them." Commenting further on how cases usually come to his attention, he said, "The grapevine is faster than your ears . . . I'm one of the last people that ever gets a complaint. About 90 percent of the complaints I get are indirect. Somebody says, 'So-and-so's been beefing about that.' "

CASE 4   THE CASE OF THE OBSTINATE NURSE

Informant: Promotion director.

Facts: Despite warnings placed on the car by the security guard, the nurse employed in a doctor's office in the center continued to

take up valuable parking space, parking at the curb only twenty
feet from the doctor's office instead of in the parking area designated for tenants and personnel. The nurse told the center manager and the council of merchants that it was none of their concern.
The landlord advised the doctor by letter that if further violations
occurred, he would have to leave the center. The doctor spoke to
his nurse. She continued parking at the curb.

Outcome: When she had received three more warnings, the
center manager sent a letter to the doctor requesting the premises
at the end of the month. The doctor asked if he could stay if he
dismissed his nurse, and was told he could. He dismissed her re-
luctantly. He said she was a good nurse.

Comment: The promotion director said it thereafter became
the unwritten rule in that center that any employee who accumulated three parking warnings (I did not think to ask over what
period of time) would be dismissed.

CASE 5   THE CASE OF THE MANIPULATED MERCHANTS

Informant: Shopping-center manager.

Facts: The manager of a major store in the center, while not a
director on the merchants' council, was active on its advertising
committee. He proposed at a weekly meeting that all the merchants hold a five-day flower show on the mall, during which they
could put out "throwaways" advertising the specials they would
run during that week only. The other merchants liked the idea
and began to develop the plan. Just before the flower show was
scheduled to open, a small merchant learned from a newspaper
space salesman that the major was coming out with a big newspaper section at the same time as the show. The small merchant
went to the center manager with this information. The center
manager called the large merchant, who confirmed it. On the day
that the "throwaways" on the flower show were put out announcing the individual merchants' specials, the big store announced

Dispute Settlement in an American Supermarket 299

a major, week-long sales event that overshadowed the merchandising of the rest of the stores in the center.

Outcome: Everybody talked about the incident, but it was never brought into the open. The consensus was that the big store had conceived the idea of the flower show only to augment its own major promotional effort with advertising monies and specials put out by the other stores. All the merchants felt bad about it. They recognized there had been no lease violation and that all the stores were free to spend their own money for promotion as they liked, but they objected that the major had not told them about his plans so they could have geared their activity to his. Fortunately, everybody did a good business that week.

While the incident was never brought up in any kind of meeting, the informant said an understanding was arrived at with the merchants that the center management would assume responsibility in the future for knowing what promotions were being planned by the major stores, so that this could not happen again. Asked how he could do this, the informant said he and his staff ask the major merchants what they are planning, when they are coming out with circulars, and so forth.

"Do you ask them this in meetings?"

"No, just when we see them. We make it our business to keep informed about their advertising and promotion plans." The manager is able to do this because he is continually in touch with his tenants. He reported a Rotary Club organized entirely within the center; 52 merchants meet together every week.

"We're very close here. It's just like a little town. Now, at lunch today I talked to seven of my tenants . . ."

[14]

Legal and Social Norms in Discipline and Dismissal

By M. Mellish and N. Collis-Squires *

WHILE undertaking work on the operation of disciplinary procedures we have been increasingly struck by the gap between what those who rationalise the dismissal decisions of tribunals say about industrial discipline and our own observations of disciplinary practice. Existing rationalisations seem to us partial and to ignore a whole welter of relevant sociological literature. Not surprisingly, they fail to analyse those variations and differences in policy which they observe and their policy conclusions consequently seem facile or ambiguous. If these dangers are to be avoided and the proper policy implications drawn from tribunal cases, some attempt must be made to develop a coherent framework for examining the *social* norms of industrial discipline and relating the *legal* norms established by courts and tribunals to these.

The corrective approach and its policy derivatives

To begin with, we need to see what approaches to industrial discipline have been adopted. Some books on dismissal law [1] do not deal with this issue at all, but most either explicity or implicity suggest that since 1972 the law has encouraged the adoption of a " corrective approach." [2] This phrase was introduced to Britain by Steve Anderman in his broadsheet *Voluntary Dismissal Procedures and the Industrial Relations Act* [3] where he said that the Act marked a shift from an older " punitive " approach to discipline to a more enlightened " corrective " approach. The punitive approach to discipline favoured harsh but irregular penalties and its purpose was to deter the offending worker and his mates from committing an offence or further offence. The punitive approach was said to ignore the educational possibilities of a disciplinary policy, in contrast to the corrective approach which " assumes employees generally are willing to abide by well-established, equitable standards of behaviour," [4] and " views discipline largely in terms of fostering self-discipline amongst employees." The basic tenets of the corrective approach are that disciplinary rules should be well-known and accepted,

---

* Industrial Relations Research Unit, Social Science Research Council, University of Warwick.

1 For example, D. Jackson, *Unfair Dismissal* (Cambridge, 1975), while dealing with many questions raised by unfair dismissal law, makes no attempt to treat the norms of industrial discipline embodied in the new law.

2 We would include in this category analyses like that of Mark Freedland, " Reasonableness of Dismissal, the Code of Practice, and Good Personnel Management " (1975) 4 I.L.J., 116, although this tries consciously to adopt a wide-ranging criterion for reasonableness which would involve substantive as well as procedural aspects of management. We would see this approach as a development of the " corrective approach " rather than an alternative to it.

3 London, 1972.   4 *Ibid.*, pp. 57–58.

and a series of warnings and lesser punishments should normally precede dismissal. There should be a careful investigation of the facts before any punishment takes place, and the worker involved should be accorded the rights of natural justice, " notably a right to a fair hearing, a right to be represented, and a right of appeal." [5] Dismissal and disciplinary procedures should be agreed and preferably go further " by incorporating employee and trade union representatives into the higher levels of procedure as joint adjudicators."

The corrective approach was quickly endorsed by the Department of Employment (D.E.) in its Manpower Paper *In Working Order*, which claimed to have noticed a shift among employers from a punitive to a corrective approach.[6] More convincing was Anderman's own later work, *Unfair Dismissals and the Law*,[7] which cogently analysed how tribunals have applied some of the elements of his corrective approach, although in one area—that of joint control and administration of discipline— tribunals and courts seem less committed than Anderman.

The appeal of the corrective approach is that it offers a way of analysing and categorising tribunal decision *and* of saying something positive about the way discipline operates in practice. In short, it links the legal and social norms of discipline. But however useful it is in ordering and cataloguing legal decisions, we will argue that it is a hindrance to understanding how discipline operates in practice.

Criticisms of the corrective approach

To begin with, it seems a pity that the dichotomy between punitive and corrective discipline was developed without reference either to historical analysis of industrial discipline or to recent sociological literature. A cursory reading of history would have shown that discipline of old was not unremittingly punitive, but had many corrective elements.[8] For example, the new industrial entrepreneurs of the nineteenth century gained a reputation as severe disciplinarians ready to dismiss, fine, or worse, at a moment's notice for anything they saw as an offence or a challenge. But these same entrepreneurs had also to try to win the co-operation of their new industrial workers by concessions like time off on traditional feast days. And they tried to inculcate the norms of the new industrial discipline by sponsoring religious and secular education. Such a historical perspective would have been useful in its own right, but even more so because it would have stressed the point that corrective and punitive discipline can, and perhaps always did, co-exist.

This point would have come even more strongly from contemporary

---

[5] *Ibid.*   [6] London, 1973.   [7] *Ibid.*
[8] See, for example, E. P. Thompson, *The Making of the English Working Class* (Harmondsworth, 1968); S. Pollard, *The Genesis of Modern Management* (London, 1965), Clark Kerr *et al.*, " The Labour Problem in Economic Development," *International Labour Review* (March 1955).

sociological literature. The distinction between corrective and punitive discipline is almost identical to that made by Alvin Gouldner in his well-known *Patterns of Industrial Bureaucracy* [9] between " Representative Bureaucracy " and " Punishment-Centred Bureaucracy." Representative Bureaucracy, he said, is characterised by rules which both management and employees are committed to, albeit for different reasons. These rules are initiated by both groups. Their breach is usually ascribed to " well-intentioned carelessness " and thus is to be corrected by education rather than punishment. Such rules are enforced by both management and workers and supported by the informal rules and values of both groups.

Punishment-Centred Bureaucracy is characterised by rules which are initiated by one side only and viewed by the other as an imposition. Breach of such rules is usually viewed by the enforcer as deliberate and wilful and therefore requiring punishment to deter repetition. What distinguishes Punishment-Centred Bureaucracy from Representative Bureaucracy is not just the more ready resort to punishment in the former. It is also the perception of the rule, by those not initiating it, as an imposition. It is also worth noting that, while punishment is normally considered a management prerogative, in Gouldner's classification a Punishment-Centred Rule can equally arise from the workforce and be supported by their industrial sanctions.

To these two types of bureaucracy Gouldner added a third which the corrective/punitive dichotomy ignores, " Mock-Bureaucracy." This is characterised by rules which *both* management and employees customarily evade or ignore. Such rules are seen as imposed by some outside agency,[10] and breach of such a rule is seen as natural and the rule is not enforced by management or workers.

Gouldner was classifying " ideal types " and normally rules would be seen as being more of one type than another. Also a rule will not necessarily remain one type for ever. The dynamics of industrial organisations can mean that what is a representative rule one day may become a punishment-centred rule the next, as either management or workers withdraw support from it. Again while mock-bureaucratic rules will normally be ignored, one form of industrial pressure open to either management or workers is the sudden insistence that such rules be adhered to.[11] Indeed, Gouldner's well-known analysis of an " Indulgency Pattern " exercised by management, and the circumstances of its withdrawal, indicate a complex relationship between formal and informal rules which we will need to return to. What needs to be stressed here is that Gouldner's analysis shows that different patterns of bureaucracy

[9] Toronto, 1964.
[10] The particular example Gouldner gave was of a no-smoking rule insisted upon by an insurance company.
[11] A good example here would be a work-to-rule by railwaymen.

can and do co-exist in any organisation. The rules which characterise such different patterns, and the different ways these rules are enforced, cannot be explained in terms of older values being replaced by newer ones, but have to be analysed in terms of the functions such rules serve different sections of management or employees and the type of response evoked.

It is this type of analysis which the corrective/punitive dichotomy fails to make and it is from this failure that the weaknesses of the corrective approach arise. Broadly these are fourfold. Firstly, it concentrates on the *procedures* for handling discipline and on procedural reform, and gives inadequate treatment to the *substantive* rules which any procedure has to enforce. Secondly, it seems committed in a fairly uncritical way to the unmitigated advantages of formalising disciplinary procedures. Thirdly, it views discipline almost exclusively from a management perspective—even when it is stressing the value of joint union-management procedures in this area. And fourthly, it attempts to separate discipline from the wider issues of control and as a result individualises what can be a collective issue.

Dealing with these criticisms in more detail, we look first at the concentration on procedures. Such a concentration has been an essential element in the general proposals for industrial relations reform since Donovan.[12] In fact, procedural reform in the area of disciplinary dismissals has been high on the agenda of reform since the earlier report of the National Joint Advisory Council to the Minister of Labour in 1967.[13] This concentration is reflected especially in the weight given to procedural reform in the Code of Practice. It is true that both Anderman's *Voluntary Dismissal Procedures and the Industrial Relations Act* and the D.E.'s *In Working Order* are aware that overhauling disciplinary procedures has implications for *substantive* disciplinary rules with which such procedures deal. *Voluntary Dismissal Procedures and the Industrial Relations Act* said that employers should consider an explicit disciplinary code, but its concern with such a code and the problems it raises lasted only a few paragraphs. The D.E. study did devote a chapter to describing how different types of offence are dealt with and even suggested that " a disciplinary policy will be unsuccessful if there is no agreement on the definition of offences," [14] but its policy conclusions were much more muted and again gave much greater weight to procedural reform. One reason for the concentration on procedures is the fact that procedural reform is the easiest policy generalisation that can be made; the highly variegated pattern of substantive disciplinary rules and the means of their enforcement inhibit general recommendations

---

[12] *Report of the Royal Commission on Trade Unions and Employers' Associations, 1965–8*, Cmnd. 3623 (London, 1968), Chap. IX.
[13] *Dismissal Procedures* (London, 1967).
[14] *Op. cit.*, p. 11.

168   *M. Mellish and N. Collis-Squires*

about them. Even so, the quoted works do seem much " softer " on the question of joint control over the drawing up of substantive rules than they do about the administration of such rules. In fact, whatever else dismissal law has done, it has not encouraged new joint agreements on substantive rules of behaviour.

Even if there seem good reasons for concentrating on procedures, procedures in themselves tell us little about the disciplinary process. The most comprehensive and model set of procedures can, and occasionally do, collect dust in personnel managers' offices. Procedures may be operated, or ignored, for motives other than the settlement of issues technically falling within their scope. For example, " sticking to the rules " or " applying the procedure " can be a tactic used by either management or employees during disputes.

This last example also raises the second criticism mentioned, the strong attachment to formalisation in the corrective approach. Again, this is very apparent in the Code of Practice and the virtues of formalising disciplinary rules and procedures were especially stressed by the D.E. Paper.

> In contrast to custom and practice a formal system of rules and procedure clarifies the responsibilities of management, unions and employees, and their relationship with one another. . . . Clearly the drawing-up of a completely comprehensive list of offences is impracticable, but the main ones, particularly those with regard to time-keeping, can be codified fairly precisely.[15]

Now it is clear that the formalising of disciplinary practice has been a widespread result of unfair dismissal law, and for many employers the new duties to ensure that records are kept, warnings given, and hearings recorded, are what they understand as the law's requirements. But is is equally clear that while employers see this as an extra administrative burden, most do not see it as otherwise changing their previous practice.[16] Of itself there seems no good reason why formalisation—" the codifying " of disciplinary rules, as the D.E. put it—should change the attitudes of either management or employees. In fact, there are several possible types of relationship between formal rules and procedures on the one hand and informal rules and practice on the other, and those who urge formalisation should be aware of these.[17]

Even the D.E. urged that formality should not be pursued at the expense of flexibility, and in a similar vein tribunals have ruled that employers should exhibit both consistency in their action and a concern for mitigating circumstances in individual cases. This indicates one possible set of relationships between formal and informal rules, what we may

---

[15] *Ibid.*, p. 49.
[16] B. Weekes, M. Mellish, L. Dickens and J. Lloyd, *Industrial Relations and the Limits of Law* (Oxford, 1975), Chap. 1.
[17] We are much indebted to a colleague at the Unit, Michael Terry, and his unpublished paper, *Formalisation of Plant Procedures and Shop Floor Bargaining.*

term *supplementary*. Most formal rules allow for the exercise of discretion, and as long as this is exercised in accordance with parties'
common values, the officious bystander should evoke the same response
on noting its exercise as he would in observing an implied term in a
contract.

But there are other possible relationships between formal and informal
rules. William Brown's study, *Piecework Bargaining*,[18] shows how informal rules – as well as wages – may " drift," in other words the number
of informal rules may grow and their leniency towards worker control
and behaviour may be enhanced. In Brown's study this often happened
where there were no formal *agreements* but the drift of informal rules
nevertheless subverted formal management *rules*:

A ratefixer who regularly fails to prevent workers slowing down their
machines before a work study is likely to find a strike on his hands when he
starts trying to dictate how fast they should be run, even if he is officially
supposed to do that. A foreman who overlooks the misrecording of work
or the pilfering of components for a period of time will find it difficult to
tighten up his controls on these matters.[19]

Informal rules here do not supplement formal rules, they govern
behaviour, often in the absence of formal agreements. In so doing they
may *supplant* formal rules. It is clear from the Brown study that such
informal rules do not arise randomly. Workers have a natural bias
towards rules which enhance their own control of the working environment and towards rules which are lenient to their own behaviour. Lower
levels of management may have few sanctions against employees and
must use concessions in order to get co-operation in achieving production targets. Individual concessions quickly become precedents and
may then be established as informal, custom and practice rules. In
this situation attempts by senior management to " tighten up "—for
example in the area of timekeeping where the D.E. thought the possibilities especially attractive—may flounder because of the relationships
of informal co-operation and interdependence between foremen and
employees. Another colleague at the Unit noticed just such an event
when a company introduced a new formal agreement on timekeeping.
The standards of lateness and the procedure for dealing with cases of
lateness set by this agreement were quickly replaced by informal rules
established by foremen under pressure from workers.[20]

Finally on formality one other possibility must be observed. We have
seen that informal rules can supplement or supplant formal rules. It can
also happen that formal rules or agreements represent "no more than
' snapshots' of the current state of the (informal) transactional rules
already in being."[21] If the rules which govern behaviour are effectively

---

18 London, 1973.   19 *Ibid.*, p. 99.
20 M. Terry, *op. cit.*   21 W. Brown, *op. cit.*, p. 85.

170   *M. Mellish and N. Collis-Squires*

those established by custom and practice and these rules originate in the bargaining strengths and weaknesses of management and workers on the shopfloor, then "outside" attempts by senior management to codify rules and formalise procedures are not, in themselves, likely to have much effect on behaviour.

The third criticism of the corrective approach is that it views discipline almost exclusively from a management perspective. Since it is the legal rights of employers to dismiss which are limited by unfair dismissal law, this is perhaps not surprising. But the corrective approach goes further by suggesting that it is management's stance which is crucial in determining behaviour, and therefore it is management which is urged to reform. This itself assumes that management has both the will to reform and the freedom of action to do so, and that—in this area of discipline and dismissal—unions are at least passive (and generally enthusiastic) recipients of such reform. There is some evidence to show how and why this is not always so.[22] In areas where workers are poorly organised or not organised at all, management has felt no need to introduce new forms of joint control in disciplinary procedures. Conversely where workers are strongly organised they have been reluctant to negotiate away the control they do exercise.

Another criticism of the "management-eye" view of discipline is that it ignores other—sometimes more important—forms of discipline at work, those imposed by unions or fellow workers. Sometimes—and the steel and merchant shipping industries offer examples—this discipline may be complementary to that of employers. In other cases—and Fleet Street newspapers are an example—it may rather be the situation that discipline along with other "managerial functions," like hiring workers and organising work for them, may be done by lay union officials[23] These may be seen as extreme examples, but as one contribution to the continuing debate on the closed shop has indicated, the inter-relationship between management and union discipline is widespread.[24] This is *not* to say that union discipline is a mere substitute for that of employers. It is well-accepted now that unions exist to promote the separate interests of workpeople in the latters' conflicts with employers. Various studies of union rules and shop floor organisation indicate that a major purpose of union discipline is the maintenance of unity, the precondition of effective collective action, and some rules that unions or work groups enforce, for example, rules limiting the speed or output of work, may directly contradict formal management rules. Two important conclusions for industrial discipline follow. Firstly, that the union—or fellow workers—may be a greater disciplinary force upon the individual worker

22 B. Weekes *et al.*, *op. cit.*, Chap. 1.
23 See K. Sisson, *Industrial Relations in Fleet Street* (Oxford, 1975).
24 B. Weekes *et al.*, *op cit.*, Chap. 2.

than the employer, and the norms they enforce may be significantly at variance with the norms of discipline preferred by the employer. And secondly, that the employer may have to work through the mediation of the union or work group to achieve his ends.

The final criticism of the corrective approach is that it attempts to separate discipline from the wider issue of control, and as a result individualises what may be a collective issue. The concern of reformists since Donovan has been that discipline and dismissal could and should be taken out of the area of industrial conflict, and this concern itself rests on the notion that discipline is an individual issue involving the transgression of common standards rather than a collective issue requiring a negotiated settlement between two opposing collective viewpoints. In its paper *In Working Order* the D.E. distinguishes between "so called group indiscipline" which it says "normally results from a widespread rejection of a working arrangement or rule," [25] and "individual indiscipline" which "indicates merely a personal deviation from standards generally accepted by other employees." Group indiscipline, it says, is to be resolved by the negotiation of new work standards—by what is called distributive bargaining.[26] But the burden of the D.E. study is with describing the most acceptable form of procedures for individual discipline, a procedure which "unlike other procedures is not fundamentally a procedure for the resolution of a disagreement; to a large extent it is investigatory." Thus the D.E. sees the role of personnel departments —as courts have done—as a judicial one. Thus also it recommends that disciplinary procedures are best hived off from the external stages of industry-wide procedures both to enable speed, but also because "whereas a wage dispute may derive from and have repercussions outside a particular workplace, discipline is *by nature* a matter of local occurrence and significance" (our italics). For similar reasons the D.E. suggests that disciplinary procedures should be hived off from normal disputes procedures "because this may involve full time officials and senior management at an early stage and this will inevitably tend to magnify what is *essentially* a domestic issue into a full scale confrontation" (our italics).

By this view discipline and dismissal are to be treated as an individual

---

[25] *Op. cit.,* p. 1.

[26] We are here using a distinction made by Walton and R. B. McKersie between distributive and integrative bargaining—see *A Behavioural Theory of Labor Negotiations* (New York, 1965). According to these authors distributive bargaining describes situations where there is a clear conflict of interests between parties. Gains made by one side are losses to the other. Bargaining here does not solve common problems but only determines how gains and losses are distributed between parties. Indeed distributive bargaining is what is ⸱ ordinarily understood by the term bargaining. Integrative bargaining, in contrast, involves parties coming together in search of a common solution of mutual benefit; it "integrates" parties. For Walton and McKersie integrative bargaining was inappropriate for wage negotiations but appropriate, at least in the American context in which they wrote, for seniority and job security questions. For a very different view see R. Harding, *Job Control and Union Structure* (Rotterdam, 1972).

172   *M. Mellish and N. Collis-Squires*

issue to be settled by a judicial or at least essentially integrative [27] form of settlement. It is interesting here, however, that despite its own orientation the D.E. study found evidence of disciplinary issues being bargained over like any other. In joint disciplinary committees it noted a tendency for management to suggest a more severe penalty than it thought necessary " in order to allow a margin to bargain over." Employee representatives as a result nearly always sought a reduction in the penalty. " In other words, the joint committee institutionalised a fairly straightforward bargaining process rather than formalised a judicial process." [28]

Discipline is not always an individual issue, it can be a collective one. Moreover, the distinction in many situations lies not, as the D.E. suggests, in the intrinsic nature of the issue, but rather in the values, goals and power of parties in respect of *any* issue. This may be seen by contrasting two phenomena common enough in their own industries, piecework " fiddling " in engineering and the shop assistant caught with a hand in the till. Lord Tangley thought the latter was " an obvious case of gross misconduct " justifying dismissal.[29] It is normally viewed and treated as an individual issue by a judicial or quasi-judicial method of settlement. In contrast, piecework " fiddling " is more often and more easily seen as raising collective issues which have to be dealt with—if at all—by straightforward bargaining.

An alternative view

We hope that the outlines of an alternative view of discipline should be apparent from the criticisms of the corrective approach. Broadly our view is that what is a disciplinary issue depends in part on what management care to treat as such. This itself will depend on the interest they have in controlling any particular aspect of employee behaviour and on their use, habitual or otherwise, of disciplinary rules to control behaviour. But it will also depend on whether employees collectively allow an issue to be treated as an individual one. This in turn will depend in part on their bargaining interests, strength and history.

We can illustrate this view by giving some examples from our current research. In particular these concern absenteeism and timekeeping and involve port transport employers whom we visited. Most of them had employed the majority of their workers in gangs on a casual basis until 1967, and most had traditionally paid them according to the amount of tonnage the gang cleared. The combination of casual working, a gang system and piecework, together with the collective bargaining strength of dockers, had meant that many aspects of operational control were, by

---

[27] *Ibid.*   [28] *Op. cit.*, p. 36.
[29] Royal Commission on Trade Unions and Employers' Associations, *Minutes of Evidence 31–50*, p. 1327, para. 4727.

1967, exercised by the gangs themselves. They were presented with the jobs and left to decide how best and how quickly to do them.[30] One particular firm we visited exhibited in 1975 many of the traditional features of dock work as we have described them. The unloading of ships at this firm was still done by gangs of workers. The size of such gangs was traditional and it often meant that they had more men than the work required. The size was, however, subject to negotiation and had recently been reduced for some work to allow the employer to take on new business. This firm also continued to pay shipworkers according to the tonnage their gang cleared. Additional payments were made for overtime after 5 p.m. and weekend working. Another traditional feature of employment at this firm was a series of highly complicated rotas for work which determined where a ship's gang was to work on a given day.[31]

This firm had formal rules on timekeeping and unauthorised absence which were not exceptional. For all that various informal practices were noticed. One of these was called the " hop system." It involved shipworkers taking time off and being covered by their mates. It was called a system because the practice was done regularly and members of the gang had their own informal rotas for deciding whose day off it was. It goes without saying that this system relied on individuals not being reported absent. Generally they were not reported, but very occasionally reports were made, and when this occurred—it was suggested—it was because such reports were one way gang members had of ". keeping in line " an individual who was not pulling his weight in the gang.

The " hop system " of shipworkers was not possible for other work at this firm because gangs were of a much smaller size. But here regular overtime was expected. This was ensured by dockers working a " quiet period " for a time in the early afternoon. This was a period of anything up to an hour or more when little or no work was done in order that the employer would " order " overtime for the two-hour period between 5 p.m. and 7 p.m. Once such orders were given it was then custom and practice to work what was called a " job and finish," a system by which employees went home as soon as their given task was completed. In practice this meant that workers would often go home at 6 o'clock or even earlier, although two hours overtime had been " ordered " and was paid for.

While the docks may be an exceptional industry, similar practices might be shown from other industries, *e.g.* the use of " blow-time " and

---

[30] See M. Mellish, *The Docks after Devlin* (London, 1972), and D. Wilson, *Dockers: The Impact of Technical Change* (London, 1972).

[31] These rotas like others in this particular port originated in the variable features of work which meant that some jobs were good (*i.e.* they required little effort or paid high tonnage or overtime bonuses) and some were bad. Workers had long insisted on rotas to ensure equal distribution of these jobs. See M. Mellish, *op. cit.*, Chaps. 5 and 16.

174   *M. Mellish and N. Collis-Squires*

" reserve workers " on assembly work. The docks' examples indicate a number of points. First, they show features of management's control system. Whatever rules management had about timekeeping and absenteeism, it had decided—at least on shipwork—to rely on incentive bonus schemes to ensure that work was done and, by default, to allow men themselves to decide how many men in the gang should be present and when work should start. On the other work mentioned management had been subject to not unusual pressures aimed at stabilising and enhancing earnings, and again in endorsing " job and finish " it accepted workers' right to determine the pace of the job and the time when it should end. Whatever the benefits for workers such control brought them, it did give them responsibility for controlling the behaviour of their own members. Generally this would be done by informal work group pressures, but occasionally it would involve the use of formal procedures which could result in fines or worse by management.[32] Workers' control over the time of work was not complete. There were some limits beyond which overtime would not be ordered, and on shipwork overtime orders generally required the approval of the relevant shipping company's agent, which was not always forthcoming. But if management wanted to control absenteeism or change timekeeping practices, it could not simply rely on formal rules. It would have to negotiate new manning standards and probably a new payment system as well. The issues were collective ones which would only become individual if workers themselves reported the absence of a colleague or aquiesced in action taken against an individual.

The docks example highlights the main points we would want to make about the nature of discipline, but two others need to be added. Firstly, technology has often been seen as an influence on the type of control management tries to exercise, and the means it uses.[33] Two other firms we studied had technologically advanced facilities for handling containers. These employed relatively few workers for the volume of traffic handled and container work had caused the breakdown of traditional gangs, as well as the abolition of piecework and daily overtime in new pay and shift work agreements. As a result management norms about timekeeping and absence from work were not subject to the same group pressures and were more readily operated against individuals. The importance of technology should not be overemphasised, however, since this had to operate via the medium of existing social organisations of employers and employees. This meant, for example, that management

---

[32] One interesting example of such a use cited to us involved the " fixing " of an unpopular foreman. He was dismissed for the theft of a bottle of whisky. Although senior management was convinced that the man concerned was first plied with alcohol and then had the offending bottle " planted " upon his person, it had no choice but to dismiss.

[33] See J. Woodward, *Industrial Organisations: Theory and Practice* (London, 1965).

norms on output were successfully challenged by some groups and accepted by others. Also the influence of technology is not simple or one way. In one of these two container firms management said that formal disciplinary procedures were now even more difficult to operate because the new technology meant that personal contact and control by managers over dockers were minimised, and the new shift work which accompanied the new technology meant that any procedure was likely to be delayed by problems in getting all relevant parties together. Even more than before foreman had to rely on informal sanctions and concessions to get the co-operation from dockers that they required.

Finally, there is a cultural definition of what is a disciplinary offence, which may or may not be shared by management and employees at any one place of work. The D.E. study noted that in some industries fighting was considered a serious offence while in other " tough " occupations it was accepted as normal. There was some uncertainty about the status of fighting as an offence in one of the dock firms we visited, but in others they were clear it was a serious matter. In most dock firms that we visited, however, swearing at supervisors was not considered an offence, though clearly it would be in other industries.

Conclusions and implications

Our studies convince us that discipline is not a special area of industrial relations because of the individual nature of the issues involved and the essentially integrative method of solving them. What makes a matter an individual disciplinary issue rather than a collective bargaining issue is firstly the extent to which management tries to control any given feature of the behaviour of their employees (whether it be timekeeping, output, respect for supervisors, or whatever). It will also depend on the manner in which such a control is sought. For example, increased effort from workers can be sought either by enforcement of a given set of rules by management personnel or else by reliance on incentive payment schemes, in which management-initiated discipline will not be involved. The O.M.E. reported that where " measured daywork schemes replaced traditional piecework schemes, foremen were given new responsibilities for cracking down on individuals who failed to meet output targets.[34] As well as management initiatives, what determines the status of an issue is the collective response of employees. This will depend on their organisation and also on the bargaining strength which they think they have and their history of using this strength. It will depend on whether they can identify with the individual concerned and whether they support or are indifferent to any action taken against him by management. These factors will be interrelated in any given situation and also will operate in an historical context in which the values of parties about what

[34] Office of Manpower Economics, *Measured Daywork* (London, 1973).

they *should* and their perception about what they *can* do will be formed.

The implications of this view of discipline for the operation of dismissal law are largely negative. It says that the factors which determine whether a dispute is an individual or a collective one are complex and it cannot be supposed that tribunals either could or would take all these into account in attempting to understand any case before them.

To begin with, tribunals are not normally concerned with disciplinary action short of dismissal, although this may be as important to employees as dismissal itself.[35] Also tribunals operate on very different principles to those of organised groups of employees. Following through our examples of absenteeism and timekeeping, a typical tribunal might act as follows. It would ensure that the factual case against an employee was proven; it might insist that an employer inquired into the circumstances of the individual's offence before dismissing him; it would probably insist that an employer warned an employee prior to dismissal; and it might decide that an individual should be given the right to explain any transgression and appeal against any decision to dismiss to more senior management. What a typical tribunal would *not* do is question the appropriateness of a rule on absence or timekeeping as organised employees might.

More than this, though, the tribunal has a duty to settle the individual complaint it receives and so it necessarily treats it in relative isolation from the bargaining context whence it came. Tribunals in effect individualise what can be collective disputes. The view that the law operates to individualise conflicts has been expressed in relation to other fields of law.[36] In dismissal cases tribunals offer individual remedies for individual complaints. Moreover, the tribunal is only used after the dismissal of one or more complainants and generally it is not able to achieve reinstatement.[37] Individual cases might be test cases for other individuals, but otherwise they can scarcely be part of a collective strategy by a group engaged in a group conflict with an employer. The individualising of conflicts in dismissal law is not accidental. Since Donovan the intention

---

[35] The relationship between dismissal and other forms of disciplinary sanctions may not be the simple progression that the law seems to assume. One result of greater legal restrictions on dismissal may be an increase in other forms of disciplinary action and the principles upon which such action is taken do not appear to be the concern of the law (subject to the limited applicability of contract law and the Truck Acts).

[36] Richard White in *Social Needs and Legal Action* (London, 1973). White said of the legal aid system: " The working principle on which the scheme is operated of comparing the applicant with the hypothetical example of the prudent unassisted litigant has the effect of individualising all conflicts and preventing the use of litigation and the legal system to advance group interests." He also makes a useful distinction between three models of the general relationship between law and society, in one of which the individualising of group conflicts is a major purpose of the law.

[37] The possibilities of such a use are clearly greater if a " status quo " rule applied preventing dismissal until after a tribunal hearing. See S. Anderman, "The ' Status Quo ' Issue and Industrial Disputes Procedures: Some Implications for Labour Law " (1975) 4 I.L.J. 131.

of unfair dismissal law has been to take dismissal questions out of the area of collective industrial disputes by providing an alternative individual remedy. One can scarcely express surprise or criticism of tribunals if this is how the law operates.

But there is in fact good reason to suppose that the effects of law are much less dramatic than this individualising would suggest. The law clearly does provide an individual remedy, but one that is generally used by those who have no collective alternative. These will generally be the unorganised or those with little collective strength.[38] Elsewhere employees will continue to define an issue as an individual or collective one for the reasons suggested above. It is extremely unlikely that where employees have a collective interest in a certain practice which contravenes employer's rules, they will let an employer enforce such rules—albeit with procedural and other safeguards insisted on by tribunals—simply because of the availability of tribunals in cases where procedures or good personnel management practices have not been followed. If this does not suggest positive improvements to be made in the law, it does suggest reasons why industrial disputes over discipline and dismissal have probably not declined since the introduction of unfair dismissal law and indeed there is no reason to suggest that the extension of this law by the Employment Protection Act will cause the number to diminish.

The variance between social and legal norms of discipline and dismissal that we have noted suggests that the general view that the law provides a statutory floor of rights for individual employees needs refining. Two corollaries of this view are that the law provides individual rights where collective bargaining is absent and that it provides a base upon which unions can build by collective bargaining. The " holes " in the statutory floor of rights through which the unorganised and the unqualified can slip have been noted in other contexts.[39] We would further suggest, from the example of unfair dismissal law, that the type of remedies the law gives individuals and the principles on which these are given may differ not only in *extent* but also in *kind* from those achieved by collective bargaining. This means, firstly, that individuals do not get—in the tribunal machinery—a sort of legal substitute for collective bargaining, and, secondly, that the legal principles enumerated in tribunals are not always seen as appropriate in collective bargaining situations. One implication of this may be that law which promotes collective bargaining directly may improve individual rights in employment more than law which gives employees individual rights against an employer.

---

[38] B. Weekes *et al., op. cit.,* Chap. 1.
[39] See R. Fryer, " The Myths of the Redundancy Payments Act " (1973) 2 I.L.J. 1, and B. Weekes *et al., op. cit.,* Appendix I.

[15]

International Journal of the Sociology of Law 1982, **10**, 365 – 383

Factory Law: The Changing Disciplinary Technology of Industrial Social Control

STUART HENRY

Department of Social Studies, Trent Polytechnic, Nottingham, U.K.

The factory is an establishment with its own code with all the characteristics of a legal code. It contains norms of every description, not excluding criminal law, and it establishes special organs and jurisdiction. Labour regulations and the conventions valid within economic enterprises deserve just as well to be treated as legal institutions as the manorial law of the feudal epoch. This too was based upon private rule, upon the will of a Lord ... The same applies to factory law, the general regulations of labour in economic enterprises. No exposition of our legal order can be complete without it, it regulates the relations of a large part of the population (Karl Renner, 1949, pp. 114–115).

Discipline ... is a type of power, a modality for its exercise, comprising a whole set of instruments, techniques, procedures, levels of application, targets; it is a 'physics' or an anatomy of power, a technology (Michel Foucault, 1977, p. 215).

Introduction

This paper examines the changes during the past two decades in the form of disciplinary technology used in British factories [1]. In the last 20 years British governments have given considerable attention to the reform of workplace discipline (A.C.A.S., 1977; Ashdown & Baker, 1973; Dawson, 1969; Dept. of Employment, 1972; Donovan, 1968; Min. of Labour, 1961; N.J.A.C., 1967) and companies and organizations have apparently responded by revising their internal disciplinary structure (I.P.M., 1979; Henry, 1981a). There are two views on these changes. Consensus theorists (A.C.A.S., 1977; Anderman, 1972; Ashdown & Baker, 1973) see them as constructive moves away from a punitive, authoritarian form of private disciplinary justice. This had emerged as early industrialists attempted to establish control over the new industrial

0194 – 6595/82/040365 + 19 $03.00/0
© 1982 Academic Press Inc. (London) Limited.

366   *S. Henry*

proletariat's traditional social orientation to work, in which time off on Mondays and feast days, as well as flexible working arrangements, were seen as a right. Harsh, rigid and irregular disciplinary sanctions were directed at individual rule-breakers, in order to exact retribution and to deter the offender and his fellow workers from committing such "offences".

The cost of skilled labour, the decline of morale and efficiency following abuses of the punitive system, and the growth of unions, were seen as responsible for an abandonment of this model in favour of "a more corrective/democratic", due process-like approach, emphasizing representation, education, and rights of appeal (Anderman, 1972; Ashdown & Baker, 1973; Jones, 1961). Here an attempt is made to 'educate' employees through the quasi-judicial application of formalized rules and a series of 'progressive sanctions' designed to persuade them to see the "error of their ways", to "adhere to company rules" and "to accept that disciplinary action needs to be taken against offenders" (Ashdown & Baker, 1973, p. 1).

The second interpretation of the change in disciplinary technology is that of the conflict of interests or pluralist theorists (Gouldner, 1954; Mellish & Collis-Squires, 1976) who argue that distinctions between individual and collective rule breaking and between punitive and corrective discipline, are ideological devices serving to individualise a collective issue and mask the battle between competing interest groups fought out both formally and informally through collective bargaining:

> What is a disciplinary issue depends in part on what management care to treat as such . . . on the interests they have in controlling any particular aspect of employee behaviour and on their use, habitual or otherwise of disciplinary rules to control behaviour. But it will also depend on whether employees collectively allow an issue to be treated as an individual one. This in turn will depend in part on their bargaining interests, strength and history (Mellish & Collis-Squires, 1976, p. 172).

They argue that in the struggle, discipline itself can become a resource. Procedures may be operated or ignored for reasons other than the settlement of disputes falling within their scope; " 'sticking to the rules' or 'applying the procedure' can be a tactic used by either management or employees during disputes" (ibid., p. 168).

A Radical Perspective on Changes in Disciplinary Technology

As Brown (1978) has observed, the pluralist analysis fails to recognize the extent of marked inequalities in conditions and opportunity between employers and employees, treating them as if they were equals. In disciplinary matters, employers can make procedural concessions without forfeiting their fundamental power base. Procedural control can even be devolved, or shared, as in the case of paternalistic companies and those embracing "industrial democracy'', since the fundamental conflicts of interests are protected through the management's retention of rights over the creation of factory rules (Henry, 1982a, 1983). In the few cases where rule-making has been devolved, this is always a partial process and is restricted to those areas least likely to affect the political and economic structure of the factory such as health and safety at work and sick pay schemes. Decentralization and democratization of this kind are part of the phenomenon of ''conservative conflict'' whereby participation is co-option, strengthening legitimation of the overall process of control (Abel, 1981).

An adequate analysis of discipline must be sensitive to both its directly coercive and its more ideological aspects, both at the level of the particular factory and in the context of total social control. It must identify who is exercising the power and for what ends; who makes the rules and whose interests they protect; who applies the rules and administers the disciplinary technology; and what purpose is served by involving employees in such administration. Crucially, the analysis must seek to explain why it is that most employees appear to go about their work in a self-disciplined way, adhering to company rules that are not their rules, behaving in ways that are not their ways, and accepting disciplinary action taken against their fellow employees.

Such an analysis was begun by Renner (1949) developing Marx, and has recently been elaborated by Kinsey (1979) and Lea (1979). These critics argue that where workers voluntarily accept position of equality in bargaining and employment contracts, this is nothing less than the furtherance of the process whereby labour is subjugated to capital. Kinsey's (1979) neo-Rennarian perspective, for example, offers a view of the development of capitalist discipline which occurs in three distinct historical phases: (i) co-operation with the few; (ii) physical coercion of all; and (iii) coercion of the few and voluntary co-operation of the majority. Since the evidence I shall draw on and the subsequent analysis develops the last phase of this process, it is worth taking a closer look at Kinsey's argument.

Following Marx and Renner, Kinsey argues that during the first period of manufacturing that characterized the formation of capitalism, skilled artisans and craftspeople co-operated in the workshop. They had power based on their protected inter-dependence. Throughout this period, the workshop owner had constantly to wrestle with the insubordination of workers. The second period came with the transition to factory production and the replacement of skills by machines which rendered workers homogeneous, interchangeable, and thereby replaceable. Factory owners no longer needed to control workers directly by law, but simply had to preserve the freedom of the individual, under law, to sell his labour power. Workers then had to choose between the authority of the capitalist inside the factory or economic need outside the factory gates. In this period a new form of co-operation is established within the factory in the form of the 'factory code' or company rules. This is not, says Kinsey, the power physically to control labour, but the power to organize and

368   *S. Henry*

co-ordinate production. All that is now required for discipline is the coercion of the 'free' market.

The final period is the establishment of capitalist discipline as automatic and self-regulating. In advanced capitalist production the voluntary contract in which employer and employee participate as formal equals becomes the generalized form of control and organisation of the labour process. The compulsion of the worker to sell his labour voluntarily is apparently removed and the worker consents. "It is with this coincidence of organization and control that discipline, properly so called, obtains" (Kinsey, 1979, p. 60).

Whilst this radical analysis is a considerable advance on the consensus and pluralist perspectives, it falls short of explaining the changes in disciplinary technology in the third period of capitalism, particularly those that have occurred since the mid-1960s. This period has seen not only a change in function of factory law but also in its *form*, towards the quasi-judicial, due process-like, corrective approach. It is this change in form that I shall now examine, following in part the arguments developed by Paskukanis (1978).

Changes in Disciplinary Technology: The Growth of State Intervention

In Britain until the early 1960s, discipline had remained outside the state's concern. It was considered a matter for management to decide internally and privately. As Martin (1962) found, even when employees broke state criminal laws, as well as company rules, as in the case of employee theft, seventy per cent of employers preferred to settle the matter privately, rather than call in the police and they were allowed to do so (Henry, 1978, 1979). However, by the mid-1960s the state entered into the industrial arena directly, as an attempt was made to respond to the growth of unofficial strikes and disputes. Research suggested that some of these disputes arose from the arbitrary use of informal private discipline. Government reports and surveys revealed that only a small minority of firms operated a formal procedure (Dawson, 1969; Donovan, 1968; N.J.A.C., 1967). Reform was encouraged towards formalization such that the notorious Industrial Relations Act, 1971 included provision for "employee protection" should the internal handling of a disciplinary case be deemed "unfair". Guidelines on what counted as fair and on how to reform disciplinary machinery toward the preferred due process-like form, appeared in various government documents and codes of practice published throughout the seventies (A.C.A.S., 1977; Ashdown & Baker, 1973; Dept. of Employment, 1972), in the Employment Protection Acts, and in the decisions of the newly established industrial tribunals. Nor was this quasi-judicial response to increasing disputes surprising for, as Pashukanis has said, "the juridicial element in the regulation of human conduct enters where the isolation and opposition of interests begins" (Arthur, 1978, p. 13).

In what follows I propose to examine the evidence available on changes in internal disciplinary technology that have occurred over the 10 year period 1968 to 1978. I shall draw on the survey data collected between 1965 and 1969 and compare it with data gathered between 1978 and 1979. I shall make the comparison by examining three key areas of change: (1) formalization of rules and procedures; (2) participation in the creation of rules and the administration of procedures; and (3) attitudes towards crime and punishment.

Formalization of Rules and Procedures

It is clear from the evidence that a dramatic change has taken place in the form of disciplinary technology during the period in question, towards the formalization of rules and procedures. In 1967, the N.J.A.C. reported that only 17% of the 373 firms in its survey had formal procedures (N.J.A.C., 1967), whereas Dawson's more reliable and wide-ranging survey of 1100 companies found that only 8% had formal procedures (Dawson, 1969). In contrast, Dickens *et al.* (1979) found that 72% of their 1000 employers surveyed had formal procedures. The Institute of Personnel Management's (I.P.M., 1979) survey of 273 companies found 98% had formal procedures, and my own survey of top industrial companies revealed that 95% of the 40 respondents from a sample of 174 had formal rules and procedures (Henry, 1981a, 1983). Both I.P.M. and myself specifically sampled large firms, and the sampling of Dawson and Dickens *et al.* across the range shows that large employers are more likely to have written formal rules and procedures. Dawson (1969, p. 63) for example, found that only 2% of firms with under 50 employees had formal procedures but that this increased with company size such that 19% of those with 500 or more employees had formalized disciplinary procedures. Similarly, though reflecting the massive increase in formalization, Dickens *et al.* showed that 51% of employers with under 10 employees had formalized compared with 99% of those with over 500 employees (Dickens *et al.*, 1979, p. 6).

The evidence also supports the view that formalization took place as a result of government and legislative pressure. Dickens *et al.*'s study shows that 12% of the procedures which did not exist before were introduced after the employer faced an unfair dismissal complaint. The I.P.M. study found that 50% of the companies surveyed had made changes to their disciplinary procedures in the two years subsequent to the 1977 A.C.A.S. *Code of Practice* and that these changes most typically involved: staging procedures, incorporating records, providing appeals machinery and stating the reasons for discipline.

My own survey [2] found that 14% of companies had been involved in unfair dismissals legislation and that 33% had changed their procedures since the 1977 Code. From an interview with one of the managers we can see how the change of form took place, while the underlying function of the new disciplinary technology remained the same:

> The form our discipline takes is that adopted in the Code of Practice, since going about these things in a different way might lead towards an Industrial Tribunal. It makes some sense to adopt the approach the tribunals consider appropriate ... We had disciplinary procedures for some years which pre-dated the Code ... The Code does in fact reflect the practice of industry ... But certainly the Code raised questions which we had to consider and we had to adopt similar provisions in our agreements. So, yes, there has been a pressure on us to mould things into the shape of the Code, but only minor things. The general philosophy is identical to the Code.

The same manager also pointed out the significance of the changes in the form of disciplinary technology to his company:

> Its main impact on us has been to enable the manager to more effectively manage, in the secure knowledge that he is behaving in a way that is regarded as reasonable. What legislation has given us is the means by which we can dismiss someone fairly, as a result of his own misconduct.

From this evidence, then, it can be seen that the importance of the increased formalization is in giving confidence and security to management in their handling of dismissals cases. The new disciplinary technology provides the 'legitimate' means to dismiss.

A further important feature of the new disciplinary technology is that its implementation is always partial rather than comprehensive. For example, rules and procedures do not necessarily apply equally to all employees. I.P.M. found that 5% of the companies with formal procedures for employees did not have formal procedures for staff or white-collar employees (I.P.M., 1979, p. 7). I found that 25% of companies had a category of employee that came under a different set of formal rules, the differences being between 'management and staff', 'staff and non-unionized staff' or 'monthly and weekly paid employees' (see also Unterberger & Unterberger, 1978).

In addition, if what is formalized is largely procedural, then this is less significant than the codification of offences and of penalties. My survey, for example, found that 40% of companies with formalized rules and procedures, failed to specify the penalties in the procedure on the grounds that to do so would have denied them "flexibility".

Ultimately, of course, whatever the degree of formalization, the actual application of procedure is always subject to a variety of informal interpretations. Neither managements nor unions are bound by rule books since these require interpretation and application to particular circumstances. Regardless of what is defined as unacceptable conduct in the rule book, or as the correct procedural response, actions may find alternative definitions at the workplace level, by co-workers, stewards, local union officials and by managements. A manager I interviewed illustrated this countervailing source of definitions for rule and procedure:

> We have a problem trying to achieve consistency, and one which requires
> constant education of both management and employees ... One
> manager may feel that an employee leaving his place of work is a dire sin
> and should entail being sacked; another may feel it's not at all that serious
> and perhaps a warning is sufficient ... Then there'll be the manager who
> want's to short-circuit the procedural steps ... and another who will
> convince himself that he's given somebody a warning, when in fact he'd
> been so oblique in his reference to misconduct that the chap probably
> thought he'd earned some praise.

Clearly, therefore, adopting a formal procedure does not necessarily mean
fully adopting the corrective, due process-like approach. Rather, that formal
and informal co-exist under the explicit umbrella of a formalized disciplinary
technology and it is this duality of existence that renders the new technological
disciplinary form significant. This is even more the case with the partial
adoption of participation in the construction and administration of
disciplinary technology.

Participation in Rule Creation

As with formalization, participation can occur in varying degrees of
completeness. The due process-like model typicaly has representative
participation only in its warning, procedural and appeals stages, and crucially
important, not in its rule making or sanctioning stages. Unfortunately there is
little empirical evidence on participation in rule-making 10 years ago.
However, evidence available on the situation in 1978 shows that participation
is relatively uncommon at the rule-making stage, even in large companies
which seem generally to evince the most developed form of the dominant
trend. The I.P.M. survey, for example, showed that only 25% of companies
jointly agreed disciplinary rules with trade unions or staff associations; a
further 30% consult such bodies and 12% merely notify the trade union
concerned. In 19% of cases, trade unions are excluded from formulation of
disciplinary rules altogether (I.P.M., 1979, p. 21). Indeed, the I.P.M. survey
also confirmed that involvement in the formulation of the rules is greatest in
medium to large companies: 19% of firms under 500 in size had agreed the
rules with trade unions compared with 30% of those between 3000 and
10,000 employees in size (I.P.M., 1979, p. 24). As I.P.M. say, "These
figures suggest that many companies and unions regard disciplinary rules as a
matter for management to decide alone" (I.P.M., 1979, p. 21).

In my own survey of large firms, I found that 57% of companies said that
they agreed the rules with the trade unions and as many as 82% had accepted
those rules. But agreement took the form of management generating rules for
union consideration, approval or veto. A manager I interviewed explained,

> Unions tend to be reactive. That's the nature of their role, to react to
> decisions or proposals .... If you ask the unions to come forward with a

> set of proposals, what does come forward, if anything comes forward at
> all, is not a suitable set that you can work with. It's not the way they've
> been brought up. They're not skilled at that sort of thing. Using words
> requires skill. Whereas many of them are skilled advocates, give them a
> pen and paper and they dry up, so it tends to work best if management
> come forward with proposals ... These are amended or whatever and
> eventually a new set of rules is arrived at.

From this we can see that agreement does not mean participation in rule
creation and is further evidence of how apparent changes can be partial and
consequently misleading.

Participation in Establishing Procedures

In 1969, Dawson found that 65% of all procedures were decided on and
initiated unilaterally by management; 20% had resulted from consultation
and negotiation with trade unions. By 1978 I.P.M. found that 38% of
companies negotiated with trade unions or staff associations over disciplinary
procedure, 25% consulted trade unions, while 12% notified unions and only
15% excluded them altogether from the formulation of procedures. My own
survey shows a similar rate of participation in the creation of procedures, with
70% of companies agreeing procedure with the union and a further 15%
saying that the unions had accepted their procedures.

As is the case with rule creation, I.P.M. found that negotiation of procedures with trade unions increased with company size: whereas only 16% of
companies under 500 employees in size had negotiated procedures and a
further 13% had consulted, as many as 52% of companies between 3000 and
10,000 in size had negotiated procedures and a further 27% had consultation.
As I.P.M. conclude, "unions and staff associations are involved to a greater
extent in the formulation of disciplinary procedures than in drawing up
disciplinary rules" (I.P.M., 1979. pp. 17–20).

Participation in Administration

By far the greatest degree of participation occurs in the application of the rules
and the administration of procedures. Even in 1969, Dawson found as many
as 47% of companies having some degree of involvement with unions in
administering disciplinary matters; 9% having set up a joint management-
union appeals committee, although 53% of managements said that they had
no contact with unions at all (Dawson, 1969, p. 78). Again, involvement was
greatly affected by company size: only 18% of companies with under 50
employees had contact with unions, compared with 86% of those with over
500 employees. Furthermore, 38% of these large companies had joint
committees formed between management and trade unions to decide on cases
of appeal against dismissal.

By 1978, I.P.M. found that most companies consulted trade unions at the earliest stages, not just appeal. Their survey found that only 3% did not consult unions at all and that 67% allowed consultation at the first formal warning stage and only 9% left consultation until the appeal stage. Moreover, 77% of companies allowed union representatives to attend appeals and a surprising 44% of companies had a union representative present and involved in the decision to dismiss. I.P.M. say, ''The results of the survey confirm that most companies find it desirable to consult trade unions or staff associations from the earliest stages of disciplinary action, not just at the stage or the official appeals stage'' (I.P.M., 1979, p. 38). My own survey endorsed this finding with no less than 100% of respondents giving the employee the right to be accompanied by a union representative or fellow employee in an advocate role at the formal disciplinary hearing.

The Purpose of Participation

In order to establish the significance of the participatory component of the new form of disciplinary technology, I asked respondents whether they considered the practice valuable and why. 47% thought that participation was valuable and gave the following reasons: it made the outcome of discipline less troublesome and more easy to secure; it was seen as more just and acceptable; and gave the workers greater responsibility. One employer for example, felt that involving workers ''takes the acrimony out of a potential industrial relations problem and, if employees participate throughout the procedure, it assists in reducing the number of appeals against dismissal''. Another felt that participation was a ''safeguard against any residual element of autocratic management'' while others said that where ''justice was seen to be done'' and ''impartiality and fairness is seen to be applied'', then there is a ''better acceptance of discipline'' which is in turn ''strengthened by union participation'' and which is necessary for rules and procedures to be enforceable and effective. Some pointed out that overall participation in discipline gave a ''sense of involvement and responsibility'' which one felt was useful ''provided that the commitment to worker participation succeeds in overcoming the individual urge to disobey reasonable rules of conduct''. For others participation provided an opportunity ''to communicate the company's attitude to offences and offenders''.

In contrast, 40% did not see the value of participation and took the view that the ''onus/initiative on performance/attitudes/behaviour, rests firmly with management'', that the matter was a ''management prerogative'', and that the union role should only be to ''see that the rules are applied reasonably and equitably''. Others felt that ''workers did not want to participate in discipline'' because ''it places them in an invidious position, which they do not like and will not accept''.

The evidence suggests therefore, that formal participation in disciplinary procedure has increased, especially in large companies. Where it is favoured this seems to be for largely instrumental reasons in facilitating the legitimate application of company disciplinary policy; where it is disfavoured this appears to be because of a fear that it will undermine management's ability to control. The tension between these opposing positions is an important dilemma for management and one to which we will return later.

Automatic Employee Self-Discipline

Unfortunately there are no survey data on informal employee self-discipline in earlier studies. I asked respondents to my survey about both formal and informal employee self-discipline. Although 57% of the sample said they had no formal employee self-discipline, 18% said that there was some and 8% said that there was a lot. In contrast, only 22% said there was no informal employee self discipline; 57% said there was some and a further 3% admitted that there was a lot.

The form employee self-discipline took varied from observing behavioural standards such as "good attendance records", "without using clocks", "awareness of time keeping", "dress", "the importance of moral standards" and "deciding on their own work priorities" and "their own levels of acceptable behaviour", to collective disciplinary action which was taken against peers who deviated. The latter form of collectivized peer-group discipline was especially apparent where work was structured into small teams or gangs, working for pooled bonuses. Under such circumstances, said one employer, "employees wish to be seen contributing to their working groups and are reluctant to disrupt the normal pattern" since, as another pointed out, "equal effort is required by gang members". Here there can be "pressure from other workers on slackers" or "sanctions on people whom the team don't feel are pulling their weight". This pressure can be informal, "from colleagues to the offending employee" or more formally by "shop stewards who make points cautioning members who break company rules" and whom they "get to toe the line" by either having a "quiet word" or in extreme cases, "advising local district officers of the union".

So, structuring of working arrangements into a collective form can encourage automatic employee self-discipline, and this can be underpinned by co-opting the trade union. But such co-option flows naturally from the partial participating role conceded to unions as representative negotiators. As a manager explained:

> Trade unionists are as anxious as anybody else to have rules. Their representatives will often argue very strongly that unless I take some disciplinary action and sack the person, I will lose all co-operation with the union movement. They have an interest in maintaining control and discipline because it reflects on control of their own members. Maintenance of discipline and order is as important in the union hierarchy

as it is in the management hierarchy. It's the idea of certainty. If you are not certain of what the outcome of a particular action is going to be, then you are less able to control your own membership. You are saying, 'Now look, I'm the person that you deal with. I'm the one who says what can and can't be done, because that's important to me. I need that power in order to negotiate'. Anyone who breaks the norms set down by the union representative and gets away with it threatens the union's power.

Overall then, the examination of participation shows that while this has increased its purpose is instrumental. Underlying it is a degree of informal employee self-discipline, which appears voluntary but which is encouraged by the organization of work into group structures that stimulate competitive, materialistic, and protective employee response and which lead to peer-group sanctioning as trade unions are ultimately co-opted into the new form of disciplinary technology.

Crime and Punishment at Work

Behaviour seen as offensive has remained remarkably consistent over a 20 year period. Those offences considered as gross misconduct and likely to lead to dismissal are, in rank order of perceived seriousness: theft of company property, clocking offences, violence and assault, fraud and the falsification of records, fighting, damage to property, drunkenness, safety offences, and refusal to obey an order (Henry, 1982b; I.P.M., 1979; Plumridge, 1964, 1966). It is the sanctioning policy against rule breakers that gives the greatest insight into changes in the disciplinary technology. It will be recalled that a shift from harsh punitive sanctions to progressive corrective sanctions was characteristic of a move towards a due process-like form of internal disciplinary technology. The most commonly used penalties in the 1960s were warnings and dismissals and to a lesser extent disciplinary suspension. Even less use was made of precautionary suspension with or without pay and there is little evidence of the use of demotion, transfer, fines or deductions. (Dawson, 1969; N.J.A.C., 1967; Plumridge, 1964). As Wedderburn & Davis (1969, p. 140) said in 1969, "It seems clear that management prerogatives to fire first and listen afterwards are still closely guarded."

However, it is important to note that even in 1964 Plumridge found that 58% of the firms he surveyed had available, disciplinary suspension without pay and in 69% of these the maximum penalty was three days though overall the range was from one day to four weeks. He said that this was being introduced because of the need to have a substantial penalty for offences where dismissal was too severe and because of the need to retain some flexibility in negotiating over disciplinary cases in strongly unionized firms: "If strong opposition to dismiss is aroused, it is a big step down to reinstate the offender with a reprimand" (Plumridge, 1964, p. 103).

I.P.M. showed that the sanctions used in 1978 were substantially the same as those used 20 years earlier, and so too was their frequency of use. Those most commonly used were: warnings (94%), dismissal (89%), summary dismissal, (74%) suspension with pay (68%), suspension without pay (53%), transfer (29%), down grading (27%) and withholding payments (15%). I.P.M. also showed that of those who suspend without pay, 74% do so for up to four days. My own survey confirmed the general range of sanctions, but it also incorporated a depth study into the disciplinary records of one large (10,000 employees) 'paternalistically' organized company. This showed that sanctions short of dismissal have always been available. For example the entry in the records book for May 26th, 1920 was:

Laziness at class and in school	Suspended 1 week
Stealing and smoking offences	Suspended 1 week
Drinking/drunk	Suspended 3 days
Falsifying time sheets	Suspended 3 days
Falsely claiming wages	Suspended 3 days

Similarly, the entry for November 18, 1920 include "Fines for stealing 3 oz of foodstuffs, £7. 10d or 51 days; suspension 3 days for smoking" (Henry, 1982b).

This evidence suggests that corrective, due process-type sanctions were available, and were being used in some large companies prior to any government intervention. Moreover, that any general change towards corrective sanctions was already underway before the government pressure of the late 1960s and early 1970s and that while this pressure might have accelerated the change, it also came about as a product of the attempt to overcome the difficulty of securing swift dismissals in the face of the growing collective strength of trade unions, the general increase in the scale of company operations, and the general trend towards pluralism in industrial relations.

A key issue is whether the new corrective sanctions were additions to, or substitutes for, the punitive sanctions of the earlier disciplinary technology. If the former, then the increased use of corrective sanctions could be seen as an increase in the overall punitive effect of disciplinary technology to which employees have become susceptible. If, however, the corrective sanctions were substitutions, then more support is given to the argument that there has been genuine change in the form of disciplinary technology towards the due process-like approach. The best evidence available on this is from Daniel and Stilgoe (1978) which supports the latter argument. In a comparison between the studies of the 1960s and their own research, they show that the rate of dismissals has fallen since the introduction of unfair dismissals legislation: "The chief change was that there were substantially fewer plants having relatively high rates" (ibid., p. 60). They point out that in 1969, a minority of establishments had a relatively very high rate of dismissals. 7% of workplaces dismissed as many as 11% or more of their employees. 13% had dismissed more than 6% of employees. However, by 1977 only 5% of the smaller companies had dismissed as many as 3.5% or more of their workforce. Daniel & Stilgoe conclude that rates of dismissal fell over the period and there was a marked reduction in the number of establishments having high levels of dismissal.

Ideological Domination and the New Form of Disciplinary Technology

The evidence examined in each of the three areas investigated, formalization, participation, and sanctioning, supports the view that there has been a change toward the new due process-like form of disciplinary technology. Rules and procedures have been formalized, participation has increased and sanctions have become more corrective and less punitive. But we have also seen that the change is neither complete nor comprehensive, but is selective and instrumental. Formalizing rules and procedures but not penalties, retains the management's flexibility. Rules, like law, require interpretation and application to specific circumstances. The involvement of the state in this process ultimately serves to strengthen employers' confidence, security and power. Mere formalization of itself is not evidence of increased justice, and partial formalization, even less so.

With participation, however, partial implementation is even more significant since it is greatest in those areas where it least affects management's overall freedom of control. Thus we have seen how unions participate far more in creating procedures than in making rules, and far more in representing employees, than in deciding their fate. Where unions do participate in decision-making this is at the appeals stage, where their control is limited and shared with management and their presence confers legitimacy on both the earlier managerial decision, and importantly, on the overall disciplinary technology.

The greater use now made of corrective rather than punitive sanctions seems merely to reflect that managements no longer need to resort to harsh measures in order to achieve social control. Crude repressive justice alone is only necessary when subtler forms of control would be ignored or when more sophisticated techniques break down. But the total control package of factory law consists of a combination of both coercive/punitive and ideological/corrective techniques, which together form the new disciplinary technology which reaffirms and reproduces the order of the factory and the existing power relations within it. The punitive or repressive component of discipline attempts to change the behaviour of individual rule-breakers, while the ideological element produces and mobilizes assent to the existing factory order. Such repressive and ideological components of domination are, as Hunt (1976, p. 182) says, in no sense alternatives. "On the contrary, they are interdependent; they interact and reinforce each other."

An adequate analysis of discipline, then, must be sensitive to both its coercive and ideological aspects. The fundamental flaw of earlier analyses is that they fail to draw out the ideological implications. It is not enough, for example, to explain away the recent changes in disciplinary technology as part of the ongoing struggle between conflicting interest groups. Such a view does not do justice to fundamental changes in the balance of power between these groups. The intervention of the state and the courts in support of one particular form of disciplinary technology has provided a sophistication of ideological dominance that was absent from the earlier, more simplistic, punitive/coercive approaches. Nor is it enough to argue that increased participation of unions in the disciplinary process has enabled them to mitigate the sanctions on individuals who without representation would have suffered harsher treatment. This is bought cheaply at the cost of generalized conformity and co-operation to factory law, expressed as a greater preparedness to accept issues as individual rather than collective ones and to accept corrective sanctions as better than punitive ones. The tragedy is that the pluralist interpretation of disciplinary development is so captured by its own insightful realism that it fails to perceive changes in the total power relationship. The irony is that these changes take place in the shadow of pluralistic protection which itself becomes part of the ideological mystifiction process strengthening the total structure of control.

The neo-Rennerian interpretation of disciplinary change is certainly a considerable advance on the consensus and pluralist analyses in that it addresses the ideological implications of changes in the function of disciplinary technology. However, it does not go far enough into precisely *how* the disciplinary technology subjugates labour, nor, more importantly, into the changes in the *form* of that technology that help bring about automatic and self-regulating discipline. In what follows I shall discuss the changes in form that take place in the last phase of the process described by the neo-Rennerians as being heralded by the transformation from a crude, semi-automatic form to a more sophisticated, fully automatic and self-regulating form.

This final phase in the development of capitalist disciplinary technology can be seen best as occurring in three distinct stages, each corresponding to three distinct disciplinary forms. The first stage sees the internal disciplinary technology in a coercive form, reflecting its earlier external form. This is the period of punitive authoritarian discipline in which management acts rapidly and forcefully against individual acts of deviance, and through summary, arbitrary, and harsh punitive sanctions, instils sufficient fear to deter the majority of employees from identifying the act as a collective one, requiring renegotiation of the rules or strike action. This situation seems likely to prevail until there is sufficient change in the external conditions of employment towards giving employees rights in law which are elaborated, as in the Employment Protection Acts, Contracts of Employment Acts, and the rights by precedent of decisions of industrial tribunals, which can involve other rights such as those given by Equal Pay, Sex Discrimination Acts, etc. Under such conditions we witness a pressure towards a transition to the second stage of semi-autonomous disciplinary technology.

This change is achieved by shifting emphasis from the coercive, punitive form to the corrective, representative form, with its greater reliance on ideological legitimation. This is why, as we have seen above, there is the adoption of a formalized, written set of rules and procedure; rules are claimed to reflect the views and standards of the company as a whole; sounding out and consultation of union views occurs prior to rule creation; there is a high degree of union/employee participation in the application of the rules through the procedures; and the right to be heard, represented, and to an appeal are essential components in the due process-like form, as is the shift toward corrective sanctions. Indeed, it is within this second stage, with its emphasis on ideological rather than coercive domination, that we can best interpret the role of the state. Its consensus account of disciplinary change; its recommendations to adopt a corrective, representative due process-like form of disciplinary machinery; and its underwriting of this code through state law and industrial tribunals, serves the ideological function of legitimating the change in the form of disciplinary technology. However, it is with the evidence of informal control and peer-group sanctioning that we gain insight into what will be the future third and final stage in the internal reorganization of capitalist discipline to its automatic form.

Conclusion: The Future Form of Capitalist Disciplinary Technology

In the two previous stages, the ultimate disciplinary action is always taken by the management even where it is legitimated through union participation. This means that up to this point we still have a semi-autonomous form of disciplinary technology. However, the recognition that informal peer group disciplinary sanctions can be co-opted to support the overall disciplinary policy of a company, and that doing so is actually more effective than the use of managerial forms of control, marks a distinctive shift into the third and final stage. This comprises a move towards the institutionalization of collective bargaining techniques into the disciplinary technology, a move which holds "participation", "decentralization" and employee "responsibility" as the core concepts, where deviance at work is perceived as a collective issue to be bargained over between management and unions with the aim of reaching a negotiated settlement and with joint management-worker bodies disciplining individual workers. In short, a participative disciplinary technology becomes the ultimate form of capitalist control (Abel, 1981, 1982; Henry, 1981b; Santos, 1980). As was seen in the evidence on informal discipline above, this change is already beginning to occur to a degree which is not explicable within the framework of the corrective-representative, due process-like model, and is particularly evident where production techniques have been reorganized along democratic, collectivist and team-work lines [3].

It is here then, that voluntary, autonomous, self-regulating disciplinary technology reaches its maturity in late capitalism. This last stage sees ideological domination so complete that the coercive element is transferred from management to the workers, who dispense it on their fellows. In the final scenario, then, prospective employees are faced with both external and internal disciplinary technology. Externally they are offered a voluntary contract of employment to be signed on a one-to-one basis with the employer. Once this is signed, they have agreed to accept the factory law and become subject to its internal discipline technology. They had no part in creating either of these instruments, nor will their future employment allow them to influence either. But they may achieve the dubious honour of serving to administer both against their fellow employees, while simultaneously conferring legitimacy on the particular decision of this 'court' of private justice and on the total system of factory social control. Such is the comprehensive character of the coincidence of external and internal forms of disciplinary technology that constitutes the due process-like form of automatic self discipline. But we can see also the contradictions of this system.

In order that the capitalist rule of law can achieve this most sophisticated and mature form of voluntary, autonomous self-regulation, it is necessary that it maximize legitimacy. This is ultimately best achieved by co-opting employees, as we have seen, into an active participatory role in the administration of the technology. However, participation brings not only self-discipline and self-control, but also self-confidence, self-respect and individual, if limited, autonomy. The issue is whether co-option, of itself, separates as a class those workers who do the disciplining from those of their fellow workers who are disciplined. The management dilemma is that if separation occurs then legitimacy is partly lost; if it does not and legitimacy is maintained and maximized, then the employees involved in constructing and administering the new disciplinary technology on their fellows are the nearest to being aware that the rules they are enforcing are not their rules. The irony then, is that the point at which labour is nearest to being most ideologically and coercively subordinated under a fully autonomous, self-regulating disciplinary technology, is the point at which it is nearest to being free; being collectively aware of its autonomous potential (Santos, 1980). As such the transition to the new participatory form of disciplinary technology must herald the final stage of capitalist social control and the penultimate stage of the process whereby the existing relations of production are undermined and replaced.

Notes

1 This paper is based on research supported by the Social Science Research Council, Grant No. HR 5907 carried out at Middlesex Polytechnic's Centre for Occupational and Community Research. It was originally presented in an earlier

form in February 1981, to the C.O.C.R. Seminar whose members I would like to thank for their constructive comments, especially Nigel South and David Binns.

2 This was a one in five postal questionnaire survey addressed to personnel managers of a random sample of the top 1000 British manufacturing companies (by turnover), which resulted in a 23% response rate after the exclusion of holding companies. The effective sample size was 173 resulting in 40 completed questionnaires, but also included depth interviews with managers and employees in an additional 14 companies ranging from large paternalistically organized capitalist enterprises to small-scale producer co-operatives employing less than 10 workers. (See Henry, 1981a, 1983). The average size of companies in the survey was 2623 employees, with a median company size of 1500 employees and with 77% of respondents being between 500 and 10,000 in size (Henry, 1981a). Similarly, only 14% of the I.P.M. (1979) sample was smaller than 500 employees, with 67% of the sample being between 500 and 10,000 employees in size.

3 The co-option of informal relations, social networks and informalised face-to-face interaction is occurring in a number of areas of social life. In law it is characterized by delegalization, decentralization and the back-to-gemeinschaft and access-to-justice movements. For uncritical accounts of this movement see Cappeletti (1978–1981), Danzig (1973), Fisher (1975), Henry (1978), Longmire (1981) and Whelan (1981). For critical reviews of this area see Abel (1981, 1982), Brady (1981), Kamenka and Tay (1978), Santos (1980) and South & Scratten (1981). The same process has parallels in all other aspects of social life involving state institutions. See Henry (1981b).

References

Abel, R. L. (1981) Conservative conflict and the reproduction of capitalism: the role of informal justice. *International Journal of the Sociology of Law*, **9**, 245–267.

Abel, R. L. (Ed.) (1982) *The Politics of Informal Justice: The American Experience*. New York: Academic Press.

A.C.A.S. (Advisory Conciliation and Arbitration Service) (1977) *Disciplinary Practice and Procedures in Employment* (The Code of Practice). London: H.M.S.O.

Arthur, C. J. (1978) Editor's introduction. In *Law and Marxism: A General Theory* (E. B. Pashukanis). London: Ink Links, pp. 9–31.

Anderman, S. D. (1972) *Voluntary Dismissals Procedure and the Industrial Relations Act*. London: P.E.P.

Ashdown, R. & Baker, K. (1973) *In Working Order: A Study of Industrial Discipline*. Dept. of Employment, London: H.M.S.O.

Brady, J. P. (1981) Sorting out the exile's confusion: or dialogue on popular justice. *Contemporary Crisis* **5**, 31–38.

Brown, R. K. (1978) Work. In *Work Urbanism and Inequality* (P. Abrahams). London: Weidenfeld and Nicolson.

Cappelletti, M. (Ed.) (1978–81) *Access to Justice*. 4 vols. Milan: Sijthoff Giuffre.

Danzig, R. (1973) Towards the creation of a complementary decentralised system of criminal justice. *Stanford Law Review* **26**, 1–54.

Daniel, W. W. & Stilgoe, E. (1978) *The Impact of Employment Protection Laws*. London: Policy Studies Institute.

382   S. Henry

Dawson, S. J. (1969) Disciplinary and Dismissals Practice and Procedures. Unpublished Government Social Survey.

Department of Employment (1972) *The Code of Industrial Relations Practice.* London: H.M.S.O.

Dickens, L. *et al.* (1979) A response to the government working papers on amendments to employment protection legislation. Coventry: *Mimeo* Industrial Relations Research Unit, University of Warwick.

Donovan, Lord (1968) *Report of the Royal Commission on Trades Unions and Employers' Associations.* London: H.M.S.O.

Fisher, E. A. (1975) Community courts an alternative to coventional criminal adjudication. *American University Law Review* **24**, 1253–1291.

Foucault, M. (1977) *Discipline and Punish.* Allen Lane: Harmondsworth.

Gouldner, A. (1954) *Patterns of Industrial Bureaucracy.* New York: Free Press.

Henry, S. (1978) *The Hidden Economy.* Oxford: Martin Robertson.

Henry, S. (1979) Controlling the hidden economy. **Employee Relations 1**, 11–22.

Henry, S. (1981a) Discipline at work: basic results from a survey. Enfield: *Mimeo* Centre for Occupational and Community Research, Middlesex Polytechnic.

Henry, S. (Ed.) (1981b) *Informal Institutions: Alternative Networks in the Corporate State.* New York: St. Martin's Press.

Henry, S. (1982a) Models of industrial discipline: variations in the technology of informal social control. Enfield: *Mimeo* Centre for Occupational and Community Research, Middlesex Polytechnic.

Henry, S. (1982b) Changes in attitudes to crime and punishment at work. Enfield: *Mimeo* Centre for Occupational and Community Research, Middlesex Polytechnic.

Henry, S. (1983) *Private Justice.* London: Routledge and Kegan Paul, (forthcoming).

Hunt, A. (1976) Law, state and class struggle. *Marxism Today* June, 178–187.

I.P.M. (Institute of Personnel Management) (1979) *Disciplinary Procedures and Practice.* London: Institute of Personnel Management.

Jones, D. L. (1961) *Arbitration and Industrial Discipline.* University of Michigan: Ann Arbor.

Kamenka, E. & Tay, A. E-S. (1978) Socialism, anarchism and the law. In *Law and Society: the Crisis in Legal Ideals* (E. Kamenka, R. Brown & A. E-S. Tay). London: Edward Arnold, pp. 48–80.

Kinsey, R. (1979) Despotism and legality. In *Capitalism and the Rule of Law* (B. Fine *et al.*). London: Hutchinson, pp. 46–64.

Lea, J. (1979) Discipline and capitalist development. In *Capitalism and the Rule of Law* (B. Fine *et al.*). London: Hutchinson, pp. 76–89.

Longmire, D. R. (1981) A popular justice system: a radical alternative to the traditional criminal justice system. *Contemporary Crises* **5**, 15–30.

Martin, J. P. (1962) *Offenders as Employees.* London: Macmillan.

Mellish, M. & Collis-Squires, N. (1976) Legal and social norms in discipline and dismissal. *Industrial Law Journal* **5**, 164–177.

Ministry of Labour (1961) *Dismissal Procedures: A Report.* London: H.M.S.O.

N.J.A.C. (National Joint Advisory Council) (1967) *Dismissal Procedures: Report of a Committee.* London: H.M.S.O.

Pashukanis, E. B. (1978) *Law and Marxism: A General Theory.* London: Ink Links.

Plumridge, M. D. (1964) Disciplinary Practice in Industry. *Unpublished Ph.D. thesis* University of Manchester.

Plumrdige, M. D. (1966) Disciplinary practice. *Personnel Management* **XLVIII**, 138–142.

Renner, K. (1949) *The Institutions of Private Law and their Social Functions.* London: Routledge and Kegan Paul.

Santos, B. S. (1980) Law and community: the changing nature of state power in late capitalism. *International Journal of the Sociology of Law* **8**, 379–397.

South, N. & Scratton, P. (1981) Capitalist discipline, private justice and the hidden economy. Enfield: *Mimeo* Middlesex Polytechnic.

Unterberger, I. & Unterberger, S. (1978) Disciplining professional employees. *Industrial Relations* **17**, 353–359.

Wedderburn, K. W. & Davis, P. L. (1969) *Employment Grievances and Disputes Procedure in Britain.* Berkeley: University of California.

Whelan, C. (1981) Informalising judicial procedures. In *Informal Institutions* (S. Henry). New York: St. Martin's Press, pp. 166–178.

Date received: November 1981

[16]

COMMUNITY JUSTICE, CAPITALIST SOCIETY, AND HUMAN AGENCY: THE DIALECTICS OF COLLECTIVE LAW IN THE COOPERATIVE

STUART HENRY*

This paper examines the relationship between social structures and community justice. It rejects both those arguments that see community justice as independent experiments for the development of an alternative system of justice and those that see such experiments as functioning solely in the interests of dominant legal and social structures. Based on a study of the collective justice systems of a variety of small-scale cooperatives, the paper develops a theory in which community justice is shown to be ambiguously related to the larger system in which it is set and to the groups and individuals who make up that system. This ambiguity, it is argued, is capable of transforming the wider structure, and the theory allows us to glimpse a potential for broad-based socio-legal change.

This paper is about the relationship between the structure of whole societies and the rules and sanctions of collective social forms existing within them. Taking the recent debate over the role of informal community justice as a starting point, the paper moves through a series of critical arguments toward the development of a new theoretical perspective for the analysis of the relations between social structure and collective normative orders. It concedes that advocates of community justice (Danzig, 1973; Fisher, 1975; Longmire, 1981) have been justly criticized for ignoring the influences of a society's wider political and social structure. But it also argues that the critics

* This paper is the outcome of my dialectical interchanges with a number of scholars, each of whom has claimed some of my territory as I have claimed some of theirs. Their influence should be apparent throughout but I acknowledge special thanks to Richard Abel, Richard Lempert, Rue Bendall, Peter Fitzpatrick, Nigel South and Brian Hipkin. An earlier version of the paper was presented at a meeting of the Research Committee on the Sociology of Law, International Sociological Association Conference, University of Antwerp, September 9, 1983. The present version, in somewhat shortened form, was presented to the American Society of Criminology Conference in Cincinnati, Ohio, November 7, 1984. I wish to thank the British Economic and Social Research Council for funding the research on which the paper was based with grant no. HR5907/2.

(Brady, 1981; Abel, 1981; 1982a; Santos, 1980) are wrong when they claim that the power and influence of the wider society is so pervasive that it necessarily shapes and constrains all but the most radical normative orders, using institutions of community justice to sap the strength of any serious challenge to the overall system.

My view is that the independence of community justice institutions is not an either/or phenomenon. The positions of both the advocates and critics of community justice are partial perspectives rather than fundamentally conflicting ones. Recognizing this, I attempt to resolve the debate over the role of community justice institutions by formulating a theory that acknowledges the integrity of both social structures and local normative orders and recognizes that relations at each level are affected by those at the other in a dialectical fashion.[1]

The paper begins with a discussion of the theoretical limitations of much of the current thinking about community justice. Then I build on a series of stimulating articles by Peter Fitzpatrick (1983a; 1983b; 1984) to develop an integrated theoretical perspective that posits a dialectical relationship between social elements and more encompassing forms. Finally, I speculate on the implications of the theory I have developed for the attainment of socialist legality. Throughout, the argument is illustrated with data on the collective justice systems of a group of cooperatives that I studied.[2]

I. THEORETICAL LIMITATIONS IN THINKING ABOUT COMMUNITY JUSTICE

The sense that the system of law in capitalist societies has become increasingly formalized, bureaucratic, and routine

---

[1] By dialectical I mean that local normative orders cannot be separated from the total society because they are integral to it in the sense that some of the relationships of the local order are some of the relationships of the totality and vice versa. There is a constant movement and tension between the whole and the parts, and both part and whole change with changes in the other. Thus, the parts and the whole may be described as "codetermining." Although there is a considerable tradition in the sociology of law for relating the normative orders of groups and organizations to the law and structure of the wider society (see for example Gierke, 1913; Ross, 1932; Renner, 1949; Ehrlich, 1936), with the exception of Gurvitch (1947) this has rarely been done in a dialectical fashion.

[2] The research on cooperatives entailed tape-recorded unstructured interviews with 27 members of 12 different housing, producer, and consumer cooperatives; correspondence with 81 housing cooperatives and 20 producer cooperatives; and attending 19 meetings of one housing cooperative over a four-month period, during which disciplinary issues were discussed and disciplinary action was taken. The data were gathered in England in 1979 and 1980.

(Danzig, 1973) has led a number of writers to propose various forms of decentralized informal justice. Two not completely separable goals are sought. The first is to increase most people's contact with and access to legal functionaries (Galanter, 1974). Here the call is for "access to justice" and "justice with a human face" (Capelletti and Garth, 1978), through the introduction of informal dispute processing institutions such as arbitration, conciliation, and mediation (Eckhoff, 1966). Cynically summarized, this goal requires no more than that judges and lawyers discard their wigs and robes. It has been described by Whelan (1981) as "informalizing law."

The second goal is to achieve greater popular involvement in the justice system through increasing participation in the actual administration of law (Versele, 1969). Some who advocate this goal also call for the increased use of arbitration or mediation, but the favored institutional forms are community-based, democratically structured popular courts or tribunals (Christie, 1976). Although some say these should form "a complementary decentralized system of criminal justice" (Danzig, 1973) that only handles certain matters (Statsky, 1974), others favor "independent alternatives" (Fisher, 1975). Thus, Fisher (1975: 1278) takes the view that "A true community court . . . should be an alternative to the formal system" and "remain independent of any political organization and influence if it is to operate effectively as an instrument of justice." Likewise, Longmire (1981: 22) argues for "popular" radical alternatives that are "a complete replacement for, rather than complement to, the existing law enforcement system."

There have been a number of criticisms of proposals for increasing democratic participation in the administration of justice by introducing local popular courts that dispense collective justice. The most virulent attack has come from those who have analyzed the proposed changes from a societal or "macro" perspective. This group includes both supporters of the existing system of law in capitalist society and, perhaps surprisingly, those who are radically opposed to existing arrangements and would prefer a socialist society.

Kamenka and Tay (1975; 1978) are the leading defenders of the status quo. They dismiss the yearning for community and its concomitant personification of law, with its preference for "people's courts" and "people's judges," as a sentimental, romantic, utopian quest to return to the dark ages, and as no more than a "humanizing cosmetic" for the growing bureaucratic practices in law—one that contains "great dangers to liberty and human dignity." Indeed, they ridicule the growing disenchantment with objectivity and with those rational legal methods that hold that people must be judged by universal principles grounded in long pondered and carefully recorded experience. Kamenka and Tay believe the move to community justice reflects the excessive growth of bureaucratic regulation, and they argue that the resultant "crisis in legal ideology" can be resolved by fighting the drift to bureaucracy and returning to an earlier equilibrium in which capitalist legality, embodying due process principles, was the core integrative mechanism of society.

Those critics who are opposed to the existing organization of society and its system of law acknowledge that community justice institutions may well increase popular participation in the administration of law. They believe, however, that in doing so these institutions help maintain the overall system of societal organization because they are concerned only with relations between individuals and small groups, and not with relations between larger powerful collectivities like multinational corporations or those between social classes. Community justice institutions, these critics tell us, do not confront fundamental social problems; they serve to reinforce existing social arrangements and to preserve the stability of the state rather than to reallocate power between groups. For example, Brady (1981) believes that popular justice, community participation, and neighborhood justice are being actively promoted and funded by the very government agencies their supporters criticize precisely because these forms of citizen participation actually serve the dominant legal order, handling low priority cases that would otherwise lay claim to professional and judicial resources. Moreover, according to Abel (1981; 1982a), the restriction of alternative dispute settlement mechanisms to trivial and systemically inconsequential matters—such as neighborhood disputes over noise, pets, and fences—coupled with a mandate for intervention that treats disputants as atomized individuals, has the effect of dispersing conflict. Any discontent is channeled away from societal-level class and structural issues toward personal and individual conflicts. Abel argues that under the guise of providing more humane, more accessible justice, informalism in law shapes conflict so that essentially political struggles about the ownership and distribution of property are translated into interpersonal disputes that draw attention away from the capitalist structure of domination and exploitation. Echoing this view, Brady (1981: 31) says that the true nature of popular justice is revealed by the fact that whenever experiments in popular justice begin to challenge powerful interests, they are abandoned by government. They serve merely to "extend the legitimacy and power of the state in a time of fiscal and political crisis."

The positions of both the radical and conservative critics of community justice are themselves open to criticism. As Nelken (1982) points out, Kamenka and Tay's position, that the eclipse of due process law by both bureaucratic and informal community-based developments has led to a crisis in legal ideology, is neither clear nor well founded. Indeed, Kamenka and Tay (1975: 141) note an inevitable tendency toward coexistence among the community, due process, and bureaucratic kinds of law "in all, or at least most societies." This seemingly calls into question their assertion that "in the western world there is no doubt that the immediate trend is toward the immeasurable strengthening and extension of the bureaucratic administrative strain" (1975: 142). In short, Kamenka and Tay recognize the integral nature of community and bureaucratic forms to law in a capitalist society, but they apparently do not recognize that by their own analysis changes in one element might be expected to give rise to changes in another as the system returns to equilibrium.

The critics from the left, on the other hand, are guilty of both one-sidedness and inconsistency. In suggesting that capitalist society inevitably shapes systems of community justice to serve its ends and maintain the existing social order, these critics (Abel, 1981; Brady, 1981) overemphasize social structural influences and underplay the degree of autonomy that community justice institutions can have. Santos (1980) recognizes this when he points out that informal institutions of community justice do not merely reflect the ideology of capitalism, but instead symbolize ideals of participation, self-government, and real community, which express popular aspirations. Whether such sentiments can be coopted into the wider social control system of a society without meaningfully affecting that overall system is what is at issue in this paper. As I shall demonstrate in the next section, I believe that cooptation cuts both ways.

The inconsistency of the argument becomes clear when we contrast the radical critics' analysis of community justice with their proposals for a structural transformation from capitalism

towards socialism and a concomitant transformation from
capitalist to decentralized socialist legality. Here the
independence that was denied to institutions of community
justice is granted to conflicting normative orders. Thus, Brady
envisions social movements for equality that seek to bring
about social change through raising consciousness, challenging
social and economic inequalities, and criticizing the state and its
justice system. Similarly, Abel (1981) sees the possibility of
radical conflict in capitalist society only in those non-legal
institutions that "transform parties, disaggregating those that
were corporate and organizing previously atomistic individuals"
(Abel, 1981: 255). In neither vision does the pervasive power of
capitalism coopt the movement and lead it to serve systemic
needs. In neither case do the authors explain why the
cooptation that they see as inevitable in the case of institutions
of community justice does not endanger other movements
whose premises differ from those of the dominant capitalist
order. Abel (1982b), in particular, recognizes that the
transformation to a socialist order may be gradual and that
partial advances are meaningful accomplishments, but he, like
others writing from the radical perspective, fails to recognize
the possibility that community justice institutions themselves
may represent a gradual and partial transformation of the
capitalist system of dispute processing.

II. TOWARDS AN INTEGRATED THEORETICAL PERSPECTIVE

The structural analyses of radical theorists such as Abel,
Santos, and Brady reflect an overly mechanistic and
deterministic theory of change that focuses on only one aspect
of the link between social structure and dispute resolution
processes. To develop a more convincing perspective without
discarding the insights of the structural theorists requires us,
first, to allow for the possibility of mutually interconnecting
relationships between parts and wholes, in this case between
local normative orders and capitalist legality, and second, to
consider the relationship between human agency and legal and
normative orders.

A useful starting point for addressing the first issue is
Moore's concept of the semi-autonomous field, a social unit
which can "generate rules and customs and symbols internally"
and "has the means to induce or coerce compliance," but which
is also "vulnerable to rules and decisions and other forces
emanating from the larger world by which it is surrounded"

since "it is set in a larger matrix which can and does invade it" (Moore, 1978: 55). Fitzpatrick draws on Moore's concept and argues that semi-autonomous fields have their own discrete normative orders which, as in the case of the family, both shape and are shaped by state legal order:

> the state legal order itself is profoundly affected by the family and its legal order. There is a constituent interaction of legal orders and of their framing social fields. One side of the interaction cannot be reduced to the other. Nor can both sides be reduced to some third element such as the capitalist mode of production (1983a: 159).

As Fitzpatrick argues elsewhere,

> It is not . . . so much that family relations function in support of relations of reproduction within the totality; family relations *are* some of those relations of reproduction . . . the family cannot be reduced to this totality or seen as only subordinate to it (Fitzpatrick, 1983b: 8).

In his latest statement, Fitzpatrick (1984: 115) offers a sophisticated elaboration of this approach as he introduces the dialectical concept of "integral plurality." Here, "state law is integrally constituted in relation to a plurality of social forms."[3] Drawing on an interpretation of Hegel's concept of dialectic,[4] Fitzpatrick argues that state legal orders tend both to converge with and maintain a distance from other social forms. Relations with state law tend to converge because, "Elements of law *are* elements of the other social form and vice versa" (Fitzpatrick, 1984: 122). For example, custom and law can have the same imperatives for behavior because law has incorporated custom into its codes and derives support from such incorporation. During incorporation, Fitzpatrick argues, "law transforms the elements of custom that it appropriates into its own image and likeness" (1984: 122). This process of appropriation and transformation involves mutual influences,

---

[3] Fitzpatrick does not in this paper distinguish between a social form and the normative order it generates. He uses the term "social form" for either case. In an earlier paper discussing legal pluralism in the Third World he does make the distinction, but his dialectical theory of "integral plurality" is less well developed. See Fitzpatrick (1983a).

[4] Use of the dialectic is, as Fitzpatrick points out, not new, even in Hegel's formulation and Marx's reformulation. Moreover, the idea has been employed in fields ranging from the philosophy of Sartre to the biology of Lewontin *et al.* (1984). For a sociological overview of the use of the concept see Schneider (1971). A concern for dialectic processes is not necessarily associated with any one interpretation of events nor with radical politics. See, for example, Van den Berghe (1963) and Kettler *et al.* (1984). For a useful discussion of the politics of dialectics see Carr (1983). For one of the clearest expositions of the dialectic method of analysis see Swingewood (1975).

such that "Law in turn supports other social forms but becomes in the process part of the other forms" (1984: 122). These mutual relations can have both supportive and opposing aspects, as is illustrated by my study of the normative orders of cooperatives in capitalist society.

Cooperatives develop their own normative orders, which are partially rooted in their own social forms and, to this extent, tend to be organized along different lines than state law. The coops surveyed in my study generally developed normative orders similar to those that Abel (1982b) describes as consistent with the needs of decentralized socialism, and to that Schwartz (1954; 1957) found in his study of the Israeli kibbutz. For example, in most of the coops studied, a decision about someone who had broken the coop rules was made by a general meeting of the cooperative. It was felt that coop members should take personal responsibility on an equal basis within the collective structure and, through their shared individual contributions, reach a collective decision.

Efforts at social control in the coops I examined, like those in the kibbutz Schwartz (1954: 476) studied, "must be considered informal rather than legal." Written rules were thought to be incompatible with the kinds of spontaneous, collective decision-making that provide the only context in which individuals can be fully and personally responsible, so rules were generally not fixed in advance or written down. As a member of a housing cooperative said to me, "the cooperative spirit is actually doing the right thing without the formality." This, as a member of an electronics commune explained, took the form of a continual openness to correction, which by its nature forestalls disciplinary problems: "All the time I'm asking them what they think about the standard of what I'm doing." Thus, as in the kibbutz (Schwartz, 1954: 477), social control was a consequence of "continuous face-to-face interaction." This is not, however, necessarily effective. For example, three members of the electronics commune left,

> because they had trouble fitting in with the way the rest of us worked. . . . They were told in the way the rest of us are always criticizing each other. This hurt their pride too much and they left.

Similarly, a member of a housing coop described how "people had just had just enough" of two

> obnoxious sort of dominant figures . . . and people decided to give them the boot by no other way than making them feel unwelcome at committee meetings.

Nor are social control efforts in coops limited to purely informal, interpersonal messages. For example, in dealing with those who failed to pay their rent, a housing cooperative in my study found that the relatively more formalized collective meeting was useful because, "If friends are there, they find out you're not paying rent; then there's much more pressure to pay . . . group pressure." Here, consistent with the findings of Schwartz (1957) and Rosner (1973), an organized forum focuses the control effort, but the sanction remains one of collective opinion.

Schwartz (1954: 473) also argued that when disturbing behavior is not adequately controlled through the informal process, law develops, in the sense of control by "specialized functionaries who are socially delegated the task of intra-group control." Schwartz thought that this development came at the expense of collective justice, but my evidence, consistent with that of Shapiro (1976), suggests that this tendency toward "legalistic" control coexists with informal controls. Thus, when a member accused of breaking a cardinal coop rule by "not participating" fails to attend the collective meeting, discipline is conducted in a communal way, via a "visit" from a delegation of the collective. A number of housing cooperatives used this system, with varying success, to encourage their members to pay their rent arrears. While such systems have legalistic elements (Shapiro, 1976), they may be institutionalized in a spirit of collective justice that is alien to the spirit of capitalist legality. For example, at one of the regular housing coop meetings that I attended, volunteers were invited to go on a "visit." There was much humor and joking, showing self-consciousness about how the visit might be viewed. One member asked, "What is it going to be then? A knee job?" Another replied, "They're not going to break his legs, just bruise him a little—where it can't be seen!"

Social forms like the cooperative and associated institutions of collective communal justice have complex relations with state law and the wider capitalist society in which they are embedded. Relations of support and opposition may simultaneously exist. For example, in spite of its proclaimed opposition to the existing structure of capitalist society, a housing cooperative is likely to benefit from laws that provide its members with certain rights, such as privacy and freedom from harassment. Similarly, even though its method of production and scheme of income distribution are diametrically opposed to the predominant forms of capitalist society, a workers' cooperative may depend on contract and corporate law for rights that are essential in dealings with its customers and suppliers as well as with its own members (Weisbrod, 1980). As Shapiro (1976: 429) observes of the kibbutz:

> The possibility that the kibbutz will not prevent the initiation of police action . . . has a subtle influence in strengthening internal controls in the kibbutz. This parallels the way in which tribal societies use the colonial power to strengthen traditional leaders.

Insofar as the rules and sanctions that constitute the conflicting normative order of a cooperative are concerned with fundamentally different issues from those of state law, such as rules enforcing participation in coop activities and rules against individual domination of the collective, enforcement of the cooperative's rules will only occasionally lend support to the larger normative order (as when a member is socially sanctioned for stealing by shaming and ostracism). However, a conflicting normative order can support state law by its very separation from it. As Fitzpatrick points out, "Law . . . assumes some separate, some autonomous identity in positive constitutive relations with other social forms. . . . Law would not be what it is if related social forms were not what they are (and vice versa)" (Fitzpatrick, 1984: 123). This should be understood in the same sense as Durkheim's famous dictum on the functional role of crime: "Crime brings together upright consciences and concentrates them" (Durkheim, 1893: 102). By this Durkheim meant that crime provides an occasion for the celebration and maintenance of law by evoking collective shock and generating a cohesive response against activities defined as unacceptable. We might say, to paraphrase Durkheim, that conflicting normative orders bring together capitalist legality and concentrate it. A good illustration of this can be found in one housing cooperative's use of the "visits" system for controlling its rent arrears. When a group of coop members are sent to another's house, without prior warning, to discuss why that member has not paid rent, the visit is intimidating and can provoke hostility on both sides. As one member explained:

> It freaked me out. We went as a group of six and stood around shuffling our feet feeling very uncomfortable. . . . One girl in particular . . . was taken aback and abusive. . . . If there isn't hostility, then the person who is being visited is bound to get overwhelmed. It is rather intimidating when six people suddenly descend on you with no prior notice at all. It's not a good forum to discuss personal things

like, "Are you going to pay your rent?" and "Why are
you not paying it?"

Not only does such an experience reinforce for both the
visitors and the visited the capitalist view of credit and debt,
but it also demonstrates the value of capitalist legality's
impersonal, rational, and predictable procedures. As a result it
may infuse aspects of capitalist legality into the collective
system. Weisbrod (1980), for example, shows how nineteenth-
century American utopian communistic religious societies used
an orthodox legal framework to "create and defend their quite
unorthodox institutions" (Weisbrod, 1980: 11) and "they tended
to use that device with considerable sensitivity" (Weisbrod,
1980: xv). Similarly, the visits system of communal control was
sufficiently stressful and insufficiently rewarding that the
housing cooperative discussed above switched to a rationally
organized model in which the ultimate sanction was the use of
state law. The following extract from an interview with one of
the members shows how state law can support the cooperative
even though the cooperative's normative order conflicts in
many ways with the ideology that underlies the state's legal
norms:

> We reached a stage then when we sent out eviction
> notices and nobody believed we'd carry them out.
> People just saw it as an empty threat . . . and
> meetings just delayed things further. We invited them
> to come along and explain. But I mean you can talk
> till you're blue in the arse and still nothing gets done
> about it. . . . Then the visits were a bloody disaster.
> There was a rumpus which was over totally personal
> things. It had nothing to do with rent. . . . The
> reason for people getting at each other's throats about
> those visiting and calling them the "heavy mob" was
> because of their own personal feelings towards those
> people that came. . . . You see, the problem when
> you're trying to use discipline or just logic is that
> people get in the way. . . . To run an efficient rent
> system you've got to get the human element out as
> much as possible because that's what messes the whole
> thing up—people's emotions. . . . A system where you
> don't have to go and explain why you haven't paid and
> involve yourself in totally irrelevant personal problems
> has to be preferable. . . . So that's why we introduced
> the new system. Now, if they are four weeks behind
> with their rent, they get a warning letter; if they're
> eight weeks behind, they get a notice to quit, and when
> that expires, we take court proceedings. Of course the
> main objection . . . is "Oh that's a bit heavy, isn't it?"
> or, if it's a possession order, "getting the law involved."
> But if the law wasn't involved, people wouldn't be

> secure in their short-life housing. . . . So the law is
> already involved. . . . I'd much rather not get the law
> involved. . . . I think it's a drag giving credibility to
> the law in this sense because the law doesn't
> particularly like coops or the people who are in
> them. . . . We are allowing the police to harass our
> members, more or less, which is very heavy, but
> there's no option. . . . If there isn't another way, then
> you've got to do it.

Note the dialectical aspect. By resorting to ordinary landlord-
tenant law, the cooperative helps validate for both society and
its members a body of law to which it is, in principle,
fundamentally opposed. At the same time, it is supported by
that law; thus, an institution providing an alternative to
capitalist forms of landlord-tenant organizations becomes more
viable and more likely to be heard.

Finally, conflicting normative orders like that of the
cooperative and the capitalist state may challenge and oppose
each other. Fitzpatrick identifies two ways in which this may
occur. The first and more obvious way is by "outright
rejection," as when state law restricts the activities of
conflicting normative orders. For example, the law may
demand that worker cooperatives shape their disciplinary
actions to the practices of capitalist industry, or the judgmental
and compensation standards of capitalist legality may apply
when individuals sue their former cooperatives for unfair
dismissals (Weisbrod, 1980).

Law may, on the other hand, accept the validity of other
norms within their own spheres:

> law sets and maintains an autonomy for opposing
> social forms keeping them apart from itself and
> purporting to exercise an overall control, but this
> control is merely occasional and marginal. . . . In this
> limited nature of its involvement with other social
> forms, law accepts the integrity of that which it
> "controls." Its penetration is bounded by the integrity
> of the opposing social form (Fitzpatrick, 1984: 126).

Thus, cooperatives may have the right to police their own
members even to the point of harassing or otherwise
victimizing them because the law refuses to intervene in
matters that are seen as the "private" concern of the coop and
its members. In these circumstances cooperatives can reject
and to some extent undercut capitalist legality. For example,
by invading members' privacy and subjecting them to
intimidation, as in the case of "visits," the collective justice of

the coop rejects, sometimes contemptuously, state laws that
elevate individual protections over group aims.

Thus, Fitzpatrick concludes that, "law is the unsettled
resultant of relations with a plurality of social forms and in this
law's identity is constantly and inherently subject to challenge
and change" (Fitzpatrick, 1984: 138). The same is true of
alternative normative orders in their relations with state law.

Fitzpatrick's contribution to dialectical or integrated
theorizing in his series of well crafted expositions increases our
understanding of law by enabling us to grasp the complexity of
the relations between the law of society and the normative
orders of the social forms that make up a society. Before
examining the implications of this analysis for socio-legal
change, I should like to point to a number of areas where
Fitzpatrick's theory of integral plurality might be developed
and to illustrate with the aid of examples from my research on
collective justice within cooperatives how these developments
might be used to examine the relations between law and
normative orders.

III. INCORPORATING THE ACTION-STRUCTURE DIALECTIC

Fitzpatrick does not tell us what counts as a social form or
what counts as a normative order. It is possible to abstract
parts from a whole, such that what is originally seen as a part
becomes the whole. A cooperative, for example, is both a part
of the capitalist society and a whole made up of its own
constituent parts such as factions and subgroups. These parts
may be similarly broken down until only individuals remain.
At all levels, however, each element is a part of something
larger that exists in relation to both the larger whole from
which it is extracted and to the other parts that make up the
original whole.

The possibility of this dual perspective raises two crucial
issues. First, how far should one abstract parts from wholes or,
to put the question another way, how many stages of
abstraction should there be? Second, how does one
meaningfully and intelligibly cope with the myriad of mutually
supportive and opposing relations between parts and wholes
that may exist at different levels of abstraction? Fitzpatrick's
analysis does not go beyond the first stage to consider the
constituents of the parts he examines. In particular, his
analysis never penetrates to the level of the individual and so
ignores all relations of human agency. Thus, in discussing the

dialectical relations between law and social forms, Fitzpatrick talks of law maintaining an identity, having an autonomy, etc., but he ignores the fact that it is through human interaction that law relates to other normative orders. Social action and the social structure, social action and the law, and social action and particular normative orders all exist in mutually constitutive relations. Ignoring the action-structure dialectic can lead one to take for granted the forms institutions take and to overlook the implications of the fact that institutions are social constructions.

Theorists have addressed these issues in different ways (see Giddens, 1979; 1982; 1984; Collins, 1981; Knorr-Cetina, 1981; Archer, 1982). Giddens, for example, argues that any examination of structure without reference to human agency or to agency without reference to structure is essentially misleading because action and structure presuppose one another in a mutually dependent relationship. He argues that the structural properties of societies are both the medium and the outcome of the practices that constitute these societies and that structure both enables and constrains actions that can change it. Each action is at once new and performed in an historical context that, without either barring or mandating the action, shapes it by setting constraints and providing the medium through which the meanings of action are expressed. Thus, Giddens maintains, "institutions do not just work behind the backs of the social actors who produce and reproduce them"; rather, "all social actors, no matter how lowly have some degree of penetration of the social forms which oppress them" (Giddens, 1979: 72).

Incorporating this insight into Fitzpatrick's theory provides a more coherent perspective that not only recognizes the dialectical relationship between state law and other normative orders but also considers the relationship between these orders and the structures in which they are embedded, on the one hand, and social action as human agency, on the other. Humans, in other words, are shaped by and shape the groups in which they are involved just as these groups are shaped by and shape the larger social structure. A theory that seeks to explain institutions of communal justice and their place in capitalist society must recognize this.

Just as the social institution is an abstraction from social structure, it is possible to identify a second level of abstraction, which I shall refer to as "factions," and a third level which, following Giddens (1979; 1982), I shall describe as "human agency." The structural correlates of these abstractions are the subgroups that exist within institutions and the individuals who are members of subgroups.[5]

Factions

Take the case of a workers' cooperative as an illustration. Factions are formed by all subgroups within a cooperative, whatever their basis. Thus, within a cooperative of foreign language teachers one faction was "a little clique who did not attempt to consult other members of the cooperative." Factions can include as few as two members who have common interests they seek to promote. The coalition strategies that such interest groups generate may be accommodated, or they can split a group. A member of a collective designing software for computers spoke of the inevitability of factions: "Find some equilibrium size, which might be 7, 10, 15. . . . Anything bigger than that and problems start to arise, so the best thing is to split."

Factions, like the social institutions of which they are a part, may generate their own rules and sanctions that specify acceptable ways of proceeding. These ways of proceeding may apply only to faction members, or the faction may seek to impose behavior it legitimates on the larger institution. What is legitimated at the factional level may, but need not, reflect the core norms of the embedding institution. A cooperative that expressly adopts informal reintegrative disciplinary procedures may or may not generate factional forms that espouse similar norms. Thus, a clique within a cooperative that is committed to reintegrative collective justice may legitimate for its members formalized, elitist, and hierarchical methods of social control. This may create tensions that transform both the clique and the cooperative. As a member of a cooperative arts group said:

> We are actually struggling with two systems, and the fact that we have two systems means we never fully commit ourselves to either. There are the two different wheels. They [elite clique] will always step in if you want them to. They will always say, "I'll wield

---

[5] While for sociological purposes the individual is the irreducible minimum, one could in principle identify groups within groups within groups and corresponding levels of abstraction. For theoretical purposes, I think we need only recognize the following levels: (1) the encompassing state with its institutions of capitalist legality; (2) semi-autonomous institutions of communal justice and their alternative normative orders; (3) subgroups of these institutions with particularistic norms and interests; and (4) individuals as motivated social actors.

the big stick." It's there in the background. . . . To
that extent we are not using one or the other.

Here, the elite clique's willingness to eject those who fail to
abide by the cooperative's rules at one level serves the interests
of the cooperative but at another contradicts the cooperative's
core ethic and basic organizing principles. Harsh discipline by
the elite faction may induce particular individuals to conform
to particular rules but in the process may reduce the overall
level of compliance with cooperative norms. For example, an
elite clique's effort to enforce participation may diminish the
average member's involvement both by making the cooperative
less attractive and by reducing the average member's
responsibility for social control. The result is likely to be a
reduced willingness to participate and even greater need to
resort to the use of discipline. The cooperative may hang
together because of attractions extraneous to the cooperative
ideal, such as access to markets, or such factionally legitimated
activity may cause the coop to collapse:

> We put together this motion: "Every member of the
> coop shall assign themselves to one predetermined
> area of work in List A within which their skills may
> lay, and can be called upon to utilize their skills and
> assist in the running of the coop. Anyone who
> persistently fails to help when asked will have their
> membership questioned by the participation
> subcommittee. . . . In addition no member shall be
> exempt from assisting in any one of the activities in
> List B."
>
> On precisely this motion people just happened to
> be wandering out. They were going home to tea or
> something and the finger was pointed: "These people
> are leaving the meeting. Isn't it a disgrace?" Well
> there was no evidence to suggest that they were acting
> in the wrong way so they took offense. They said,
> "Fuck you!"

Human Agency

Factions are, of course, composed of individuals whose
action, following Giddens, I shall refer to as "human agency":

> To be a human agent is to have power to be able to
> "make a difference" in the world. . . . In any
> relationship which may be involved in a social system,
> the most seemingly "powerless" individuals are able to
> mobilize resources whereby they carve out "spaces of
> control" in respect of their day-to-day lives and in
> respect of the activities of the more powerful. . . .
> There are many ways in which the seemingly
> powerless, in particular contexts, may be able to

influence the activities of those who appear to hold complete power over them; or in which the weak are able to mobilize resources against the strong. . . . Anyone who participates in a social relationship . . . necessarily sustains some control over the character of that relationship or system . . . actors in subordinate positions are never wholly dependent, and are often very adept in converting whatever resources they possess into some degree of control over the conditions of reproduction of the system. In all social systems there is a dialectic of control, such that there are normally continually shifting balances of resources altering the overall distribution of power . . . an agent who does not participate in the dialectic of control *ipso facto* ceases to *be* an agent (Giddens, 1982: 197-99).

The social action of individuals, like social action at each level we have examined, may conform to special sets of rules. The normative order rooted in human agency is that which is referred to as "personal self-control," "self-discipline," or "conscience." It is not, of course, independent either of the person in whom it is rooted or of other social forms with which it exists in a dialectical relationship.

The personal rules that human agents adopt are like the rules of the various subgroups we have discussed in that they both shape and are shaped by the groups of which they are a part. When association with a group is voluntary, as it is with a cooperative or a faction, one would expect personal norms and values to be largely congruent with those of the group to which the person belongs. However, groups have multifaceted attractions, and individuals are complex characters. Thus, human action may both support and challenge the core norms of membership groups, sometimes at the same time. For example, one member of a housing cooperative that I studied was renowned for excusing his rent arrears by blaming his uncooperative behavior on the wider structure of capitalism. In doing so, he confirmed the cooperative ideology while threatening its financial stability. The material advantages of this dual posture led inevitably to resentment, concern, and suspicion:

People think "Oh he's got a lot of problems!" But it's only because we know about his problems, because he's made damn sure everybody knows about them, whereas other people in the coop . . . who've got really serious problems . . . haven't made it their business to say so.

A member of the same cooperative explained that they were particularly vulnerable to this kind of individualistic exploitation because

> None of us wants to get our fingers burned or to be seen to be heavy so what happens? . . . We'd be nice to them and make an arrangement for them to pay. . . . We start feeling sorry for them. "Ah poor dears. They've got all these problems. Let's make it easier for them. . . . Perhaps we ought to restructure the coop to make it more accessible!"

A member of a wholefood coop explained how this kind of toleration could eventually be disastrous:

> Because everybody believes in being nice to everyone, one person could put a complete spanner in the works. . . . Apart from being bad from the financial side . . . it can have a very negative effect on all the other people.

Moreover, individuals subject to the collective discipline of the normative order can challenge it by arguing that individual vindictiveness rather than collective concerns is the motivating force. Cooperatives are especially vulnerable to such defenses because the members all know one another intimately. As a member of another housing cooperative said of those with rent arrears:

> The individuals concerned almost expect to be taken to task but they are surprised and resentful when they see . . . a comrade knocking on the door. Quite a lot react aggressively . . . feel that they have to hit back. People think they are victimized.

This can be seen in the account of a member of an arts collective who blamed her expulsion on a feud she was having with the wife of a member of the disciplinary committee:

> It seemed to me that it was rigged all the way through by these people—this particular woman who wanted me out. She'd got a lever through her husband to every committee.

Another member of the same collective pointed out that the size and close-knit nature of coop relations meant that

> it's more likely than you might imagine . . . [that] the committee you get is possibly going to be influenced in that kind of way.

One may ask why organizations like cooperatives contain members and factions whose rules of proceeding contradict core cooperative norms and threaten to destroy it. The reasons are too numerous and complex to explicate here, but one aspect must be mentioned. The wider capitalist order both stimulates and supports the oppositional actions of both the human agents

and factions that are found in cooperatives. Thus, the social
structure threatens oppositional institutions from below. These
institutions are not foredoomed to failure, but even when they
are not overtly challenged by capitalist society, they have a
constant struggle to maintain themselves. As a member of a
theatre cooperative expressed it:

> Specialization is exactly the sort of contradiction that
> happens when you try and behave in a way that is
> contradicted by life . . . by the particular form of our
> society. . . . You can't avoid it.

A member of a housing coop pointed out that it is difficult
for people used to a hierarchical system to suddenly change
their whole approach and assumptions. They expect a landlord
and tenant relationship and cannot imagine how Joe and Mabel
from up the road can actually evict them, nor can Joe and
Mabel easily contemplate this!

> It's a question of people having been traditionally in a
> very weak position, and suddenly they are in a position
> of power but are not aware of it . . . cannot
> comprehend it.

Others point to contamination by the sexist divisions in the
wider capitalist society. A member of the electronics commune
made the point this way:

> Meetings themselves are sexist. . . . The men seem to
> enjoy meetings as a sort of social interaction, a bit like
> being down the pub together or boys in the back room,
> and . . . it's quite a strong interaction for them. . . .
> The women are stronger in terms of one-to-one
> interaction during the course of the ordinary
> productive process, of talking, just sort of chatting over
> the shoulder. . . . Both are methods for achieving the
> same thing, which is to find opinions, interact, and
> through that you could make decisions. But if you're
> then going to say meetings are how this coop makes its
> decisions, it may be that there is a slight sexual bias to
> it.

Undoubtedly, one of the most important ways in which the
wider capitalist society can be seen as shaping the collective is
through the necessary interaction of its members with other
capitalist organizations. A member of a wholefood coop, for
example, noted that the wider capitalist structure means that
cooperatives have to compete with capitalist companies on their
terms:

> Profit means . . . having a surplus at the end of the
> year rather than a deficit. And if you keep having a
> deficit, you go bankrupt. . . . I see a lot of
> cooperatives very concerned with the superficial image

> of whether or not they are a kind of far out place . . .
> no authority structure, everybody just does their own
> thing. They're not actually concerned with building
> something up that is strong, that is actually going to
> generate some money and take the capitalists on at
> their own game.

A member of the theatre collective also accepted the
inevitability of some capitalist contamination:

> No more do I believe we operate perfectly as a
> collective could operate. Obviously its contradicted by
> lots of things in the outside world. We are on one level
> a cooperative experimenting with new ways of doing
> things and on another we are a small company . . .
> concerned with developing plays. . . .   One thing
> beyond anything else that makes that possible is
> economic survival. If you want to eat and do
> community theatre, it's necessary to earn money, and
> that means endless concessions. . . . In order to exist
> legally there are certain accounting skills which you
> must have. . . .   For Greg, who's learning about
> performing, to interest himself in the details of
> administration would destroy his ability to perform.
> Everything would numb out into a vague
> blandness. . . . It's clearly a division of labor, but I
> don't think a division of labor necessarily means a
> division of experience, nor does it imply hierarchy.

It is, however, as I have already suggested, a mistake to
explain entirely in structural terms the tendencies toward
individualism, factionalism, specialization, and sexist role
allocation that existed in the cooperatives I studied and were
reflected in their normative orders. Human agency was also
important. People are different in their abilities, motives, and
values, and these differences both as an inescapable fact and as
particular constellations of personalities necessarily affect the
organizations that people create.[6] As a member of an
electronics commune put it:

> Although we are very much a coop of equals, I do
> think we inevitably move away from this ideal . . .
> because we are all different people with different
> levels of confidence to work.

Another member of the electronics commune observed:

> Even if you think you've got a consensus system, it is
> possible to find that people with the strongest
> personalities so often carry everyone else with them

---

[6] This is not the same as saying that people are naturally different;
rather, humans have the capacity to differentiate themselves and to make the
differences significant.

that it's almost as if they control the direction in which
we go.

And a member of the computer collective said:

I think a division of labor has to be inevitable in some
fields. . . . There's going to be some things that I
might find interesting that . . . somebody else doesn't.

The wider system of capitalism, with its individualist
rewards and competitive ethic, may strengthen and lend
support to these kinds of differentiation, but this does not mean
that capitalism determines how or the extent to which
differentiation proceeds within collectives, nor does it mean
that collectives or other efforts at communal government are
doomed to fail or inevitably to support the capitalist enterprise.
The tendency toward differentiation that is associated with
human agency is, no doubt, reinforced by the encompassing
capitalist system, but it exists under socialism as well. And
from this human agency arise the values associated with
communalism and the commitment to work toward collective
ends.

IV. CONCLUSION

In conclusion, let me sketch the most important
implications of this paper for those who espouse socialism and
who, like Abel (1982b), believe that the creation of small-scale
collectives is fundamental to achieving it. First, my study of
cooperatives suggests that in a capitalist society even radically
independent collective structures are permeated by influences
of the larger system. Second, we have seen that such collective
institutions are especially vulnerable to crisis and collapse.
This is not due just to the mutually opposing relations that the
collective and its normative order have with the capitalist
society and its law. It stems also from the sometimes anti-
communitarian tendencies of factions and individuals within
these institutions, which may be fostered by the wider society
and its law. Third, the number of institutions, such as
cooperatives and collectives, that are organized around
principles inconsistent with capitalism is small in relation to
the number of institutions permeated by the capitalist ethic.
Even if it were possible for communally oriented institutions to
remain free of capitalist influences, we could not expect these
forms to be a vanguard for total social change unless we had
some reason to believe that the example or efforts of such
institutions would transform capitalist institutional structures.
Abel offers neither theoretical support for this expectation nor

evidence that communal institutions have such effects. This study provides both, but not in the direct way that this expectation suggests. Alternative institutions and their associated normative orders do not work transformations on capitalist structures and rule systems but instead interact with them in a dialectical way such that both the alternative system and the capitalist order are vulnerable to incremental reformulations. Since capitalist rules and institutions predominate among the norms and organizations of capitalist society, the greatest potential for a social transformation lies in these dialectical processes. At one level the communitarian concerns of human agents are likely to interject more communal elements into capitalist society by penetrating and modifying capitalist institutions than are injected through the creation of alternative collective structures. At another level institutions of communal justice within employee work groups, neighborhood residence groups, mutual support, and self-help groups, none of which challenge the core organizing principles of capitalist society, are likely to do more to modify the shape of capitalist legality than the collective justice of cooperatives, communes, and other more socialistically oriented orders that are rarely encountered within capitalism and are generally marginal in the larger society. Indeed, capitalism may, as we have seen, successfully undercut opposing orders, but it cannot destroy its own institutions and therefore must continually contend with opposing internal tendencies. Thus, it is likely that the collective justice of factions that form within capitalism has a degree of persistence that is not found in conflicting orders. An implication of these observations is that, short of revolution, change towards socialist legality is more likely to be fostered by mechanisms of communal justice within institutions that do not challenge the basic premises of capitalism than through the development of more radical conflicting institutions.

Those who value socialist forms of interpersonal government should recognize that the desired communal collective form is already an existing, if unacknowledged, underemphasized, and undervalued, component of the capitalist legal order. Failing to see this, those who espouse socialism will miss the most promising ways of institutionalizing schemes of socialist legality. Moreover, in evaluating attempts to institutionalize socialist legality, those who are blind to the integrative perspective are likely to be continually frustrated by what are in fact inevitable imperfections in the socialist ideal and will not recognize what they have achieved.

The spirit with which the movement toward socialist legality in capitalist society must proceed, if it is to proceed at all, is nicely captured in the remarks of a member of a theatre collective whom I interviewed:

> We are trying to glimpse possible relationships in the present world. Unless you know what it would be like to have a society where people cooperate, unless you've got some glimpse of it, I really don't see what you're doing trying to get it. Or even if you manage to get it, what on earth are you going to do with it? . . . The only way things change, in my experience—all the things I'm referring to are a very intricate set of relationships ranging from personal ones to huge ones involving organizations—is in an imaginative, cooperative, creative way, where someone offers a possibility with a degree of conviction, energy, and forethought about how that possibility will be organized, so that it becomes evident to the other people that that's what happens. I really want to make it mundane, because I think it's very important to make it mundane. I don't want to end up talking about mass party organization. I'm not convinced that someone running a socialist center, however *au fait* he is with contemporary political ideas, is going to be able to handle society better than Sue Smith, who's 19, because she's doing it now. You know, she's actually trying to work out what happens when she's got a better idea than someone who is older than her, or apparently usually knows better, and how to explain to them without causing an argument and wasted time.

In conclusion, then, I would invert Abel's (1982b) observation that "partial advances need not await a total victory." Total victory is contingent upon partial advances, but such advances will be inconsequential in bringing about the desired end if they are restricted to peripheral institutions that reject capitalism at their core. While such advances are a form of progress, broad-based change requires transformations within mainstream institutions that do not begin by challenging the premises of capitalism and the capitalist legal order. As I have tried to show in this paper, there exists the potential for such broad-based change. It is rooted in the ability of human agents to "make a difference," and in the dialectical interplay of factions and the groups that contain them. Ironically, forces that often undercut bold attempts to achieve socialist legality, like those in the collective systems I studied, provide the greatest hope of ultimately achieving it.

326 COMMUNITY JUSTICE

REFERENCES

ABEL, Richard L. (1981) "Conservative Conflict and the Reproduction of Capitalism: The Role of Informal Justice," 9 *International Journal of the Sociology of Law* 245.
—— (1982a) *The Politics of Informal Justice*, 2 vols. London and New York: Academic Press.
—— (1982b) "A Socialist Approach to Risk," 41 *Maryland Law Review* 695.
ARCHER, Margaret S. (1982) "Morphogenesis Versus Structuration: On Combining Structure and Action," 33 *British Journal of Sociology* 455.
BRADY, James P. (1981) "Sorting Out the Exile's Confusion: Or a Dialogue on Popular Justice," 5 *Contemporary Crisis* 31.
CAPPELETTI, Mauro and Bryant GARTH (1978) *Access to Justice: A World Survey.* Milan: Sijthoff Giuffre.
CARR, Jerry (1983) "The Synthesis of Functionalism and Conflict Theory: A Study in the Metaphysics of Sociological Dialectics," 7 *Quarterly Journal of Ideology* 14.
CHRISTIE, Nils (1976) *Conflicts as Property.* Sheffield: The University Centre for Criminology.
COLLINS, Randall (1981) "On the Microfoundations of Macrosociology," 86 *American Journal of Sociology* 984.
DANZIG, Richard (1973) "Toward the Creation of a Complementary, Decentralized System of Criminal Justice," 26 *Stanford Law Review* 1.
DURKHEIM, Emile (1893) *The Division of Labor in Society.* Chicago: The Free Press.
ECKHOFF, Torstein (1966) "The Mediator, the Judge and the Administrator in Conflict Resolution," 10 *Acta Sociologica* 148.
EHRLICH, Eugen (1936) *Fundamental Principles of the Sociology of Law.* Cambridge, MA: Harvard University Press.
FISHER, Eric (1975) "Community Courts: An Alternative to Conventional Criminal Adjudication," 24 *American University Law Review* 1253.
FITZPATRICK, Peter (1983a) "Law, Plurality and Underdevelopment," in D. Sugarman (ed.), *Legality, Ideology and the State.* London: Academic Press.
—— (1983b) "Marxism and Legal Pluralism," 1 *Australian Journal of Law and Society* 45.
—— (1984) "Law and Societies," 22 *Osgood Hall Law Journal* 115.
GALANTER, Marc (1974) "Why the 'Haves' Come out Ahead: Speculations on the Limits of Legal Change," 9 *Law & Society Review* 95.
GIDDENS, Anthony (1979) *Central Problems in Social Theory: Action, Structure and Contradiction in Social Analysis.* London: Macmillan.
—— (1982) *Profiles and Critiques in Social Theory.* London: Macmillan.
—— (1984) *The Constitution of Society.* Cambridge: Polity Press.
GIERKE, Otto von (1913) *Political Theories of the Middle Age.* Cambridge: University Press.
GURVITCH, Georges (1947) *Sociology of Law.* London: Routledge and Kegan Paul.
HENRY, Stuart (1983) *Private Justice: Towards Integrated Theorising in the Sociology of Law.* London: Routledge and Kegan Paul.
KAMENKA, Eugene and Alice Erh-Soon TAY (1975) "Beyond Bourgeois Individualism: The Contemporary Crisis in Law and Legal Ideology," in E. Kamenka and R.S. Neale (eds.), *Feudalism, Capitalism and Beyond.* London: Edward Arnold.
—— (1978) "Socialism, Anarchism and Law," in E. Kamenka, R. Brown and A. Tay (eds.), *Law and Society: The Crisis in Legal Ideals.* London: Edward Arnold.
KETTLER, David, Volker MEJA and Nico STEHR (1984) "Karl Mannheim and Conservatism: The Ancestry of Historical Thinking," 49 *American Sociological Review* 71.
KNORR-CETINA, Karen (1981) "Introduction: The Micro Sociological Challenge of Macro Sociology: Toward a Reconstruction of Social Theory and Methodology," in K. Knorr-Cetina and A. Cicourel (eds.), *Advances in*

Social Theory and Methodology: Toward an Integration of Micro- and Macro-Sociologies. London: Routledge and Kegan Paul.
LEWONTIN, R.C., Steven ROSE and Leon J. KAMIN (1984) *Not in Our Genes: Biology, Ideology and Human Nature.* New York: Pantheon.
LONGMIRE, Dennis R. (1981) "A Popular Justice System: A Radical Alternative to the Traditional Criminal Justice System," 5 *Contemporary Crisis* 15.
MOORE, Sally Falk (1978) *Law as Process.* London: Routledge and Kegan Paul.
NELKEN, David (1982) "Is There a Crisis in Law and Legal Ideology?" 9 *Journal of Law and Society* 177.
RENNER, Karl (1949) *The Institutions of Private Law and Their Social Functions.* London: Routledge and Kegan Paul.
ROSNER, Menahem (1973) "Direct Democracy in the Kibbutz," in R. Kanter (ed.), *Communes: Creating and Managing the Collective Life.* New York: Harper.
ROSS, Edward A. (1932) *Social Control: A Survey of the Foundations of Order.* New York: Macmillan.
SANTOS, Boaventura de Sousa (1980) "Law and Community: The Changing Nature of State Power in Late Capitalism," 8 *International Journal of the Sociology of Law* 379.
SCHNEIDER, Louis (1971) "Dialectic in Sociology," 36 *American Sociological Review* 667.
SCHWARTZ, Richard D. (1954) "Social Factors in the Development of Legal Control: A Case Study of Two Israeli Settlements," 63 *Yale Law Journal* 471.
—— (1957) "Democracy and Collectivism in the Kibbutz," 5 *Social Problems* 137.
SHAPIRO, Allan E. (1976) "Law in the Kibbutz: A Reappraisal," 10 *Law & Society Review* 415.
STATSKY, William P. (1974) "Community Courts: Decentralizing Juvenile Jurisprudence," 3 *Capital University Law Review* 1.
SWINGEWOOD, Alan (1975) *Marx and Modern Social Theory.* London: Macmillan.
VAN DEN BERGHE, Pierre (1963) "Dialectic and Functionalism: Towards a Theoretical Synthesis," 28 *American Sociological Review* 695.
VERSELE, Severin-Carolos (1969) "Public Participation in the Administration of Criminal Justice," 27 *International Review of Criminal Policy* 9.
WEISBROD, Carol (1980) *The Boundaries of Utopia.* New York: Pantheon.
WHELAN, Christopher J. (1981) "Informalising Judicial Procedures," in S. Henry (ed.), *Informal Institutions.* New York: St. Martin's Press.

[17]

SOCIAL PROBLEMS, Vol. 30, No. 5, June 1983

A PRIVATE NETWORK OF SOCIAL CONTROL: INSURANCE INVESTIGATION UNITS*

SUSAN GUARINO GHEZZI
Boston College

Fraud investigation units have sprung up within insurance companies across the United States to counter corporate losses due to fraud and the restrictions imposed on the industry by government regulations. This paper looks at the birth, operating strategies, and effectiveness of these units in three automobile insurance companies in Massachusetts. Because fraud cases are rarely brought to court, these units operate as a kind of private police. They exchange information with the public police and other companies and circumvent judicial control, often using investigative procedures which would render the evidence they collect inadmissible in court. Recent legislation has strengthened their power and cut off avenues of redress once available to wronged policyholders.

Federal government control of insurance fraud in the United States has existed since the mail fraud statute was added to the postal laws and regulations in 1872 (Comstock, 1969). Since most insurance claims are handled by mail, the statute controls fraud by prohibiting use of the mails to carry schemes to defraud. In addition, over the past century a number of states have enacted their own statutes designating insurance fraud as illegal. Yet because of the circumstantial nature of insurance fraud, defrauders have rarely been identified or prosecuted. One study estimated the annual cost of insurance fraud at $1.5 billion (Bureau of National Affairs, 1976). In Massachusetts, the number of auto theft claims had swelled to an unprecedented level by 1975, when it was estimated that 25 percent of all reported thefts were fraudulent (Governor's Task Force on Automobile Theft, 1980). This led the Massachusetts office of the Kemper Company, located in Quincy, to devise a system to detect fraudulent claims. The first Special Investigation Unit (SIU), as the insurance industry's in-house teams have come to be called, was set up by Kemper in 1976. Since then, every major insurance company in the state has implemented a similar unit, mainly for auto insurance fraud. In addition, scaled-down versions of SIUs are now appearing throughout the United States.

This paper examines why the insurance industry set up SIUs and how they operate. I focus on events in Massachusetts because this was the birthplace of the units. The state's unique regulatory environment has encouraged both fraudulent activity and privately funded solutions to the problem of fraud.

In 1979 and 1980 I conducted 30 in-depth interviews with investigators, SIU supervisors, claims managers, attorneys, and insurance executives from the New England offices of three insurance companies. The companies, which I call X, Y, and Z, were selected by means of the snowball sampling technique. The claims manager of Company Y, whom I contacted first, suggested I look at Companies X and Z as well; "connections" between the three companies facilitated access. The companies vary in size (ranging from an approximate ranking of 15th to 50th in the United States) and maturity of their SIUs (ranging from several years in one company to newly implemented in another). All three are veteran companies that entered the United States' market before the First World War; two companies are international. In addition to interviewing I examined a small sample of investigative reports and other documents from all three companies, attended seminars and films sponsored by the insurance industry on how to detect

* This is a revised version of a paper presented at the annual meeting of the Eastern Sociological Society in Philadelphia, March 1982. The author thanks Stephen Pfohl, David Karp, Paul Gray, Sally Heffentreyer, and the anonymous *Social Problems* reviewers for their comments. Correspondence to: Department of Sociology, Boston College, Chestnut Hill, MA 02167.

522
GHEZZI

and control those who commit crimes against insurance companies, and accompanied an SIU supervisor from Company Y while he was investigating a typical case. Data not attributed to other sources comes from my research.

This paper is divided into four sections. The first section examines why the SIU emerged. I suggest that the SIU is the result of regulation, legislation and public police indifference to the growing problem of insurance fraud. The second section describes how SIUs are organized and how they operate. In the third segment I discuss the profitability of SIUs and their deterrent effect. The paper's final component describes how the insurance industry has cultivated channels of influence which facilitate the investigation process. I show how recent legislation has increased the SIUs' control while decreasing the recourse of policyholders.

BIRTH OF THE SIUs

Auto insurance in the United States is provided solely by private industry. In no state is it mandatory for motorists to purchase theft or accident coverage; liability coverage, on the other hand, is either compulsory or "quasi-compulsory"[1] (Kulp and Hall, 1968:421). The insurance industry is regulated by state agencies and by certain federal authorities. The state regulatory authorities are responsible for protecting customers against overcharging or unfair discrimination, while regulating the business in such a way as to encourage companies to make necessary insurance protection available to the public. In many states auto rates must be approved in advance by the regulator; in other states, rate changes may be made without prior regulatory approval (Insurance Information Institute, 1981–82). Various federal agencies (e.g., Federal Trade Commission, Department of Justice, Internal Revenue Service) monitor such areas of insurance activity as advertising, antitrust matters, and insurance accounting (Kulp and Hall, 1968).

The regulation of insurance in Massachusetts is unique in two respects. First, the powers of the state Commissioner of Insurance exceed those of his colleagues in virtually every other state. With one exception,[2] Massachusetts is the only state in which the commissioner has the authority to set the rates for auto insurance. New rates are determined by the commissioner each year. In other states, the commissioner's powers are limited to review or approval of rate changes submitted by the insurance industry. Second, Massachusetts was the first and only state to forbid insurers from denying any type of auto insurance to any motorist, including people convicted of automobile theft or fraud. In 1970 the state legislature approved the "mandatory offer law" (Massachusetts G.L.c. 175, sections 22E and 22F) which guarantees auto insurance to all applicants, and which provides that repeat, known defrauders pay the same rate for theft coverage as "honest" policyholders.

Five factors help explain why Massachusetts was the birthplace of SIUs in the U.S. insurance industry:

1) Massachusetts came under regulation of the mandatory offer law when it became effective in 1972.

2) In the 10 years preceding the birth of SIUs in Massachusetts, its rate of automobile theft was the highest in the United States (U.S. Department of Justice, 1968–77). The insurance industry regards the mandatory offer law as largely responsible for the state's unenviable distinction as "auto theft capital of the world" (Ancipink, 1980:99). In the first three years after the mandatory offer law took effect, the number of automobile theft claims in the state more than

---

1. Even in states where auto liability insurance is not made compulsory through legislation, it is mandatory for all practical purposes. Drivers without such insurance risk losing their driving privileges as a result of financial inability to satisfy judgements made against them.
2. The state of Texas.

doubled—from 23,800 in 1972 to 56,400 in 1975 (Governor's Task Force on Automobile Theft, 1980:22).

3) Since 1926 the price of automobile insurance in Massachusetts has been set by the state's Commissioner of Insurance. From 1975 to 1979 this position was held by a liberal economist who, in the view of insurance industry executives, set prices too low to keep pace with the rising costs of automobile theft.

4) Despite state regulation, Massachusetts' auto insurance rates are among the highest in the United States. Because of territorial and demographic distinctions, inter-state comparisons of auto insurance rates are difficult to determine. However, the Governor's Task Force on Automobile Theft (1980:xxii) reported that Massachusetts' rates for auto theft insurance were the highest in the nation. The cost of insurance has created highly publicized tensions between the insurance industry and state consumer groups. Policyholders have responded to these steep rates by submitting large numbers of padded and fraudulent claims in an attempt to recapture part of their premium expenses. As a result, fraudulent claims have produced even higher rates.

5) The mandatory offer law allows an insurance company to voluntarily select those policies it wants to insure by itself ("good risks") and those policies it wants to pass on to the Massachusetts Motor Vehicle Reinsurance Facility ("bad risks"). Facility losses are pooled, and each company is charged for a share of facility losses according to the percentage of total auto business which it writes in the state. This way, companies do not risk substantial losses on any given policy which has been ceded to the facility since all companies contribute towards paying claims submitted on such policies. A substantial number of auto policies are unloaded onto the facility each year—roughly half of all policies in 1982. Insurance companies' claims departments have less incentive to settle claims profitably, since losses are divided among all of the companies in the state. This widespread sharing of losses has created a laxness in claims handling which encourages fraudulent activity (Ancipink, 1980).

The state's facility system means that the companies writing the most automobile insurance in Massachusetts are forced to assume the bulk of the bad risks. The state's larger companies have seen their profits stripped away by the facility. For example, Company Y had a profitable 43.8 percent loss ratio (losses per premiums) in 1978 on the policies it volunteered to insure itself. However, their total loss ratio, including their bill for pooled facility losses, was 71 percent, which meant the company lost $2.5 million after operating expenses and income from investment. Other leading writers of personal automobile insurance in the state found themselves in similar situations (Ancipink, 1980). If Massachusetts companies could turn down applicants for insurance, as insurance companies do in other states, their results might have been profitable.

Faced with such a situation, insurance companies in Massachusetts found they had few options. Massachusetts law forbids companies from withdrawing from a line of business they have already undertaken unless they surrender their license to do business within the state. Small companies with little business in other lines are unlikely to dissolve themselves. And while national companies have the option of shutting down state agencies, corporate policy-makers are usually reluctant to make such dramatic changes. Company Y considered reducing its exposure in Massachusetts by releasing certain agents but decided instead to work for the dissolution of state regulatory controls.

Another option was to appeal to traditional law enforcement services for help in combatting insurance fraud. Companies that tried this approach, however, had little success. A claims manager with Company Y explained why:

> Law enforcement has decided: "You insurance guys deal with that problem. We've got so many murders and robberies and street crimes to fight. We don't have the budget; we don't have support publicly to go in and start prosecuting insurance fraud." So we ended up taking on the job ourselves.

524   GHEZZI

SIUs are a result of the insurance industry's decision to "take on the job" of fighting fraud. In effect, SIUs are a type of private police force.[3] The insurance companies realized that their normal, claims-adjusting procedures were not sufficient to investigate complex and potentially fraudulent claims. They realized that their adjusting staffs, generally overburdened and without specific training in how to detect fraud, could not be expected to cope with the problem. So, between 1976 and 1979, the companies I studied set up SIUs to tighten claims procedures and fill the void left by the public law enforcement agencies. "Routine" claims continued to be handled by the regular claims adjusting staff. But staffs of specially trained investigators began examining any claims that looked suspicious. Moreover, the three companies' SIUs began developing a mutually supportive, informal network to exchange information and technical expertise.

HOW THE SIUs WORK

When a car is stolen or involved in an accident, the owner fills out a "first report of loss" with the insurance agent. The agent turns the report over to the company's adjusting office which begins the process of settling the claim. The company sends an appraiser to inspect the car, if it has been in an accident, and the adjusting office uses the appraiser's report to calculate the amount the company should pay to the owner. It is at this stage that irregularities must be detected and, if necessary, the case referred to the SIU.

All three companies I studied had trained their adjusting staffs to recognize suspicious claims. I read a copy of a speech that a Company Y claims manager delivered to an audience of insurance agents. He explained:

> We have developed a profile [of a typical defrauder] which sits on every adjuster's desk. . . . After many months, we have finally educated our [adjusting] staff to be suspicious of anything that shows up in the profile. And when they get suspicious, to do a real thorough investigation. We have changed our standards for the investigation of auto theft losses. No longer can they be handled by a desk adjuster. Face-to-face contact must be made with each insured and a detailed investigation must be concluded. These are our standards.

The profile of the typical defrauder is similar to profiles used by airport personnel to identify hijackers. Burdened by heavy caseloads and hindered by limited investigative training, insurance adjusters use the profile to screen their cases for referral to the SIU. The profile describes a single man, in his 20s, who is self-employed or unemployed, and who exhibits an aggressive attitude: "they yell on the phone, they bang their fists on the desk when they come into the office, they demand immediate payment," said an investigator with Company X. In addition to the profile, adjusters may use a check-list with point scores for various "symptoms" of fraud.

Adjusting staff are trained to spot a number of symptoms of automobile fraud. Urban policyholders often try to avoid the higher rates charged to city residents by giving false, lower-rate, suburban addresses when taking out a policy, a lie that will probably not be discovered until a claim is submitted. At such time claimants must provide a telephone number where they can

---

3. The void created by the absence of public policing has been a *raison d'être* for private police forces in the United States since the mid-19th century. Historically, private police have been instrumental in penetrating areas in which public police were either unable or unwilling to become involved. Pinkerton's, the first private detective agency in the United States, was founded in 1830. In its early years, Pinkerton's major business involved protecting the railroads and their express carriers. At the time, there was no national, centralized police force in the United States capable of moving quickly across jurisdictional boundaries. Thus, Pinkerton's and similar agencies grew out of the necessity for a national police force. See Becker (1974), Spitzer (1982), and Spitzer and Scull (1977) for theoretical analyses of private police emergence. See Draper (1978), Kakalik and Wildhorn (1971a), and Klare (1975) for the qualifications, specializations, and resources of private police. See Braun and Lee (1971), Kakalik and Wildhorn (1971b), and Scott and McPherson (1971) for the legal definitions of private policing. See Kakalik and Wildhorn (1971c) for regulatory controls on private police.

be reached. The claims staff are tipped off to the fraud when they see an urban telephone number and a suburban address. Likewise, when someone with little or no accident insurance submits a theft claim, the adjuster refers the case to the SIU in case the claimant is trying to obtain compensation for accident damage by falsely claiming a theft.[4]

The companies hired SIU agents on the basis of two criteria: a background in insurance adjusting and some exposure to the criminal justice system, usually a bachelor's degree in criminology. In addition, Company X's personnel profile suggested that investigators be men, and that they be "intelligent, confident, determined, unflapable, [and have a] firm telephone manner and appearance." Company Y preferred former police officers as SIU managers.

The SIU begins its investigation by visiting the claimant at home and tape-recording a statement. As Company Y's SIU supervisor explained,

When a case comes in, it's assigned by me to one of my investigators, and that investigator is required to contact the insured within 24 hours, and go out and take a signed statement. Now by going out, I mean go right out to the insured's home, not having the insured come into the office, or meeting him outside — meet him at his home surroundings. This gives the investigator a chance to see (1) that [the insured] does live there; (2) what type of neighborhood [it is]; and (3) the overall background that the insured has — we look at the economic structure and get a feel from the type of premises they live at.

The statement taken from the claimant includes both responses to standard questions (e.g., "what was the location of your car when it was stolen?") and to questions pertaining to the particular case. The investigator verifies all of the information provided by the claimant through the use of standard police methods, such as contacting the claimant's employer, friends, and neighbors. Said one investigator with Company X:

A good source is kids riding by on their bikes. Kids are sharp — they notice more than you'd think. You ask them if they ever saw a car in the driveway, and they'll say, "yeah, it was a green car." And sometimes they're sharp and they'll say "yeah, it was a green Oldsmobile." Then you ask them what kind of shape it was in, and they'll say "that was the car with the big dent in the rear" or "that was the car with all the damage in the front end."

When investigators with Company Y interviewed claimants or third parties, they did not introduce themselves as "investigators" but said only that they were "with" that company. They tried to show, in some way, that they were just "working stiffs trying to do a job." For example, investigators might say they needed a signed statement because "my boss is breathing down my neck." Or they might call the insurance company a "big rip-off" and charge that no one receives a fair deal from it.

Company Y's claims manager described a typical investigation handled by the SIU:

A man purchases a 1981 Lincoln Continental second-hand. The car had been stolen from the previous owner but later recovered. The new owner insures the car for theft and accident damage. A month later the owner reports that it has been stolen a second time and submits a claim to the insurance company. The case is referred to the SIU because of the possibility that the car was already damaged as a result of the original theft when sold to the current owner. The SIU considers the possibility of fraud: perhaps the Lincoln was actually a total wreck when purchased by the claimant. The claimant may have paid a minimal price for the wreck, and obtained a proof of ownership (title) from the previous owner. The title would not indicate that the vehicle was a total loss, and with the title the new owner could register and insure the car, since neither the Registry of Motor Vehicles nor the insurance company looks at the car. Then the new owner claims that the car has been stolen and wrecked in the process, and seeks its full market value from the insurance company. The claimant may even induce a body shop to claim that they repaired the damage from the first theft before the car was again stolen.

---

4. For a typology of schemes to defraud insurance companies, see Reichman (1982).

526   GHEZZI

An investigator with Company X explained how the SIU would handle the case:

First what we do is take the statement of the insured, hoping or expecting that he'll say the car was in excellent condition prior to the [second] theft. We know it was a total loss, but we won't say we're aware of that. The way we know the actual condition of the car is we have the title—this can be obtained from the registry. On the title is a list of previous owners. We go to the previous owner's insurance company, which has a loss file on the individual. We then request copies of the damage appraisal, and pictures of the damaged vehicle. There is a problem here with the Privacy Act of 1979, because some companies are afraid of being sued by giving out this information. So some companies won't give copies of the appraisal and pictures of the vehicle, but we do. We've never been sued—in fact we just won a case where the insured tried to apply the Privacy Act.

. . . Meanwhile, we find out that [the car] was a total loss. Then we ask the insured and the [body] shop about its condition. If the insured and the shop tell you it was in good condition, then you probably have them. The shop will say they rebuilt the car. Now this could be true, and often is. The key is documentation—you need to have documentation that the car was rebuilt. The shop must be able to supply you with receipts that are itemized—not just "car rebuilt: $500." If there is no breakdown on the receipt, it proves nothing.

The biggest help is the inspection sticker. If the insured said he was driving the car, he must have had an inspection sticker. But most of these people forget about the inspection sticker. We ask them where they got their car inspected, and it throws them off guard. They say they don't know or they can't remember. Some can tell you Joe's garage, but it could be a conspiracy between the insured and the garage. You go and check with the shop, and it turns out they have falsified the record of inspections. You find out it's been falsified when you go to the registry and check on inspections. They have sheets which list the insured's name, license plate number, and sticker number. If no sticker was issued, then you've caught them in a lie. This is not conclusive proof for denial in itself, but you pair this with no accurate proof of repair, and you've got a case [for denial of payment]. Then you go to neighbors' houses, knock on the doors, ask them if they recall seeing the insured's car and determine from them what condition it was in.

The investigator presents his evidence to his supervisor and they decide how to proceed. Another resource available to SIUs in cases such as this is the National Automobile Theft Bureau (NATB), a private firm which is funded by member insurance companies. These companies supply information to the NATB when a car is stolen and when an insurance company sells a salvaged vehicle. This enables SIUs to monitor people who submit claims to other companies, or who buy wrecks and then submit claims for them.[5]

The SIUs spend an average of three weeks investigating each case. Then they recommend that the claim be either paid or denied. If the claim is denied, the claimant may file suit against the company. Although exact figures were not available, respondents from the companies I studied reported that suits against them were rare. (Roughly 10 percent of total dollars denied to claimants are ever paid following litigation.) Criminal court action taken by Massachusetts insurance companies against claimants is also rare. Due to the circumstantial nature of insurance fraud, respondents estimated that since the inception of SIUs, fewer than 5 percent of the cases they investigate are presented to the district attorney. A case must be airtight and involve a lot of money or a large number of defrauders before the district attorney is usually willing to prosecute.

MONEY SAVED AND DETERRENCE

How cost-efficient are SIUs? Company Z found that between 1979 and 1982 they spent under $100,000 on total overhead costs and saved over $300,000. Company X reported a similar cost-benefit ratio for each year since their SIU was implemented. Company Y was reluctant to report

---

5. According to Company Y executives, the insurance industry is also working to create a central computerized indexing system of all companies' losses. This system would detect multiple policies on the same vehicle and help identify and track down defrauders who move from company to company. Sharing information in this way would reduce the vulnerability of smaller insurance companies which lack the resources to set up their own SIUs.

its savings and, like the other companies, stressed that the dollar value of SIUs cannot account for their deterrent value, which they believed to be high. For example, an attorney with Company Y said that between 1977 and 1981 their reported auto thefts dropped over 50 percent, while state-wide the decline was only about 10 percent. This suggests that people who plan to have their cars stolen go elsewhere for insurance.

SIUs act as deterrents in two ways. First, regardless of the outcome of an investigation, a claimant may be sufficiently rattled by the experience to think twice about doing anything which would again arouse the company's suspicion. One investigator noted that even when an SIU probe fails to produce enough evidence for a denial of payment, ". . . at least I would think that the fact that we investigated is gonna make that insured think, and he won't [commit fraud] again." Commented another investigator and former insurance adjuster:

> The main value our unit can provide is deterrence. The adjusters are unable to do this. Insurance adjusting becomes an assembly-line job. . . . The insured will say, "I was at the movies when my car was stolen" and the adjuster won't even ask what movie he went to.

A second way that SIUs act as a deterrent is by alerting potential defrauders that a particular company has a fraud investigation unit. Company X's SIU supervisor commented:

> We rely mostly on word of mouth—the people who would commit fraud usually have friends who did, and word gets around that [our company] is the roughest company to deal with.

An executive with Company Y was even more explicit:

> Because so much [insurance fraud] is undetectable, and because we get deterred still in some areas for trying to detect it, the most effective method we will have in terms of a potential for actual success is psychological warfare. That means publicly advertising in the media and everywhere else that at least our company has gumshoes all over the place, running around detecting people, with the help of a profile that we scientifically develop. And if we could convince enough people that the risks inherent in filing a fraudulent claim are greater than what you could recover from it, I think you would see an incredible drop in the number of loss dollars that we pay out.

All three companies were careful in handling the public image of the SIUs. While they ran articles in insurance trade magazines and occasionally gave interviews to a local radio or TV station, the companies generally avoided publicizing the SIUs. Company Z's supervisor explained that because of the tensions that existed between Massachusetts consumer groups and the insurance industry over high rates, his company was apprehensive about public reaction to SIUs. The supervisor from Company X expressed his company's concern that public information on defrauding insurance companies could be read as a "how-to" for future defrauders.

EVOLVING RELATIONS WITH THE STATE

The emergence of SIUs has brought the insurance industry into contact with government in two areas: jurisdiction and legislation. The insurance companies I studied had tried to improve the position of their SIUs vis-a-vis the Massachusetts government in two stages. First, they tried to reduce the potential for conflict over common "turf" between the state as a consumer protector and the SIUs as private police forces. Then they tried to ensure that SIU control over common turf would triumph over state control. I look at each stage in turn.

Relations With State Agencies

In principle, SIUs and the state government's regulatory apparatus—in Massachusetts, the department of consumer affairs of the state Commission of Insurance—work at cross purposes. The consumer department is designed to receive complaints from policyholders about the handling of their claims, and to act on the policyholders' behalf in obtaining fair settlements. In practice, however, the department is hampered by a lack of staff and resources, as are most such

528   GHEZZI

regulatory agencies (Barnet and Muller, 1974:262; Domhoff, 1974; Kimball, 1969). As a result, the insurance industry is in a position to influence regulatory policy in Massachusetts. For example, one of the companies I studied donated "$5,000 to [gubinatorial] candidate [Edward J.] King within days of his election—a little insurance of their own, perhaps, that their man [Stephen] Clifford would indeed get the nod [as insurance commissioner]." Clifford was immediately appointed to the post, and "as pawn for the industry, was to undo the reforms of the [Governor Michael] Dukakis years." However, Clifford was forced to resign shortly after accepting his appointment when "the media reported that Clifford had been involved in real estate deals with a convicted arsonist" (Loth, 1981:6).

Company Y had worked diligently to "neutralize" conflict with the insurance department and thereby co-opt regulatory personnel.[6] An executive from Company Y explained their tactic:

> We found that complaints that come in against us [also went to the State Commission of Insurance]. So what we do—if you can't beat 'em, why not join 'em? So we beat the crowd. We run to the insurance department and say, "we've got this case we're investigating, this is why we're not gonna pay. You may get a complaint, here's what we got, what do you think?" Well, right away when you ask the Insurance Department, or the person who is responsible for that area, "what do you think about it?", he feels flattered, plus the fact that he feels like he's participating, plus when he does get a complaint he's a lot more receptive to our position. And [that person] doesn't put us behind the eight ball as long as we don't procrastinate. And [as long as] we get the investigation done in the time frame given to us, he's not about to come down on us.

Investigators are also aided by the very group the SIUs were developed to supplant—the public police. SIU investigators with Company Y developed contacts within public law enforcement circles which facilitated the transfer of relevant information which might otherwise have been off limits. This was part of the rationale behind Company Y's policy of recruiting former police officers as SIU managers. An executive with Company Y explained:

> Getting law officers on our team, they may not always have the ability to get into certain areas or form contacts but—[pause] there are their friends. So what it does is open up the doors for us so we can work both sides of the street.

There are three reasons why the work of SIU investigators, unlike that of police, is rarely scrutinized in court: (1) The nature of insurance fraud investigation is such that restitution can be made without resorting to prosecution, simply by a company's refusal to pay a claimant. (2) It is difficult to conclusively prove charges of fraud in court because the vast bulk of evidence is circumstantial. (3) The number of prosecutions is limited by the standards and caseloads of the district attorney's office.

Avoiding legal action offers SIUs the path of least resistance. By being able to successfully deny claims while circumventing judicial checks and controls, the SIU is implicitly granted the power to investigate as they see fit.[7] In so doing, SIU investigators routinely and with the full knowledge of their supervisors, obtain evidence through procedures which would render the evidence inadmissable in court. One company's investigators reported their unit's "selective harassment" of certain suspects and the use or threatened use of polygraph tests to encourage claimants to negotiate their demands. Another SIU used a voice stress test on the claimant's tape recorded statement to determine if they should proceed with the investigation. One company had illegally tape recorded telephone conversations. What is crucial here is not the types of activities

---

6. Serber (1975) documents strategies used by the insurance industry in Pennsylvania to influence that state's regulatory agency, the Pennsylvania Department of Insurance.
7. As Skolnick (1966) observed in his study of urban patrolmen, police feel free to violate the rights of a suspect when they do not intend to have the case prosecuted.

which SIU investigators engage in, but the fact that these activities are not systematically monitored by any reviewing body.

Capitalizing on Legislative Influence

State tort laws, such as libel and defamation of character, are civil laws designed to restrain private investigative activity by offering the public recourse to lawsuits as a weapon of self-defense. In practice, few successful civil suits have been initiated against private police because of consumer ignorance or indigence (Kakalik and Wildhorn, 1971c). Yet the fear of lawsuit is the only control device available to the consumer. As of this writing, however, five states including Massachusetts have passed legislation specifically protecting insurance investigators from tort accusation in criminal court cases. In 1980, reinforced by the recommendations of Governor King's auto theft task force (which was chaired by an insurance executive), the insurance industry succeeded in forcing several amendments to Massachusetts law. Massachusetts G.L.c. 175, section 1130 was amended to grant insurance companies immunity from civil or criminal liability should the company attempt to prosecute the case. This legislation makes it impossible for injured parties to seek retribution from insurance investigators when their cases are brought to criminal court.

In addition, the state legislature created a new criminal offense, G.L.c. 266, section 111B, which prohibits filing a fraudulent insurance claim falsely alleging auto theft (fabricated theft). The statute mandates a minimum jail term of one year for repeat offenders and requires restitution to the insurance company. Similarly, G.L.c. 266, section 27A was amended to mandate a minimum one year in jail for repeat offenders convicted of stealing a car for insurance fraud purposes [actual auto theft]. The statute also requires restitution to the insurance company. While conclusive proof of guilt is difficult to obtain, given the circumstantial nature of insurance fraud, the insurance industry views these amendments as legislative victories which increase its investigative command.

The Massachusetts insurance industry was less successful in another area of legislation—repealing the state's mandatory offer law. In 1980 one large insurance company spent $1 million on a publicity campaign designed to neutralize criticism of the industry by consumer groups (Loth, 1981). This company founded the Coalition for Auto Insurance Reform (CAIR), directed by a professional grass-roots organizer, to mobilize public support to reverse the mandatory offer law. The campaign included radio commercials, advertisements in suburban weekly newspapers, talk-show appearances, public speeches, plastic key chains, and bumper stickers. Industry pressure persuaded Governor King to introduce a bill in March, 1981, aimed at repealing the law. King's bill was defeated in the state legislature; some charged that the governor's entire legislative package had in fact been dictated by the insurance industry (Loth, 1981).

CONCLUSION

The successful development of privately financed and operated policing networks is symbolic of the resources, technology, and outside support available at the corporate level. The insurance industry's SIUs have succeeded both in controlling the behavior of individuals and in meeting the challenges of government regulation of the industry. While the public law enforcement agencies have not been willing to actively participate in the struggle to control insurance fraud, the insurance industry has shrewdly cultivated existing channels of influence and control to win support for its investigative policies.

The emergence of SIUs in the United States insurance industry since 1976 raises an important issue: when the state is unable or unwilling to allot valuable resources to contain criminal behavior, who has access to the technology and organizational resources required to efficiently

530   GHEZZI

fight crime? Small companies have fewer resources to protect themselves with, and are thus more vulnerable to fraud. It is likely that smaller insurance companies unknowingly absorb defrauders who have been deterred by larger companies' SIUs. At the same time, consumers have had little success in regulating corporate fraud and deception (Edelhertz, 1978; Geis, 1973; Nader, 1973; Stone, 1975). Magnuson and Carper (1968) describe the extent to which consumers are vulnerable to the fraudulent and deceptive selling practices of businesses. Even when statutes exist, enforcement is so rare that the laws are virtually impotent. The void in controlling corporate fraud exists for essentially the same reasons that insurance fraud is overlooked by public police: overburdened case loads and the difficulty of proving beyond a reasonable doubt that deceptive practices have indeed taken place. Yet, for various reasons, victimized consumers have been reluctant to mobilize their energies against the corporate community (Edelhertz, 1978; Magnuson and Carper, 1968).

The insurance industry has succeeded in designing and implementing a network of law enforcement which, to its advantage, exists outside of the law. Through co-optation, manipulation, and "neutralization" of outside circles, SIUs have penetrated and in effect joined ranks with existing networks of social control. Thus, SIUs possess the authority of police but are not subject to judicial monitoring. Industry influence in the legislature ensures that SIUs will maintain their position of control. Moreover, consumers whose rights are violated by SIUs will probably see such avenues of redress as lawsuits continue to diminish.

REFERENCES

Ancipink, Patricia
    1980   "Auto insurance in Massachusetts: A no-exit maze." Best's Review: Property/Casualty Insurance
            Edition 81(3):28–100.
Barnet, Richard J., and Ronald E. Muller
    1974   Global Reach. New York: Simon and Schuster.
Becker, Theodore M.
    1974   "The place of private police in society: An area of research for the social sciences." Social Prob-
            lems 21 (February):438–453.
Braun, Michael, and David J. Lee
    1971   "Private police forces: Legal powers and limitations." University of Chicago Law Review 38
            (Spring):558–582.
Bureau of National Affairs
    1976   "White collar justice." Criminal Law Reporter 19(2):3.
Comstock, Anthony
    1969   Frauds Exposed. Montclair, N.J.: Patterson Smith.
    [1880]
Domhoff, G. William
    1974   Who Rules America? Englewood Cliffs, N.J.: Prentice-Hall.
Draper, Hilary
    1978   Private Police. Atlantic Highlands, N.J.: Humanities Press.
Edelhertz, Herbert
    1978   "The nature, impact, and prosecution of white-collar crime." Pp. 44–65 in John M. Johnson and
            Jack D. Douglas (eds.), Crime at the Top. Philadelphia: J.B. Lippincott Co.
Geis, Gilbert
    1973   "Deterring corporate crime." Pp. 182–197 in Ralph Nader and Mark J. Green (eds.), Corporate
            Power in America. New York: Grossman.
Governor's Task Force on Automobile Theft
    1980   Auto Theft in Massachusetts—An Executive Response. Boston: Government Printing Office.
Insurance Information Institute
    1981-   Insurance Facts. New York: Insurance Information Institute.
    82
Kakalik, James S., and Sorrel Wildhorn
    1971a   The Private Police Industry: Its Nature and Extent. Santa Monica, California: Rand Corporation.
    1971b   Current Regulation of Private Police: Regulatory Agency Experience and Views. Santa Monica,
             California: Rand Corporation.
    1971c   The Law and Private Police. Santa Monica, California: Rand Corporation.

Kimball, Spencer L.
1969 "The regulation of insurance." Pp. 3-16 in Spencer L. Kimball and Herbert S. Denenberg (eds.), Insurance, Government, and Social Policy. Homewood, IL: Richard D. Irwin.

Klare, Michael T.
1975 "The boom in private police." Nation, November 15:486-491.

Kulp, C.A., and John W. Hall
1968 Casualty Insurance. Fourth edition. New York: The Ronald Press Company.

Loth, Renee
1981 "Protection money." The Boston Phoenix, May 5:1-27.

Magnuson, Warren G., and Jean Carper
1968 The Dark Side of the Marketplace. Englewood Cliffs, N.J.: Prentice-Hall.

Nader, Ralph
1973 Bitter Wages: The Nader Report. New York: Grossman.

Reichman, Nancy
1982 "Insurance fraud: Fabricated crimes, contrived losses, and other deceptive acts." Paper presented at the 32nd annual meeting of the Society for the Study of Social Problems, San Francisco, September 3-6.

Scott, Thomas, M., and Marlys McPherson
1971 "The development of the private sector of the criminal justice system." Law and Society Review 6 (November):267-288.

Serber, David
1975 "Regulating reform: The social organization of insurance regulation." The Insurgent Sociologist 5(3):83-105.

Skolnick, Jerome H.
1966 Justice Without Trial. New York: John Wiley and Sons.

Spitzer, Steven
1982 "Prevention, protection, and coercion for profit: The privatization of enforcement in America." Paper presented at the 32nd annual meeting of the Society for the Study of Social Problems, San Francisco, September 3-6.

Spitzer, Steven, and Andrew Scull
1977 "Privatization and capitalist development: The case of the private police." Social Problems 25(1):18-29.

Stone, Christopher
1975 Where the Law Ends. New York: Harper and Row.

U.S. Department of Justice
1968- Crime in the United States—Uniform Crime Reports. Washington, D.C.: U.S. Government Print-
77 ing Office.

Statutes Cited

Revised Statutes of the United States (18)1
1872 Title XLVI, Chapter 3, section 3894 (June 8):763.

Massachusetts General Laws
1970 G.L.c. 175, sections 22E and 22F (August 24):119-121.
1980 G.L.c. 175, section 1130 (July 10):138-140.

Annotated Laws of Massachusetts
1980 ALM G.L.c. 266, section 111B (July 10):58-59.

[18]

MEDICINE AS AN INSTITUTION OF SOCIAL CONTROL *

Irving Kenneth Zola

The theme of this essay is that medicine is becoming a major institution of social control, nudging aside, if not incorporating, the more traditional institutions of religion and law. It is becoming the new repository of truth, the place where absolute and often final judgments are made by supposedly morally neutral and objective experts. And these judgments are made, not in the name of virtue or legitimacy, but in the name of health. Moreover, this is not occurring through the political power physicians hold or can influence, but is largely an insidious and often undramatic phenomenon accomplished by 'medicalizing' much of daily living, by making medicine and the labels 'healthy' and 'ill' *relevant* to an ever increasing part of human existence.

Although many have noted aspects of this process, by confining their concern to the field of psychiatry, these criticisms have been misplaced.[1] For psychiatry has by no means distorted the mandate of medicine, but indeed, though perhaps at a pace faster than other medical specialities, is following instead some of the basic claims and directions of that profession. Nor is this extension into society the result of any professional 'imperialism', for this leads us to think of the issue in terms of misguided human efforts or motives. If we search for the 'why' of this phenomenon, we will see instead that it is rooted in our increasingly complex technological and bureaucratic system—a system which has led us down the path of the reluctant reliance on the expert.[2]

Quite frankly, what is presented in the following pages is not a

*This paper was written while the author was a consultant in residence at the Netherlands Institute for Preventive Medicine, Leiden. For their general encouragement and the opportunity to pursue this topic I will always be grateful.
It was presented at the Medical Sociology Conference of the British Sociological Association at Weston-Super-Mare in November 1971. My special thanks for their extensive editorial and substantive comments go to Egon Bittner, Mara Sanadi, Alwyn Smith, and Bruce Wheaton.

Irving Kenneth Zola

definitive argument but rather a case in progress. As such it draws
heavily on observations made in the United States, though similar
murmurings have long been echoed elsewhere.[3]

An Historical Perspective

The involvement of medicine in the management of society is not
new. It did not appear full-blown one day in the mid-twentieth century.
As Sigerist[4] has aptly claimed, medicine at base was always not only a
social science but an occupation whose very practice was inextricably
interwoven into society. This interdependence is perhaps best seen in
two branches of medicine which have had a built-in social emphasis
from the very start—psychiatry[5] and public health/preventive medicine.[6] Public health was always committed to changing social aspects
of life—from sanitary to housing to working conditions—and often
used the arm of the state (i.e. through laws and legal power) to gain its
ends (e.g. quarantines, vaccinations). Psychiatry's involvement in
society is a bit more difficult to trace, but taking the histories of psychiatry as data, then one notes the almost universal reference to one of
the early pioneers, a physician named Johan Weyer. His, and thus
psychiatry's involvement in social problems lay in the objection that
witches ought not to be burned; for they were not possessed by the
devil, but rather bedeviled by their problems—namely they were in-
sane. From its early concern with the issue of insanity as a defence in
criminal proceedings, psychiatry has grown to become the most dominant rehabilitative perspective in dealing with society's 'legal' deviants.
Psychiatry, like public health, has also used the legal powers of the
state in the accomplishment of its goals (i.e. the cure of the patient)
through the legal proceedings of involuntary commitment and its concomitant removal of certain rights and privileges.

This is not to say, however, that the rest of medicine has been
'socially' uninvolved. For a rereading of history makes it seem a matter
of degree. Medicine has long had both a *de jure* and a *de facto*
relation to institutions of social control. The *de jure* relationship is
seen in the idea of reportable diseases, wherein, if certain phenomena
occur in his practice, the physician is required to report them to the
appropriate authorities. While this seems somewhat straightforward
and even functional where certain highly contagious diseases are concerned, it is less clear where the possible spread of infection is not the
primary issue (e.g. with gunshot wounds, attempted suicide, drug use

Medicine as an Institution of Social Control

and what is now called child abuse). The *de facto* relation to social control can be argued through a brief look at the disruptions of the last two or three American Medical Association Conventions. For there the American Medical Association members—and really all ancillary health professions—were accused of practicing social control (the term used by the accusers was genocide) in first, *whom* they have traditionally treated with *what*—giving *better* treatment to more favoured clientele; and secondly, *what* they have treated—a more subtle form of discrimination in that, with limited resources, by focusing on some disease others are neglected. Here the accusation was that medicine has focused on the diseases of the rich and the established —cancer, heart disease, stroke—and ignored the diseases of the poor, such as malnutrition and still high infant mortality.

The Myth of Accountability.

Even if we acknowledge such a growing medical involvement, it is easy to regard it as primarily a 'good' one—which involves the steady destigmatization of many human and social problems. Thus Barbara Wootton was able to conclude:

> 'Without question . . . in the contemporary attitude toward antisocial behaviour, psychiatry and humanitarianism have marched hand in hand. Just because it is so much in keeping with the mental atmosphere of a scientifically-minded age, the medical treatment of social deviants has been a most powerful, perhaps even the most powerful, reinforcement of humanitarian impulses; for today the prestige of humane proposals is immensely enhanced if these are expressed in the idiom of medical science.'[7]

The assumption is thus readily made that such medical involvement in social problems leads to their removal from religious and legal scrutiny and thus from moral and punitive consequences. In turn the problems are placed under medical and scientific scrutiny and thus in objective and therapeutic circumstances.

The fact that we cling to such a hope is at least partly due to two cultural-historical blindspots—one regarding our notion of punishment and the other our notion of moral responsibility. Regarding the first, if there is one insight into human behaviour that the twentieth century should have firmly implanted, it is that punishment cannot be seen in merely physical terms, nor only from the perspective of the giver. Granted that capital offences are on the decrease, that whipping and torture seem to be disappearing, as is the use of chains and other physical restraints, yet our ability if not willingness to inflict human

Irving Kenneth Zola

anguish on one another does not seem similarly on the wane. The most effective forms of brain-washing deny any physical contact and the concept of relativism tells much about the psychological costs of even relative deprivation of tangible and intangible wants. Thus, when an individual because of his 'disease' and its treatment is forbidden to have intercourse with fellow human beings, is confined until cured, is forced to undergo certain medical procedures for his own good, perhaps deprived forever of the right to have sexual relations and/or produce children, *then* it is difficult for that patient *not* to view what is happening to him as punishment. This does not mean that medicine is the latest form of twentieth century torture, but merely that pain and suffering take many forms, and that the removal of a despicable inhumane procedure by current standards does not necessarily mean that its replacement will be all that beneficial. In part, the satisfaction in seeing the chains cast off by Pinel may have allowed us for far too long to neglect examining with what they had been replaced.

It is the second issue, that of responsibility, which requires more elaboration, for it is argued here that the medical model has had its greatest impact in the lifting of moral condemnation from the individual. While some sceptics note that while the individual is no longer condemned his disease still *is*, they do not go far enough. Most analysts have tried to make a distinction between illness and crime on the issue of personal responsibility.[8] The criminal is thought to be responsible and therefore accountable (or punishable) for his act, while the sick person is not. While the distinction does exist, it seems to be more a quantitative one rather than a qualitative one, with moral judgments but a pinprick below the surface. For instance, while it is probably true that individuals are no longer directly condemned for being sick, it does seem that much of this condemnation is merely displaced. Though his immoral character is not demonstrated in his having a disease, it becomes evident in what he does about it. Without seeming ludicrous, if one listed the traits of people who break appointments, fail to follow treatment regimen, or even delay in seeking medical aid, one finds a long list of 'personal flaws'. Such people seem to be ever ignorant of the consequences of certain diseases, inaccurate as to symptomatology, unable to plan ahead or find time, burdened with shame, guilt, neurotic tendencies, haunted with traumatic medical experiences or members of some lower status minority group—religious, ethnic, racial or socio-economic. In short, they appear to be a sorely troubled if

Medicine as an Institution of Social Control

not disreputable group of people.

The argument need not rest at this level of analysis, for it is not clear that the issues of morality and individual responsibility have been fully banished from the etiological scene itself. At the same time as the label 'illness' is being used to attribute 'diminished responsibility' to a whole host of phenomena, the issue of 'personal responsibility' seems to be re-emerging within medicine itself. Regardless of the truth and insights of the concepts of stress and the perspective of psychosomatics, whatever else they do, they bring man, *not* bacteria to the centre of the stage and lead thereby to a re-examination of the individual's rôle in his own demise, disability and even recovery.

The case, however, need not be confined to professional concepts and their degree of acceptance, for we can look at the beliefs of the man in the street. As most surveys have reported, when an individual is asked what caused his diabetes, heart disease, upper respiratory infection, etc., we may be comforted by the scientific terminology if not the accuracy of his answers. Yet if we follow this questioning with the probe: 'Why did you get X now?', or 'Of all the people in your community, family etc. who were exposed to X, why did you get . . . ?', then the rational scientific veneer is pierced and the concern with personal and moral responsibility emerges quite strikingly. Indeed the issue 'why me?' becomes of great concern and is generally expressed in quite moral terms of what they did wrong. It is possible to argue that here we are seeing a residue and that it will surely be different in the new generation. A recent experiment I conducted should cast some doubt on this. I asked a class of forty undergraduates, mostly aged seventeen, eighteen and nineteen, to recall the last time they were sick, disabled, or hurt and then to record how they did or would have communicated this experience to a child under the age of five. The purpose of the assignment had nothing to do with the issue of responsibility and it is worth noting that there was no difference in the nature of the response between those who had or had not actually encountered children during their 'illness'. The responses speak for themselves.

The opening words of the sick, injured person to the query of the child were:
'I feel bad'
'I feel bad all over'
'I have a bad leg'
'I have a bad eye'
'I have a bad stomach ache'
'I have a bad pain'
'I have a bad cold'

Irving Kenneth Zola

The reply of the child was inevitable:
'What did you do wrong?'
The 'ill person' in no case corrected the child's perspective but rather joined it at that level.
On bacteria
> 'There are good germs and bad germs and sometimes the bad germs . . .'

On catching a cold
> 'Well you know sometimes when your mother says, "Wrap up or be careful or you'll catch a cold", well I . . .'

On an eye sore
> 'When you use certain kinds of things (mascara) near your eye you must be very careful and I was not . . .'

On a leg injury
> 'You've always got to watch where you're going and I . . .'

Finally to the treatment phase:
On how drugs work
> 'You take this medicine and it attacks the bad parts . . .'

On how wounds are healed
> 'Within our body there are good forces and bad ones and when there is an injury, all the good ones . . .'

On pus
> 'That's the way the body gets rid of all its bad things . . .'

On general recovery
> 'If you are good and do all the things the doctor and your mother tell you, you will get better'.

In short, on nearly every level, from getting sick to recovering, a moral battle raged. This seems more than the mere anthropomorphizing of a phenomenon to communicate it more simply to children. Frankly it seems hard to believe that the English language is so poor that a *moral* rhetoric is needed to describe a supposedly amoral phenomenon—illness.

In short, despite hopes to the contrary, the rhetoric of illness by itself seems to provide no absolution from individual responsibility, accountability and moral judgment.

The Medicalizing of Society

Perhaps it is possible that medicine is not devoid of a potential for moralizing and social control. The first question becomes: 'what means are available to exercise it?' Freidson has stated a major aspect of the process most succinctly:

> 'The medical profession has first claim to jurisdiction over the label of illness and *anything* to which it may be attached, irrespective of its capacity to deal with it effectively.'[9]

For illustrative purposes this 'attaching' process may be categorized in four concrete ways: first, through the expansion of what in life is deemed relevant to the good practice of medicine; secondly, through

Medicine as an Institution of Social Control

the retention of absolute control over certain technical procedures; thirdly, through the retention of near absolute access to certain 'taboo' areas; and finally, through the expansion of what in medicine is deemed relevant to the good practice of life.

1. *The expansion of what in life is deemed relevant to the good practice of medicine*

The change of medicine's commitment from a specific etiological model of disease to a multi-causal one and the greater acceptance of the concepts of comprehensive medicine, psychosomatics, etc., have enormously expanded that which is or can be relevant to the understanding, treatment and even prevention of disease. Thus it is no longer necessary for the patient merely to divulge the symptoms of his body, but also the symptoms of daily living, his habits and his worries. Part of this is greatly facilitated in the 'age of the computer', for what might be too embarassing, or take too long, or be inefficient in a face-to-face encounter can now be asked and analyzed impersonally by the machine, and moreover be done before the patient ever sees the physician. With the advent of the computer a certain guarantee of privacy is necessarily lost, for while many physicians might have probed similar issues, the only place where the data were stored was in the mind of the doctor, and only rarely in the medical record. The computer, on the other hand, has a retrievable, transmittable and almost inexhaustible memory.

It is not merely, however, the nature of the data needed to make more accurate diagnoses and treatments, but the perspective which accompanies it—a perspective which pushes the physician far beyond his office and the exercise of technical skills. To rehabilitate or at least alleviate many of the ravages of chronic disease, it has become increasingly necessary to intervene to change permanently the habits of a patient's lifetime—be it of working, sleeping, playing or eating. In prevention the 'extension into life' becomes even deeper, since the very idea of primary prevention means getting there *before* the disease process starts. The physician must not only seek out his clientele but once found must often convince them that they must do something *now* and perhaps at a time when the potential patient feels well or not especially troubled. If this in itself does not get the prevention-oriented physician involved in the workings of society, then the nature of 'effective' mechanisms for intervention surely does, as illustrated by the

Irving Kenneth Zola

statement of a physician trying to deal with health problems in the ghetto:

> 'Any effort to improve the health of ghetto residents cannot be separated from equal and simultaneous efforts to remove the multiple social, political and economic restraints currently imposed on inner city residents.'[10]

Certain forms of social intervention and control emerge even when medicine comes to grips with some of its more traditional problems like heart disease and cancer. An increasing number of physicians feel that a change in diet may be the most effective deterrent to a number of cardio-vascular complications. They are, however, so perplexed as to how to get the general population to follow their recomendations that a leading article in a national magazine was entitled 'To Save the Heart: Diet by Decree?'[11] It is obvious that there is an increasing pressure for more explicit sanctions against the tobacco companies and against high users to force both to desist. And what will be the implications of even stronger evidence which links age at parity, frequency of sexual intercourse, or the lack of male circumcision to the incidence of cervical cancer, can be left to our imagination!

2. *Through the retention of absolute control over certain technical procedures*

In particular this refers to skills which in certain jurisdictions are the very operational and legal definition of the practice of medicine— the right to do surgery and prescribe drugs. Both of these take medicine far beyond concern with ordinary organic disease.

In surgery this is seen in several different sub-specialities. The plastic surgeon has at least participated in, if not helped perpetuate, certain aesthetic standards. What once was a practice confined to restoration has now expanded beyond the correction of certain traumatic or even congenital deformities to the creation of new physical properties, from size of nose to size of breast, as well as dealing with certain phenomena—wrinkles, sagging, etc.—formerly associated with the 'natural' process of ageing. Alterations in sexual and reproductive functioning have long been a medical concern. Yet today the frequency of hysterectomies seems not so highly correlated as one might think with the presence of organic disease. (What avenues the very possibility of sex change will open is anyone's guess.) Transplantations, despite their still relative infrequency, have had a tremendous effect on our very notions of death and dying. And at the other end of life's continuum,

Medicine as an Institution of Social Control

since abortion is still essentially a surgical procedure, it is to the physician-surgeon that society is turning (and the physician-surgeon accepting) for criteria and guidelines.

In the exclusive right to prescribe and thus pronounce on and and regulate drugs, the power of the physician is even more awesome. Forgetting for the moment our obsession with youth's 'illegal' use of drugs, any observer can see, judging by sales alone, that the greatest increase in drug use over the last ten years has not been in the realm of treating any organic disease but in treating a large number of psychosocial states. Thus we have drugs for nearly every mood:

    to help us sleep or keep us awake
    to enhance our appetite or decrease it
    to tone down our energy level or to increase it
    to relieve our depression or stimulate our interest.

Recently the newspapers and more popular magazines, including some medical and scientific ones, have carried articles about drugs which may be effective peace pills or anti-aggression tablets, enhance our memory, our perception, our intelligence and our vision (spiritually or otherwise). This led to the easy prediction:

    'We will see new drugs, more targeted, more specific and more potent than anything we have . . . And many of these would be for people we would call healthy.'[12]

This statement incidentally was made not by a visionary science fiction writer but by a former commissioner of the United States Food and Drug Administration.

3. *Through the retention of near absolute access to certain 'taboo' areas*

These 'taboo' areas refer to medicine's almost exclusive licence to examine and treat that most personal of individual possessions—the inner workings of our bodies and minds. My contention is that if anything can be shown in some way to effect the workings of the body and to a lesser extent the mind, then it can be labelled an 'illness' itself or jurisdictionally 'a medical problem'. In a sheer statistical sense the import of this is especially great if we look at only four such problems—ageing, drug addiction, alcoholism and pregnancy. The first and last were once regarded as normal natural processes and the middle two as human foibles and weaknesses. Now this has changed and to some extent medical specialities have emerged to meet these new needs. Numerically this expands medicine's involvement not only in a longer

Irving Kenneth Zola

span of human existence, but it opens the possibility of medicine's services to millions if not billions of people. In the United States at least, the implication of declaring alcoholism a disease (the possible import of a pending Supreme Court decision as well as laws currently being introduced into several state legislatures) would reduce arrests in many jurisdictions by ten to fifty per cent. and transfer such 'offenders' when 'discovered' directly to a medical facility. It is pregnancy, however, which produces the most illuminating illustration. For, again in the United States, it was barely seventy years ago that virtually all births and the concomitants of birth occurred outside the hospital as well as outside medical supervision. I do not frankly have a documentary history, but as this medical claim was solidified, so too was medicine's claim to a whole host of related processes: not only to birth but to prenatal, postnatal, and pediatric care; not only to conception but to infertility; not only to the process of reproduction but to the process and problems of sexual activity itself; not only when life begins (in the issue of abortion) but whether it should be allowed to begin at all (e.g. in genetic counselling).

Partly through this foothold in the 'taboo' areas and partly through the simple reduction of other resources, the physician is increasingly becoming the choice for help for many with personal and social problems. Thus a recent British study reported that within a five year period there had been a notable increase (from twenty-five to forty-one per cent.) in the proportion of the population willing to consult the physician with a personal problem.[13]

4. *Through the expansion of what in medicine is deemed relevant to the good practice of life*

Though in some ways this is the most powerful of all 'the medicalizing of society' processes, the point can be made simply. Here we refer to the use of medical rhetoric and evidence in the arguments to advance any cause. For what Wootton attributed to psychiatry is no less true of medicine. To paraphrase her, today the prestige of *any* proposal is immensely enhanced, if not justified, when it is expressed in the idiom of medical science. To say that many who use such labels are not professionals only begs the issue, for the public is only taking its cues from professionals who increasingly have been extending their expertise into the social sphere or have called for such an extension.[14] In politics one hears of the healthy or unhealthy economy or state.

Medicine as an Institution of Social Control

More concretely, the physical and mental health of American presidential candidates has been an issue in the last four elections and a recent book claimed to link faulty political decisions with faulty health.[15] For years we knew that the environment was unattractive, polluted, noisy and in certain ways dying, but now we learn that its death may not be unrelated to our own demise. To end with a rather mundane if depressing example, there has always been a constant battle between school authorities and their charges on the basis of dress and such habits as smoking, but recently the issue was happily resolved for a local school administration when they declared that such restrictions were necessary for reasons of health.

The Potential and Consequences of Medical Control

The list of daily activities to which health can be related is ever growing and with the current operating perspective of medicine it seems infinitely expandable. The reasons are manifold. It is not merely that medicine has extended its jurisdiction to cover new problems,[16] or that doctors are professionally committed to finding disease,[17] nor even that society keeps creating disease.[18] For if none of these obtained today we would still find medicine exerting an enormous influence on society. The most powerful empirical stimulus for this is the realization of how much everyone has or believes he has something organically wrong with him, or put more positively, how much can be done to make one feel, look or function better.

The rates of 'clinical entities' found on surveys or by periodic health examinations range upwards from fifty to eighty per cent. of the population studied.[19] The Peckham study found that only nine per cent. of their study group were free from clinical disorder. Moreover, they were even wary of this figure and noted in a footnote that, first, some of these nine per cent. had subsequently died of a heart attack, and, secondly, that the majority of those without disorder were under the age of five.[20] We used to rationalize that this high level of prevalence did not, however, translate itself into action since not only are rates of medical utilization not astonishingly high but they also have not gone up appreciably. Some recent studies, however, indicate that we may have been looking in the wrong place for this medical action. It has been noted in the United States and the United Kingdom that within a given twenty-four to thirty-six hour period, from fifty to eighty per cent. of the adult population have taken one or more 'medical' drugs.[21]

497

Irving Kenneth Zola

The belief in the omnipresence of disorder is further enhanced by a reading of the scientific, pharmacological and medical literature, for there one finds a growing litany of indictments of 'unhealthy' life activities. From sex to food, from aspirins to clothes, from driving your car to riding the surf, it seems that under certain conditions, or in combination with certain other substances or activities or if done too much or too little, virtually anything can lead to certain medical problems. In short, I at least have finally been convinced that living is injurious to health. This remark is not meant as facetiously as it may sound. But rather every aspect of our daily life has in it elements of risk to health.

These facts take on particular importance not only when health becomes a paramount value in society, but also a phenomenon whose diagnosis and treatment has been restricted to a certain group. For this means that that group, perhaps unwittingly, is in a position to exercise great control and influence about what we should and should not do to attain that 'paramount value'.

Freidson in his recent book *Profession of Medicine* has very cogently analyzed why the expert in general and the medical expert in particular should be granted a certain autonomy in his researches, his diagnosis and his recommended treatments.[22] On the other hand, when it comes to constraining or directing human behaviour *because* of the data of his researches, diagnosis, and treatment, a different situation obtains. For in these kinds of decisions it seems that too often the physician is guided not by his technical knowledge but by his values, or values latent in his very techniques.

Perhaps this issue of values can be clarified by reference to some not so randomly chosen medical problems: drug safety, genetic counselling and automated multiphasic testing.

The issue of drug safety should seem straightforward, but both words in that phrase apparently can have some interesting flexibility— namely what is a drug and what is safe. During Prohibition in the United States alcohol was medically regarded as a drug and was often prescribed as a medicine. Yet in recent years, when the issue of dangerous substances and drugs has come up for discussion in medical circles, alcohol has been officially excluded from the debate. As for safety, many have applauded the A.M.A.'s judicious position in declaring the need for much more extensive, longitudinal research on marihuana and their unwillingness to back legalization until much more data are in. This applause might be muted if the public read the 1970

Medicine as an Institution of Social Control

Food and Drug Administration's 'Blue Ribbon' Committee Report on the safety, quality and efficacy of *all* medical drugs commercially and legally on the market since 1938.[23] Though appalled at the lack and quality of evidence of any sort, few recommendations were made for the withdrawal of drugs from the market. Moreover there are no recorded cases of anyone dying from an overdose or of extensive adverse side effects from marihuana use, but the literature on the adverse effects of a whole host of 'medical drugs' on the market today is legion.

It would seem that the value positions of those on both sides of the abortion issue needs little documenting, but let us pause briefly at a field where 'harder' scientists are at work—genetics. The issue of genetic counselling, or whether life should be allowed to begin at all, can only be an ever increasing one. As we learn more and more about congenital, inherited disorders or predispositions, and as the population size for whatever reason becomes more limited, then, inevitably, there will follow an attempt to improve the quality of the population which shall be produced. At a conference on the more limited concern of what to do when there is a documented probability of the offspring of certain unions being damaged, a position was taken that it was not necessary to pass laws or bar marriages that might produce such offspring. Recognizing the power and influence of medicine and the doctor, one of those present argued:

> 'There is no reason why sensible people could not be dissuaded from marrying if they know that one out of four of their children is likely to inherit a disease.'[24]

There are in this statement certain values on marriage and what it is or could be that, while they may be popular, are not necessarily shared by all. Thus, in addition to presenting the argument against marriage, it would seem that the doctor should—if he were to engage in the issue at all—present at the same time some of the other alternatives:

> Some 'parents' could be willing to live with the risk that out of four children, three may turn out fine.
> Depending on the diagnostic procedures available they could take the risk and if indications were negative abort.
> If this risk were too great but the desire to bear children was there, and depending on the type of problem, artificial insemination might be a possibility.
> Barring all these and not wanting to take any risk, they could adopt children.
> Finally, there is the option of being married without having any children.

It is perhaps appropriate to end with a seemingly innocuous and technical advance in medicine, automatic multiphasic testing. It has

Irving Kenneth Zola

been a procedure hailed as a boon to aid the doctor if not replace him. While some have questioned the validity of all those test-results and still others fear that it will lead to second class medicine for already underprivileged populations, it is apparent that its major use to date and in the future may not be in promoting health or detecting disease to prevent it. Thus three large institutions are now or are planning to make use of this method, not to treat people, but to 'deselect' them. The armed services use it to weed out the physically and mentally unfit, insurance companies to reject 'uninsurables' and large industrial firms to point out 'high risks'. At a recent conference representatives of these same institutions were asked what responsibility they did or would recognize to those whom they have just informed that they have been 'rejected' because of some physical or mental anomaly. They calmly and universally stated: none—neither to provide them with any appropriate aid nor even to ensure that they get or be put in touch with any help.

Conclusion

C. S. Lewis warned us more than a quarter of a century ago that 'man's power over Nature is really the power of some men over other men, with Nature as their instrument.' The same could be said regarding man's power over health and illness, for the labels health and illness are remarkable 'depoliticizers' of an issue. By locating the source and the treatment of problems in an individual, other levels of intervention are effectively closed. By the very acceptance of a specific behaviour as an 'illness' and the definition of illness as an undesirable state, the issue becomes not whether to deal with a particular problem, but *how* and *when*.[25] Thus the debate over homosexuality, drugs or abortion becomes focused on the degree of sickness attached to the phenomenon in question or the extent of the health risk involved. And the more principled, more perplexing, or even moral issue, of *what* freedom should an individual have over his or her own body is shunted aside.

As stated in the very beginning this 'medicalizing of society' is as much a result of medicine's potential as it is of society's wish for medicine to use that potential. Why then has the focus been more on the medical potential than on the social desire? In part it is a function of space, but also of political expediency. For the time rapidly may be approaching when recourse to the populace's wishes may be impossible.

Medicine as an Institution of Social Control

Let me illustrate this with the statements of two medical scientists who, if they read this essay, would probably dismiss all my fears as groundless. The first was commenting on the ethical, moral, and legal procedures of the sex change operation:

'Physicians generally consider it unethical to destroy or alter tissue except in the presence of disease or deformity. The interference with a person's natural procreative function entails definite moral tenets, by which not only physicians but also the general public are influenced. The administration of physical harm as treatment for mental or behavioral problems —as corporal punishment, lobotomy for unmanageable psychotics and sterilization of criminals—is abhorrent in our society.'[26]

Here he states, as almost an absolute condition of human nature, something which is at best a recent phenomenon. He seems to forget that there were laws promulgating just such procedures through much of the twentieth century, that within the past few years at least one Californian jurist ordered the sterilization of an unwed mother as a condition of probation, and that such procedures were done by Nazi scientists and physicians as part of a series of medical experiments. More recently, there is the misguided patriotism of the cancer researchers under contract to the United States Department of Defence who allowed their dying patients to be exposed to massive doses of radiation to analyze the psychological and physical results of simulated nuclear fall-out. True the experiments were stopped, but not until they had been going on for *eleven* years.

The second statement is by Francis Crick at a conference on the implications of certain genetic findings:

'Some of the wild genetic proposals will never be adopted because the people will simply not stand for them.'[27]

Note where his emphasis is: on the people not the scientist. In order, however, for the people to be concerned, to act and to protest, they must first be aware of what is going on. Yet in the very privatized nature of medical practice, plus the continued emphasis that certain expert judgments must be free from public scrutiny, there are certain processes which will prevent the public from ever knowing what has taken place and thus from doing something about it. Let me cite two examples.

Recently, in a European country, I overheard the following conversation in a kidney dialysis unit. The chief was being questioned about whether or not there were self-help groups among his patients. 'No' he almost shouted 'that is the last thing we want. Already the patients are sharing to much knowledge while they sit in the waiting room, thus making our task increasingly difficult. We are working now on a procedure to prevent them from ever meeting with one another.'

Irving Kenneth Zola

The second example removes certain information even further from public view.

> The issue of fluoridation in the U.S. has been for many years a hot political one. It was in the political arena because, in order to fluoridate local water supplies, the decision in many jurisdictions had to be put to a popular referendum. And when it was, it was often defeated. A solution was found and a series of state laws were passed to make fluoridation a public health decision and to be treated, as all other public health decisions, by the medical officers best qualified to decide questions of such a technical, scientific and medical nature.

Thus the issue at base here is the question of what factors are actually of a solely technical, scientific and medical nature !

To return to our opening caution, this paper is not an attack on medicine so much as on a situation in which we find ourselves in the latter part of the twentieth century; for the medical area is the arena or the example *par excellence* of today's identity crisis—what is or will become of man. It is the battleground, not because there are visible threats and oppressors, but because they are almost invisible; not because the perspective, tools and practitioners of medicine and the other helping professions are evil, but because they are not. It is so frightening because there are elements here of the banality of evil so uncomfortably written about by Hannah Arendt.[28] But here the danger is greater, for not only is the process masked as a technical, scientific, objective one, but one done for our own good. A few years ago a physician speculated on what, based on current knowledge, would be the composite picture of an individual with a low risk of developing atherosclerosis or coronary-artery disease. He would be:

> ' . . . an effeminate municipal worker or embalmer completely lacking in physical or mental alertness and without drive, ambition, or competitive spirit; who has never attempted to meet a deadline of any kind; a man with poor appetite, subsisting on fruits and vegetables laced with corn and whale oil, detesting tobacco, spurning ownership of radio, television, or motorcar, with full head of hair but scrawny and unathletic appearance, yet constantly straining his puny muscles by exercise. Low in income, blood pressure, blood sugar, uric acid and cholesterol, he has been taking nicotinic acid, pyridoxine, and long term anto-coagulant therapy ever since his prophylactic castration.'[29]

Thus I fear with Freidson:

> 'A profession and a society which are so concerned with physical and functional wellbeing as to sacrifice civil liberty and moral integrity must inevitably press for a 'scientific' environment similar to that provided laying hens on progressive chicken farms—hens who produce eggs industriously and have no disease or other cares.'[30]

Nor does it really matter that if, instead of the above depressing picture, we were guaranteed six more inches in height, thirty more

Medicine as an Institution of Social Control

years of life, or drugs to expand our potentialities and potencies; we should still be able to ask: what do six more inches matter, in what kind of environment will the thirty additional years be spent, or who will decide what potentialities and potencies will be expanded and what curbed.

I must confess that given the road down which so much expertise has taken us, I am willing to live with some of the frustrations and even mistakes that will follow when the authority for many decisions becomes shared with those whose lives and activities are involved. For I am convinced that patients have so much to teach to their doctors as do students their professors and children their parents.

Brandeis University.

[1] T. Szasz: *The Myth of Mental Illness*, Harper and Row, New York, 1961; and R. Leifer: *In the Name of Mental Health*, Science House, New York, 1969.

[2] E.g. A. Toffler: *Future Shock*, Random House, New York, 1970; and P. E. Slater: *The Pursuit of Loneliness*, Beacon Press, Boston, 1970.

[3] Such as B. Wootton: *Social Science and Social Pathology*, Allen and Unwin, London, 1959.

[4] H. Sigerist: *Civilization and Disease*, Cornell University Press, New York, 1943.

[5] M. Foucault: *Madness and Civilization*, Pantheon, New York, 1965; and Szasz: *op. cit.*

[6] G. Rosen: *A History of Public Health*, MD Publications, New York, 1955; and G. Rosen: 'The Evolution of Social Medicine', in H. E. Freeman, S. Levine and L. G. Reeder (eds.): *Handbook of Medical Sociology*, Prentice-Hall, Englewood Cliffs, N.J., 1963, pp. 17-61.

[7] Wootton: *op. cit.*, p. 206.

[8] Two excellent discussions are found in V. Aubert and S. Messinger: 'The Criminal and the Sick', *Inquiry*, Vol. 1, 1958, pp. 137-160; and E. Freidson: *Profession of Medicine*, Dodd-Mead, New York, 1970, pp. 205-277.

[9] Freidson: *op. cit.*, p. 251.

[10] J. C. Norman: 'Medicine in the Ghetto', *New Engl. J. Med.*, Vol. 281, 1969, p. 1271.

[11] 'To Save the Heart; Diet by Decree?', *Time Magazine*, 10th January, 1968, p. 42.

[12] J. L. Goddard quoted in the *Boston Globe*, August 7th, 1966.

[13] K. Dunnell and A. Cartwright: *Medicine Takers, Prescribers and Hoarders*, in press.

Irving Kenneth Zola

[14] E.g. S. Alinsky: 'The Poor and the Powerful', in *Poverty and Mental Health,* Psychiat. Res. Rep. No. 21 of the Amer. Psychiat. Ass., January 1967; and B. Wedge: 'Psychiatry and International Affairs', *Science,* Vol. 157, 1961, pp. 281-285.

[15] H. L'Etang: *The Pathology of Leadership,* Hawthorne Books, New York, 1970.

[16] Szasz: *op. cit.;* and Leifer: *op. cit.*

[17] Freidson: *op. cit.;* and T. Scheff: 'Preferred Errors in Diagnoses', *Medical Care,* Vol. 2, 1964, pp. 166-172.

[18] R. Dubos: *The Mirage of Health,* Doubleday, Garden City, N.Y., 1959; and R. Dubos: *Man Adapting,* Yale University Press, 1965.

[19] E.g. the general summaries of J. W. Meigs: 'Occupational Medicine', *New Engl. J. Med.,* Vol. 264, 1961, pp. 861-867; and G. S. Siegel: *Periodic Health Examinations—Abstracts from the Literature,* Publ. Hlth. Serv. Publ. No. 1010, U.S. Government Printing Office, Washington D.C., 1963.

[20] I. H. Pearse and L. H. Crocker: *Biologists in Search of Material,* Faber and Faber, London, 1938; and I. H. Pearse and L. H. Crocker: *The Peckham Experiment,* Allen and Unwin, London, 1949.

[21] Dunnell and Cartwright: *op. cit.;* and K. White, A. Andjelkovic, R. J. C. Pearson, J. H. Mabry, A. Ross and O. K. Sagan: 'International Comparisons of Medical Care Utilization', *New Engl. J. of Med.,* Vol. 277, 1967, pp. 516-522.

[22] Freidson: *op. cit.*

[23] *Drug Efficiency Study—Final Report to the Commissioner of Food and Drugs,* Food and Drug Adm. Med. Nat. Res. Council, Nat. Acad. Sci., Washington D.C., 1969.

[24] Reported in L. Eisenberg: 'Genetics and the Survival of the Unfit', *Harper's Magazine,* Vol. 232, 1966, p. 57.

[25] This general case is argued more specifically in I. K. Zola: *Medicine, Morality, and Social Problems—Some Implications of the Label Mental Illness,* Paper presented at the Amer. Ortho-Psychiat. Ass., March 20-23, 1968.

[26] D. H. Russell: 'The Sex Conversion Controversy', *New Engl. J. Med.,* Vol. 279, 1968, p. 536.

[27] F. Crick reported in *Time Magazine,* April 19th, 1971.

[28] H. Arendt: *Eichmann in Jerusalem—A Report on the Banality of Evil,* Viking Press, New York, 1963.

[29] G. S. Myers quoted in L. Lasagna: *Life, Death and the Doctor,* Alfred Knouf, New York, 1968, pp. 215-216.

[30] Freidson: *op. cit., p.* 354.

[19]

Peter Conrad

Types of medical social control

Abstract   In recent years there has been considerable interest in the social control
aspects of medicine. While medical social control has been conceptualized in several ways, the concern here is with the medical control of
deviant behavior, an aspect of what has been called the medicalization
of deviance. Medical social control is defined as the ways in which
medicine functions (wittingly or unwittingly) to secure adherence to
social norms: specifically by using medical means or authority to
minimize, eliminate or normalize deviant behavior. This paper cata-
logues and illustrates a broad range of medical control of deviance,
and in so doing conceptualizes three major types of medical social
control: medical technology, medical collaboration, and medical
ideology. Numerous examples are provided for each. These concepts
aid in revealing the breadth of medical social control and the extent
and limitations of professional dominance over the medical social
control of deviance.

In recent years there has been considerable interest in the social control
aspects of medicine. Medicine was first conceptualized as an agent of
social control by Parsons (1) in his seminal essay on the 'sick role'.
Freidson (2) and Zola (3) have elucidated the jurisdictional mandate
the medical profession has over anything that can be labeled an illness,
regardless of its ability to deal with it effectively. The boundaries of
medicine are elastic and increasingly expansive (4), and some analysts
have expressed concern at the increasing medicalization of life (5).
While medical social control has been conceptualized in several ways,
including professional control of colleagues (6) and control of the
micro-politics of doctor-patient interaction (7), the focus here is
narrower. My concern is with the medical control of deviant behavior,
an aspect of what has been called the medicalization of deviance (8, 9).
Thus, by medical social control I mean the ways in which medicine
functions (wittingly or unwittingly) to secure adherence to social
norms; specifically, by using medical means to minimize, eliminate, or
normalize deviant behavior. While there has been considerable research
on medical social control, there has been no attempt to order and
analyze the variety of medical controls. The purpose of this paper is to
cataglogue and illustrate the broad range of medical controls of deviance,

Sociology of Health and Illness Vol. 1 No. 1 1979
© R. K. P. 1979   0141-9889/79/0101-0001 $1.50/1

2   Conrad

conceptualize three major types of medical social control, and explicate the relation of the medical profession to these types of social control.

On the most abstract level, medical social control is the acceptance of a medical perspective as the dominant definition of certain phenomena. When medical perspectives of problems and their solutions become dominant, they diminish competing definitions. This is particularly true of problems related to bodily functioning and in areas where medical technology can demonstrate effectiveness (e.g., immunization, contraception, anti-bacterial drugs), and is increasingly the case for behavioral and social problems (10). This underlies the construction of medical norms (e.g., what is healthy) and the 'enforcement' of both medical and social norms. Medical social control also includes medical advice, counsel, and information that is part of the general stock of knowledge: eat a well-balanced diet, cigarette smoking causes cancer, overweight increases health risks, exercising regularly is healthy, teeth should be brushed twice daily, etc. Such aphorisms, even when unheeded, serve as roadsigns for desirable behavior. At a more concrete level, medical social control is professional medical intervention qua medical treatment (although it may include some types of self-treatment). This intervention aims at returning sick individuals to a state of health and to their conventional social roles, adjusting them to new (e.g., impaired) roles, or, short of these, making individuals more comfortable with their condition [cf. 1, 2]. Medical social control of deviant behavior is usually a variant of medical intervention that seeks to eliminate, modify, isolate or regulate behavior, socially defined as deviant, with medical means and in the name of health.

Traditionally, psychiatry and public health have served as modes of medical control. Psychiatry's social control functions with mental illness, especially in terms of institutionalization, have been widely analyzed (e.g., 11, 12). Recently it has been argued that psychotherapy itself is an agent of social control and a supporter of the status quo (13, 14). Public health medicine's mandate, the control and elimination of conditions and diseases that are deemed a threat to the health of a community, is more diffuse. It operates as a control agent by setting and enforcing certain 'health' standards in the home, workplace, and community (food, water, sanitation, etc.) and by identifying, preventing, treating, and, if necessary, isolating persons with communicable diseases (15). The clearest example of the latter is the detection of venereal disease. Indeed, public health has exerted considerable coercive power in attempting to prevent the spread of infectious disease.

There are a number of types of medical control of deviance. The most common forms of medical social control include medicalizing deviant behavior – i.e., defining the behavior as an illness or a symptom of an illness or underlying disease – and subsequent direct medical intervention (9). This medical social control takes three general forms: medical technology, medical collaboration, and medical ideology. These 'ideal types' are not entirely discrete. We separate them here in an attempt to 'unpack' the elements of medical social control and catalogue the range of possible controls.

The growth of specialized and technological medicine and the concomitant development of *medical technology* has produced an armamentarium of medical controls. Psychotechnologies, which include various forms of medical and behavioral technologies (16), are the most common types of medical control of deviance. Since the emergence of phenothiazine medications in the early 1950s for the treatment and control of mental disorder. there has been a virtual explosion in the development and use of psychoactive medications that control behavioral deviance: tranquilizers like Librium and Valium for anxiety, nervousness, and general malaise; stimulant medications for hyperactive children: amphetamines for overeating and obesity; Antabuse for alcoholism: Methadone for heroin, and many others.[1] These pharmaceutical discoveries, aggressively promoted by a highly profitable and powerful drug industry (17), often become the treatment of choice for deviant behavior. They are easily administered, under professional medical control, quite potent in their effects (i.e.. controlling, modifying, and even eliminating behavior), and are generally less expensive than other treatments and controls (e.g., hospitalization, altering environments, long-term psychotherapy).

Psychosurgery, surgical procedures meant to correct certain 'brain dysfunctions' alleged to cause deviant behavior, was developed first in the early 1930s as prefrontal lobotomy as a treatment for mental illness. Early forms of psychosurgery fell into disrepute in the' early 1950s because the 'side effects' (general passivity, difficulty with abstract thinking) were deemed too undesirable and many patients remained institutionalized (and besides, new psychoactive medications were becoming available to control the mentally ill). During this period, however, approximately 40,000 to 50,000 such operations were performed in the United States. In the late 1960 a new and technologically more sophisticated variant of psycho-surgery (including laser technology and brain implants) emerged and was heralded by some as a treatment of uncontrollable violent outbursts (18, 19). While psychosurgery for violence has been criticized from both within the medical profession and without (20) and relatively few operations have actually been performed. in 1976 a blue-ribbon national commission reporting to the US Department of Health, Education and Welfare endorsed the use of

4   Conrad

psychosurgery as having 'potential merit' and judged its risks 'not excessive'. This may encourage an increased utilization of this form of medical control.[2]

Behavior modification. a psychotechnology based on B. F. Skinner and other behaviorist learning theories, has been adopted by some medical professionals as a treatment modality. A variety of types and variations of behavior modification exist (token economies, positive reinforcement schedules, aversive conditioning, operant conditioning, etc.). While they are not medical technologies per se, these have been used by physicians for the treatment of mental illness. mental retardation. homosexuality, violence, hyperactive children. autism, phobias. alcoholism, drug addiction. and other disorders. An irony of the medical use of behavior modification is that behaviorism explicitly denies the medical model (that behavior is a symptom of illness) and adopts an environmental, albeit still individual, solution to the problem. This has not, however, hindered its adoption by medical professionals, perhaps because physicians frequently have been only able to treat 'symptoms' rather than causes, anyway.

Human genetics is one of the most exciting and rapidly expanding areas of medical knowledge. Genetic screening and genetic counseling are becoming more commonplace. Genetic causes are proposed for such a variety of human problems as alcoholism, hyperactivity. learning disabilities. schizophrenia. mania-depressive psychosis. homosexuality. and mental retardation. At this point in time. apart from specific genetic disorders such as pheylketonuria (PKU) and certain forms of retardation, genetic explanations tend to be general theories. with only minimal (if any) empirical support. and are not the level at which medical intervention occurs. The most well-publicized genetic theory of deviant behaviour is that an XYY chromosome arrangement is a determinant factor in 'criminal tendencies'. While this XYY research has been severely questioned (21) the controversy surrounding it may be a harbinger of things to come. Genetic anomalies may be discovered to have a correlation with deviant behavior and may become a causal explanation for this behavior. Medical control. in the form of genetic counseling (22), may discourage parents from having offspring with a high risk (e.g.. 25 per cent) of genetic impairment. Clearly, the potentials for medical control go far beyond present use; one could imagine the possibility of licensing selected parents (with proper genes) to have children, and further manipulating gene arrangements to produce or eliminate certain traits.

Medicine acts not only as an independent agent of social control (as above) but frequently *medical collaboration* with other authorities serves social control functions. Such collaboration includes roles as information provider. gatekeeper, institutional agent, and technician. These interdependent medical control functions highlight the interwoven position of medicine in the fabric of society. Historically, medical personnel have reported information on gunshot wounds and venereal disease to state authorities. More recently, these have been extended to reporting 'child abuse' to child welfare or law enforcement agencies.

The medical profession's status as official designator of the 'sick role', which imbues the physician with authority to define particular kinds of deviance as illness and exempt the patient from certain role obligations. is a general gatekeeping and social control task. In some instances the physician functions as a specific gatekeeper for special exemptions from conventional norms: here the exemptions are authorized due to illness, disease or disability. The classic example is the so-called 'insanity defense' in capital crime cases. Other more commonplace examples include: medical deferment from the draft or a medical discharge from the military; requiring doctors' notes to legitimize missing an examination or excessive absences in school; and, before abortion was legalized, obtaining two psychiatrists' letters testifying to the therapeutic necessity of the abortion. Halleck (13) has termed this 'the power of medical excuse'. In a slightly different vein, but still forms of gatekeeping and medical excuse, are medical examinations for disability or workman's compensation benefits. Medical reports required for insurance coverage and employment, or medical certification of an epileptic as seizure-free to obtain a driver's license, are also gatekeeping activities.

Physicians in total instutitons have one or two roles. In some institutions. such as schools for the retarded or mental hospitals, they are usually the administrative authority; in others, such as the military or prisons, they are employees of the administration. In total institutions. medicine's roles as an agent of social control (for the institution) is more apparent. In both the military and prisons, physicians have the power to confer the sick role and to offer medical excuse for deviance (cf. 23, 24). For example, medical discharges and sick call are available designations for deviant behavior. As physicians are in the hire of and paid by the institution, it is difficult for them to be fully an agent of the patient, engendering built-in role strains. An extreme example is in wartime conflict when the physician's mandate is to return the soldier to combat duty as soon as possible. Under some circumstances, physicians act as direct agents of control by prescribing medications to control unruly or disorderly inmates or to help a 'neurotic' adjust to the conditions of total institution. In such cases, 'captive professionals' (23) are more likely to become the agent of the institution than the agent of the individual patient.

6   Conrad

Under rather rare circumstances, physicians may become 'mere technicians', applying the sanctions of another authority who hires their medical skills. An extreme, although more complex, example would be the behavior of the experimental and death physicians in Nazi Germany. A more mundane example is physicians who perform court-ordered sterilizations (24). Perhaps one could imagine sometime in the future, if the death penalty becomes commonplace again, physicians administering drugs as the 'humanitarian' and painless executioner.[3]

Medical ideology is a type of social control that involves defining a behavior or condition as an illness primarily because of the social and ideological benefits accrued by conceptualizing it in medical terms. It includes adopting medical or quasi-medical imagery or vocabulary in conceptualizing and treating the problem. Medical ideology uses medical authority by way of language. The latent functions of medical ideology may benefit the individual or the dominant interests in society or both, but are quite separate from any organic basis for illness or any available treatment. Waitzkin and Waterman (25) call one latent function of medicalization 'secondary gain', arguing that assumption of the sick role can fulfill personality and individual needs (e.g., gaining nurturance or attention) or legitimize personal failure (25). One of the most important functions of the disease model of alcoholism and to a lesser extent drug addiction is the secondary gain of removing blame from, and constructing a shield against condemnation of, individuals for their deviant behavior. Alcoholics Anonymous, a non-medical quasi-religious self-help organization, adopted a variant of the medical model of alcoholism quite independently from the medical profession. One suspects the secondary gain serves their purposes well.

Disease designations can support social interests and institutions. A poignant example is prominent New Orleans physician S. W. Cartwright's antebellum conceptualization of the disease drapetomania, a condition that only affected slaves. Its major symptom was running away from their masters (27). Medical conceptions and controls often support dominant social values and morality: the 19th-century Victorian conceptualization of the illness of and addiction to masturbation and the medical treatments developed to control this disease make chilling reading in the 1970s (28). The recent Soviet labeling of political dissidents as mentally ill is a further example of the manipulation of illness designations to support dominant political and social institutions (29). These examples highlight the socio-political nature of illness designations in general (30).

In actual operation, the types of medical social control described above do not necessarily exist as discrete entities, but are found in combination with one another. For example, court-ordered sterilization or medical prescribing of drugs to unruly nursing home patients combines both technological and collaborative aspects of medical control; legitimating disability status is both ideological and collaborative; and treating Soviet dissidents with drugs for their mental illness combines all three aspects of medical social control. We treat them as analytically separate to explicate and clarify the various faces of medical social control.

Medical social control and the medical profession

This section of the paper discusses the relation of the medical profession to each type of medical social control. Given the dominance of the medical profession in western society (2, 31), one might suspect that medical control of deviance was squarely in the hands of the medical profession. A number of writers have assumed medical hegemony, monopoly or imperialism in the expansion of the sphere of medical control (4, 32). While in individual cases this may present an accurate picture, upon closer inspection we find that the determination and control of each of these controls varies considerably. We identify three factors affecting the medical profession's control of medical controls: the necessity of active involvement of medical professionals, the ability of non-medical segments of society to limit or demand medical social control, and the source of instigation of medical control.

Medical technology and collaboration both require the active participation of medical professionals. Only the medical profession has the license and mandate to legally use behavior-controlling drugs and to perform surgery. Without the involvement of physicians, medical technology cannot be implemented. Medical ideology, on the other hand, can exist without the active participation of medical professionals. Frequently non-medical groups, such as Alcoholics Anonymous and the early juvenile court (33), adopt a medical ideology or rhetoric in their social control work. The involvement of the medical profession is marginal at best, and more likely, non-existent. Fledgling professions or semi-professions (34) may adopt a medical ideology in their work in order to benefit from the prestigious cloak of medicine and enhance their own professional status.

The ability of agents outside of medicine to require or limit the use of medical controls varies for the three types of control. The application of medical technology by and large belongs solely to the medical profession. This medical monopoly may be somewhat restricted by governmental regulatory agencies such as the Food and Drug Administration, by the courts, or through special legislation. But the actual limitations

8   Conrad

on medical control by these agencies is limited – it is usually the result of a specific controversy (e.g.. XYZ research with newborns). the specific restrictions of a specific drug, or a specific legal issue (e.g., informed consent and psychosurgery). Generally speaking, the professional dominance of medicine is most evident here, as the extra-medical agents must engage in battle if they wish to limit the medical profession's primacy in the use of medical technology. Medical collaboration by definition involves some relationship with another institution. In nearly all examples of medical collaboration cited above, medicine performs reporting, definitional or technical tasks for another institution. Physicians are significantly constrained by these relationships: they may be required to report information (as in child abuse) or may have their range of medical judgment limited by the demands of the 'collaborating' institution (as in the military). Medical dominance and professional freedom in use of expertise is thus significantly curtailed in collaborative social control. Medical ideology can be greatly affected by non-medical agents in society. Although medical professionals may use medical ideology as social control. it is not the sole property of the medical profession or its related professions. Self-help organizations like Alcoholics Anonymous or weight-reducing groups (35) can adapt or develop their own quasi-medical theories apart from medical professionals. These theories may of course be challenged by medical professionals. but here the challenge must come at the instigation of the medical profession.[4] The medical profession claims, but has no ownership of, medical rhetoric and vocabulary. It can be used by other organizations independently of the medical profession. Physicians may disown or challenge a particular use of medical vocabulary, but they must challenge it through the media. courts. the legislature or in some other public arena.

Finally, source of instigation varies for the three types of social control. Medical technology includes surgical procedures, drugs and technological innovations. While psychoactive drugs and advanced medical apparatuses are often invented and promoted by corporate interests, they only can be implemented by medical professionals. (This is why the pharmaceutical industry spends 25 percent of its gross budget on physician advertising.) The implementation of surgical procedures by physicians is among the most laissez-faire of modern medicine.(36). Physicians may not be the original instigators of specific medical technologies, but they are invariably in control of its implementation. Medical collaboration is nearly always instigated outside the medical profession. Even in the case of child abuse where some physicians championed the cause (37), it was the state's passage of mandatory reporting laws that instigated the use of medical control.

With medical excusing or gatekeeping tasks, as well as with much medical work in institutions, medical control occurs at the instigation of agents outside the medical profession. Medical ideology may be instigated either inside or outside the medical profession: physicians' entrepreneurship of new diagnoses or disorders, or non-medical adoption of medical definitions, rhetoric or vocabulary may extend medical ideology.

To summarize, while many analysts have written of the professional dominance of medicine, our analysis reveals that only in terms of medical technology does the medical profession maintain dominant and monopolistic control. When medicine operates in a collaborative role, it shares control with other institutions or performs work in the service of another institution. Medical ideology may arise independently from the medical profession; for the medical profession to maintain dominance over this form of social control, it must publicly challenge those groups utilizing medical ideology.

Conclusion

This paper presented medical technology, collaboration and ideology as three types of medical social control. It suggests that the dominance of the medical profession in the utilization of medical social control is limited to medical technology and that the medical profession's power and control are shared or diminished with medical collaboration and ideology.

It is clear that the enormous expansion of medicine in the past fifty years has meant that the number of possible ways in which problems could be medicalized has increased. Yet, we can only speculate on the amount of medicalized deviant behavior and the extent of medical social control. We need further examination of the 'natural history' of the emergence and decline of medical social control mechanisms, the 'battles' over social control turfs between medicine and competing control agencies, and the extent to which there is actual utilization of medical social control. It is important to discover and explicate the linkages between medicine and other social control agencies and how they support one another. We will then have a better understanding of medicine's jurisdication over deviant behavior and its operation as an agent of social control.

Department of Sociology
Drake University

10   Conrad

Notes

My thanks to Joseph W. Schneider and anonymous reviewers for comments on an earlier draft of this paper.

1. Another pharmaceutical innovation, birth control pills, also functions as a medical control: in this case, the control of reproduction. There is little doubt that 'the pill' has played a significant part in the alleged sexual revolutions since the 1960s and the redefinition of sexual deviance.
2. A number of other surgical interventions for deviance have been developed in recent years. Surgery for 'gender dysphoria' (trans-sexuality) and 'intestinal by-pass' operations for obesity are both examples of the medicalization of deviance and surgical intervention. The legalization of abortions also has medicalized and legitimated an activity that was formerly deviant and brought it under medical-surgical control.
3. It is worth noting that in the recent Gary Gilmore execution, a physician was involved: he designated the spot where the heartbeat was loudest and measured vital signs during the execution.
4. If these non-medical practitioners overextend their work to include that which is part of the legislated medical monopoly, they may be subject to prosecution for practicing medicine without a license.

References

1. Parsons, T. 1951 *The Social System*. New York: Free Press.
2. Freidson, E. 1970 *Profession of Medicine*. New York: Dodd, Mead.
3. Zola, I. K. 1975 'In the Name of Health and Illness: On Some Socio-political Consequences of Medical Influence.' *Social Science and Medicine*, 9:83–87.
4. Ehrenreich, B. and Ehrenreich, J. 1975 'Medicine and Social Control.' In *Welfare in America: Controlling the 'Dangerous' Classes* (edited by B. R. Mandell), pp.138–167. Englewood Cliffs, N.J.: Prentice–Hall.
5. Illich, I. 1976 *Medical Nemesis*. New York: Pantheon.
6. Freidson, E. 1975 *Doctoring Together*. New York: Elsevier.
7. Waitzkin, H. and Stoeckle, J. 1976 'Information Control and the Micro-politics of Health Care: Summary of an Ongoing Project.' *Social Science and Medicine*, 10:263–76.
8. Pitts, J. 1968 'Social Control: The Concept.' In *International Encyclopedia of Social Sciences*, No. 14 (edited by D. Sills). New York: Macmillan.
9. Conrad, P. 1975 'The Discovery of Hyperkinesis: Notes on the Medicalization of Deviant Behavior.' *Social Problems*, 23:12–21.
10. Mechanic, D. 1973 'Health and Illness in Technological Societies.' *Hastings Center Studies*, 1:7–18.
11. Szsaz, T. 1970 *Manufacture of Madness*. New York: Harper and Row.
12. Miller, K. 1976 *Managing Madness*. New York: Free Press.
13. Halleck, S. 1970 *The Politics of Therapy*. New York: Science House.
14. Hurvitz, N. 1973 'Psychotherapy as a Means of Social Control.' *Journal of Consulting and Clinical Psychology*, 40:232–39.

Types of medical social control 11

15. Rosen, G. 1972 'The Evolution of Social Medicine.' In *Handbook of Medical Sociology* (edited by H. E. Freeman, S. Levine and L. Reeder), pp.30–60. Englewood Cliffs, N.J.: Prentice-Hall.

16. Chorover, S. 1973 'Big Brother and Psychotechnology.' *Psychology Today*, 43–54.

17. Goddard, J. 1973 'The Medical Business.' *Scientific American*, 229:161–68.

18. Mark, V. and Ervin, F. 1970 *Violence and the Brain*. New York: Harper and Row.

19. Delgado, J. M. R. 1971 *Physical Control of the Mind*. New York: Harper and Row.

20. Chorover, S. 1974 'Psychosurgery: A Neuro Psychological Perspective.' *Boston University Law Review*, 74:231–48.

21. Fox, R. G. 1971 'The XYY Offender: A Modern Myth?' *Journal of Criminal Law, Criminology and Police Science*, 62:1–15.

22. Sorenson, J. 1974 'Biomedical Innovation, Uncertainty, and Doctor–Patient Interaction.' *Journal of Health and Social Behavior*, 15:366–74.

23. Daniels, A. K. 1969 'The Captive Professional: Bureaucratic Limitation in the Practice of Military Psychiatry.' *Journal of Health and Social Behavior*, 10:255–65.

24. Kittrie, N. 1971 *The Right to be Different*. Baltimore: Johns Hopkins Press.

25. Waitzkin, H. K. and Waterman, B. 1974 *The Exploitation of Illness in Capitalist Society*. Indianapolis: Bobbs-Merrill.

26. Shuval, J. T. and Antonovosky, A. 1973 'Illness: A Mechanism for Coping with Failure.' *Social Science and Medicine*, 7:259–65.

27. Cartwright, S. W. 1851 'Report on the Diseases and Physical Peculiarities of the Negro Race.' *New Orleans Medical and Surgical Journal*, 7:691–715.

28. Englehardt, H., jr. 1974 'The Disease of Masturbation: Values and the Concept of Disease.' *Bulletin of History of Medicine*, 48:234–48.

29. Conrad, P. 1977 'Soviet Dissidents, Ideological Deviance, and Mental Hospitalization.' Paper presented at Midwest Sociological Society Meetings, April.

30. Zola, I. K. 1972 'Medicine as an Institution of Social Control.' *Sociological Review*, 20:487–504.

31. Freidson, E. 1970 *Professional Dominance*. Chicago: Aldine.

32. Radelet, M. 1977 'Medical Hegemony as Social Control: The Use of Tranquilizers.' Paper presented at the meetings of the Society for the Study of Social Problems.

33. Platt, A. 1969 *The Child Savers*. Chicago: University of Chicago Press.

34. Chalfant, P. 1976 'Unindicted Co-Conspirators in the Medicalization of Deviance: The Role of a Semi-Profession.' Paper presented at the meetings of the American Sociological Association.

35. Millman, M. Personal communication.

36. Millman, M. 1977 *The Unkindest Cut: Life in the Backrooms of Medicine*. New York: William Morrow.

37. Pfohl, S. 1977 'The "Discovery" of Child Abuse.' *Social Problems*, 24:310–23.

Name Index